KU-521-803

NICHOLAS HILLIARD

An Unknown Youth

Leaning against a Tree among Roses

c. 1588

NICHOLAS HILLIARD

by

ERNA AUERBACH

ROUTLEDGE & KEGAN PAUL
London

First published 1961
by Routledge and Kegan Paul Ltd
Broadway House, 68-74 Carter Lane
London, E.C.4

Made and printed in Great Britain by
William Clowes and Sons, Limited
London and Beccles

© Erna Auerbach 1961

No part of this book may be reproduced
in any form without permission from
the publisher, except for the quotation
of brief passages in criticism

B 61- 09475

HERTFORDSHIRE
COUNTY LIBRARY

1953885

To
EMMA AUERBACH
in memoriam

CONTENTS

PLATES

Plates

xi

Plates

Plates

xiv

Plates

xvi

Plates

THE FOLLOWING PLATES ARE ALSO REPRODUCED
IN FULL COLOUR

xvii

PREFACE

NICHOLAS HILLIARD holds a unique position in the history of English painting. At a time when the mysteries of painting and limning were much under foreign influence, that great Elizabethan, the son of an English goldsmith and a goldsmith himself, created his own unmistakable style and thus added a new, indigenous, element to the development of English art in the sixteenth century. The charm of his miniatures, carried out with accomplished craftsmanship and superb artistic touch, is well known; less known is the remarkable influence which Hilliard exercised on his contemporaries, an influence which far transcends the limited sphere of miniature painting and goldsmiths' work. The purpose of this study, founded on intensive research into the history of painting in England in the sixteenth century, is to indicate Hilliard's position in the development of English art of that period by giving a detailed account of the life and work of this great artist.

I am greatly indebted to the Worshipful Company of Goldsmiths who by their generous encouragement and support made possible the publication of this study. They further kindly granted permission to study their records and other documents and thereby enabled me to ascertain biographical facts about Hilliard which hitherto were unknown, facts which established his close connection with the Company's activities and the goldsmiths' craft.

Research in the history of art, like every other branch of human knowledge, is a continuous process and every student owes much to those who studied his subject before him. I am particularly indebted to the following: Mr. Graham Reynolds, Keeper of the Department of Engraving, Illustration and Design and Paintings, Victoria and Albert Museum, who in 1947 arranged a memorable exhibition of Hilliard's works and by his various publications has done much to add to our present knowledge of the great artist's work; Mr. Carl Winter, Director of the Fitzwilliam Museum, Cambridge, an enthusiastic admirer of Nicholas Hilliard, who unstintingly let me profit from his great knowledge and the published and unpublished results of his research; Mr. John Pope-Hennessy, Keeper of the Department of Architecture and Sculpture, Victoria and Albert Museum, who published a profound appreciation of Hilliard's artistic position in the context of European Art; Mr. Noel Blakiston, Principal Assistant Keeper in the Public Record Office, who greatly assisted me in the search of documentary material; he also kindly allowed me to use his own notes and the material which he had collected over the years.

My thanks are further due to Sir Herbert Read who was always ready to give me the benefit of his wise judgment on the many problems which beset the path of my research.

I received valuable information on the subject-matter of this work from the following: Mr. C. K. Adams, Director of the National Portrait Gallery, and Mr. D. T. Piper, Assistant Keeper of the same Museum; Mr. E. F. Croft Murray, Keeper of the Department of Prints and Drawings, British Museum; Mr. P. H. Hulton, Assistant Keeper of the same Department, and Mr. G. H. Tait, Assistant Keeper of the Department of British and Medieval Antiquities, also of the British Museum; and further Professor E. K. Waterhouse, Director of the Barber Institute of Fine Arts; Mr. Robert Hutchison, Keeper of the Scottish National Portrait Gallery; Mr. G. R. Batho, Assistant Lecturer, University of Sheffield; Dr. R. Churchill Blackie, Curator of the Royal Albert Memorial Museum, Exeter; Mr. J. W. Goodison, Keeper of the Fitzwilliam Museum, Mr. C. van Hasselt, of the same Museum; Mr. J. G. Philip, Secretary of the Bodleian Library; Mr. John Woodward, of the City of Birmingham Museum and Art Gallery; and Mr. T. S. Wragge, Keeper of Works of Art, Chatsworth. Sir Owen Morshead, sometime Librarian of Windsor Castle, and Miss Scott Elliot kindly granted me access to the Royal Collection of miniatures.

I also received useful assistance from abroad, in particular from M. Jean Adhémar, of the Cabinet des Estampes, Bibliothèque Nationale, Paris; Mr. R. de Broglie, Curator of the Musée Condé, Chantilly; Professor W. G. Constable, sometime Curator of Paintings, Museum of Fine Arts, Boston; Dr. H. Gerson, Director of the Rijksbureau voor Kunsthistorische Documentatie, The Hague; Dr. C. Nordenfalk, of the National Museum, Stockholm, and Dr. A. B. de Vries, Director of the Mauritshuis, The Hague.

It would be impossible to name all those who have helped me in various respects but I should like to mention Mr. T. J. Brown, Assistant Keeper of the Department of Manuscripts of the British Museum; Mr. R. W. Elmore, of the City of London College; Miss Lorna MacEchern, Secretary to the Duke of Buccleuch; Miss Nellie McNeill O'Farrell, Miss Carolyn Merion, Mr. Francis Needham and Miss Clare Talbot, Librarian of Hatfield House.

THE PLATES

Her Majesty the Queen graciously permitted the reproduction of photographs of miniatures in the Royal Collection at Windsor Castle.

Preface

Her Majesty the Queen of the Netherlands kindly consented to the reproduction of miniatures in the Archives of the Royal House of the Netherlands.

The following private owners gave their courteous permission to reproduce and take photographs of works of art in their possession: the Marquess of Anglesey, the Viscount Bearsted, the Earl of Beauchamp, the Duke of Bedford, the Duke of Buccleuch and Queensberry, Mr. J. N. Bryson, Miss M. R. Bulkeley, Mr. A. D. R. Caroe, the Marchioness of Cholmondeley, Dr. Louis C. G. Clarke, the Earl of Derby, Mr. Simon Wingfield Digby, Mr. Alan Evans, Mr. Brinsley Ford, Mr. and Mrs. E. H. Heckett, Mrs. Doris Herschorn, Dr. M. E. Kronenberg, the Hon. Hugh de B. Lawson Johnston, the Hon. H. Lawson-Tancred, the Earl of Leicester, Lady Lucas, Lt.-Col. Sir George Meyrick, Col. Sir John Carew Pole, Bt., the Duke of Portland, the Earl of Powis, the Earl of Radnor, Lorth Rothschild, the Duke of Rutland, the Marquess of Salisbury, Mr. Harry G. Sperling, the Rev. and Mrs. J. E. Strickland, the late Earl of Verulam, the Earl of Warwick, Mrs. Ward-Boughton-Leigh, and Lord Wharton.

Pictures, miniatures and other works of art in the custody of Public bodies are reproduced by courtesy of the following: The Berkeley Estates Company, Berkeley Castle; the Barber Institute of Fine Arts, Birmingham; Museum of Fine Arts, Boston; the Trustees of the National Museum of Cardiff; Cambridge: the Master and Fellows of Emmanuel College, the Syndics of the Fitzwilliam Museum, the Council of the Senate of the University of Cambridge; the Cleveland Museum of Art; Musée Condé, Chantilly; the National Gallery of Ireland, Dublin; the Trustees of the National Galleries of Scotland, Edinburgh; the Rector of the Parish Church of St. Sidwell, Exeter; the Royal Albert Memorial Museum, Exeter; the Trustees of the National Maritime Museum, Greenwich; the Mauritshuis, The Hague; the Nelson Gallery-Atkins Museum (Starr Coll.), Kansas City; the Walker Art Gallery, Liverpool; London: the Trustees of the British Museum; the Worshipful Company of Mercers, the Governors of St. Olave's Grammar School, the Trustees of the National Portrait Gallery, the Keeper of the Public Record Office, the Victoria and Albert Museum; the Trustees of the National Gallery of Victoria (Felton Bequest), Melbourne; the Metropolitan Museum of Art (Fletcher Fund, 1935), New York; the Bibliothèque Nationale, Paris; the Bodleian Library, Oxford; the Mildred Anna Williams Collection at the California Palace of the Legion of Honor, San Francisco; the National Museum, Stockholm; Kunsthistorisches Museum, Vienna.

Reproductions from photographs of the Victoria and Albert Museum and the Public Record Office are Crown Copyright, reproduced by permission of the Controller of H.M. Stationery Office.

London, 1960.   E.A.

ABBREVIATIONS

Amsterdam, *The Triumph of Mannerism*, 1955	Amsterdam, Rijksmuseum: De Triomf van het Maniërisme, Exhibition, 1955.
Auerbach, *More Light on Nicholas Hilliard*	Auerbach, Erna, "More Light on Nicholas Hilliard". See Bibliography, No. 6.
—*Portraits of Elizabeth I*	Auerbach, Erna, "Portraits of Elizabeth I". See Bibliography, No. 8.
—*Tudor Artists*	Auerbach, Erna, *Tudor Artists*, 1954. See Bibliography, No. 9.
—*Tudor Portraits*	Auerbach, Erna, "Some Tudor Portraits at the Royal Academy", See Bibliography, No. 10.
Blakiston, *Nicholas Hilliard and Queen Elizabeth's Third Great Seal*	Blakiston, Noel, "Nicholas Hilliard and Queen Elizabeth's Third Great Seal". See Bibliography, No. 11.
—*Nicholas Hilliard at Court*	Blakiston, Noel, "Nicholas Hilliard at Court". See Bibliography, No. 13.
B.M.	British Museum.
Brussels, 1912	Williamson, George C., *La Miniature Anglaise*, 1913, Catalogue de l'Exposition de la Miniature à Bruxelles en 1912. See Bibliography, No. 69.
B.F.A.C., 1889	Burlington Fine Arts Club, Exhibition of Portrait Miniatures, 1889.
B.F.A.C., 1909	Burlington Fine Arts Club, Exhibition illustrative of Early English Portraiture, 1909.
B.F.A.C., 1926	Burlington Fine Arts Club, Exhibition of Late Elizabethan Art, 1926.
B.F.A.C., 1933	Burlington Fine Arts Club, Exhibition of Elizabethan Art, 1933.
Burl. Mag.	*The Burlington Magazine*, various volumes.
Cat.	Catalogue.
Cecil Pap.	Manuscripts in the possession of the Marquess of Salisbury at Hatfield House.
Coll.	Collection.
Conn.	*The Connoisseur*
Cust	Cust, Sir Lionel, *Windsor Castle, Portrait Miniatures*. See Bibliography, No. 19.

Exeter, 1957	Exhibition of Exeter Silversmiths Domestic Silver of the 16th to 18th Centuries, 1957.
Exeter Mus.	Royal Albert Memorial Museum, Exeter.
Farquhar, *Nicholas Hilliard*	Farquhar, Helen, "Nicholas Hilliard: Embosser of Medals of Gold". See Bibliography, No. 25.
—*Phoenix Badge*	Farquhar, Helen, "John Rutlinger and the Phoenix Badge of Queen Elizabeth". See Bibliography, No. 26.
—*Portraiture of Stuart Monarchs*	Farquhar, Helen, "Portraiture of our Stuart Monarchs on their Coins and Medals". See Bibliography, No. 27.
Goulding	Goulding, R. W., "The Welbeck Abbey Miniatures". See Bibliography, No. 30.
Gower, II	Gower, Lord Ronald, *The Great Historic Galleries of England*, Vol. II. See Bibliography, No. 31.
Harl. Soc.	Harleian Society, Publications of
Haydocke	Haydocke, Richard, *Tracte containing the Artes of curious Paintinge, Caruinge, Buildinge*. Oxford, 1598. See Bibliography, No. 32.
Huguenot Society	Huguenot Society, the Publications of the
Kennedy	Kennedy, H. A., "Early English Portrait Miniatures in the Collection of the Duke of Buccleuch". See Bibliography, No. 36.
Lit.	Literature
Liverpool, Kings and Queens, 1953	Walker Art Gallery, Liverpool, Exhibition of Kings, and Queens of England, 1953.
Long	Long, Basil S., *British Miniaturists 1520–1860*. See Bibliography, No. 38.
— *Notes*	Long, Basil S., Manuscript Notes on the Collection of Miniatures of the Duke of Buccleuch at Drumlanrig Castle.
Mackay	Mackay, Andrew, *The Collection of Miniatures in Montagu House*. See Bibliography, No. 39.
Manchester, 1857	Manchester Art Treasures Exhibition
Med. Ill.	*Medallic Illustrations of the History of Great Britain and Ireland to the Death of George II*. See Bibliography, No. 41.
Meres	Meres, Francis, *Palladis Tamia*, Wit's Treasury, being the second part of Wit's Commonwealth. See Bibliography, No. 42.
Minutes	Goldsmiths' Company, Wardens' Accounts and Court Minutes, various volumes.
MSS.	Manuscripts
Mus.	Museum
Norgate	Norgate, Edward, *Miniatura or the Art of Limning*. See Bibliography, No. 44.

O'Donoghue	O'Donoghue, F. N., *A Descriptive and Classified Catalogue of Portraits of Queen Elizabeth*. See Bibliography, No. 45.
Piper, *Essex*	Piper, David, "The 1590 Lumley Inventory: Hilliard, Segar and the Earl of Essex", I and II. See Bibliography, No. 49.
P.C.C.	Prerogative Court of Canterbury, Wills.
Pope-Hennessy, *Lecture*	Pope-Hennessy, John, *A Lecture on Nicholas Hilliard*. See Bibliography, No. 50.
—*Treatise*	Pope-Hennessy, John, "Nicholas Hilliard and Mannerist Art Theory". See Bibliography, No. 51.
Prov.	Provenance.
P.R.O.	Public Record Office
Documents:	
A.O.1	Exchequer and Audit Department, Declared Accounts.
A.O.3	Various Accounts.
C.2	Chancery Proceedings Series I., Elizabeth to Charles I.
C.24	Chancery Depositions
C.33	Chancery, Entry Books of Decrees and Orders.
C.54	Chancery Close Rolls.
C.66	Chancery Patent Rolls.
E.36	Exchequer: Treasury of Receipt, Miscellaneous Books.
E.101	King's Remembrancer, Accounts, Various.
E.178	King's Remembrancer, Special Commissions of Enquiry.
E.179	King's Remembrancer, Subsidy Rolls, etc.
E.351	Exchequer: Declared Accounts
E.371	Exchequer: Originalia Rolls.
E.403	Exchequer: of Receipt, Issues, Enrolments, Registers.
E.407	Exchequer: of Receipt, Miscellanea
K.B.27	King's Bench, Coram Rege Rolls.
P.C.2	Privy Council Office, Registers.
Req.2	Court of Requests, Proceedings.
S.P.12	State Papers, Domestic, Elizabeth.
S.P.13	State Papers, Domestic, Elizabeth (Cases).
S.P.14	State Papers, Domestic, James I.
Sta.Cha.4, 5	Star Chamber, Proceedings, Mary. Elizabeth.
R.A.	Royal Academy of Arts, London
R.A., 1934	Royal Academy of Arts, Exhibition of British Art, 1934.
R.A., 1950/1	Exhibition of Works by Holbein and other Masters of the sixteenth and seventeenth centuries, 1950/51.
R.A., Kings and Queens	Kings and Queens A.D. 653–1953, Diploma Gallery, London, 1953.

R.A., British Portraits, 1956/7	British Portrait Exhibition, 1956/7.
Radnor	Catalogue of the pictures in the Collection of the Earl of Radnor. See Bibliography, No. 53.
Reynolds *Catalogue*, 1947	Reynolds, Graham, *Nicholas Hilliard and Isaac Oliver, an Exhibition.* See Bibliography, No. 56.
—*Conn. Guide*	Reynolds, Graham, *The Connoisseur Period Guides*, The Tudor Period . . . See Bibliography, No. 57.
—*Miniatures*	Reynolds, Graham, *English Portrait Miniatures*, 1952. See Bibliography, No. 58.
—*Walpole Society*	Reynolds, Graham, "Portraits by Nicholas Hilliard and his Assistants of King James I and his Family." See Bibliography, No. 59.
Scharf	Scharf, George, *A Descriptive and Historical Catalogue of the Collection of Pictures at Knowsley Hall.* See Bibliography, No. 60.
South Kens. Mus., 1862	Special Exhibition of Works of Art at the South Kensington Museum, Section II, 1862.
South Kens. Mus., 1865	Special Exhibition of Portrait Miniatures on Loan at the South Kensington Museum, 1865.
The Hague, The Age of Shakespeare, 1958	Den Haag, Gemeentemuseum, Exhibition: De Eeuw van Shakespeare Toen Elizabeth Regeerde, 1958.
Treasures of Cambridge, 1959	Treasures of Cambridge, Exhibition, organised by the Worshipful Company of Goldsmiths, Goldsmiths' Hall, London, 1959.
Treatise	Hilliard, Nicholas, *A Treatise* concerning the Arte of Limning writ by N. Hilliard, MS. Copy in the Library of the University of Edinburgh, dated 1624.
Treatise, Walpole Society	Hilliard, Nicholas, "A Treatise concerning the Arte of Limning." See Bibliography, No. 65.
Tudor, 1890	Exhibition of the Royal House of Tudor, The New Gallery, 1890.
Vanderdoort's Cat.	Vanderdoort, Abraham, *A Catalogue and Description of King Charles the First's Capital Collection of Pictures and Limnings*, etc. See Bibliography, No. 66.
Vertue	Vertue, George, "Note Books", *The Walpole Society* publications, 6 volumes, 1930–1955. See Bibliography, No. 67.
V. & A.	Victoria and Albert Museum.
Williamson, *Portrait Miniatures*	Williamson, George C., *The History of Portrait Miniatures.* See Bibliography, No. 70.
—*Pierpont Morgan Cat.*	Williamson, George C., Catalogue of the Collection of Miniatures, the Property of John Pierpont Morgan, I. See Bibliography, No. 71.
Winter, *Eliz. Miniatures*	Winter, Carl, *Elizabethan Miniatures.* See Bibliography, No. 73.

I

NICHOLAS HILLIARD

THE MAN

HIS DESCENT AND EARLY TRAINING

A T THE beginning of the sixteenth century Devon and Cornwall were amongst the most active counties of England. Protestantism, the new discoveries beyond the sea, and the rise of a new gentry were transforming the social structure of the West.[1] A strong generation of men emerged, sustained by the new religion, guided by the spirit of adventure, and rapidly acquiring a taste for the new wealth which resulted from the pursuits of the seafarers who set out from the Western shores and the prolonged but not unprofitable struggle with Spain. One of the centres of this new activity was Exeter, where trade increased, the crafts assumed greater influence than ever before, and the incorporated guilds took a leading part in the administration of the city. This was the Exeter in which Nicholas Hilliard was born in the year 1547.

On 9 June 1549, for the last time in the West, the adherents of the Roman faith started a revolt against the reformed religion. This was the "Prayer Book Rebellion" which led to the siege of Exeter. "In the City were two sorts of people, the one and the greater nomber were of the old stampe and of the Romyshe religion: The other, being of the lesser nomber, were of a contrary mind and disposition for they wholye replyed themselves to the reformed religion."[2] This is reported by an eyewitness, John Vowell *alias* Hoker, who was Chamberlain of Exeter in 1553 and gave us the description of the ancient city.

---

[1] A. L. Rowse, *The West in English History* (1949), pp. 67–74 and *Tudor Cornwall* (1941) p. 319.
[2] John Vowell *alias* Hoker, "The Description of the Citie of Exeter", *The Devon and Cornwall Record Society*, Exeter, II, 1919, pp. 71 and 77.

It is in his story of the siege of Exeter that the name of Richard, Nicholas' father, is mentioned for the first time. John Vowell describes skirmishes from the besieged city and continues:

> But amonge theime all was John being of that Companye [e.g. of those adhering to the reformed religion] and servant to Richard Helyerd of the same, Goldesmithe and a flemynge borne had the best successe.

When attacked, Richard's apprentice John apparently pretended to be wounded, took his attacker by surprise, killed him and returned into the city with what he had taken from him.

Thus we learn that Richard Hilliard, who was born in 1518/19, practised as a goldsmith in the city of Exeter in 1549 and had a Flemish apprentice, and that both were supporters of the reformed church. We further know that Richard later held high office in the city administration: he was a bailiff in 1556 and a sheriff in 1568.

From medieval times goldsmiths are known to have worked in the city of Exeter where they combined their craft with that of bankers and moneylenders, like the goldsmiths of London. The early existence of the goldsmith's craft in Exeter is evidenced by the Chapel of All Hallows "in Aurifabria" built in the thirteenth century and the name "Goldsmith Street" in the centre of the city, but the incorporation of the goldsmiths of Exeter into a Guild or Company took place only at about 1700. The reason for this was that the Goldsmiths' Company in London had the sole jurisdiction over all works of gold and silver within the kingdom of England,[1] so that a local Guild could not yet legally be formed. That an inspection of the quality and standard of the gold and silver ware in the West country was undertaken by officers of the London Gold-smiths' Company, emerges from the Company's Minutes.[2] In summer 1571 assayers seem to have examined the standard of purity and to have established a strict rule. Bonds for "true workmanship" were signed and the list of the gold-smiths of Exeter who were so bound is headed by Richard Hilliard. Apparently as a result of this severe control the town-mark, namely the Roman capital X surmounted by a crown and sometimes adorned by dots, was added to the initials of the individual maker.

Before this mark was introduced, Richard Hilliard had made two chalices with covers for the churches of St. Sidwell and St. Edmund on the Bridge which bear his mark, "RH", in a circle, with a concentric ring of dots, and which may be dated to 1571. He is thus the earliest goldsmith of Exeter whose work has been identified. The craftsmanship of these chalices is of fine quality

---

[1] *Transactions of the Devonshire Association*, Vol. 44, 1912, pp. 439ff.
[2] Book K-L,2, pp. 74–6 and 147.

and the simple ornamental band below the cover is true to the Exeter Elizabethan style.

Quite recently an even earlier work of Richard Hilliard has been found and exhibited, a richly ornamented "font-shaped" silver standing dish, dated between 1560 and 1565,[1] and, furthermore, a seal-topped spoon has been added to his *œuvre*. These specimens of goldsmiths' work, coming from the hand of Nicholas' father, will be discussed more fully in a later chapter.[2]

Judging from the portrait miniature of Richard Hilliard, painted by his son Nicholas in 1577,[3] he was the type of well-to-do craftsman and citizen. He was married to Laurence, the daughter of John Wall, a goldsmith, who has always been thought to have lived in London. Although his name appears in the Minutes of the Goldsmiths' Company of London, he is mentioned therein as "John Wall of Exet' Goldsmythe" and whilst he may have had certain connections with London, there is no proof that he ever actually practised as a goldsmith in the Metropolis.

The search into John Wall's history in London and Exeter has produced further facts of interest for Hilliard's background. According to the Minutes of the Goldsmiths' Company,[4] on 8 August 1535, Mr. Cromwell, secretary to the "Kinges Grace", sent for the Wardens and "for the goldsmythes of Exeter whose names be here vnder wrytten . . .". Amongst the goldsmiths of Exeter and other parts of the West were three Englishmen and one Dutchman. They all

> went vnto Canburye where the sayd Mr. Secretary laye . . . Mr. Fythwylliam the Tresurer of the Kynges house was wth hym in his Orcharde. And then and there one John Wall of Exet' Goldsmythe cam before theym, and presented stuff he had taken in Somerset, Devonshire and Cornwall together with Henry Atwell. . . .

Letters patent had been granted to John Wall and Henry Atwell at Westminster on 13 February 1534 according to which gold and silver ware found in the West country had to be taken to Goldsmith's Hall, London, to be assayed in the presence of John Wall who had to give a bond. But only a short time afterwards, in 1535, the Wardens attempted to deprive John Wall of the patent of the search and to obtain it for themselves, and decided that the Lord Chancellor's favour should be asked for.[5] The Wardens were not successful on this occasion, but when on 31 October 1542, John Wall brought in bad silver

[1] Exeter, 1957, Cat. Nos. 43 and 66. Mr. Churchill Blackie showed me the pieces in his care and kindly gave me full information about the Exhibition.
[2] See Chapter VI.
[3] V. & A.
[4] Books E and F (1532–42), pp. 57 and 58.
[5] *Ibid.*, p. 91.

which "by Indentur and by vertu of the King's letters patent" he had pur-
chased of the late Earl of Essex, the Wardens asked him to bring in the document and succeeded: it was then declared "that thys day at Westminster in
Chancery John Wall of Exeter resigned and surrendered the King's patent and
that he should be rewarded not above 5*l*."[1] From this struggle with the Company it is clear that Nicholas' grandfather on his mother's side was also a goldsmith of high standing and considerable means.

Documents kept in Exeter throw further light on the life and career of Richard Hilliard, Nicholas' father. The most important fact that emerges from them
is that Richard became a Freeman on 6 September 1546 and that he had been
an apprentice of John Wall.[2] Here again, as often amongst craftsmen at that
period, the apprentice married his master's daughter. Richard's marriage took
place probably at the time when he had set up his own practice as a goldsmith.
He seems also to have gained financial advantages by his marriage. After the
death of John Wall, the landlord of the latter granted to Richard the house and
garden in the parish of St. Pancras, Exeter, formerly held by John Wall;[3] it
was this land which carried the patronage of the benefice or parsonage of St.
Pancras that Richard later bequeathed to his son Nicholas.

Richard does not, however, appear to have lived during his married life in
the house in St. Pancras, but he lived in the parish of St. George. Although the
Registers of that parish have not survived for that period his name appears
regularly in the assessments for the parish of St. George in the Subsidy Rolls
from 1557/8 to 1586. His activities can also be followed in the reports of the
City Council. He was elected a member on 21 September 1562[4] and from that
date until 22 September 1579 he was present at almost all the meetings. On that
day,[5] at a meeting of the City Council, it was recorded that he was overtaken
by illness and honourably discharged from future service; it was "ordered" that,
on his application, he be "cleared of the Company of this House [the City
Council] grates and freely" and as a special favour he was given "canon bread
as in times past". He was to live yet another fifteen years.

From these entries it is clear that Richard was highly respected in his home
town and that he lived in comfortable circumstances. The goldsmith tradition
was well established in the family and Nicholas as a child, surrounded by younger
brothers and sisters, grew up in the atmosphere of a workshop which must have
had a strange fascination for a boy of his particular gifts and talents. His brother

[1] Book F, pp. 232–3.
[2] The Mayor's Court Book (1545–57), f. 56a.
[3] Calendar of Misc. Rolls, 22.m.1b. 12 April 1549.
[4] Act Book III, p. 90.
[5] *Ibid.*, pp. 430–1.

Jeremy likewise followed his father's calling and settled down in Exeter as a practising goldsmith. He lived in the same parish, St. George's, and his name appears first jointly with that of his father, and then alone.[1] He, too, had considerable means.

Nicholas, however, had more ambitious plans. His ambitions led him from the West country to the Metropolis. It has always been a matter of speculation where, when, and with whom Nicholas had his training. Yet the precise answer is contained in the closely written manuscript pages of the Minutes of the Goldsmiths' Company: he was not apprenticed, as is often assumed, to John Wall, his grandfather on his mother's side, but to Robert Brandon. It is recorded that on Friday, 13 November 1562, the Court of the Goldsmiths' Company in London received 5s. from Robert Brandon "for the presentment of Thomas Sammon and *Nicholas Helyard*, his apprentices."[2] Robert Brandon was, of course, Nicholas' future father-in-law.

At that time Nicholas was 15 years old, the usual age for a boy to become apprenticed to a master craftsman. The date 1562 is significant: three small miniatures have survived which Hilliard painted in 1560, two years before he began to train as a goldsmith. Naturally, he watched his father exercising his craft in his workshop and may well have worked a little himself there; we would have no record of this. It is quite certain that Robert Brandon was the first London goldsmith to whom Hilliard was apprenticed, because had he been serving previously with another goldsmith, the entry in the words of the Goldsmiths' Company Books in London would state that he was "set over" by another member of the Company. The fact that he painted three delightful miniatures, two portraits of himself at the age of 13[3] and one of the Duke of Somerset,[4] before he trained as a goldsmith, gives welcome support to the theory, founded on the artistic style of his miniatures,[5] that he first learned his craft from a limner who had a wide practice in illuminating all kinds of secular documents. This explains the calligraphic character of his lettering and the frequent use of gold, likewise in Hilliard's later miniatures. The limnings of 1560 are reminiscent of the round portraits decorating the *Guerre Gallique* of *c.* 1519, usually ascribed to Jean Clouet, but Holbein's influence is also noticeable.

We gain a clear picture of Robert Brandon's personality and career from the Minutes of the Goldsmiths' Company and from various legal documents. On 30 January 1547/8 Robert Brandon applied to become a brother of the Company

[1] Assessment Rolls, 1582–c. 1630.
[2] Minutes, Book K, pt. I, 1557–66, p. 207.
[3] In the possession of the Duke of Portland and the Duke of Buccleuch.
[4] In the possession of the Duke of Buccleuch.
[5] Auerbach, *Tudor Artists* (1954), pp. 120–1.

and offered to pay 40s. for this privilege. This was granted and a week later he was admitted as a freeman and paid the usual fee of 3s. on taking the oath.[1] He apparently had no claim to become a freeman by patrimony or apprenticeship, but was admitted by favour, which means that he must have come from outside the Company. He was highly successful: already in 1558/9 he, together with Affabell Partridge, appeared on the royal payroll.[2] As the Queen's goldsmith and jeweller Brandon subsequently received regular payments. In 1560 a royal warrant was granted to him requesting him to collect some money for the Mint.[3] According to a list of members of the Goldsmiths' Company, Brandon was elected a liveryman in 1561 and lived during that time in Cheapside in a house which had the poetic name of "the gylt lyon with the fyerbrand".[4] As in those days apprentices lived with their master, it can be assumed that young Nicholas also lived there. Brandon was a man of substantial means, a servant of the Queen, and a man of influence with the Company.[5]

Nicholas remained with Brandon for the customary seven years. On Friday, 29 July 1569, he became a freeman of the Goldsmiths' Company and took his oath.[6] Shortly afterwards, on 7 April 1570, he himself tried to engage an apprentice: the widow of another goldsmith, Charles Byrte, agreed that her late husband's apprentice, John Cobbold, should be "sett over" to Nicholas, to dwell and serve with him. After Hilliard had paid 40s. to the widow "for her good wyll herein" and given her an obligation for another 20s. in a year's time to come, the application was granted on 14 April 1570.[7]

Apart from John Cobbold, Hilliard had at least one other apprentice during his early years as master goldsmith, namely Gualter Reynoldes, who was a foreigner anxious to increase his knowledge of the goldsmith's craft in this country.[8]

The Minutes of the Goldsmiths' Company further record that on 23 February 1570/1 Agnes Rutlingen, the wife of John, goldsmith and engraver, promised to deliver

> vnto Thomas Clerke a booke of portraitures wthin this sennyght wholle and perfett, wch is now in the handes of Nichas Helliard,

and that Thomas Clerke was to give her 20s. for it.[9] Whatever this book of

---

[1] Minutes, Books G, H and I, pp. 30–1.   [2] P.R.O., E. 405/125ff.
[3] S.P. 12/14 (15 Oct. 1560).
[4] Minutes, Books K–L, 1566–73, p. 455 and p. 462.
[5] In a Subsidy Roll for St. Foster's Parish, Robert Brandon was assessed in 1563 at 100l. and paid 5l. taxes. See P.R.O., E. 179/145/219.
[6] Minutes, Book K–L, p. 5.   [7] *Ibid.*, pp. 23 and 24.
[8] Auerbach, *More Light on Nicholas Hilliard*, p.168.
[9] *Ibid.*, p. 167.

portraitures may have been, whether it contained drawings, engravings or miniatures, it is the first entry that connects Hilliard at this early date with the art in which he afterwards excelled. It also makes it clear that he collaborated with a fellow-goldsmith and engraver although we have no details of their joint work. It is, of course, possible that they worked only on the decoration of the cover of the book. John Rutlingen is mentioned again in the Court Minutes of the Goldsmiths' Company on 6 April 1571, when he "promised to finish a book of gold on Thursday next or before if he can, which book he has to make for Mr. Lannyson to the use of my lord of Leicester".[1] The meaning of "book of gold" is as ambiguous as that of "portraitures", but the fact that this was a commission for the Earl of Leicester is of interest.

Immediately below this entry, under the same date, there appears a mention of Hilliard which is recorded here in full in view of its biographical importance:

> And also the same tyme the said Cradock[2] delyuered into the handes of Mr Wardens a Jewell of gold, and 4 litle rynges of gold wch he receaued of Ni'chas and John Hellyard brethern in earnest of a bargayne betweene him and them, to the ende the same iewell and ringes shall remayne in the handes of Mr Wardens tyll the controuersie betweene him and the said brethern touchynge the said bargayne be fully determined by the award of 2 indifferent persones by bothe parties to be indifferently chosen, And they to be bound in 20*l.* a peece to stand to the order of the same arbitrators. And if they can make no ende, then Mr Wardens to be Umpiers. Wherevnto the said Cradock agreed, if the said brethern wyll agree to the same. The Jewell and rynges aforesaid are thies. Viz. A rose of gold enameled wt a diamond in it, and a pearle hangynge at it: A litle rynge of gold wth a parrett vpon it. 2 litle rynges of gold wth ragged staves in them. And a litle rynge of gold wt an emerald peane in it.[3]

As this dispute between Cradock and the brothers Hilliard is not mentioned again in the records, we must assume that it was settled amicably.

The above entry is important because it shows that shortly before Hilliard painted the portrait miniature of Queen Elizabeth, dated 1572, he actively worked as a goldsmith, perhaps jointly with his brother. In view of this fact and his connection with the royal Court, it is interesting to learn that one of the pieces in dispute with Cradock was an enamelled rose of gold with a diamond in the centre and a pearl hanging therefrom.

A few observations may be added on Nicholas' brother John of whom no record has appeared so far in the printed sources. He must have been very near

[1] Book K–L, p. 62.
[2] One Edmund Cradock, goldsmith.
[3] For the expression "parrett" we should read "parroll", a rope; a "ragged staves" is in the language of the goldsmith a setting pierced with holes and a "peane" is an "heraldic sable".

in age to Nicholas, for he became a freeman of the Goldsmiths' Company less than two months after Nicholas. It is recorded that the Wardens received on 5 September 1569

> 3*s* of John Helliard late thapprentice of Mr. Edward Gylberd for his othe.[1]

The two brothers must have gone to London together, were apprenticed to two different goldsmiths and may have started to practise their craft together after having completed their apprenticeship. Edmund Cradock, who was older than the Hilliard brothers, was, incidentally, also apprenticed to Robert Brandon.

One further reference to Nicholas' brother John may be noted. According to legal proceedings[2] which Hilliard started against one William Alcock, brother and executor of a deceased fellow goldsmith Richard, on 30 April 1580, he alleged that about eight years before, his brother John had borrowed 13*l*. from Richard Alcock and that he, Nicholas, had taken out a bond of 20*l*. jointly with his brother John to guarantee the payment of John's debt; the further details of this case do not interest us, but these facts make it clear that Nicholas readily pledged his credit for his brother. This nonchalance in money matters is a lovable trend in Hilliard's character which we shall often note on later occasions. John Hilliard fades out of the picture again, and in his father's will of 1586 he is not mentioned.

Two other brothers of Nicholas are referred to in later proceedings in the same Court when Hilliard sued one Thomas Brigham. These references probably concern Jeremy, the goldsmith of Exeter, and the younger brother Ezechiel who was a clergyman. In an interrogatory a witness is asked if he had told Thomas Brigham

> that one of the plaintiff's brothers, that then dwelt in the west Countrye Beinge in London at the plaintif Hilliardes Howse within a short tyme after the defendant's monye was paid to the plaintif, was verye ernest wth the plaintif hys brother, for hym selfe or for his frend to gett the said revercon and put this defendant Thomas Brigham from yt. And did you not farther saye to this defendant Brigham as followeth, or to the lik effect vzt. That an other brother of the plaintif Hilliard being a student and then redye to go beyond seas to travel, contendid with his Brother perswadinge the plaintiff not to lett anye man have the Bargayne before the defendant, partlye for your sake and for that the plaintif had reserved the defendant's monye for it.[3]

---

[1] Minutes, Book K–L, p. 10.
[2] In the Court of Requests, Req. 2/219/55.
[3] Req. 2/224/38. These proceedings are mentioned by Blakiston, *Nicholas Hilliard at Court*.

8

Although the answer to this interrogatory was in the negative, the facts mentioned therein, which must have occurred shortly after 3 May 1583, give us an idea of Hilliard's hospitality to his brothers from Devon and indicate that he kept open house in London for his family.

Hilliard's portrait miniature of the Queen, dated 1572, is surely based on a sitting which Elizabeth must have granted him. He was, therefore, already in that year in the royal service. Probably he had started to work for the Queen immediately after he became a free goldsmith in 1569. In any event, Nicholas Hilliard's delightful rectangular miniature of Elizabeth in State robes at Welbeck Abbey must have been painted at that time. It is so finished and accomplished in quality that it may be considered the masterpiece at the end of his training. It is likely that he was introduced to the royal patron by his master Robert Brandon who himself was in the service of the Queen. As early as 9 January 1573, Nicholas received a first token of encouragement from the Crown for "his good, true and loyal service" in the grant of the reversion for a lease of the rectory and church of Clyve in Somerset.[1] In the same year, on 11 October, a further reward of 100*l.* was granted to him under a warrant of the Privy Seal.[2] It is probably no mere coincidence that the entry of the latter in the Exchequer records follows one of very many grants to Robert Brandon, "her Majesties goldsmith and jeweller", bearing the date 27 September 1573.

More miniatures, some of them dated, are known to have been painted by Hilliard during 1572–4 and several entries in the Court Minutes of the Goldsmiths' Company reflect his expanding activities as a goldsmith.

In 1573, on 8 June, Nicholas' apprentice John Cobbold became a freeman of the Goldsmiths' Company after William Smyth had taken *his* place as Nicholas' apprentice on the previous 13 March.[3]

In the same year the Wardens and assistants of the Goldsmiths' Company showed Nicholas a first sign of appreciation. On 9 June, 1573,

> the reversion of the house wherein Nichas Johnson now dwelleth in Gutterlane was graunted to Nichas Hellyard. He after the deceasse of the said Johnson, if he fortunes to over lyve the same Johnson, to have a lease of the said house for 21 years from thens to come.[4]

This is the first reference to the house "The Maydenhead" in Gutter Lane into which he moved some five years later; in which he lived for 35 years

---

[1] C. 66/1096. Cf. Auerbach, *Portraits of Elizabeth I*, p. 202. Clyve probably means Cleeve.
[2] E. 403/2559, fol. 62.
[3] Minutes, Book K–L., pt. 2, pp. 149 and 140.
[4] *Ibid.* p. 150. This grant was copied on 21 February 1574/5 (Book L., p. 224) and delivered to Hilliard. On the same day Mr. Brandon's lease of his house in Chepe was renewed for 30 years.

and the lease of which Hilliard was so anxious to have renewed approximately 25 years later.

Nicholas Johnson, whose house was thus granted to Hilliard in reversion, was a respected goldsmith and from 1558 until his death in 1577 or 1578 one of the "rentners" of the Company who collected the money every quarter of the year and delivered it to the Wardens and their assistants.[1] From an earlier document[2] we not only learn the name of the house, but also gain an impression, if not of the whole house, yet of part of it. On 3 October 1558 Johnson agreed to share the "tenement in Gutterlane called Maydenhead and belonging to the Companie" with the widow of a goldsmith, as long as she lived. Johnson

> should have and enjoy: for him. his wif and familie: 3 chambers whereof 2 have chymneis wt a privie and a shopp benethe for an entraunce into the said rowmes. And also that his wif or maydee one daye in every weke shall have the use and occupyinge of the Kytchen there for theire necessarie washynge.

Thus, the house, which was to be Hilliard's later, had a good many rooms, some comfort at least, and a shop underneath with an entrance where we may imagine some jewellery was displayed.

After the death of Johnson, Hilliard came into possession of the house in Gutter Lane, that is approximately in 1578 after his return from France.

Two more apprentices were engaged by Hilliard during these early years: William Franke, who probably was a German, was "set over" to him on 20 July 1573,[3] and one John Pickrynge was presented as his apprentice on 21 March 1574/5.[4]

The year 1576 was important in Hilliard's life. The bond between him and Robert Brandon became firmer and their relationship grew more intimate. On 15 July Alice Brandon, Robert's beautiful daughter, was married to Nicholas in St. Vedast, Foster Lane. He was 29 and she was 20. When in 1562, as a boy of 15, he first met her, she was only a child, 6 years old, and we can well imagine how they both grew up together in her father's house. Such is her charm and beauty as immortalised by her husband in the lovely miniature in the Victoria and Albert Museum, painted in 1578, that we are not surprised that Hilliard who was so responsive to women's graces fell in love with her. Nicholas in his self-portrait, dated a year after his wedding, is likewise good-looking and his appearance as a daring, elegant courtier must have attracted the young girl, the more so as he was at the threshold of a splendid career.

In late autumn of the same year Nicholas set out on his journey to France and took his young wife with him.

[1] Book K, pt. 1, p. 58.
[2] *Ibid.*, p. 64.
[3] Book L, pt. 2, p. 157.
[4] *Ibid.*, p. 226.

HILLIARD IN PARIS

Until recently no conclusive documentary evidence was known of Nicholas Hilliard's stay in France. Only an entry in an account of the domestic officers of the Duc d'Alençon, from 1562 to 1584, can be taken as a reference to our artist. Under the heading of "Vallets de chambre à 2 cent livres de gages" we find one "Nicolas Béliart, peintre anglois, en 1577".[1] That "Béliart" was in fact Heliard or Hilliard is now established by two letters from the English ambassador in Paris, Sir Amyas Poulet. In the first of these letters, dated at St. Dye beside Bloys, on 8 December 1576, and addressed to John Peter, auditor of the Exchequer,[2] Poulet requests financial support from the authorities. When explaining his expenses he asks the Exchequer to consider that his train has been great

> by reason of dyuers Gentlemen recomended unto me by the Queenes Matie as Maister Doctor Cesar, Mr Throgmorton and Mr Helyer besides those of myn owne companie.

"Mr. Helyer", is of course, Nicholas Hilliard. This is made even clearer in Poulet's second letter, addressed to Walsingham and dated 19 February 1577/8 in which he writes:[3]

> Helyard means nothing less than to leave her Majesty's service; having repaired hither, as he says, with no other intent than to increase his knowledge by this voyage, and upon hope to get a piece of money of the lords and ladies here for his better maintenance in England at his return. He would have been back by this time if he had not been disappointed by some misfortunes. He intends to go shortly, and carry his wife with him.

The following facts emerge from these letters: *first*, Hilliard went to Paris with the recommendation of his royal mistress; *secondly*, his departure from England to France must have taken place between his wedding day, 15 July 1576, and 8 December of the same year, the date of the first letter; *thirdly*, Hilliard, together with his wife, was still in Paris in February 1578, although he intended to depart before long; *fourthly*, he was personally known to the English ambassador in Paris and probably, at least at the beginning, financially supported by him; *fifthly*, Hilliard's visit to Paris was so successful that, during part of it, he became

[1] An account of the status of the "officiers domestiques de Monseyneur François, duc d'Alençon, fils du Roy Henri II depuis l'an 1562 jusques en 1584", Bibliothèque Nationale, MSS. Fonds Français, 7856, fols. 1207 and 1239.

[2] E. 407/73. See Noel Blakiston, "Nicholas Hilliard in France", *Gaz. des Beaux-Arts*, July 1958, pp. 298–300.

[3] Cal. of State Papers, Foreign, 1577–8, No. 653; see Blakiston, *Nicholas Hilliard as a Traveller*, p. 169.

attached to the court of the Duc d'Alençon, and finally, in February 1578, the Queen grew impatient and was anxious to have her much needed painter back.

Of these conclusions, the second is particularly important: until the two letters referred to earlier were found by Mr. Blakiston, it was thought that Hilliard stayed in France only one year, namely from 1577 onwards. It is now clear that he stayed there two years and went to Paris directly after his marriage in 1576.

This conclusion is corroborated by Nicholas Hilliard's own statement in the proceedings in the Court of Requests against Alcock which were mentioned earlier.[1] It will be recollected that these proceedings concerned an obligation which Nicholas had undertaken on behalf of his brother John, approximately in 1572. In his submissions to the Court he states that after incurring this liability he lived for four years at least in London and thereafter he went overseas where he remained for two years. These are the relevant extracts from the documents:

> After wch tyme yor sayde Subjecte was for the space of fowre yeres at the leste comorante here in London. . . . Sythens wch tyme yor sayde Subjecte vppon ocasion by lycence of yor highnesse wente beyonde the Seas where he remayned two yeres. . . .

That Hilliard had a great reputation with the Goldsmiths' Company even at that early date can be seen from Alcock's statement to the Court that he is "standing too much uppon his reputacon".

Hilliard's presence in England from 1569 to 1572 is further accounted for by the references to him in the Minutes of the Goldsmiths' Company. Since it is most unlikely that he travelled abroad during the years of his apprenticeship, i.e. from 1562 to 1569, his visit to France was a highly important event in his life; it was in all probability his first and only visit abroad. Whether, when in Paris, Hilliard travelled to other countries on the Continent, we do not know.

It has generally been thought that Nicholas and Alice returned to England before the baptism of their first son Daniel at St. Vedast, Foster Lane, London, on 16 May 1578. However, new research shows that this view is not in harmony with the facts. It appears that Alice returned to England alone in time, it may be, for the birth and baptism of her eldest son, but that Nicholas was detained in France, probably against his will. On 16 June 1578 Poulet wrote from the French capital to the Earl of Hertford[2] that Hilliard had asked him to inform the Earl that he would have finished the Earl's jewel—we do not know what it was—

[1] See p. 8, *ante*.
[2] Bodleian, MSS. Add. c. 82., Poulet's letterbook.

12

long before "if God had not visited him with sickness" and that he would complete the work within three weeks and then either "bring or send it" to Lord Hertford.

At that date Hilliard was thus uncertain whether he could leave France three weeks later, but two months later he was still abroad. That follows from an entry in the Court Minutes of the Goldsmiths' Company, dated 22 August 1578.[1] On that date William Franke, Hilliard's apprentice, applied to be made free of the Company, but the Wardens could not grant the application, because "the said Hilliard, his master, is at this present beyond the seas". For that reason Franke

> was willyd by Mr Warden Brandon to staye for this syxe weekes, in the meane tyme the saied Mr Warden promysed to wright unto his saied master in his Behalfe and to certyfye him of his answere.

Whether Hilliard returned as a result of his father-in-law's communication or gave his approval by writing, is not known: on 3 November 1578, Franke became a freeman of the Company.[2]

What do we know of Hilliard's life in France and about the people he met? At the English Embassy Nicholas must have known the young noblemen who, under the care of Sir Amyas Poulet, learned French, diplomacy and the ways of the world. From Poulet's correspondence we learn how seriously the ambassador took his responsibility to supervise his charges.[3] At the Embassy, Hilliard must have met Francis Bacon who stayed and worked there from 1576 to 1579. We may well imagine how Hilliard enjoyed talking to this cultured young man who had just come down from Trinity College, Cambridge.

So much for the English circle. The French people with whom he was in touch were equally persons of consequence. Being in the service of the Duc d'Alençon, Hilliard was as close to the Court as was possible. His master was a man of great intellect and culture though of somewhat ambiguous character. Just when Hilliard entered into his service, there was a period of truce between the Duke and his brother, King Henri III, but, apart therefrom, there was much intrigue and discord at the French Court. In 1575, the Duke was considered to be the leader of the "mécontents" and was imprisoned. Intrigues that the King started against him led to a rapprochement between the Duke and his sister Marguerite, Queen of Navarre. They often met, and it is quite possible that Hilliard too became acquainted with the Court of Navarre at Béarn, which was smaller but not less brilliant than that of Paris. Both the Duke and the English

[1] Book L, 2, p. 412.   [2] *Ibid.*, p. 420.
[3] See various entries in Cal. State Papers, Foreign, 1577 ff., as regards Sir George Speake's son: Copy-book of Sir Amias Poulet's Letters, 1577, Roxburghe Club, 1896, p. 15.

Embassy certainly went as far south as Poitiers in the summer of 1577. This is the more important as we learn that Hilliard was personally known to Jacques Gaultier, the painter who at one time at least was closely connected with the Queen of Navarre and who painted the decorations in Bordeaux for the entry of Marguerite in September 1578.[1] That Jacques Gaultier had met Hilliard, perhaps in Paris, before he moved further south, we learn from a letter by the French painter, dated 12 January 1592/3 and written from Bordeaux. The letter was addressed to Anthony Bacon in England who himself had stayed in France from 1579 to 1592. In a postscript[2] Gaultier sent greetings to "Monsieur Hyllart paintre et orfeuvre de la Royne s'il est près de vous" (painter and goldsmith of the [English] Queen if he is near you) and asked him to send him a pound of paint of which he enclosed a sample. Jacques' son "L. Gautier", who in August 1592 sent some portrait drawings to Anthony Bacon, was at the same time in the service of the Condés. If the view advanced elsewhere[3] is correct, that he can be identified as the famous engraver Léonard Gautier, he was probably in Paris during Hilliard's stay in France and may have met him there. Léonard Gaultier is supposed to be the son-in-law of André Caron who, together with Germain Pilon, was at that time the most influential artist at the Court of Henri III.

In Paris Hilliard knew the poet Pierre Ronsard[4]—we have his own word for this—who was one of the founders of the Académie de Paris, which, from 1576, was seated at the King's Court in the Louvre. When Charles IX entered Paris, Ronsard supervised the decorations, together with Niccolò dell' Abbate and Germain Pilon. There is considerable affinity in spirit between Hilliard and Ronsard; both were artists of the Renaissance who attempted to harmonise the medieval and the classic concept of art in their work.

The most interesting work which Hilliard executed in France and which has survived are the portraits of the Duke and Duchess of Nevers on the cover of the book containing the constitution of the "Fondation du duc de Nivernois" which provided for the marriage of sixty poor maidens. The suggestion that Hilliard drew those portraits, the artistic value of which will be examined later,[5] originated from Blaise de Vigenère, the well-known man of letters who was connected with the Duke of Nevers for many years. Hilliard learned from Blaise de Vigenère, who was in charge of the production of the book, that he was

[1] Jacques Gaultier was appointed painter to the City of Bordeaux on 22 August 1579.
[2] The letter has been published by Noel Blakiston, "Nicholas Hilliard and Bordeaux", *The Times Literary Supplement*, 28 July 1950, p. 469. See also E. Auerbach, "English Engraving in the Reign of James I", pp. 97–8.
[3] *Ibid.*, p. 98.
[4] Ronsard himself had been to Scotland and England as a child and was an Anglophil.
[5] See chapter III.

dissatisfied with the portraits which were engraved first by Master Bernard and then by Master Georges, and desired that he, Hilliard, should be entrusted with the task of replacing them by his own portrait engravings, though it might be necessary to insert new pieces of boxwood, and it even was suggested that the Duke should travel to Paris to sit for the English artist. In an unsigned letter from Paris, dated 20 February 1577/8, Blaise de Vigenère[1] advised the Duke of Nevers[2] of the progress of the decorated copy of the book on vellum, and complained that he found it difficult to trace the whereabouts of the "peintre anglois"; he had stayed before with "maistre Herman l'orfèvre"[3] where it was thought that he had left for the Court, but he was then discovered hidden in the house of "maistre Georges, le peintre de la reyne",[4] where Blaise de Vigenère found him and discussed with him the execution of the portraits on the cover of the book of the Foundation. Why Hilliard went into hiding we do not know; it may, however, be recorded that only a day before Blaise de Vigenère's letter, Poulet had written to the Queen and advised her of "some misfortunes" that had disappointed her limner during that period and had delayed his imminent departure.

Blaise de Vigenère was a great personal friend and admirer of Hilliard, particularly as a miniature portraitist. In the letter to the Duke of Nevers he writes:

A ce propos, le dit peintre angloys est tenu pour l'un des plus excellents dont on aye mémoire au moins en petit volume, et puisque vous l'avez en main, ie serois bien d'advis . . . de vous faire portraire en une planche de bouys, plus grand assès que vous n'estes icy, que, si cela vous estoit agréable, nous passerions encore oultre a retirer les princes et illustres personnages de ce temps, hommes et femmes, et en faire un livre complet, car je ferois les éloges et sommaires de leur vie, à l'immitation des anciens, et de leur race et maison, lequel seroit d'un costé, et le portrait avec les armoiries au dessoubz d'un aultre, ce qui seroit plus à propos, pour perpétuer leur mémoire à jamais, que les médailles des anciens, car nous avons l'imprimerie qu'il ignoroient.

[1] Who has been identified as author of this letter in Auerbach, *More Light on Nicholas Hilliard*, p. 166. Denyse Metral, *Blaise de Vigenère, Archéologue et Critique d'Art (1523–96)*, 1939, pp. 51 and 299, has come to the same conclusion.

[2] Henri Bouchot, "La Préparation et la Publication d'un livre illustré au XVIe siècle", Bibliothèque de l'École des Chartes, LIII, Paris, 1892, p. 612.

[3] "Maistre Herman l'orfèvre" is probably Germain Pilon, the most eminent goldsmith and sculptor of Henri III. M. Adhémar drew my attention to another possibility; Pierre Hotman, mentioned 1557–71, Registre Ville de Paris, Vaisselle d'Argent portée à la Monnoye 1562–68. (Bque Nle. MSS. Fonds Moreau No. 1060 Y5/38 & No. 14). M. Adhémar assumes that "Herman" may be a misspelling for "Hotman", but I think that "Herman" may be mis-read or misspelled for "Germain".

[4] "Maistre Georges, le peintre de la reyne" was, according to Dimier, Georges of Ghent or Georges van der Straeten, a Fleming who was a fashionable Court painter in the fifteen-seventies.

Vigenère, the secretary to the Duke of Nevers, was, therefore, thinking of a book of engraved portraits and suggested that Hilliard should be entrusted with this task. It was probably never made, but one is reminded of the "book of portraitures" which Hilliard had in his hands in 1570/1, jointly with Rutlingen, and which also may have contained—so it would seem to follow—portraits in the form of engravings.

Walpole[1] mentions the following eulogy of Hilliard, likewise from the pen of Blaise de Vigenère:

> Telle estoit aussi l'écriture et les traits d'un peintre Anglois nommé Oeillarde, d'autant plus à emerveiller, que cele se faisoit avec un pinceau fait des poils de la queue d'un escureuil, qui ne resiste ni ne soutient pas comme feroit une plume de corbeau, qui est très ferme.

Here the neatness of Hilliard's line was admired. The eulogy, quoted by Walpole, assumes a new importance, as it is now evident that the French author knew the English artist personally and may have watched him working.

Further, Blaise de Vigenère was an eminent author of critical essays on the philosophy of the visual arts. He had a wide knowledge, not only of the world of antiquities, but also of contemporary French art, and sculptors such as Goujon and Pilon were greatly admired by him.[2] In view of the fact that Hilliard himself was interested in the theory of art—as can be seen in his *Treatise*—his meeting with this "wise man" and their exchange of ideas must have proved most beneficial to him.

HIS RETURN TO LONDON: 1579—84

Hilliard returned to London at some time between the end of August 1578 and 30 April 1579. On that day an indenture was made in London between him and Robert Brandon which Hilliard signed in person on 14 July 1579 before the Lord Chancellor[3] and which makes it clear that Hilliard's hope, of which Poulet wrote in his letter to Walsingham, "to get a piece of money of the lords and ladies" in France "for his better maintenance in England at his return" had failed. According to that bond Hilliard was to borrow 70*l.* from his father-in-law for one year on the security of property in St. George's in Exeter which was in the possession of Hilliard's father Richard and which formerly belonged to

---

[1] *Anecdotes* (1888), p. 173.

[2] See *La Suite de Philostrate*, Paris, 1602; the chapter "Du desseing et portraiture" is most revealing.

[3] C. 54/1055.

the Earl of Oxford; the bond provided that if the money was repaid on the due date it should be invalid but if it was not so repaid the property should be forfeited to Brandon, and Hilliard and "Alice now his wife" should have no further rights in this matter. We do not know whether Hilliard was able to redeem his property. The strict terms on which Brandon lent the money to his son-in-law are remarkable, particularly when one considers the circumstances, viz. that Nicholas and Alice had just returned from abroad, and the short term of the loan.

Shortly after his return from France, Hilliard must have begun to take an interest in the unfortunate speculation in gold mining in Scotland. He was involved in that transaction by two Flemish artists, Cornelis Devosse and Arnold or Arthur van Brounckhurst[1], with one of whom he might have come into touch already in or about 1572. We know a good deal about them and the Scottish adventure from *The Discoverie and Historie of the Gold Mynes in Scotland* written in 1619 by a London goldsmith, Stephen Atkinson.[2] A short extract is as follows:

> The late Queene Elizabeth, of a famous memory, was possessed often with a good opinion of the Gold Mines in Scotland, (vizt) about some forty yeares past. Long before Mr Bulmer had intelligence [1608], one Cornelius Devosse, a most cunninge pictur maker, and excellent in arte for triall of meneralls and menerall stones, sometimes dwelling in London, a young man, well acquainted with Mr Nicholas Hilliard, a goldsmith, then principall drawer of small pictures to the late Queene Elizabeth, procured the same Hilliard to adventure with him into Scotland, and to send his servant and freind as an agent thither, by name Arthur Van-Brounck-hurst; for at that time there was a great report and fame that went of the naturall gold gotten within the Kingdom of Scotland. And Brounckhurst being known to be a good artist, skilful and well seene in all sorts of stones, especially in meneralls and menerall stones, then Mr Hilliard ceased not, untill he had procured pattent, which was graunted unto Cornelius Devosse mad upon reasonable Conditions an assignement unto Arthur Van-Brunckhurst, who, after that powerfull, sett sondry workemen to worke without any trouble or molestation.

Hilliard, who as we know from his deal with Brandon was in need of money, apparently attempted to supplement his income as painter and gold-smith by other means. He used his considerable influence at the Court for the purpose of procuring a patent for his two associates in business in which he participated. Cornelius Devosse was not only a "picture maker" but also an influential merchant and a shareholder in the Company of Mines Royal, and on 4 March 1567/8 received a grant from James, Earl of Murray, Regent of

[1] *Tudor Artists*, pp. 107, 117, 142–3, 152, 161.
[2] Edited by Gilbert Laing Meason, Bannatyne Club, ed. 1825.

Scotland, to search and develop the Crawford Moor Mines for the production of gold for nineteen years.[1]

From a letter of December 1566 written by Thurland to Cecil we learn that Devosse was a somewhat dubious character. He appears to have reported on the gold finds more optimistically than was justified, in order to obtain more money from his partners in London. Hilliard appears to have been a dupe of this unscrupulous speculator.[2]

Devosse later disposed of his shares in the Mines Royal and formed a similar company in Scotland of which he and his London friends held ten parts. During the regency of the Earl of Morton he was forced to renew his patent. It was probably at that time, presumably in 1578 or 1579, that Hilliard and Devosse came to an agreement with van Brounckhurst according to which the latter was to go to Scotland to search for gold and bring it back safely to England. But the Earl of Morton did not allow the export of gold from Scotland and in September 1580 Brounckhurst was compelled to become principal painter to the King of Scotland

> to draw all the small and great pictures for his Majesty. And by this meanes, Mr Hilliard and Cornelius Devosse lost all their chardges, and never since got any recompence, to Mr Hilliard's great hinderance, as he saith, who yet liveth, and confirmeth the same.

We can believe Atkinson, who knew Hilliard, that the latter was disappointed at the failure of an adventure inspired by the typical Elizabethan fever for gold.

From 1579 to 1592 no minute books of the Goldsmiths' Company have survived, but in the Apprentice Books of the Company[3] we find a most interesting entry:

> Memorandom that I Rowland Lockey son of Lenard Lockey of thi paresh of St Brids in Flitstrete crasbomaker haue put myself prentice to Nicolas Hilliard for the terme of 8 yiers biginning at the fest of St Meghel in anno dni 1581
>
> by me Rouland Lockey

That this versatile artist was held in high esteem as a painter by contemporary Elizabethan writers is well known, and we also know from Richard Haydock's translation of Lomazzo's *Trattato dell' Arte della Pittura* (1598)[4] that he was a pupil of Hilliard. This entry in the Apprentice Book for 1581 provides documentary evidence of that fact and also of the length of Lockey's apprenticeship.

[1] Register of the Privy Council of Scotland, Vol. I, No. 97, p. 612.
[2] M. B. Donald, *Elizabethan Copper* (1955), p. 86.
[3] The Apprentice Books start in 1578 and in the first volume cover the period from 1578 to 1648; see *ibid.*, p. 30.
[4] *Tudor Artists*, p. 175.

From 1580 to 1584 Hilliard was actively engaged in painting miniatures for the Queen and members of the Court. Many of his best miniatures which have survived bear date of that period. Evidence of Leicester's interest in him is found in a letter which the Earl addressed from the Court to Sir Walter Mildmay, Chancellor of the Exchequer, on 28 June, presumably in 1582.[1] In this letter, which Leicester apparently gave Hilliard as bearer, he states that the Queen had given a lease to the painter for his services during the past two years and asked the Chancellor to expedite its execution. This letter indicates "a personal intervention by the queen's favourite on behalf of the ever needy limner."[2] As Hilliard received on 15 October 1582 the grant of a lease of a warren at Milbroke, tithes at Lockington, and the manor of Yelvertoft,[3] Leicester's intervention proved successful. The letter further implies that both Leicester and the artist were at that time actually at Court. This is again confirmed by interrogatories in proceedings started by Hilliard against one Thomas Brigham[4] in which a witness was asked whether he knew who first induced Hilliard to procure the place as Falconer for the defendant's brother—which happened in 1583—and "where and at what house Her Majesty lay at, when first the plaintiff Hilliard began his suit". This shows that the painter had knowledge of, and probably access to, the houses in which the Queen lived during her progresses through the country.

Meanwhile Hilliard's family increased and one child after another was born to his beautiful wife: Daniel, the first-born, was baptised on 16 May 1578, Elizabeth on 4 October 1579, Francis on 24 December 1580, Laurence on 5 March 1582, Lettice on 25 May 1583, Penelope on 31 October 1586, and Robert on 30 March 1588. On 27 December 1584 a still-born child of Nicholas Hilliard was buried.[5] The names which Hilliard gave to some of his children make it probable, as Mr. Blakiston suggested,[6] that eminent members of the Queen's Court acted as their god-parents; one is reminded of *Elizabeth*, the Queen, of Sir *Francis* Knollys, of *Lettice*, Lord Leicester's second wife, of *Penelope*, Lady Rich, and, of course, of *Robert*, Lord Leicester, or *Robert*, 2nd Earl of Essex. *Laurence*, alone, refers to the family and repeats the name of Hilliard's mother.

The year 1584 was again most eventful for Hilliard. He was by now well established at the Court, so well indeed, that nobody could rival him in the

---

[1] S.P. 46/XVII, f. 63, published by Mr. Blakiston, *Nicholas Hilliard at Court*, p. 17.
[2] As Mr. Blakiston has pointed out, *ibid.*, p. 17.
[3] C. 66/1214.
[4] Req. 2/224/38.
[5] Registers of St. Vedast, Foster Lane, Harl. Soc. Registers, XXIX.
[6] Blakiston, *ibid.*

execution of miniatures. When in that year a patent of monopoly for the painting of portraits of the Queen was drafted in favour of George Gower, the Serjeant Painter, Hilliard's name was especially included:[1]

> Exceptinge only one Nichas Hilliard, to whome it shall or maie be lawfull to exercyse and make purtraicts, pictures, or proporcons of our body and person in small compasse in lymnynge only, and not otherwise.

Whatever the origin of this draft of which no enrolment as patent has been found, whether it was drafted on the Queen's initiative or was a petition by the two painters, it clearly shows that the royal goldsmith enjoyed absolute supremacy in the field of portrait miniature painting.

In the same year, 1584, Hilliard was honoured by the royal command to make the Second Great Seal for the Queen. This commission was the ideal task for Hilliard as it gave him an opportunity of combining his skill as a portraitist and a goldsmith. Hilliard was to make the Great Seal in conjunction with Dericke Anthony, graver to the Mint. The Queen's commission runs:[2]

> You shall embosse . . . patterns for a new Great Seal according to the last pattern made upon parchment by you Our servant Hilliard. . . . And by the same pattern you shall work, engrave, sink, finish and bring to perfection ready to be used . . . such a new Great Seal in silver.

The Queen who, like every reigning sovereign of that period, was personally interested in her Great Seal, the matrix of which she constantly used to handle, not only asked her limner to create her likeness but also—in collaboration with Dericke Anthony—to engrave it and to carry out the actual goldsmith's work. It was not only honour and artistic satisfaction that Hilliard gained from this commission but also the envy of the official graver of the Mint, for when he was asked to accept a commission from the Earl of Salisbury for work which was within the scope of the Serjeant Painter, he hesitated and remembered: "For I had once envy enough about a Great Seal for my doing well in other men's offices."[3]

But the envy of his colleagues was not Hilliard's worst predicament. When he worked on the Great Seal, he was again in financial trouble, a difficulty of which he could not free himself during almost his whole life. In an undated letter to Lord Burghley or Sir Robert Cecil—the addressee is not mentioned—in which he

---

[1] *Tudor Artists*, pp. 109 and 168.
[2] S.P. 15/28, No. 86. Blakiston, *Nicholas Hilliard and Queen Elizabeth's Third Great Seal*, pp. 101ff. *Tudor Artists*, pp. 111, 130, 151 and 168.
[3] Hist. MSS. Com. Salisbury MSS., Pt. XVIII, p. 409. This letter is undated but by internal evidence assigned to 1606 (No. 119/8). See p. 37 *post*.

asked his patron to intervene in his favour when threatened with arrest, Hilliard again mentions the eventful happenings of that period:

> . . . And what so ever is unpayed of the principall, I will presently paye him. as I have often offered to doo. but he refusethe it because when I was in truble attending the Queen Matie about the great Seale 4 yeres past, I fayled the last payment of my bond wch is 48*s* for wch my bond is forfeted in 20*l*. I beseche your honors, do me not so hard measure as to cause me to paye the forfeture. . . .[1]

This letter does not mention the name of the person who pressed Hilliard for payment, but some light is thrown on this matter if it is connected with some contemporary proceedings in the Orphans' Court and in Chancery. On 4 March 1584/5, Nicholas Hilliard, John Ballet, John Bent, all three goldsmiths, and William Freeman, Innholder, signed three recognizances by which they undertook jointly and severally to pay to "Robert Brandon goldsmith and Chamberlain of London" certain sums for moneys belonging to orphans which are named in the documents.[2] Apparently the orphans' moneys were managed by the Chamberlain and profitably invested by him by being lent out to trustworthy citizens. The moneys to which the three recognizances refer were:

Orphans' moneys	*Payable by the Borrowers*
36*l*. 12*s*. 1*d*.	44*l*.
26*l*. 7*s*. 6*d*.	38*l*.
33*l*. 6*s*. 8*d*.	42*l*.
————	————
96*l*. 6*s*. 3*d*.	124*l*.

The four signatures of the borrowers to these documents were headed by Hilliard and he signed his name in the distinctive style which we know so well from inscriptions on some of his miniatures. (*See reproduction overleaf*)

Altogether the sum payable by the four borrowers came to approximately 100*l*. which is the amount mentioned by Hilliard in the petition to Lord Burghley or his son to which reference has been made. This was not the only transaction relating to orphans' moneys with which Hilliard was concerned, as

---

[1] Petition 782 (Hist. MSS. Com. Salisbury MSS. IX, p. 436). The Calendar ascribes this petition to 1599 and gives only an abstract of three lines with a wrong interpretation. This letter written 4 years after he was working on the Great Seal, must be dated between *c.* 1588 and 1590.

[2] City Record Office, JOR. 21, Proc. of Com. Council of the Corporation of London, fol. 416, 7. The names of the orphans were: George, son of George Myller, girder, Winifred, daughter of Tymothy Cockerell, painter-stainer, and the orphan children of W. Methold, mercer.

is shown by an entry in the records of the Orphans' Court of 9 March 1584/5[1] when the sum of 30*l.* belonging to one of the orphans was to be paid to him.

Hilliard himself gives some indication about the investment of the orphans' money in which he took part, when in the above-mentioned petition he states

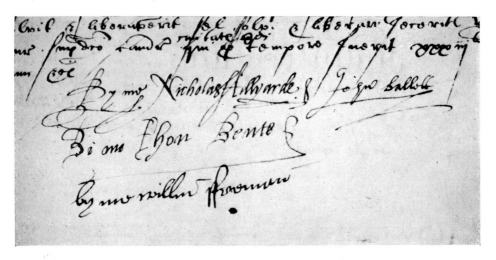

Hilliard's signature

that the aldermen were apparently under an obligation to his opponent who is unnamed in the petition and continues:

> and my lords' if the Aldermen have doone the man any such wrong for wch they
> woold agayne pleasure him, they maye at all tymes doo him suche a pleasure,
> fynding suerties as I did/ to have of the Orphants mony paying the due intrest/ if
> the suertyes be good it is never refused neither can they by statute take above 9*l.*
> in the 100th/

It follows that at that time—1584/5—Hilliard was still on good terms with his father-in-law, Robert Brandon, the powerful Chamberlain of the City of London.

However, it appears that Hilliard, the incorrigible financial optimist, was unable to honour his undertakings in the orphans' bonds and that the orphans' moneys were repaid by one of the co-sureties, John Ballet, a goldsmith of substance and a warden of the Goldsmiths' Company. On 17 January 1588/9 Hilliard and John Maryett appeared in Chancery and acknowledged their indebtedness in the sum of 200*l.* to John Ballet as the result of the failure of Hilliard and others to honour the three orphans' recognizances of 4 March

[1] City Record Office, Rep. 21, fols. 147–8.

1584/5; apparently John Maryett stood surety for Hilliard. But at least this financial wangle seems to have ended happily: on 28 March 1590, in Chancery, John Ballet declared himself to be satisfied and the new bond was cancelled.[1]

It is quite possible that the influential unnamed opponent whom Hilliard mentions in his petition to Lord Burghley or Sir Robert Cecil was none other than John Ballet. This conclusion is supported by an entry in the minutes of the Goldsmiths' Company of 27 May 1593 according to which Hilliard mortgaged the lease of his house to Ballet, probably as security for the release in Chancery of 1590. This is the entry[2]:

> The same tyme lycence was grauntyd to Mr Warden Ballett to Alyene sell or settouer the lease of a tenement in gutter Lane late in the tenner of Nichas Hellyarde and nowe in the possessyon of the said Mr Ballett, and also the tente wth the apperto' or any part therof mentyoned in the saied lease to any person or persons whatsoever any clause or acte in the said Indenture contayned to the contrarye in anywyse not wtstandynge.

That lease Hilliard did not forfeit, because in the will of John Ballet who died shortly afterwards no mention is made of the tenement in Gutter Lane and we know that Hilliard, in the late fifteen-nineties, applied to the Goldsmiths' Company for the renewal of that lease.

It is likely that the money for the redemption of the mortgage on Hilliard's house came from yet another source, namely from one no less important than the Earl of Essex himself.

According to the Devereux Accounts the following entry, just published,[3] appears under "Gifts". Though undated, the approximate date can be derived from the preceding item which is dated "22 October 1595". This is the entry relating to Hilliard:

> (Item to) Mr deane Wood for Mr Hillyard vpon (your lordship's) letter in part of 140 for Mr Hillyards house—xx*l*.

Probably some earlier instalments were already paid towards the 140*l*.

This document provides a welcome confirmation of the theory that Ballet was Hilliard's principal creditor. The payment to "deane Wood", who was Owen Wood, Dean of Armagh, and at that time—in 1595—the second husband of "Ritch Ballet's Widow of Cheapside", was thus made to the very person on whom the mortgage on the lease of Hilliard's house devolved after the death of the original mortgagee, namely Ballet.

If the making of the Second Great Seal of Queen Elizabeth involved Hilliard in financial difficulties, it also brought him some reward: on 18 October 1587

---

[1] C. 54/1303.   [2] Minutes, Book N-O, Pt. I, p. 16.
[3] Roy C. Strong, "Queen Elizabeth, The Earl of Essex and Nicholas Hilliard", pp. 146–9.

23

he received "for good service" a reversionary lease containing lands and rents of various sizes and widely dispersed over many different counties.[1] Two of his most influential patrons, Walsingham and Lord Burghley, wrote to the Exchequer and asked that the grants of the leases be expedited. The first of these letters, written by Walsingham to Sir Walter Mildmay, Chancellor of the Exchequer, on 8 November 1586 begins as follows:[2]

> Sir,
>
> Hir Majestie is pleased to bestowe upon the bearer Nicholas Hilliarde a lease in reversion of forty poundes by the yere as well in respect of his paynes lately employed in the engraving of the great seale of Englande as for divers other services for wch as yet he never receyved any recompense or allowance.

Burghley's letter of July 1587 is interesting because it shows that Hilliard in his great financial difficulties was not without influential friends: Burghley writes to an Exchequer official[3] that since Hilliard finds himself unable to produce two sureties, the Exchequer should use him, Burghley, and the Chancellor, but should retain the bond "privately".

HILLIARD DURING THE CLOSING YEARS OF ELIZABETH'S REIGN

Very beautiful miniatures have survived of the closing years of Queen Elizabeth's reign, but they appear to have brought Hilliard small financial rewards. The usual fee for an unframed miniature was apparently 3*l*., which would be paid by any gentleman or lady at that time. In the Earl of Northumberland's accounts for 1 September 1585 to 27 November 1586 we find an entry according to which 60*s*. were paid to Hilliard for his Lordship's picture;[4] and the same amount was paid on 27 July 1592 to him for 'the drawing of one picture" by Bess of Hardwick, Countess of Shrewsbury.[5] At the same time Hilliard was still engaged on work for the Queen and on 11 December 1591 it was recorded that he received the considerable sum of 400*l*. for his good and faithful service "to be taken unto him of our free gift without any *prest* [tax] or other charge to be set upon him for the same or any part thereof ".[6] This was indeed a generous royal reward, if he really received it, which revealed the Queen's gratitude to him.

[1] C. 66/1290.
[2] E. 310/41/15.
[3] *Ibid.*
[4] U.I. 1, and U.I. 2. Extracts of these documents were made by Mr. Batho.
[5] Hardwick MSS. 7, f. 30.
[6] E. 403/2559, f. 332.

In the same year, 1591, Hilliard's father-in-law died. Robert Brandon's will,[1] a most complicated legal instrument, does not contain any provision for Nicholas or his children; on the contrary, it deliberately cuts him out from the inheritance; even the money which Brandon leaves to Alice is not left to her absolutely but is left to the Goldsmiths' Company to pay to her for her maintenance in quarterly instalments, the Elizabethan equivalent to a restraint upon anticipation. This is the relevant part of the will:

> Item I give and bequeathe to the wardenns and communaltie of the misterie of Goldesmithes of London the somm of fiftie pounde of lawefull moneie of Englande to be paide unto them within one halfe yeere nexte after my decease which I hartelie praie them by the wardens of ye saide misterie or anie of them for the time beinge to paie unto the saide Alice my daughter for and towardes her maintenaunce by sixteene pounde thirteene shillinges fower pence a yere quarterlie [sic] by evenn porconns within three yeeres nexte after my decease.

Apparently the testator trusted his son-in-law so little that he made the strictest provision for the relatively small bequest in favour of his daughter to prevent it from falling into Nicholas' hands and from being used as security by him. The intention of the testator is likewise reflected in the substitutional gifts: in the case of Alice's death the fifty pounds left to her were to be divided between the testator's son Edward and the other four daughters. As to an annuity of 50*l.* payable by the Goldsmiths' Company to his son, the testator provided that after Edward Brandon's death the money should go to his five daughters including Alice but—and this is highly significant—the ten pounds thus due to each of the five daughters contingently were to be held in the case of the death of Rebecca, Sara, Martha or Marie for their issue, but in the case of Alice's death her ten pounds should not go to her issue but were to be divided amongst the children of the other four daughters!

It follows that Brandon's feelings against Nicholas did not even soften towards his grandchildren by Nicholas and Alice. We have seen that at an earlier time, during the years of Hilliard's apprenticeship, the Chamberlain of the City of London helped and supported Nicholas and was friendly disposed towards the young couple. Why had this changed now, in 1591? It is possible that Brandon had a low opinion of the financial ability of his son-in-law who on various occasions had defaulted on his obligations and kept himself going by complicated financial operations. The real reason for Brandon's disapproval of Hilliard's careless attitude to finance—and we should not forget that the goldsmiths of those days were, to a large extent, the bankers of that period—is a clash between Nicholas' artistic temperament, the actual moving power be-

---

[1] P.C.C., 43 Sainberbe; see Auerbach, *More Light on Nicholas Hilliard*, p. 168.

hind his supreme talent, which was in evident contrast to the prudent and cautious mind which the chief administrator of the Goldsmiths' Company and the Chamberlain of the Corporation of London applied to matters of finance. In his *Treatise* Hilliard himself gives the clue to this clash when he describes the worries of the craftsman and his "liberal"—probably Brandon called it spendthrift—attitude to money:[1]

> The good workman also which is soe excelent dependeth one his owne hand, and can hardly find any workmen to worke with him, to heelpe him to keepe promise, and worke as well as himselfe, which is a great mischeefe to him. Neither is he alwayes in humore to imploye his spirits on some worke, but rather one some other. Also such men are commonly noe mysers, but liberall above theire littel degree, knowing howe bountifull God hath indued them with skill above others; also they are much given to practises, to find out newe skills, and are ever trying conclusions, which spendeth both theire time and mony, and oftenes when they have performed a rare pece of worke (which they indeede cannot afforde) they will give it awaye to some worthy personage for very affection and to be spoken of. . . .

Here is Hilliard's character, here speaks the artist, convinced of his own vocation and abounding in lovable if improvident generosity.

We learn from an inscription on Hilliard's portrait miniature of Alice that she was his first wife. But no record has been found of her death, nor are we at all sure about a second marriage. No payment to Alice can be traced after Brandon's death, owing to the gap in the minutes of the Goldsmiths' Company, but one fact is certain, namely that she was alive on 8 May 1591 when Brandon made his will. Other provisions of the will, whereby substantial sums were bequeathed to the Goldsmiths' Company and the share of Brandon's youngest daughter Lucy (whose interests were looked after by the Orphans' Court), figure in many discussions and arguments before the Wardens and their assistants of the Company in later years when records of the Company were again available.

Hilliard's name often appears in the Cecil Papers. These references are highly important and of great biographical interest. For 1593 and 1594 two such documents have survived. On 16 March 1593/4 Hilliard petitioned Sir Robert Cecil to intervene in favour of one "Abell Feckemann" who was condemned for "coyning, being drawne thereunto by Webb and one Morgan Webs man";[2] Hilliard continued in that petition that Abel "is an excellent woorkman . . . I have knowne the young man, I mean the said Abell, both [as] servant with maisters and [as] his owne man almost these five years and never heard but

---

[1] *Walpole Society*, Vol. I (1911–12), p. 41.
[2] Salisbury MSS., Vol. 22, 74. Cal. IV, p. 490. E. A. Jones, *Conn.* 1943, pp. 1–6.

very well of him . . . ". A few weeks later, on 27 May 1594, Richard Martyn addressed Robert Cecil in the same matter and emphasised that "Abell Fecnam stranger . . . is very penitent . . . being a very good workman, young and hable to do her Majes^{tie} good service, in gravinge under Mr. Hilliard who set him in work, and is to be favored as well as any of the reste, if her Majes^{tie} so think mete."[1] Since Hilliard states that he had known Abel for five years, it is possible that he had him working in his workshop when he engraved the Armada jewel; Hilliard's concern for Abel is understandable as we have his own word that it was difficult to find able assistants.

The second petition of 1593[2] addressed to William, Lord Burghley, is written by two painter-stainers, Hughe Bennett and Samuel Tompson, who had applied for a monopoly of doing the decorative work for funerals under Clarenceux. As there was no reply from the King of Arms, they submitted a year later a petition, to Robert Cecil,[3] and their letter ends as follows:

> whoe not doubting but that their sute and motion shalbe found reasonable and very necessary, are very well content that there may also be ioyned with them to perform suche works, Mr Nicholas Hillyard her Maties servant to your Honors so well knowne for his sufficiencie and care in his woorks, as we hope the rather for his sake your Honore will the more speedely graunt this desired reformation.

Three points emerge from this petition: Hilliard tried his hand at some kind of heraldic and decorative work, or, to say the least, he expressed his desire to do this work which properly pertained to the domain of the painter-stainer; two decorative painters wanted to work together with him and spoke with admiration of his "sufficiency and care"; and lastly, they knew that Hilliard was one of Sir Robert's favourites and hoped, therefore, for a "speedy grant" of their petition.

In the meantime, Richard Hilliard, Nicholas' father, had died. His will, made on 2 November 1586, was proved on 9 August 1594.[4] Richard was apparently a man of some substance and all his tenements and rights in the parish of St. Pancras were to go to his son Nicholas. His wife, Lawrence, Nicholas' mother, who survived his father and died in 1604, was the executrix of his will. Nicholas was also given Richard's best gown and a gold ring with a Cornelyn stone. Jeremias and Ezechiel were likewise provided for, but John is not mentioned. Of Nicholas' children only Frances received a legacy of

[1] Salisbury MSS., Vol. 26, 96. Cal. IV, p. 537. E. A. Jones, *ibid.*, p. 6.

[2] Cal. IV, p. 459. Salisbury MSS. 170, 51. See *Tudor Artists*, pp. 153, 188.

[3] Cal. V, 63. MS. 170, 50. See *Tudor Artists*, pp. 153, 188. The Calendar gives only a very short abstract.

[4] P.C.C., 58 Dixy.

6l. 13*s.* 4*d.* Daniel, his eldest son, does not appear in the will and it is, therefore, possible that he was not alive in 1586.

At about the same time Hilliard began his prolonged attempt to obtain a renewal of the lease of his house in Gutter Lane. Again and again he petitioned the Goldsmiths' Company and year after year his case was deferred. The first time his application appears in the minutes is on 20 February 1595/6[1] and then again on 25 May 1597,[2] 29 July 1597,[3] 19 March 1598/9[4] and two days later when "it was respited until some other time", which we may take as an adjournment *ad Kalendas Graecas*.

After having petitioned his landlords for four years in vain, help came, as so often in Hilliard's life, from the highest quarters: on his application the Lords of the Privy Council agreed on 30 June 1600 to write a strongly worded letter to the Goldsmiths' Company in favour of the Queen's limner. They wrote:[5]

> Wee understand that Nicolas Hilliarde, her Majesty's servant, being one of your Company, is also one of your tenantes of a small tenement of three poundes rent in Gutter Lane, which because he hath bin at greate charges to repayre (to the summe at the leaste of 200*l.* by reason that it was much decayed and the lightes thereof darkened with the annoyance of one of the next neighbours' buyldinge), his suite unto you is that his lease beinge neare expiration may be favorably renued for some longer terme of yeres and for some small fine, the rather for the consideracon above-mentioned of his charges and for that he is one of your owne Company. Off [*sic*] which suite her Majesty having taken notice and wishinge that the same should take effect, is pleased that we shell signifie the same unto you by these our letters, and lett you know that the favour you shew unto her servant Hilliard wilbe acceptable unto her self because with the more conveniency of his house he shalbe the better able to doe her Majesty service in the skyll and workmanshipp wherein he is employed. Wee doubt not but it will suffice that wee have signified her Majesty's pleasure in his behalf, whereunto wee neede not adde any worde of request from our selves, and yet nevertheles to shew our owne desire also that he may speede wee doe earnestly commende his suite unto you, and pray you to afforde him all the favour that you may. And so, etc. .

The letter was signed, amongst others, by Robert Cecil, Secretary, Hilliard's protector and friend. It appears from this letter that not only the Privy Councillors but the Queen herself supported Hilliard's applications and the statement that with the improvement of the working conditions in his house the royal limner and goldsmith would be in a position to serve the Queen much better

---

[1] Minutes, Books N-O, pt. I, p. 81.

[2] *Ibid.*, p. 112.

[3] *Ibid.*, p. 120.

[4] *Ibid.*, pp. 160-1; he offered to give for his lease "xx*l.* and a pyctuer wch shalbe worthe XX nobles".

[5] Acts of the Privy Council 1599–1600, p. 432.

"in the skill and workmanship wherein he is employed" made it virtually impossible for the Goldsmiths' Company to refuse the application.

The Company, it must be admitted, responded promptly to the royal wish; they granted Hilliard at once, on 4 July, the renewal of the lease for 21 years:[1]

> Mr Helliar by the mediacon of lres from the Lords of the Counsailie signifyinge her Maties pleasuer on his behalf to the Companie, a Lease of his howse in . . . . . . Lane, for 21 yeares for 30*l.* fine wch was his owne voluntarie offer to be paied vppon the ensealinge of his lease. And to make and bestowe on the Companie a faire picture in greate of her Matie to remayne in the Howse for an ornam't and remembrance aswell of their humble duties as of her princelie fauor towardes him and of his gratefulnes to the Company.

It has now been generally accepted that the reference to the "faire picture in greate of her Matie" which Hilliard was to make and bestow on the Company meant that the Queen's miniaturist should paint a life-size portrait of his royal patron. This important documentary evidence testifying to Hilliard's ability as portrait painter on a large scale is also strengthened by the remark that this picture should remain in Goldsmiths' Hall as an ornament and a lasting "remembrance". Surely a miniature could not fulfil this condition.

A few months later, on 28 November 1600, Hilliard requested the Wardens to allow him to complete the Queen's picture in summer when light was more favourable; it is further evident from the record that Hilliard had difficulty in finding the 30*l.* for the lease. This is the entry:[2]

> Mr. Hiliard made request to Mr Wardens to haue his Lease made and deliuered him vnder seale promisinge to bringe in his money, but for the quenes picture for that the wintertyme is verie vnseasonable tyme to worke yt he will make it in the Somer wch vppon the receite of his lease he will geve securitie for whose request Mr. Wardens haue promised to Comende to ther assistantes at ther next meting.

More time, however, elapsed and on 9 March 1601/2 we hear of the matter again:[3]

> At this Court Mr. Heliers letter was redd wch he brought from Sir John Fortescue and in respect of his request to haue his fyne remitted wch he sholde haue payed by his owne agreement to the howse the Company haue ordered that Sir John shalbe satisfied by Mr Wase and Mr Newman whoe are requested to attend on him to that purpose.

The fine was still not paid and the lease not sealed; but unfortunately there is no mention of Hilliard's work on the picture.

---

[1] Minutes, Book O, pt. 2, 1599–1604, p. 125. See *More Light on Nicholas Hilliard*, p. 168, and *Tudor Artists*, p. 132.

[2] Minutes, *ibid.*, p. 157.

[3] Minutes, Book O, pt. 2, 1599–1604, p. 234.

On 17 May 1602 Hilliard and some fellow goldsmiths were warned "to amend and repair their houses".[1] Only on 18 June 1602 was the final lease granted[2]:

> At this Courte Mr Wardens made theire assistantes acquainted wth the conference they hadd wth Sir John Fortescue whoe requested that Mr Hilliar might haue his lease from the expiracon of the three yeres yet to come in his owlde lease but the same beinge answered vnto by the committes to the satisfaccon of Sir John after- wardes the saide Mr Hilliar was content and referred himselfe to the favor of the Companye and yt was at this Courte ordered that yf Mr Hilliar still rest contented to the first grante and doe not otherwise make any further request then this lease that was last made to be readie and sealed wth the first.

This time it was the Lord Treasurer who intervened in favour of Hilliard. Finally, on 13 July 1602, the Company's Common Seal was affixed to his lease. When in 1610 a list of all the property owned by the Company was drawn up, Nicholas Hilliard was still mentioned as the present occupier of a "tenement in Godron Lane".[3] The commencement of his lease was stated to have been Lady Day 1602. He had it for a period of 21 years, so that the date of expiration was Lady Day 1623. The rent was three pounds per annum and the fine was "30*l*. and a Picture". The latter entry is quite exceptional in a rent book; in other cases the fine of money is supplemented by a gift in kind, such as a "buck" which is recorded in one entry, but nowhere else is a picture mentioned. This points again to the importance which the Company attached to the fulfilment by Hilliard of this condition.

Later additions to the Rent Book, written in differently coloured ink and smaller letters, yield some further information about the fate of Hilliard's property. At Michaelmas 1613—before Nicholas' lease had expired—the lease for his house was granted to "Laurence Hillyard" for 21 years at an annual rent of 3*l*. as before. But the fine was now 60*l*. He was "present occupier" after his father and had the lease until Michaelmas 1634 when it came into the hands of one Francis Ashe who had to pay 300*l*. as a fine. So much had the value of the property increased within some 30 years.

We know that Nicholas died in the parish of St. Martin-in-the-Fields where, according to his will of December 1618, he had been a parishioner for some time. It is a matter of speculation at what time exactly he moved to Westminster. No payments for rent or other subsidies have been found in the Rent Books and Accounts of that parish. Nor do we know the reason why Hilliard moved

---

[1] Minutes, Book O, pt. 2, 1599–1604, p. 239.
[2] *Ibid.*, pp. 243–4.
[3] Rent Book 1913/B. 393, f. 6. "Godron lane" is identical with "Gutter lane".

further west. Was it perhaps that he wanted to be nearer to the Court and stayed with some friends who kept house for him? Whatever the reason, it can now be assumed that he left his house in Gutter Lane shortly before or after Michaelmas 1613 and that at some unknown date thereafter he took up residence in the parish of St. Martin-in-the-Fields.

Reverting to the closing years of the sixteenth century, at last on 17 August 1599 Hilliard's struggle for a safer financial position was rewarded when by letters patent he was granted an annuity of 40*l*. a year.[1] Again it was Robert Cecil, Hilliard's faithful patron, who had obtained the grant for him. Hilliard writes on 28 July 1607[2] that the annuity will be "a good stay and comfort to him when living with his friends in the country, at the house rent and the table free". It is interesting to note, as throwing light on the remuneration of artists and their social standing, that the 40*l*. granted to the goldsmith and limner were the same amount as the pension given to the "paintrix" and limner Levina Teerlinc by Henry VIII.[3]

The payments of his annuity can be followed up in various Exchequer Accounts. He was quarterly paid 10*l*. and received the first payment at Michaelmas 1599;[4] the Christmas instalment was paid to his son Laurence and the two further payments of 1600 went again to Hilliard himself. But only shortly afterwards, on 9 December 1602, Hilliard assigned his annuity together with the letters patent to one Richard Cannon and one Richard Orrell.[5] Subsequently the name of the latter appeared in the Accounts. Richard Orrell was an official in the department of the Hanaper, with whom Hilliard might have come in touch when designing the Great Seal, and from whom he probably had borrowed money. He received the last payment recorded in this series at Christmas 1607, and at Lady Day 1608, one John Burges was paid the instalment of 10*l*.[6] Further payments to Hilliard are regularly recorded from 26 April 1611 onwards, apparently into his own hands, and the last quarterly remittance of 10*l*. was made to him at Lady Day 1618.[7] According to his will of 24 December in the same year 30*l*. of his pension was still due to him, 10*l*. of which he bequeathed to his sister Anne, the wife of Thomas Averye.

It has been known that a considerable time before 17 May 1600 Hilliard must have been working again on a new Great Seal for the Queen; for on that

[1] E. 403/2453, f. 316 and C. 66/1510 m. 34.
[2] See his letter to Robert Cecil: Salisbury MSS., 87, 25.
[3] *Tudor Artists*, pp. 187–8.
[4] E. 403/2284, f. 11; see *Tudor Artists*, p. 169.
[5] Blakiston, *Nicholas Hilliard and Queen Elizabeth's Third Great Seal*, p. 104.
[6] E. 403/2291.
[7] E. 403/2368/8 and *Tudor Artists*, p. 169.

day a draft warrant was addressed to Charles Anthony, graver of the Mint, to work, engrave and finish such seal with all possible speed, "according to a pattern which we have ready and [which] remains with Nicholas Hilliard, our servant".[1] This seal which would have been the Third Great Seal of Queen Elizabeth was never completed. That Hilliard and Charles Anthony worked on it long before that date, emerges from Charles Anthony's account roll for the period from 22 May 1606 to 30 September 1609. Allowances are granted for material, workmanship, drawing of patterns, embossing some in wax and other work in connection with "a great Seal for the late Queen Elizabeth". The account further indicates that the patterns had to be altered several times before they were approved by the Queen. The most important passage of the account roll reads:[2]

> Drawinge and embossinge sondrye paterns for the saide greate Seale viz. twoe in the yeare 1592 60s, six other patternes somewhat lesser in the yeares 1594 and 1596 60s, embossinge a patterne in white waxe for the foreside of the saide greate Seale in the yeare 1597 70s, embossinge one other patterne in white waxe after a patterne which Mr Hilliarde did lymne in parchmente in the yeare 1599 100s; embossinge a greater patterne in white waxe which after many mendings was liked by her Majestie 11l; and for makeinge sondrye patternes for the horsbacke side of the sayde greate Seale in the yeare 1600 12l. 10s. In all . . . 37l.

It has been suggested[3] that Hilliard's drawing for a Great Seal of Ireland in the British Museum, in which the Irish emblems have been only faintly drawn in, may represent one of these patterns, perhaps that "which Mr. Hilliard did lymne in parchment" and which Anthony embossed in 1599.

It is now possible, as the result of a clue found in the Salisbury Papers, to state that Hilliard must have worked on the patterns for the third Great Seal as early as 1591.[4] In these documents is a record of an examination of the luggage of one Thomas Harrison after his return from France on 4 October 1601. Harrison was apparently accused of being a Papist and, worse still, of intending to endanger the Queen's life by placing next to a metal picture of her Majesty contained in a wooden box, a kind of mercury sublimate which was poisonous and had eaten into the metal. In the course of Harrison's deposition Hilliard's name is, strangely enough, mentioned several times:

> Being further asked what Picture that is which he had in a Box of wood and of what mettall he answereth that it is a Picture of a woman but of whom he doth not know, but saythe that the mettall is of mercury congeled with vinygir, and verdygresse, and was made by Mr Hyllyard about eyght or nine yeares sythence. . . .

[1] S.P. 12/274/143 and E. 403/2560, f. 212. Blakiston, *loc. cit.*, pp. 101–7.
[2] E. 351/2890.   [3] Blakiston, *loc. cit.*, p. 107.
[4] Cecil. Pap., 88, 89.

And he further saythe the mettall of the Picture was made by Mr Hyllyard, and will with aqua fortis be dissolved again into Quycsilver, and he sayeth that the said Picture was made about the tyme that Mr Hyllyard dyd make workes for the great Seale in the tyme of Sir Xsofer Hatton.

As Sir Christopher Hatton died on 21 November 1591, Hilliard must have worked on these models even earlier.

The last passage in this deposition is likewise of great interest:[1]

Beinge asked if it be not the Picture of the Q$^{ne'}$ that wch was in mettall he answereth that he thinketh that Hilliard dyd make it emongst the moddels that he made for the seale for the Q^{nes} picture. Beinge asked if he saw Hilliard cast The Picture he confessethe he dyd not se Hyllyard make the same, but Hyllyard tellinge him how he dyd congeal the same, he requyred the said Hyllyard to gyve him one pder and so Hyllyard gave him that Picture, and after he saw the said Hyllyard make the mettall. . . .

Here it becomes clear that Hilliard practised alchemy, an obvious sideline of the goldsmiths' craft in the Elizabethan age and one especially tempting to the speculative and enquiring mind of the Queen's limner.

That Hilliard was always ready to listen to any scheme of his fellow goldsmiths and friends for the discovery or gain of precious metal is evident from his participation in the search for gold in Scotland when he became a joint venturer with Devosse and Brounckhurst. He was always ready—perhaps too rashly and indiscriminately—to give his support to a person advancing such a scheme. One of these was the goldsmith William Laborer with whom Hilliard became very friendly in later years. It is rewarding for an appreciation of Hilliard's character to examine the personality of Laborer more closely.

It appears from a deposition[2] in Chancery on 30 July 1599 that Laborer was then 39 years old, and therefore born approximately in 1560. According to the records of the Goldsmiths' Company he became apprenticed to one Robert Stanger on 10 September 1571.[3] He claims in 1603 that he was a freeman of the Goldsmiths' Company for about 22 years, which would render the period of his training rather longer than usual and would bring its termination to the year 1581.[4] On 11 September 1600 he was resident in Foster lane and in 1603 he described himself as goldsmith "of Coleharbert, London". He was in royal employment, for his name appears on the list of "artificers" who received 4 yards of red cloth for the procession of James I through the City of London

[1] Cecil Pap., 88, 89. The Calendar (XI, 406) gives only an abstract. See Blakiston, *ibid.*, p. 103 and Reynolds, *Miniatures, p. 12.*
[2] C. 24/273/38.
[3] Minutes, Book K–L, p. 82.
[4] Star Chamber Proceedings 8, James I, Bundle 9, File 5. Date: 30 May 1603.

on 15 March 1603/4.[1] In this document he is called "latten goldsmyth" and it seems that the treatment of that particular metal, i.e. a kind of brass, was his speciality. These are the bare facts of his life, but more can be gleaned about his skill and character from various lawsuits in which he was involved and from the Minutes of the Goldsmiths' Company.

Between 15 February and 26 April 1593/4 William Laborer apparently engaged a great number of apprentices and was fined 8s. for not having obeyed the rules and ordinances of the Company.[2] He was again fined the following year when he at last paid his fine and presented a new apprentice.[3] In summer 1601 allegations of forgery began to be made against him. On 12 July some spoons were taken from him. Sir Richard Martin, Master of the Mint, was asked to give his expert opinion on them, and on 15 August an indictment was preferred against Laborer for forgery. He was called to answer[4]

> for making diverse sortes of Spones of latten whereof he had whited parte wth tynne and florished an other parte wth cunninge and deuise to make them seeme better then the trew nature of the mettall can afford and to make them the more saleable and in request to be vttered and the nearer to resemble syluer and siluer and gilt in the eye of the buyer he had stamped markes vppon the steale or handle and in the boll of every spoone resemblinge very nearelye the towch of Golde-smythes Hall wherwth all plate is towched to the greate scandall and reproach of the whole socyetye wherevpon after he had ben by the whole assemblie generally reproved he was required to enter into bonde to the Company not to woorke any copper or latten any more his woorkinge tooles excepted . . . but the saide Laborer refused soe to doe makinge noe good nor sound reason therefore. wherevpon yt was agreed that my Lorde Chief Justice should be made acquainted wth his woorke and the spoones to be shewed vnto him by the wardens.

On 28 August 1602 a search was made by the Company "at Bartholomew Faire touching the abuses offered by Laborer and his accomplices" and various basins, dishes, "a great square salt with pillars" and "one Frenche bowle" were taken from his booth and shown to "Mr. Attorney in the morninge".[5] Following this search Laborer's assistants were called before the Court and required not to work for him any more in his copper works, but they avoided giving a "resolued annswere". Finally, on 9 January 1602/3, it was decided that Laborer and his assistant Henry Cooley should be prosecuted with vigour as this was necessary for the reputation of the Company. A few weeks later, on 6 February 1602/3, we learn that proceedings had been started against both goldsmiths in the Star

[1] L.C. 2/4 (5).
[2] Minutes, Book N-O, pt. 1 (1592–1599), pp. 35, 37.
[3] *Ibid.*, p. 59.
[4] *Ibid.*, p. 194.
[5] *Ibid.*, pp. 258–63.

Chamber, and Laborer sent a friend to the Wardens with the message that he was not in town and that he could not come with safety "for fear of arrest" but that he had acknowledged the order in the Star Chamber and would comply with it. Then all his assistants were informed of the order and on 25 February the Wardens reported about the state of the proceedings.[1] On 30 May 1603 Laborer and Cooley were again questioned in Star Chamber for "False marking of plate and sale of gilt brass as gold",[2] but the outcome of the proceedings is unknown.

If Laborer's character does not emerge as exactly immaculate from these proceedings, it seems that Hilliard was completely unperturbed by the accusations of forgery against his friend. For in another series of legal actions which Laborer started against a fellow-goldsmith and Warden of the Company, John Broad, and in the end won, Hilliard signed several bonds for him. This suit[3] concerned a company known as "the Mynerall and Battrye Workes" which was founded on 28 May 1568 and had several highly placed people, headed by Sir Nicholas Bacon, as its governors and promoters. The company had works for casting, melting and making metal at Isleworth. A quarrel broke out between Laborer, the plaintiff in the suit, and John Broad, the defendant, who was also a governor of the company. Laborer alleged that the company only wanted to appropriate his knowledge and skill and Broad replied that Laborer only wanted to learn the manufacturing secrets of the company. In the end it was ordered in Chancery, on 2 October 1601, that Laborer should have liberty to go to Broad's house in Isleworth and fetch "copper, latten and calamine stone" at the price which was already fixed by a commission.[4] For that purpose he had to be bound by good securities and at this point Hilliard came in; he entered into a recognizance of 200*l.* for his friend. Co-surety with Hilliard was Thomas Richardson, Hilliard's son-in-law.[5]

By what seems to be a strange coincidence, on the day when Hilliard's second lease was sealed by the Company, "the Warden Mr. Broad was absent, namely a prisoner in the Marshalsea, upon Counsel's commandement". But he was visited in prison, delivered the keys and consented to the deed.[6]

Years before these events Hilliard was friendly with another member of the "Mynerall and Battrye Workes", one Cornelius Devosse who was—as it may be recalled—also a slightly dubious character.

---

[1] Minutes, *ibid.*, p. 284.
[2] Star Ch., James I, 9/5.
[3] Commenced on 29 March 1596 in the Court of Requests, Req. 2/131/28.
[4] C. 33/100, ff. 725 and 731.
[5] C. 54/1703; see also p. 38, *post.* Further see C. 54/1676 (11 Sept. 1600).
[6] Minutes, Book N-O, p.245.

In one—rather unexpected—kind of activity the versatile Laborer appears to have excelled: in the mending of the highways. In an undated letter to the Privy Council[1] he claims at comparatively little cost to be able to mend the thirteen highways of the realm so that they will "remaine good with littell repaire, to the worldes end." In a letter of 17 June 1623, the Lords of the Privy Council asked the Justices of the Peace in Middlesex[2] to employ at once William Laborer as supervisor for the mending of the Highways in that county, as "this man hath spent much tyme and pains in this way, and offers to do Workes, with less coste, and to better purpose than others doe, that spend the Country's mony, and leave the wayes never the better for want of skill". It is possible that this directive was in response to Laborer's undated letter to the Privy Council.

The clearest indication of the friendship which bound Hilliard to his fellow-goldsmith and roadmender is contained in a letter which Hilliard wrote on 26 March 1610 to his patron and friend, Robert, Earl of Salisbury.[3] This important letter not only reveals the writer's high opinion of Laborer but also gives us one of the rare glimpses of Hilliard's charming and lovable character. He starts by stating that he had been very ill for about forty days, so ill that he feared death, and that although he had had this illness for the last thirty years, it had never tormented him so much and lasted so long as this time. The illness to which Hilliard refers was gout, a common complaint of that time. He must have suffered from it much earlier, because a witness was asked in the lawsuit against Brigham[4] whether he did not lay "sick of the gout" at a certain date, namely shortly after 1583. Hilliard then continues in the letter of 1610 that he vowed, if ever he was able to write again, to support the "honest and commendable" petition of William Laborer, goldsmith, for "the repairing of the highwayes". This is an extract from the letter to the Earl:

> It may seme straunge to yor Lp that I woold truble my head wth such a matter. But it may please yor Honor to vnderstand that the very fowndation of both this o'r scills, is in comon experience wth Goldsmiths, wch can Moulde in Sandes and Clayes, and know their natures, and how to make them firmer then they ar by nature, and we can also by o'r smale tooles invent greater for the wayes mending/ and although sum pregnant wit may perceive and imitate o'r way. Yet the playne Cuntree folke and comon laboring men, mvst not only see it doone, but often doo it them selves, or they will vnderstand it/ And fewe or none wilbe hable to enstruct the smith and the Carpent' to make suche thinges as shalbe nessessary for the

[1] S.P. 14/188/57.
[2] Cal. Acts Privy Council, 1623–5, p. 2.
[3] S.P. 14/53/43.
[4] See on pp. 8 and 19, *ante*; Req. 2/224/38, Question No. 10.

woork, wthout scill in drawing, and then once well made and in comon vse, it wilbe as easy as the plough.

Sweete Lo I haue bene ou' tedious, but as yor Hono' hath bene a greate Beawtyfyer of this City: So vouchsafe my good Lo' to be of the Highewayes also, That the rememberance of yor Honor, may be as the brightnes of the Dimund aboue all other precious stones. And looke not my Lo on the meanesse of o'r estates or imperfections of natvre, but on o'r affections and trew knowledge of yor Honor, for even Moyses had his Fault in speche, but his hart was wth God (most Faythfull) To whome I comitt yor Honor. . .

The letter, with its facility of expression and well-turned phrase, reveals the human feelings and the literary talents of the writer, of which more will have to be said later; it is to his credit that he is sufficiently honest to mention in a postscript that he expects "some profit" out of the transaction, "as we each other promised".

Hilliard's confidence in his own versatile artistic ability and the persuasiveness and force of his literary style is clear from another letter which he wrote to the Earl of Salisbury in 1606[1] and in which he requests, in spite of the claim of the Serjeant Painter, to be commissioned to trim the tomb of the late Queen Elizabeth because

as a Goldsmith, I understand howe to set foorthe and garnishe a pece of stone woork, not with muche gylding to hyde the beawty of the stone, but where it may grace the same and no more. And, having scill to make more radient cullers lyke unto Amells, then yet is to Paynters knowne, I would have taught sum one which woulde not have made it common. . . .

And indeed, when we think of Hilliard's miniatures, we realise that at least one of the secrets of their charm lies in the restrained application of gold, which in its economy adds lustre to the radiant quality of those brilliant colours which are only comparable with precious stones.

During the last years of the reign of Queen Elizabeth, Hilliard was not only awarded his pension, but also at least one grant of land, in Lancashire, the lease of which was part of the possessions of "Edward Eccleston, of Eccleston, esquire, recusant" and had a yearly value of 28*l*.[2] The date of these letters patent is 17 April 1600. But these rewards were insufficient to end Hilliard's financial difficulties and in his letter to Sir Robert Cecil of 28 July 1601[3] he goes so far as to ask his benefactor to obtain the Queen's permission for him to "depart the

[1] Cecil Pap., 119, 8. Cal. XVIII, p. 409.

[2] C. 66/1543, m. 19 and E. 371/598 rot. 86.

[3] Cecil Pap., 87.25, etc. Copy in Reynolds, *Catalogue* 1947, No. 116. Hilliard also points out that he has taught "divers bothe straungers and Englishe, wch nowe and of a long tyme have pleased the comon sorte exceeding well".

Realm for a year or two at the most"; he is confident that he will then be able to satisfy his creditors and continues:

> I maye afterwards return agayne wth credit to her highnes better service quyeted and furnished wth divers thinges for my needefull vse, wch ar not heere for any mony to be had.

Hilliard is, however, as the letter indicates, worried about the training of his son Laurence who then was approximately 20 years old; he could not keep him continuously working in his house as he used to do with the others he taught. Hilliard asks Sir Robert to take his son into his service as a secretary; he mentions, in that connection, that his son is able to speak Spanish and has "an enterance into well writing and drawing".

It is extremely unlikely that the Queen gave permission for her limner and goldsmith to leave England, since references to his continuous presence in London occur in the Minutes of the Goldsmiths' Company for that period and in connection with the renewal of the lease of his house.

About the same time, in summer 1601, Hilliard must have painted the portrait of Sir Robert Cecil, for in a letter to him of 6 May 1606 he states that he drew his picture about five years ago. In this letter Hilliard asks him again to take his son Lawrence into his service and to let him wait on his lordship in his livery at the feast of St. George. It becomes clear that Hilliard's first request in the letter of 1601 was not refused by his patron, and, to quote Hilliard's own words:[1]

> Yor L: willed me to retayne him still to perfect him more in drawinge/ wch I have doon. And he dothe his Matie now good service, bothe in Lymned pictures, and in the Medals of Golde . . .

Of another of Hilliard's children, his daughter Elizabeth, we know that she married Thomas Richardson, a wealthy and well connected young man with whom Nicholas appears to have been on good terms and with whom he transacted several property deals, one relating to property in the neighbourhood of Cordwainer Street, London, as early as approximately 1599,[2] and the other a settlement of property when Thomas intended to go to war. Thomas and Elizabeth had one child, a daughter.

HILLIARD AND THE COURT OF JAMES I

In the reign of James I payments to Hilliard are frequently mentioned in the records, which thus provide documentary evidence of the highest order of the many miniatures, portraits and goldsmith's works which he executed for his

[1] Cecil Pap., 115, 130. Cal. XVIII, 130.
[2] Close Roll of 4 April 1607, C.P. 25/2/170 and C. 54/1854.

royal patron. Only one general payment is recorded in that period: on 7 July 1604 he received 147*l.* 12*s.* as "His Majesty's free gift" out of the moneys forfeited to the late Queen.[1] The other payments refer to individual works created by Hilliard. The first of these entries occurs on 28 December 1603 where it is recorded that he received 19*l.* 10*s.* for certain pictures of James I for the ambassador of the Duke of Denmark.[2] In 1604, upon a warrant of 24 December he was paid 64*l.* 10*s.* for certain (twelve) medallions in gold made by His Majesty's command.[3] Similar payments continue to be recorded: at Michaelmas 1608 he received "for his Ma[ts] picture given to Sir Robert Carre 4*l.* for the Kings and princes pictures given to the Launcegrave of Hessen and one other of his Ma[ts] given to Mrs. Roper with crystal glasses that covered them 15*l.*, in all . . . 19*l.*"[4] On 10 July 1609 a payment of 9*l.* 5*s.* is recorded for "two pictures by him made, one of his Ma[ts] and the other of the Duke of York and delivered for his highness' service".[5] By warrant of 5 June 1611 Hilliard was rewarded with 24*l.* 12*s.* "for making two pictures and two tabletts of gold for his Ma[ts] service".[6] On 3 November 1613 he received a warrant for the payment of 12*l.* "for one tablet of gold graven and enamelled blue conteyning the picture of the Princes highness with a crystal thereon by his Ma[ts] command . . . ".[7] On 31 January 1614/5 he was paid 8*l.* for a "picture of the Prince in linen drawn to the waist with a rich crystal thereon and delivered to Mr. Murray, his highnes tutor".[8] From a warrant of 18 October 1615 we learn that he was to receive the large sum of 35*l.* "for work done by him aboute a table of his Ma[ts] picture garnished with diamondes given by his Ma[tie] to John Barkelay".[9] The last entry in this series of Accounts refers to a "small picture of his Ma[tie] delivered to Mr. Herryott his Ma[ts] jewellor" for which he received 4*l.* at Michaelmas 1618.[10] The information which we gain from these documents throws important light on the wide range of miniatures and goldsmith's work which Hilliard had to execute for James I. Many portraits of the royal family have survived, and although Hilliard certainly employed craftsmen to help him, some at least are by his hand. Only recently Mr. Graham Reynolds was able to identify the work that has come down to us with that mentioned in the documentary

1 Index 6801; E. 403/2598, f. 76.
2 A.O. 1/388/41. N. Blakiston, "Nicholas Hilliard: Some unpublished Documents" pp. 187–9.
3 Index 6801; E. 403/2598, f. 99.
4 A.O. 1/388/45; E. 351/543, m. 199.
5 E. 351/543, f. 217 and A.O. 1/389/46. *Tudor Artists, p.* 169.
6 A.O. 1/389/48 and E. 351/543, m. 252.
7 A.O. 1/389/51 and E. 351/544, m. 32.
8 A.O. 1/390/52 and E. 351/544, m. 47.
9 A.O. 1/390/53, E. 351/544, m. 65.
10 A.O. 1/390/55 and E. 351/544, m. 89.

evidence and showed that quite a considerable number of miniatures representing members of the royal family must have been from Hilliard's own hand.[1] This is the more important as at that time his former pupil Isaac Oliver gained more and more influence at the court and especially in the immediate *entourage* of the Queen. Oliver was even appointed limner to Queen Anne in 1604.[2] This may explain the absence of any mention of her portrait amongst the tasks entrusted to Hilliard.

At the beginning of this period, when Hilliard was fully engaged on work for the King, he had certainly the help of his son Laurence, but we learn from the meetings of the Goldsmiths' Company that on 7 June 1605 "Lawrence Hilliard was sworne and made free by Patrimony".[3] Only a week later, on 14 June 1605, Hilliard presented a new apprentice, Richard Osbaldeston, to the Company and paid the usual 2s. 6d. to replace his son.[4]

For the last fourteen years of his life only a few facts have come down to us and the biographical evidence becomes meagre. There still remains the uncertainty of the death of Alice Hilliard and the question of a second marriage of Nicholas. It is possible but, in the absence of further documentation in the Calendars of London Marriage Licences, not certain, that an entry in the Parish register of St. Mary at Hill, London, refers to our limner: on 3 August 1608 a "Nicholas Hilliard married Susan Gysard".[5] The name "Gysard" might be foreign; in fact, three goldsmiths with the names "Jezarde, Gezarde", "Gezardet" and "Gizard" appear in the lists of the Goldsmiths' Company as having been freemen at that time. One "Nicholas Gyssard" or "Gyffard" was granted denization in 1550[6] and various French craftsmen with similar names are mentioned in the publications of the Huguenot Society. The date would fit quite well, as it is close to the time when Hilliard left his house in Gutter Lane, which was taken over by Laurence in 1613. On the other hand, in 1608 Hilliard was already sixty-one years old. Here the matter must rest until further evidence comes to light.

In 1617 James I granted his "wel-beloved Servant Nicholas Hilliard, Gentleman, our principal Drawer for the small Purtraits and Imbosser of our Medallions of Gold" a monopoly for twelve years to make, engrave and imprint Royal portraits. He received this grant for his 'extraordinary Art and Skill in Drawing Graving and Imprinting of Pictures . . . of us and others ".[7] He was also given the sole right to sell or dispose of these pictures, whether they were drawn on

---

[1] Reynolds, *Walpole Society, p.* 17.   [2] *Tudor Artists*, p. 179.
[3] Minutes, Book O, III, 1604–11, p. 397.   [4] *Ibid.*, p. 398.
[5] Gh. L. MS. 4546. St. Mary at Hill, Parish Register.
[6] Cal. Pat. Rolls E. VI, III, p. 250.   [7] Rymer's *Foedera*, XVII, p. 15.

paper or parchment or engraved in any other medium suitable to his skill. It is stated in this patent that Hilliard himself had asked for this privilege because he did not dare to create work to the best of his ability as he was afraid it might be copied by others, much to his own loss and discredit. The whole question of a monopoly for royal portraits played an important part in the history of Court patronage in the Elizabethan and Jacobean Age. The draft patent to Gower and Hilliard has been mentioned before. The sovereign himself took great personal interest in the representation of his image and insisted that it was done properly and to his liking. In almost all important theoretical essays on art by contemporary writers, such as Blaise de Vigenère or Haydocke—to mention only two—it was recounted that Alexander had given the monopoly for his own image in sculpture to Lysippus and that for his painted portrait to Apelles.

Hilliard was able to enjoy the financial gains from his grant for only two years, and in only one case do we know that he really authorised an engraving to be done. This was the fine print of Queen Elizabeth engraved by Delaram on which it is stated that it was carried out with the permission of the royal limner.

In the same year 1617 Hilliard was imprisoned in Ludgate for a debt due to one William Pereman, a yeoman usher of the Chamber. According to proceedings in Common Pleas Hilliard was summoned to answer Pereman in a plea that he should pay him 40*l*. which he owed and which he had acknowledged in a bond on 11 July 1612.[1] Hilliard's attorney was—and this is an interesting fact—Thomas Avery, his brother-in-law. In later proceedings by his attorney he did not give any answer and denied the debt, and Pereman was given the right to recover the money. Hilliard did not pay and was imprisoned. In the Court of Requests he sued Pereman because of the damage he had suffered.[2] There is another fact of interest to be gleaned from the answer of the defendant in the latter suit: Pereman had lent 20*l*. to one Mr. John Longford, and it was a joint security taken out by Hilliard together with Longford for which Hilliard had to go to prison. It was again Hilliard's willingness to sign recognizances for his friends which led him into difficulties.

When a year later, on 24 December 1618, Hilliard made his will, the legal proceedings just mentioned must have been still in his mind.[3] He bequeathed to his sister Avery, wife of Thomas Avery, 10*l*. out of 30*l*. arrears of his pension, and further gave her 10*l*. out of 15*l*., "due and owing by Mrs. Anne Langford". Surely, this sum still outstanding in favour of the testator was likewise connected with those proceedings, since the origin of Hilliard's debt was a loan of 20*l*. by Pereman to Mr. John Longford.

[1] C.P. 40/1954, m. 605; C.P. 40/1961, m. 3529.
[2] *Notes & Queries*, Vol. 192, No. 6, p. 123.   [3] P.C.C. 2, Parker.

The rest of the will is not very revealing. He gave 20*s*. to the poor of the parish of St. Martin-in-the-Fields in the County of Middlesex, "where I now dwell", and household goods to the value of 10*l*. to "my trustie Servannte Elizabeth Deacon my Attendant in this my sicknes". This gift supports the view that he had also survived his second wife if indeed he had one. The residue of his estate was given to his "wellbeloved son Laurence Hilliard", whom he made the sole executor of his testament. The witnesses of the will were Thomas Brathwaite, John Davis, Nicholas Higgins, and Anthony Marshe, servant to John Eaton, Scrivener.

Hilliard died when 72 years old and was buried in St. Martin-in-the-Fields on 7 January 1618/9. On 23 January probate of his will was granted to his son Laurence. In the Churchwardens' Accounts of the parish of St. Martin-in-the-Fields the following entry referring to money received appears under burials in January 1618/9: "The viith day for Nicholas Hilliard 52*s*." Considering the amount of money usually paid by parishioners for funerals of their relatives, the payment of 2*l*. 12*s*. is very high and indicates that Laurence arranged for an appropriate ceremony in honour of his deceased father, this truly great English artist. No other reference to Hilliard has been found in any Churchwardens' or Overseers' Accounts of that parish. There is therefore no way to establish the exact name of the street or place where he resided. It is possible that he lived with friends or that he was granted the lease of a house, which was Crown property, by grace and favour; the Crown owned much property in Westminster, particularly in and around Charing Cross Mews.[1]

An interesting later payment to a Hilliard, probably Laurence, after his father's death, is recorded in the Salisbury Manuscripts.[2] This may well be for work Nicholas had carried out previously for his patron and his family. It is an unusually large sum.

HILLIARD'S CHARACTER AND THE OPINIONS OF OTHERS ABOUT HIM

Taking all the facts together, what is the picture of the man that emerges from these documents? Apart from his artistic talents, he certainly had a forceful personality, buoyant and full of *esprit*, generous to his friends, and never embittered by the adversity of fate—and we know financially he was more often in difficulties than not—always ready to learn and to embark in new adventures of human invention and skill. There was nothing petty about him. Just as his small

[1] The Cecil family had also property there.
[2] Private Accounts, 123/7 (1619/20). " to Mr. Hilliard in full of his bill—104*l*."

portraits were great in conception, his various letters show an unusual intensity of feeling and warm-hearted sincerity. He was surrounded by a large family, on whose members he bestowed loving care. He enjoyed life and gave with full hands when he had money to spend. He had culture and learning, and showed exquisite taste in everything he made. The radiant brilliance and gaiety of his miniatures reflect a delightful balance of mind and good-natured disposition. Moreover, he was humbly grateful for the extraordinary gift with which he had been endowed. He always emphasised that the art of limning was most suitable to be performed by "gentlemen" and "as for a naturall aptness of or to painting after the liffe, those surely which have such a gift of God ought to reioyce with humble thankfulness".[1]

His friends came from different *strata* of society, but two main groups of people with whom he was in constant touch may be noted: first, his fellow-goldsmiths, with whom he would discuss problems of exciting techniques, and new methods for the treatment of gold and metal, and whom he would join in their sometimes rash enterprises. From these friends he would borrow money and to them he would freely give securities and bonds. Whenever necessary, he would use his influence at Court on their behalf. The second class of people were courtiers. They were the great of the Elizabethan age, outstanding personalities, well known in the worlds of politics, learning and literature, "wise men" whose conversation must have given much pleasure to our artist. While they were sitting for him, they talked and discussed matters of artistic interest. The Queen herself had outspoken views on her portrait, and her wish to be painted in an open alley, where there would be no shadows, much appealed to Hilliard's idea of the importance of the line. Sir Christopher Hatton and Sir Philip Sidney, "that noble and most valiant knight, that great scoller and excellent poet" are mentioned in Hilliard's *Treatise* as his sitters and as participating in interesting arguments on artistic problems. He painted Sir Robert Cecil, Lord Leicester, the Earl of Essex, Sir Francis Knowles, the Earl of Cumberland, the Earl of Northumberland, Sir Walter Raleigh, Sir Francis Drake, to mention only a few. He certainly knew Sir Walter Mildmay, Sir Thomas Heneage and many other actors on the Elizabethan political stage. As he must have been frequently at Court, it is quite possible that he witnessed there performances of plays by Shakespeare and perhaps even knew him personally. It was a completely new phenomenon that, at the end of the sixteenth century, an English-born artist had free access to court circles where he was esteemed as the most eminent miniaturist of the age.

[1] *Walpole Society*, I, p. 170.

The privileged position which Hilliard enjoyed at Court and his unequalled fame at home and abroad were noted by many contemporary writers on art. One of them was the famous Sir John Harington whose spirited translation of Ariosto's *Orlando Furioso* into "English Heroical Verse" appeared in 1591.[1] In his annotations to the 33rd Book he speaks of Apelles who "was held in such reputation for his drawing, that Alexander the Great gave commaundement that none should make his picture but only Apelles", and he continues in a little-known passage:

> Yet I may say thus much without parciallitie, for the honour of my country, as myne author hath done for the honour of his: that we haue with vs at this day, one that for limming (which I take to be the verie perfection of that art) is comparable with any of any other country. And for the prayse that told you of Parrhasius, for taking the true lynes of the face, I thinke our countryman (I meane Mr Hilliard) is inferior to none that liues at this day: as among other things of his doing, myselfe haue seen him, in white and blacke in foure lynes only, set downe the feature of the Queenes Maiesties countenaunce: that it was euer hereby to be knowne; and he is so perfect therein (as I haue heard others tell) that he can set it downe by the Idea he hath, without any peterne; which (for all Apelles priuiledge) was more (I believe) then he could haue done for Alexander. . . .

These lines express not only Harington's justified pride that this great artist, comparable to the greatest of antiquity, is his countryman; they also provide interesting information about Hilliard's technique. We learn from them that he was so sure of the image of the Queen that he could draw her likeness from memory without a pattern. Hilliard himself refers to the problem of the "four lines" in his *Treatise* and amplifies there the points involved.

A friend of Sir John Harington, whom he called "a well-learned Gentleman and noted sonnet-writer", Henry Constable, composed in about 1590 a sonnet in honour of our limner. Constable had Roman Catholic sympathies and stayed for a long time in France; he belonged to the literary circle of Sir Philip Sidney and Edmund Bolton and was in touch with Anthony Bacon and Robert, Earl of Essex. He had intimate connections with the Countess of Shrewsbury and Penelope, Lady Rich. This sonnet, hitherto unnoticed by scholars, runs as follows:[2]

> To Mr. Hilliard: upon occasion of a picture he made of my Ladie Rich.
>
> If Michaell the archpainter now did live,
> Because that Michael he, an angell hight,
> As partiall for his fellow angels, might

---

[1] Ed. 1591, pp. 277–8. Mentioned by John Nichols, *The History and Antiquities of the County of Leicester*, Vol. III, Pt. I (1800), p. 489, based on W. Burton's *Antiquities of Leicester*.

[2] Hazlitt: ed. of Henry Constable, 1859, pp. 44–5. *Harleian Miscellany*, Vol. 9, p. 489; see also Strong, *loc. cit.* p. 146.

To Raphaelle's skill much prayse and honour give.
But if in secret I his judgment shrive,
It would confesse that no man knew aright
To give to stones and pearles true die and light,
Till first youre art with orient nature strive.
But thinke not yet you did that arte devise;
Nay, thanke my Ladie that such skill you have:
For often sprinckling her black sparckling eyes
Her lips and breast taught you The [art you gave]
To diamonds, rubies, pearls, The worth of which
Doth make the jewell which you paynt seeme Rich.

Two other poetical eulogies of Hilliard's work are known. One comes from the pen of Dr. John Donne and appears in his "Letters to severall Personages". The few lines in praise of Hilliard are contained in the opening verses of "The Storme, to Mr. Christopher Brooke".[1]

Thou which art I, ('tis nothing to be soe)
Thou which art still thy selfe, by these shalt know
Part of our passage; And, a hand, or eye
By *Hilliard* drawne, is worth an history,
By a worse painter made; and (without pride)
When by thy judgment they are dignifi'd,
My lines are such: 'This the preheminence
Of friendship onely to 'impute excellence.'

This poem was written in July or August 1597, probably in Plymouth, whereto the fleet returned after it had been damaged by a storm. Christopher Brooke was Donne's friend who shared his rooms at Lincoln's Inn. He also was a poet and his friends were Selden, Jonson, Drayton, Browne, and Davies of Hereford. Again, a circle of fashionable intellectuals to whom Hilliard must have been known, if he was not actually their friend. Prefixed to the 1635 edition of Donne's poems is his engraved portrait by William Marshall with the inscription "1591" and "ætatis suæ 18" the original of which may well have been a miniature by Hilliard.

The second is an anagram on Nicholas Hilliard's name written at the beginning of the seventeenth century. It was composed by a Frenchman and is signed: "Vottre meilleur ami, et serviteur à jamais Jehan Durant Parisien".[2] Again, a friendly link with France! The poem is based on the changing of the second "l" in Hilliard's name to "e", thus: "Nicolas Hileyart". It then re-arranges the order of the letters so as to make them read "En Christ ay la loi".

[1] *John Donne*, ed. by Herbert J. C. Grierson, 1912, p. 176.
[2] Victoria and Albert Museum, L. 964–1946. Reynolds, *Catalogue*, 1947, No. 119 B.

This anagram is beautifully written out by the famous calligrapher Peter Bales, or *Praesul Beatus* as he called himself, and gold is used for the lettering.

In 1598 Richard Haydocke's translation of Lomazzo's *Trattato* was published. It contains interesting references to Hilliard. In the notes which the translator addresses to the reader he blames "divers Honourable Personages, and even Princes" for publishing to the world, "not only unlike, but most lame, disproportioned and unseemly counterfeites . . . of their livelie persons". If only Alexander's edict were now in force again, he exclaims. He then speaks of the more industrious painters of his own country and expresses some surprise that they have achieved so much and have "attained so neere vnto the ancient perfection, with so feawe helpes, as our country (for ought I could ever learn) hath afforded them". He states that he would like to write in the skilful manner of Vasari to preserve these deserving names for eternity and that he would love to compare the lives of these English painters with those of the Italians, just as Plutarch compared the Roman captains with the "Graecians".

> Then would Mr Nicholas Hilliard's hand, so much admired amongst strangers, striue for a comparison with the milde spirit of the late worldes-wonder Raffaell Vrbine; for (to speake a truth) his perfectiô in ingenious Illuminating or Limming, the perfection of Painting, is (if I can iudge) so extraordinarie, that when I devised with my selfe the best argument to set it forth, I found none better, then to perswade him to doe it himselfe, to the viewe of all men by his pen; as hee had before vnto very many, by his learned pencell: which in the ende hee assented vnto; and by mee promiseth you a treatise of his own Practise that way, with all convenient speede. Whose true and liuely Image you may otherwise behold, more then reflected vppon the mirrours or glasses, of his two schollars Mr: Isaac Oliver for Limming and Rowland Lockey for Oyle and Lim: in some measure: Both which (I doubt not) are herein of Great Alexanders minde who reioyced more that hee had Aristotle for his Master, then Philippe to his father.[1]

Haydock again praises Hilliard's skill in his "Briefe Censvre of the Booke of Colovrs" as follows:

> . . . And in Limming, where the colours are likewise mixed wth gummes, but laied wth a thicke body and substance: wherein much arte and neatenesse is required. This was much used in former times in Churchbookes, (as is well knowne) as also in drawing by the life in small models, dealt in also of late yeares by some of our Country-men; as Shoote, Bettes etc. but brought to the rare perfection we now see, by the most ingenious, painful and skilful Master Nicholas Hilliard, and his well profiting scholler Isaacke Oliuer; whose farther commendations I referre to the curiositie of their workes.[2]

[1] Haydock, *Tracte* . . . , 1598, p. 93.
[2] *Ibid.*, p. 126.

46

Here is a contemporary opinion about the origin of the miniature, namely from the illuminations of manuscripts, a clear description of the paint used and an appreciation of the outstanding quality of Hilliard's work.

In the same year, viz. 1598, Francis Meres, in *Palladis Tamia*, made a similar comparison between Greek and English painters. He mentions Apelles, Zeuxis and Parrhasius and continues:

> as learned and skilfull Greece had these excellently renowned for their limming: so Englande hath these; Hiliard, Isaac Oliuer, and John de Creetes, very famous for their painting.

Here follows the well-known account of other English painters, including William Segar and his brother Francis, Thomas and John Bettes, Lockey, Lyne, Peake, Peter Cole, Arnolde, and Marcus.

The well-known experience that the public is inclined to overestimate foreign artists of the past and to withhold recognition from living native painters, prompts Henry Peacham, in his *The Art of Drawing with the Pen and Limning in Water Colours, etc.*, published in 1606, to write:[1]

> Nor of those of neerer and our own times, as Michael Angelo and his brother, Alberdure, Stradane, M. Hilliard and M. Isaac our own Countrimen; because their works are yet scarce dry in the world. Now least you shold esteem but basely of this art, and disdain your picture because you may haue it for a trifle (which I account a fault in many of our good workmen). . .

Here the modest charges which English painters made for their work are given as reason for the lack of fashionable public appreciation.

In Peacham's *The Gentlemans Exercise* (published in 1612), there is another reference to English painters of his time:[2]

> nor must I be ingratefully vnmindfull of mine owne countriemen, who have beene, and are able to equal the best, if occasion serued, old Mr. Hiliard, Mr. Isaac Oliuer inferior to none in Christendome for the countenance in small, my good friend Mr Peake and Mr Marques for oyle colours. . . .

Hilliard is always at the head of the list—an indication of the high reputation which he enjoyed amongst his contemporaries.

Another most interesting reference to Hilliard occurs in a book by Thomas Vaughan, entitled *Anima Magica Abscondita or a Discurse of the Universal Spirit of Nature*, which was published in 1650.[3] This is the work of a mystical philosopher who was also strongly devoted to alchemy. He writes:

> Now, if the agent which determinates and figures the Matter were not a discerning spirit it were impossible for him to produce anything at all. For let me suppose

---

[1] p. 6.   [2] pp. 6–7.

[3] *The Works of Thomas Vaughan*, ed. by A. E. Waite, p. 82. I am indebted to Mr. G. Le Breton for giving me this reference.

Hyliard with his pencil and table ready to portray a rose, if he doth not inwardly apprehend the very shape and proportion of that which he intends to limn he may as well do it without his eyes as without his intellectuals. . . .

How true this is. The writer who was born in 1622, five years after Hilliard's death, apparently died from inhaling the fumes of mercury during a chemical experiment. It is illuminating that he should have referred to Hilliard, who, we know, had himself experimented in alchemy.

This short survey of opinion about the artistic greatness of Nicholas Hilliard from the end of the sixteenth to the seventeenth centuries may be concluded by a reference to the English translation of *The Art of Painting* by the Frenchman Roger de Piles. In the edition of 1706 there is added an essay by B. Buckeridge on the English School.[1] Here we have the first full appreciation of Hilliard as a painter—he is called "Goldsmith, Carver and Limner to the Queen"—and the short hints about some of his works and their extraordinary value were duly taken up by Vertue and Walpole.

[1] p. 430.

II

THE RISE

HAVING SKETCHED the main events of Hilliard's life—as far as we know them—we now pass to consideration of his work.

Hilliard was foremost a miniaturist, and the earliest examples known to come from his hand are three small circular limned portraits which he painted in 1560, at the age of 13, before he was apprenticed to the goldsmith Robert Brandon.

In his *Treatise* he paid a tribute to King Henry VIII for calling to his Court "the most excelent painter and limner Haunce Holbean, the greatest master truly in both thosse arts after the liffe that euer was"[1] and he confessed that he always tried to imitate him. Only during his second visit to this country did Holbein paint miniature portraits, and we are informed by van Mander, the art critic, who wrote in the year 1604, that one "master Lukas" instructed Holbein in the technique of limning. The latter can be identified with Luke, the son of Gerard Horenbout, who belonged to a group of well-known Ghent-Bruges painters and illuminators. Gerard and his children, Luke and Susanna, came to the Tudor Court in the 'twenties and, with the exception of Susanna, were on the royal payroll from 1528 onwards. Gerard received the first monthly payment of 36s. 8d. in October of that year. He probably left the country after 1531.[2] His activities in these islands can, on the ground of style, be tentatively linked with some work done for Wolsey. There is also certain, slightly ambiguous, documentary evidence in support of this theory. He was mainly engaged on the illumination of manuscripts used for religious services and the decoration of the initials on the charter headings for the foundation of Wolsey's colleges. In the

---

[1] *Tudor Artists*, p. 6.

[2] *Tudor Artists*, pp. 40ff, 50ff, 171–2. See also Auerbach, "Notes on Flemish Miniaturists in England", pp. 51–3. Paget, "Gerard and Lucas Hornebolt in England", *The Burl. Mag. CI*, 1959, p. 399, gives an earlier reference to Luke, for 1525.

latter group portraits of the King and some of his courtiers including Wolsey himself were drawn in. The style of all these illuminations clearly points to the artists of the Ghent-Bruges circle. It is quite reasonable to assume that Luke likewise assisted his father in this kind of work. His monthly allowance of 55*s*. 6*d*. (for his annuity was higher than that of his father) was paid to him from October 1528 to his death in 1544. He was appointed King's Painter on 22 June 1534—the word "limner" does not appear on his patent. What exactly his duties were is not quite clear. Surely the painting of oil portraits must have been part of them, and it is evident from a posthumous payment to his wife for small portraits of Henry and Katherine Parr that he likewise painted miniatures of the members of the Court.

Only recently has an attempt been made[1] to classify two types of portrait miniatures of *Henry VIII* at the age of thirty-five in 1525/6 in their different versions, one in the Fitzwilliam Museum, at Cambridge (*Pl. 1*), the other at Windsor (*Pl. 2*). Mr. Reynolds has grouped them together with three or four other portraits, very much akin in style, and attributed them to Luke Horenbout. Although this can only be a tentative attribution, much can be said in its favour. These miniatures, originating at a time when Holbein had not yet expressed himself in this medium, are, moreover, different from his own work in style and manner. They must have been greatly appreciated at Court—otherwise they would not have been repeated so often — and it therefore seems reasonable to suppose that they were commissioned from one of the "King's Painters". They are near in conception to the Flemish School, and the three-quarter position of the head with the somehow flatly receding and foreshortened, yet clearly outlined, side of the face, is reminiscent of the portrait of *Liévin van Pottelsberghe* as a donor in the Musée des Beaux-Arts, at Ghent, which is usually attributed to Gerard, Luke's father. A similar rendering of the face appears on the Wolsey Patents. The most important miniature of this group is *Henry VIII* in the Fitzwilliam Museum. It is circular like the others, but stands on a square, separated from it by a thin gold circle, and the spandrils are decorated by censing angels, a motif which definitely establishes the link with the old tradition of manuscript illumination. Figures of putti appear frequently on the Wolsey Patents and the Gospels and Epistles in Oxford, also illuminated for the same patron. Thus, a motif used in manuscript illumination decorates the surround of a circular portrait. The transition from the manuscript page to the independent miniature becomes evident. The earliest phase in this development is noticeable in France where Jean Clouet, perhaps also of Flemish origin, illuminated the famous *Preux de Marignan* for Francis I in about 1519 with portrait roundels of

[1] Reynolds, *Conn. Guide*, pp. 127–8, pl. 69. Auerbach, *Tudor Portraits*, p. 13.

the heroes of the victory of *Marignan*.[1] In their flatness they show that they are based on chalk drawings by the same artist. But the origin of the English portrait miniature is certainly linked rather with the presence of members of the Ghent-Bruges family of illuminators in this country and at Court, and with their striking and original work for Wolsey's manuscripts and charter initials, than with any direct influence from France.

Plate 1. Henry VIII, by Luke Horenbout

Plate 2. Henry VIII, by Luke Horenbout

Plate 3. Catherine Howard, by Hans Holbein, the Younger

Compared with the miniatures ascribed to Luke Horenbout, Holbein's portraits are more precise and clear. There is compactness and character in the figure (*Pl. 3*). His line is absolutely to the point. Holbein expresses the likeness with great economy of means and little shading and his whole conception arises from a detached vision of the sitter.

[1] Pope-Hennessy, *Lecture*, p. 13 and pl. IVa.

When Hilliard painted in 1560 his earliest known miniatures as a boy of 13, seventeen years had passed since Holbein's death and sixteen since Horenbout's. Henry's reign had come to an end and his second daughter Elizabeth was now firmly established on the throne. Levina Teerlinc, daughter of Simon Benninck and another member of the Ghent-Bruges circle of illuminators, was appointed the Queen's "paintrix", an office which she already had held during Henry's reign and the reigns of Edward VI and Mary I.[1] Although she was still called the Queen's "Painter" and not her "Limner", it is clear that she painted miniatures. Amongst the many New Year gifts which she presented to the Queen, there is, e.g. "a small picture of the Trynite" or still more explicit "a Carde with the Quenis Matie and many other personages". She received her salary of 40*l.* a year until her death in 1576, and many years later, in 1599, her successor, Nicholas Hilliard, was paid exactly the same sum. Not one of the miniatures which have been ascribed to her at some time or other can definitely be identified as her work. The same must be said about the work of other limners whose names we know and who lived in the middle of the century, namely John Bettes[2] who died before 1576, John Shute[3] whose death occurred

Plate 4.   Unknown Young Girl, by an unknown artist, 1549

Plate 5.   Queen Mary I, in the manner of Hans Eworth, oil on copper

in October 1563, and Guillam Scrotes who was called "King's limner" by Strype.[4] Only a few miniatures may be mentioned here to give a general idea of the style of portraiture between the death of Henry VIII and Hilliard's rise to fame.

[1] *Tudor Artists*, pp. 153–4.   [2] *Ibid.*, pp. 186–7, etc.
[3] *Ibid.*, pp. 185–6.   [4] *Ibid.*, p. 187.

An interesting miniature has been acquired recently by the Victoria and Albert Museum. It is the circular framed likeness of an *Unknown Young Girl* (*Pl. 4*) in a frontal position, the arms symmetrically rounded, both hands clasping gloves, thus accentuating the middle line. The face is slightly turned three-quarter to the left. The date, 1549, is indicated in bold figures. The round modelling of the face and the warm colouring, together with the indication of the white ermine, render the miniature most attractive.

The beautiful oil miniature of *Queen Mary I* (*Pl. 5*) in the collection of the Duke of Buccleuch must have been painted only a few years later.[1] The frontal view of the half-length figure is again combined with the three-quarter position of the face and the likeness is brought out clearly. This style is closer to that of Eworth's portrait of the same sitter in the Society of Antiquaries than to that of Mor to whom it was ascribed formerly.

Plate 6. An Elizabethan Maundy, by an unknown artist of the middle of the sixteenth century

Plate 7. Young Girl, by an unknown artist of the middle of the sixteenth century

An Elizabethan Maundy (*Pl. 6*) within a wide oval miniature frame, painted about 1560, in the collection of the Earl of Beauchamp, was once attributed to Hilliard.[2] It is an excellent example of the Anglo-Flemish manuscript style, painted on vellum and obviously cut to fit the frame. Its manner would better

[1] R.A., British Portraits, 1956/7, No. 613.
[2] Brussels, 1912, No. 181, repr. Pl. I, 3.

agree with the name of Levina Teerlinc than with that of Hilliard, according to what we know of the origin of that woman artist. And indeed the description of one of her New Year's gifts as "a Carde the Quenis Matie and many other personages" might be a suitable title for it. Elizabeth in front is clearly recognisable, her coat with its long train is of a beautiful blue. It is in contrast to the red garment worn by the woman in front and seen from the back. The whole gathering of clergy and courtiers is colourful, fashionable and lively. The draping of the costumes, the attitudes of the onlooking crowd and the conception of space speak for a versatile limner of the Ghent-Bruges School who resided in this country.

Related in date and style to the Queen's figure on the *Maundy* miniature is a fine circular portrait of a *Young Girl* (*Pl. 7*), half-length without hands, in the Royal collection at Windsor.[1] It has been attributed to Levina Teerlinc and was supposed to represent Queen Elizabeth as princess or Lady Jane Grey. Here again we are not on safe ground, except that it tones in well with the angular

Plate 8. Katherine, Countess of Hertford, with her son, by an unknown artist of the middle of the sixteenth century (enlarged)

stiffness characteristic of the figures of the *Maundy*. The type and conception is that of the middle of the century and the straightforward position of the sitter can be compared with that on the miniature of *Edward VI* at Madresfield Court, a portrait which was often repeated. It is of an excellent quality, with a

---

[1] *Tudor Artists*, pp. 76/7. Reynolds, *Miniatures*, p. 17, suggests that it may be a copy by the youthful Hilliard of a large-scale painting by Eworth.

clear blue background and nearer to Hilliard's style, though it shows a more detailed modelling of the features than his early work.

Closely connected therewith and possibly by the same hand is the charming circular miniature *Katherine, Countess of Hertford, with her son* at Belvoir Castle (*Pl. 8*). It is beautifully composed within the round, showing the half-length

Plate 9. Robert Dudley, Earl of Leicester, in the manner of Nicholas Hilliard, *c.* 1565 (enlarged)

figures of mother and child in a lively attitude, so that both their expressive hands are visible. Here again there is that angular quaintness which is noticeable on the Windsor miniature, as well as the light and clear colouring and the exact rendering of detail; the white fur, the costume of the child and the gold-rimmed miniature the mother wears on a black ribbon are characterised with minute care.

Another most attractive circular miniature, representing *Robert Dudley, Earl of Leicester*, of about 1565 (*Pl. 9*), also at Belvoir Castle, belongs to the same group. It is attributed to Hilliard and, though the face is slightly retouched, it is of an excellent quality. Whilst it could be the work of the youthful master, perhaps a copy from an oil painting, there is rather more tone and grading of shades in it than is usual in Hilliard's early work. It is, however, related in style to the group of miniatures just discussed, though it may not be by the same hand. These few examples may be sufficient to indicate the high standard of English portrait miniatures between 1550 and 1565, even if a definite name cannot be attached to them in the present state of our knowledge.

It is of great significance that the first Self-portraits by young Hilliard of

55

1560 (*Pls. 10, 11*) have nothing to do with the style of that period. They seem rather to revert to the beginning of the century. His self-portrait at Welbeck Abbey with its dull terracotta background and the yellowish doublet, with its sweetness of expression, and with the relatively broad band bearing the inscription conveys the feeling of a flat coin or a roundel cut from a manuscript page, such as one painted by Jean Clouet. With this impression the version at Drumlanrig Castle also agrees except that the face is slightly more elongated

Plate 10.   Self-portrait, 1560

Plate 11.   Self-portrait, 1560

Plate 12.   Edward Seymour, Duke of
Somerset, 1560

and the colour scheme differs in the bright red of the background and the blue of the sleeves which are hardly visible in the picture.

The portrait miniature of *Edward Seymour* (*Pl. 12*) painted and signed by Hilliard in 1560, after Seymour's death, belongs to this group. Although the drawing itself was probably based on some pattern near to Holbein, the circular framing with the inscribed band and the particular size of the cutting is again reminiscent of the round portraits inserted on the manuscript pages of the *Preux de Marignan* by Jean Clouet. The precision of the goldsmith is still absent from these early works; it may be recalled that Hilliard had not started his apprenticeship when he drew these pictures.

56

The Rise

After what seems to be a gap of about eight or nine years, which was probably mainly due to Hilliard's apprenticeship with Robert Brandon, the series of important miniatures begins. It is heralded by the lovely rectangle representing young *Queen Elizabeth I in robes of state* at Welbeck Abbey (*Pl. 13*). Though this miniature is not signed, there can be no doubt that it is an authentic painting by Hilliard. The delicate handling of the figure, the dainty frontal face of the young Queen with the pale blue shading, the round pupils of the narrow eyes, the firm and precise line separating it from the piped ruff and then disappearing into the softness of the hair across the forehead, and finally the hair itself falling in full waves down on the shoulders and the minute and careful treatment of hands, dress and jewellery are typical of Hilliard's style and the quality of his early work. Little rubies are indicated, sometimes slightly raised, in the crown, the Tudor brooch, the girdle, the rings, and a real diamond decorates the centre of the cross on the orb. Here we see the goldsmith at work. That Hilliard really painted such a picture we learn from Vanderdoort's

Plate 13. Queen Elizabeth I in robes of state, c. 1569

Plate 14. Queen Elizabeth I, on indenture of 30 August 1559, in the manner of Nicholas Hilliard

Catalogue of the "King's limned pieces at Whitehall" (*c.* 1639) under No. 40:[1]

> Done by Hilliard, given to the King by the young Hilliard, and presented by the Earl of Pembroke, Lord Steward.
>
> Imprimis, Done upon the right light, A full forward faced picture of Queen Elizabeth in her Parliament robes, with a sceptre and globe in her hands, in a little square box, wooden frame, with a cover.

Except that the measurements given ($2\frac{1}{4}'' \times 2''$) are smaller than those of the Welbeck Abbey picture, the description fits perfectly. The size may have been slightly wider originally, but the portrait is painted on a card and was always intended to be a miniature in a rectangular frame.

There is nothing in this beautiful painting to suggest inspiration from Clouet or Holbein. Its provenance is clear: it is in the purely English tradition of secular illumination, a tradition developed two or three generations before Hilliard in the illumination of documents, such as the initials of charter headings and Plea Rolls with the image of the Sovereign. Hence the iconic frontal composition which conforms exactly to the type usually applied by limners of legal documents from the beginning of the Queen's reign to *c.* 1572.[2] Already the first illuminated portrait of young Elizabeth on the Plea Roll for Michaelmas 1558[3] had moved from the previous manner towards a more miniature-like style, and the enthroned Queen limned within the initial of an Indenture of 30 August 1559[4] (*Pl. 14*) is very close in style to the Welbeck Abbey miniature. Nor are these few examples the only ones painted in this manner. A wide range of similar illuminations existed during that period. Hilliard must have seen these limnings often and must have been acquainted with them. The close affinity of his style with that of legal illustrations proves that he had trained with a limner and may have even had a hand at limning himself in his early years. In the light of the discovery of the exact period of his apprenticeship as a goldsmith, it now becomes clear that he must have been working with a limner before 1562 when he entered Robert Brandon's workshop. This leads us to the year of the first miniatures, about 1560, and would further explain the fact that during his whole career he was so fond of calligraphy that he invariably used it whenever possible. The Welbeck Abbey miniature, which shows the highest perfection of the accomplished goldsmith, must have been painted right at the end of his apprenticeship with Brandon, in about 1569. This masterpiece

---

[1] Published in 1757 by Vertue, p. 44. O'Donoghue, p. 26, No. 1.
[2] *Tudor Artists*, pp. 119–21.
[3] K.B. 27/1188; *ibid.*, pp. 119–20, pl. 34.
[4] *Ibid.*, p. 120, pl. 35c; E. 36/277.

Plate 15. Queen Elizabeth I in robes of state, in the manner of Nicholas Hilliard, oil on panel

unites in full harmony the two trends of Hilliard's artistic training, that of the limner and that of the goldsmith.

A life-size oil painting on panel of *Queen Elizabeth in robes of state (Pl. 15)* in the great Hall of Warwick Castle resembles the miniature closely. The picture has recently been cleaned, and the impression which it now creates emphasises its resemblance to Hilliard's miniature style. Of course, caution is necessary. Though we have now learned that Hilliard painted portraits in large, we do not know his style of full-size portraiture, but we appreciate that in the sixteenth

Plate 16. A Gentleman, perhaps Oliver St. John, 1st Baron St. John of Bletsho 1571

Plate 17. An Unknown Man, aged 24 in 1572

Plate 18. An Unknown Lady, aged 18 in 1572, companion miniature to Plate 17

century the borderline between these two types of painting was fluid and an artist produced miniatures and oil paintings with the same ease. In the oil painting in Warwick Castle the dignified majesty of the youthful figure, the wide sweep of the golden mantle, shaded in dark grey, the frontal, china-like face with its light-blue modelling, the full hair falling on to the shoulders and the white horizontal and vertical lines on the dark blue background recall the effect of the miniature. In addition, the exact attitude of the hands holding the royal insignia, the pattern of dress and coat, the ruff and the wrist cuffs, the jewellery, the crown, even the tassels, are faithfully repeated. Only the treatment of the hands is slightly more clumsy, a more spatial conception of the figure is created by the darker shades of the coat, and the three-quarter-length composition is framed by an area which is a trifle wider and longer. The latter observation may perhaps lead to the assumption that the miniature in its present form was very slightly cut. The oil painting of the Queen at Warwick Castle is most impressive and of an excellent quality and one would indeed like to know who was the artist, so very close in style to our limner, who painted it.

Between 1571 and 1576 Hilliard painted a splendid series of miniatures, culminating in the portrait of Elizabeth in 1572. The earliest of this series is that of a *Gentleman, perhaps Oliver St. John, 1st Baron St. John of Bletsho* at Welbeck Abbey (*Pl. 16*). It shows the transition from the juvenile style of Hilliard to the beginning of his mature art. Still circular, it is more precise than *Edward Seymour*, and has already the typical calligraphic inscription, viz. *Anno Dni 1571. Aetatis Suae: 35* which follows along the circle of the frame. Holbein's manner is still continued, but the way in which the hat is sitting on the head and the eyes are looking in the opposite direction—to mention only a few details—already anticipates Hilliard's mature style.

In the next year, 1572, he must have gained prestige and confidence, as so many of his miniatures bear that date. With the exception of two or three in an oblong shape, they still appear in circular form. We begin with the portrait of *An Unknown Man* (*Pl. 17*), a rectangle inscribed: *Ætatis sue XXIIII Ano Dni. 1572*, in the Victoria and Albert Museum. In this miniature of a fashionably dressed young man in black against a blue background adorned with a gold inscription we already recognise the high quality of his mature style. It has been said that a French idiom has inspired the conception of this portrait;[1] while on the other hand a similarity with court portraiture by Anthonis Mor has been noticed.[2] Both influences are easily explained: the former by the rapprochement between this country and France during those years and by the wide knowledge of

[1] Pope-Hennessy, *Lecture*, p. 18, pls. VIII, IX.
[2] Reynolds, *Miniatures*, p. 18.

drawings by the Clouets at the Elizabethan Court; the latter by the fact that Mor's paintings were likewise well known in this country and that members of the nobility travelled to the Netherlands and returned with their own portraits, painted by this master. In spite of certain similarities in composition with Mor, the French influence is more important in these miniatures of Hilliard than the Flemish one, as is shown by the infinitely more elegant and gay attitude of the sitter which is less formal than the Flemish approach. The beauty of this miniature lies in the firm handling of the much foreshortened three-quarter view of the face which brings out the individual features with much clarity and precision and in some decorative elements which are Hilliard's own touch. These can be seen in the narrow slits of the eyes, the linear treatment of the hair overlapping the ear and the forehead, the lovely flourishes of the writing con-

Plate 19.   An Unknown Man, 1572

Plate 20.   An Unknown Lady, aged 52
in 1572

forming to the bizarre treatment of the ruff which protrudes beyond the slim neck below the ear and the green ribbon tied into a bow sprinkled with fanciful gold lines. The character and elegance of an Elizabethan courtier is caught in this image.

The miniature of *An Unknown Lady*, inscribed *Ætatis Suæ XVIII. Ano Dni 1572*, at Drumlanrig Castle (*Pl. 18*) may be considered the companion picture to the above-mentioned portrait. Though an eighth shorter and a tenth narrower, it is also framed as a rectangle and the flourishes of the gold lettering, the minute and accomplished rendering of the standing lace collar, the blue-green embroidery decorating the black dress with its square-cut neckline, and finally,

62

the gold chain and jewellery; all these details match *An Unknown Man*, aged 24, of the same year. Unfortunately, the face is partly repainted and the ruff is damaged in some parts. But enough is preserved to suggest the original conception which Hilliard intended to convey.

To the same series belongs the circular miniature of a man, formerly called *Earl of Devon*, dated 1572, now in the Fitzwilliam Museum (*Pl. 19*). The gold lettering follows the round of the frame and the fine head with its dark hair is of a relatively large size within the picture space, similar to that on the rectangular portraits of that year. Here is already the characteristic line of the forehead, the narrow slits of the eyes and the short lines indicating the beard.

Another miniature of *An Unknown Lady*, aged 52 in 1572, at Drumlanrig Castle (*Pl. 20*), fits well into this group and can be attributed to Hilliard, though costume and type show rather Flemish influence. The background is blue and the gold lettering stands out in a bold circle.

There can be no doubt that the culmination of the early part of this phase of Hilliard's work is his first dated portrait of *Queen Elizabeth I*, now in the National Portrait Gallery (*Pl. 21*). In the beautiful gold lettering following the curve of the upper border, standing on bright blue ground, is inscribed: *Ano Dni 1572. Ætatis suæ 38*. On either side of the face appear the capitals E and R, each surmounted by a delicately drawn crown. The round is lengthened to an oval by the addition of a mere quarter of an inch, in order to give more of the Queen's youthful figure. The whole decorative scheme is in perfect harmony, with the dainty colouring of the precisely modelled face, the jewelled head-dress, the closely fitting ruff, the black dress, cut square at the neck and partly covered by lace, the white sleeves, the white rose pinned against her left shoulder, the chain with a black ring, another chain of jewels, and a large pendant hanging from a pink ribbon. Every minute area of the miniature has a full share in the artist's vision, every single detail is really seen. Besides, the Queen's portrait has never before been given as a likeness so true to life, formulated—probably according to her own wishes—by lines rather than by shadows. One has only to think of the more tangible and plastic figure Eworth created of Elizabeth in 1569 in his oil painting *The Judgment of Paris*, to realise how much the English artist's approach differed from that of the Flemish painter.

As to the Queen's appreciation of art, Hilliard gave much credit to her in his *Treatise*. The radiant serenity that emanates from the picture, together with the truthful portrait likeness, which nobody had been able to express before, must have pleased his royal patron very much. It is therefore not surprising that the impact which this miniature made on the further development of English painting was very great. The type Hilliard thus created was taken up by illuminators of legal documents at exactly the same period,[1] and at least in one instance, in the *Pelican* portrait of Queen Elizabeth in the Walker Art Gallery, Liverpool (*Pl. 22*), probably painted *c.* 1574, the pattern of the miniature was closely followed and transposed into the larger scale of an oil painting on panel.[2] This painting—with its warm red colouring, subdued by mellow greys and a dull pink in the fan, but enlivened by the scarlet in the rose pinned on to the dress, with the particular shape of the face embedded and supported by the

Plate 21. Queen Elizabeth I, 1572

Plate 23. Queen Elizabeth I, playing the lute (enlarged)

ruff, and the arrangement of the curly hair, is extremely close to Hilliard's portrait miniature. Even the crowned Tudor rose and fleur-de-lis in the background recall the ornaments of the crowned E and R on the miniature, thus testifying to the connection with the almost heraldic and calligraphic character of Hilliard's style. Nor is this all, for a whole series of royal portraits, formulated more or less in this manner, was to follow for many years. It is of less importance whether Hilliard himself was the painter of the *Pelican* portrait or somebody else closely connected with him; what matters more is the fact that the minute technique and decorative treatment of his first realistic portrait of Elizabeth

[1] Auerbach, *Tudor Artists*, pp. 120–1, pls. 40a, b, 41.
[2] Auerbach, *Portraits of Elizabeth I*, p. 202, pl. 32, 35.

Plate 22.   Queen Elizabeth I, in the manner of Nicholas Hilliard, *Pelican* portrait,
shortly after 1572, oil on panel

"in little" profoundly modified the style of oil painting and effected the re-orientation of portraiture "in large" along the lines of miniature painting, a style which was to be in vogue for at least the next ten years. It is remarkable that he should have had such influence while only 25 years old and only discovering his artistic power.

Another portrait miniature of the Queen by Hilliard, a work of the greatest importance, belongs to this period. It is *Queen Elizabeth I playing the lute* at Berkeley Castle (*Pl. 23*). Though it was known that it existed—it was not possi-

Plate 24. Woman, called Isabel, Countess of Rutland, 1572

Plate 25. Jane Coningsby, 1574

Plate 26. An Unknown Man, aged 45 in 1574

ble to include it in the 1947 Exhibition—it had been seen by scarcely anyone before 1956, when the house in which it had been kept for generations opened its doors to the public. In a manuscript list of portraits at Berkeley Castle of 1796[1] it is mentioned under Miniatures as *Queen Elizabeth playing on a Mandoline*. The name of the artist is not indicated here, but by family tradition it was

[1] B.M., Add. MSS. 6391, fol. 56.

always called a miniature by Hilliard. Indeed, nobody else could have painted the Queen with so much grace and charm and yet such true likeness, in spite of the extremely small size of the face. This likeness is almost as accomplished as that of the miniature of *Elizabeth* in the National Portrait Gallery. Here are the carefully drawn mouth, the clearly outlined nose, the eyes looking at the

Plate 27. An Unknown Man, aged 37 in 1574

viewer, veiled by slightly heavy eyelids, a typical feature of Elizabeth's face, and the arched forehead, so characteristic of Hilliard's manner. But the shape of the Queen's face is rounder than that on the miniature of 1572 and the ruff has increased in width; the style, therefore, anticipates that of the portrait of *Alice Hilliard*. It follows that it can be dated roughly between 1574 and 1576, but before he set out for France. These features alone would be interesting, but, in addition, it is a portrait seen as a *genre* picture and a most attractive one. The Queen is seated on a throne, almost enclosed by it. There is a window-like balustrade in front of her on which she rests the rounded part of the lute which stretches right across diagonally. Some architectural accessories, such as pillars with capitals, balls and cartouches, emphasise the construction of the throne. Its back and one side wall are decoratively treated. But the most surprising feature of this lovely miniature is the precise drawing of the lute, the shadow it throws on to the horizontal parapet and the beautiful movement of the hands, which no other painter in England at this period but Nicholas Hilliard could have painted with such elegance. The miniature, limned on vellum, fitting the oval perfectly in a carefully planned composition, recalls the illuminations of charter headings and Plea Rolls and comes close to the work of the manuscript painter. Here we find an incontestable link between both these trends of art in Hilliard's work.

Plate 28. An Unknown Woman, (?) Lady Margaret Douglas, 1575

There remain to be mentioned a few more miniatures belonging to this early phase: two circular portraits of women, characterised by the same decorative qualities, one representing *Isabel, Countess of Rutland* [*?*], in the collection of the Duke of Rutland (*Pl. 24*), the other, *Jane Coningsby*, dated 1574, in the possession of Mrs. Ward-Boughton-Leigh (*Pl. 25*). The latter date is also inscribed on the fine portrait of an *Unknown Gentleman* who was aged 45 in that year, in the collection of the Duke of Buccleuch (*Pl. 26*). Lettering and treatment of features and details seem to justify the attribution to Hilliard and a certain affinity with François Clouet is therefore the more interesting. A further most attractive work of this period is the fine miniature of *An Unknown Man*, aged 37 in 1574, at Cambridge (*Pl. 27*), with its green background and smaller sized head. A similar relationship in size between the head and the circular picture area is also evident in the miniature of *An Unknown Woman*, dated 1575, in the Mauritshuis, at The Hague (*Pl. 28*), formerly ascribed to Levina Teerlinc. But the clearly formulated likeness, the close resemblance to the Cambridge miniature and the typical lettering make the attribution to Hilliard certain. There is a replica of this miniature, though considerably repainted, in the Fitzwilliam Museum, a fact which points to the importance of the sitter. As an attempt to identify the

68

lady represented, I should like to quote the description of one miniature in the Collection of Charles I from *Vanderdoort's Catalogue*:[1]

> Done by old Hilliard given to the King. Item. Done upon the right light, The third picture, written on it the year of our Lord, with golden letters, 1575, and also her age 53, being the Lady Margaret Douglas, Aunt to Queen Mary of Scotland, in a black and white mourning widow's habit, and a little plain ruff. $1\frac{3}{4} \times 0''$.

The circular miniature has a diameter of $1\frac{3}{4}''$, so even the measurements as well as the description seem to refer to this picture. The inscription in gold letters *Ano Dni 1575. Aetatis Suae* . . . gives the date, but the figures stating the age of the sitter have been overpainted. It is probable that this is a portrait of *Lady Margaret Douglas*.

Plate 29. Called Henry Howard, Earl of Northampton, 1576 (enlarged)

The beautiful miniature *called Henry Howard, Earl of Northampton* (*Pl. 29*), aged 39 in 1576, formerly in the collection of the Viscount Morpeth, is an authentic Hilliard and one which, in its precision and splendid colouring, forms a welcome close to an interesting series of miniatures which though less sophisticated than Hilliard's later works, are of an extremely high quality.

[1] See p. 58, above, 4th Book, p. 43, No. 34.

III

BROADENING OUTLOOK

SINCE HILLIARD stayed in France from autumn 1576 to at least autumn 1578 and apparently did not return to England during these two years, it is probable that the miniatures dated 1577 and 1578 were painted abroad. The two earliest and most important of them are the circular *Self-Portrait* (*Pl. 30*) and *Richard Hilliard* (*Pl. 31*) his father. The former is signed with cursive letters N.H., and both are dated 1577. Both bear inscriptions in bold gold lettering on a blue background, standing out brilliantly and following the round closely, thus firmly supporting and enclosing the figure within the circle. A precise and sharp medallic appearance is achieved. The treatment of the features of the three-quarter turned faces, gliding almost into profile, follows the same lines: clearly drawn, foreshortened cheeks, eyes fixed on the onlooker in the opposite direction, short, straight and curved brushstrokes indicating the hair, emphasise the solid and concentrated view the artist has of the sitter. As Mr. Winter stated,[1] in their medallic shape and design they are akin to some of Germain Pilon's medals, especially to those of *Charles IX* and *Henri III* (1573 and 1575). The same area is shown within the round and the heads are stretching right up to the top so that the bonnets even touch the framing border and divide, as on the medals, the curve of the inscription into two. In addition, the *Self-Portrait* resembles in style and even in some of the features Dürer's *Self-Portraits* of 1493 and 1498;[2] both miniatures reflect the admiration which Hilliard, as he himself writes in his *Treatise*, had for the exact work of the German master. The medallic quality appears for the first time on these two circular portrait miniatures which, probably, were painted under the influence of Pilon in France. That quality

[1] Winter, *Elizabethan Miniatures* (1943), p. 23.
[2] Mr. Winter first made this suggestion, see *ibid.*, p. 16.

70

was lacking in his earlier miniatures, even in those executed only a very short time before, namely in 1576.

To the same year as that in which the *Self-Portrait* and the portrait of *Richard Hilliard* were painted, namely 1577, belongs a now clearly oval portrait miniature of *An Unknown Man*, aged 52, formerly in the Warneck and T. Hugh Cobb collection (*Pl. 32*). The sitter wears a black garment with a narrow white

Plate 30. Self-Portrait, 1577 (enlarged)

frill and a tall black hat which again touches the top border. The face is full of determined expression and the portrait shows the same clear and concentrated treatment.

The last-named miniature, with its oval shape, is followed by the beautiful portrait of *Alice Hilliard (Pl. 33)*, dated 1578, which is an oval of exactly the same dimensions, but later on enlarged into a circle by a circumscription in Hilliard's own hand. This charming miniature, always acclaimed as one of the masterworks of our limner, combines the newly discovered precision with a dainty colouring and a sweet and tender expression that clearly

Plate 31. Richard Hilliard, 1577

Plate 32. An Unknown Man, aged 52 in 1577

Plate 33. Alice Hilliard, née Brandon, 1578

72

shows the refined atmosphere of the French Court. The delicate painting of the tastefully adorned dress, the French bonnet and the closely fitting lace ruff have brought a new decorative quality into the picture which is enhanced by

Plate 34. The Duke of Nevers, 1578, wood engraving

Plate 35. The Duchess of Nevers, 1578, wood engraving

the lovely gold lettering. Compared with the *Queen Elizabeth* of 1572 in the National Portrait Gallery, Alice Hilliard's portrait is definitely more French in conception than any of his earlier portraits and shows the artist's increasing ability to arrange the composition in a new fashion, where the different forms seem to be much better co-ordinated and a more coherent unity is created.

The two woodcuts inserted by Hilliard on the title page of *the Fondation du duc de Nivernois* in 1578 and representing the portraits of *The Duke of Nevers* (*Pl. 34*) and *The Duchess of Nevers* (*Pl. 35*)[1] conform to the style of the miniatures painted by Hilliard in France, in particular of Hilliard's *Self-Portrait* and that of his wife. The amount of bust visible within the area of the picture frame is the same on all four portraits, just as the three-quarter turning of the face and the opposite direction of the eyes are identical. The French character of these sitters is noticeable. Hilliard's hand is evident in the precise rendering of the features, the nose clearly outlined, the upper eyelids given in one slightly curved line, the corners of the mouth faintly turned upwards, and above all

[1] See pp. 14/5, *ante*.

in the dress of the Duchess, where the fully detailed, on this minute scale almost exaggerated ornament, is yet free from emptiness. These woodcuts likewise show Hilliard's characteristic line which sharply defines the forehead on one side, whilst it gradually vanishes into the hair on the other. His skill is the same, whether in a woodcut executed in black and white, or in a limning, painted with a fine, pointed brush on vellum in delicate colours and gold.

There were certainly other miniatures Hilliard painted in France "to get a piece of money of the lords and ladies" in Paris.[1] One of his famous sitters was probably Francis Bacon who was attached to the English Embassy from 1576 to 1579. An engraving by W. H. Worthington, showing young Bacon, and used as frontispiece to various editions of his works, the earliest of which is dated 1825, bears the additional information that it was taken from the miniature by Hilliard in the possession of "John Adair Hawkins, Esq."[2] Though the painting itself is now assumed to be lost, the engraved portrait, inscribed "1578. *Si tabula daretur digna, animum mallem. Ætatis Suæ 18*", shows in every respect the familiar features of Hilliard's style during that period.

Amongst his clientèle in Paris there must have been many members of the French nobility, but it is difficult to trace them to-day. It is possible that the miniature of *Mlle de Sourdis*, dated 1577, and formerly in the Pierpont Morgan collection,[3] is from Hilliard's hand. How close Hilliard's style of that period is to the manner of French works of art is seen, if Hilliard's portrait of *Sir Anthony Mildmay* is compared with a drawing of *Henri III* in the Bibliothèque Nationale, ascribed to François Clouet. In both cases the same elongated figure with a small head stands against a background of furniture. The difference is that Hilliard's figure has a slightly unstable, almost swaying posture, accentuated by the rhythms of the background, whereas the French drawing, with the straighter line of the legs, and the furniture square and upright, is strictly vertical and static.[4]

There is, however, one miniature, certainly depicting a Frenchman of noble origin, which, amongst the precious treasures of art in the Cabinet formerly belonging to the *Duc d'Aumale* at Chantilly, strikes the visitor as decisively English in style, in fact as being by Hilliard's hand. It is the bust portrait of a gentleman called *François de Valois, Duc d'Alençon (Pl. 36)*. It is an oval miniature with a blue background, the face turned three-quarter to the left, of a relatively

---

[1] See p. 11, *ante*.

[2] *The Works of Francis Bacon*, new ed. by Basil Montagu, 1825. An impression is in B.M. Printroom. See also Blakiston, *Nicholas Hilliard as a Traveller*, p. 169.

[3] Williamson, Pierpont Morgan, *Cat.*, I, No. 23, pl. 16, 2. Sold at Christie's, 24 June 1935, Lot 101 and at Frederick Müller's, Amsterdam, 9–11 April, 1940.

[4] For the French influence see Pope-Hennessy, *Burl. Mag.*, LXXXIII, p. 259 and C. Winter, *Burl. Mag.*, LXXXIX, p. 179. Pope-Hennessy, *Lecture*, pp. 18/19, pls. XII and XIII.

prominent size, resting on a closely fitting lace ruff, near in shape and style to that *Alice Hilliard* is wearing, with curly hair, adorned by a feather ornament, a lighter moustache and a faint indication of a beard. The flesh tints are light in colour, the eyes are gazing at the onlooker in the opposite direction and show the characteristic sweep of the upper eyelid, while the hair is treated by short brushstrokes reminiscent of Hilliard's *Self-Portrait*. The face is clearly modelled

Plate 36. François Hercule, Duc d'Alençon

and the jewels in the hair and the buttons on the doublet are rendered in gold. The identification of the miniature represents a welcome addition to Hilliard's *œuvre*.

About the provenance of this miniature not much is to be found. All we know is that the Duc d'Aumale, who resided in London from about 1848 to 1872, supplemented the collection of miniatures he had inherited from members of his family, the Condés, the Bourbons, etc. by various purchases in Paris (1861) and in London (1862), and it seems that he acquired *le Duc d'Alençon* in London from the firm of Dominique Colnaghi.[1] It was exhibited in 1865 in the Loan Exhibition of Miniatures in the South Kensington Museum (No. 386) as *François, Duc d'Alençon, afterwards Duc d'Anjou*, by an unknown artist.

Consulting reproductions of drawings representing the likeness of the famous French Duke,[2] we have to distinguish between two types: the first, a drawing by François Clouet in the Bibliothèque Nationale, of approximately 1570, shows him with a thin face and an indication of a slight beard. The second, by François Quesnel, in the same collection, of approximately 1580, represents him with a fuller face—he has put on weight—and with only a small moustache

[1] Gustave Macon, *Chantilly et le Musée Condé*, 1910, p. 239.
[2] Brocklebank Collection, French Royal Portraits, VII, pp. 13–14.

and without a beard. The miniature in Chantilly gives the likeness of the former and according to costume and style it must have been painted by Hilliard in the late fifteen-seventies. Here we have in all probability a miniature portrait which he took of his royal French patron when he was in his service in France.

Plate 37. François Hercule, Duc d'Alençon, after Nicholas Hilliard, oil

In addition, the small oil painting, commissioned by the Archduke Ferdinand for his collection of portraits, now in the Kunsthistorisches Museum, Vienna, and inscribed "Dux Alençon H" (*Pl. 37*), seems to be based on the Chantilly miniature. Hilliard portrayed the Duke again between 1581 and 1583, clearly reflecting the second likeness. This portrait will be considered later.

The miniature of *Mary Queen of Scots* (*Pl. 38*), in the collection of Mrs. Doris Herschhorn, was originally in the Royal Collection, and was painted by Hilliard *c.* 1578, probably after his return to this country. Another version is in Windsor. The likeness is supposed to be the original, taken *ad vivam*, on which the various oil portraits grouped round Oudry's *Sheffield* painting are based. As some of these are dated 1578 or 1580, the date of the miniature is approximately fixed. Since the Scottish Queen was at that time closely guarded in Sheffield, Hilliard must have painted her there or at least in this country. From the aesthetic point of view, a new breadth of conception appears, and the classic features of the Queen in widow's weeds are broadly seen and fill the small frame with amazing vitality. In this strong concentration on the individual character of the person portrayed Hilliard goes even beyond the works he had created in France.

We have seen that the miniatures which Hilliard had painted during his stay abroad were, with the exception of his *Self-Portrait* and that of his father, enclosed in an oval frame. This shape which he has tentatively tried out in his portrait of Elizabeth of 1572 had gradually become his most favoured form. With it the locket, easy to wear and to handle, and to view from close quarters, became the normal container for a miniature. Hilliard used the oval frame again when illuminating the famous Prayer Book of Queen Elizabeth, in which she herself had written six prayers, each in a different language, with the portrait of the *Duc d'Alençon* (*Pl. 39*) at the beginning and with that of the *Queen* at the

Plate 38. Mary Queen of Scots, *c.* 1578

end (*Pl. 40*). Here the miniatures appear within an oval wreath of leaves, intersected by Tudor roses, standing out from the gold ground, powdered with fleurs-de-lys, that covers the vellum page. It is as though Hilliard conceived even book illumination in terms of miniature lockets.

This Lilliputian prayer book, once the well-appreciated treasure of English

Elizabethan art, seems now lost or at least not traceable.[1] What it looked like we can only guess from a black and white facsimile, printed in 1893, in the British Museum, which is but a poor substitute for the colourful splendour of the original.

Plate 39. François Hercule, Duc d'Alençon
Frontispiece of Prayer Book, Fac. 218

Plate 41. François Hercule, Duc d'Alençon

The black and white facsimile gives us, however, an idea of the appearance of the two portraits in the original. That of the Duke stands out against the apparently plain vellum background, framed by the oval wreath on the gold

[1] See Auerbach, *Tudor Artists*, p. 121. Cf. manuscript note on Fac. 218.

78

surface; the rather fat type of the Duke agrees with Quenel's drawing of the fifteen-eighties and, in fact, the date of the illumination on the prayer book must be between 1581 and 1583, when the affair between the Queen's French

Plate 40.   Queen Elizabeth I, last page of prayer book, Fac. 218

suitor and herself had reached its climax. Although this portrait is painted on a manuscript page, it conforms, within its oval surround, in conception and style to Hilliard's independent miniatures of that period and is absolutely true to his usual manner. In addition, it helps us to identify Hilliard's miniature, wrongly called *Sir Walter Raleigh*, in the Kunsthistorisches Museum in Vienna (*Pl. 41*) as that of the *Duc d'Alençon*. This excellent portrait agrees even in detail with the illumination of the Prayer Book. That miniature, formerly in the collection of Archduke Ferdinand, has nothing to do with the small oil portrait of *Raleigh* —inscribed with the sitter's name—in the same collection, which in its turn, as we now know, is based on Hilliard's miniature, formerly in the possession of Viscount Morpeth, now in the National Portrait Gallery.[1]

[1] See pp. 95/6, *post.*

The portrait of Queen Elizabeth at the end of the Prayer Book shows her Majesty in all her charm and youthfulness and is characteristic of all portraits of her by Hilliard in that period. Only a short while ago the artist had returned home from France and the assimilation of the French idiom is evident. The Queen is seen to the waist, turned to the left, wearing a large jewelled head-dress

Plate 42.   Queen Elizabeth I, after Nicholas Hilliard (?),
engraving, Frontispiece Saxton Atlas

and a high lace ruff which leaves the black dress slightly open at the neck in a small triangular cutting. This opening at the neck was probably intended to emphasise the unmarried status of Elizabeth for the eyes of her suitor. Gilded jewels are spread over the dress and a rose is fixed on the curly yellow-brown hair.[1] The face appears fuller and rounder than that of the portrait of 1572, and its style is transitional to that of the later, more rotund likeness. It is unlikely that in 1582 or thereabouts, when this illumination was painted, the Queen was sitting to her limner for the first time since his return to England. One would

[1] Colours are described by O'Donoghue, pp. 31/2.

80

Plate 43. Queen Elizabeth I, in the manner of Nicholas Hilliard, *c.* 1575–80, oil on panel

Plate 44. Queen Elizabeth I, by Nicholas Hilliard (?), oil on panel, *c.* 1580

expect this to happen in 1578/9 and it is highly probable[1] that Hilliard designed the Queen's image for the frontispiece of the Saxton Atlas of 1579 (*Pl. 42*) and that he based her portrait in the prayer book on a renewed study *ad vivam*.

Plate 45.   An Unknown Lady, *c.* 1580

Plate 46.   An Unknown Lady, aged
21 in 1580

To illustrate further the problem of Hilliard's conception of the Queen's likeness at that period, two oil portraits, showing his influence and style, may be considered here. One is *Queen Elizabeth I*, presented in 1588/9 by Sir Vincent Skinner to the University of Cambridge (*Pl. 43*), the other a portrait of *Queen Elizabeth I*, in the possession of Lord Rothschild (*Pl. 44*). The former agrees

[1] See Auerbach, *Portraits of Elizabeth I*, p. 202.

in the slim and elongated shape of the face with the *Pelican* portrait and goes back to the likeness which Hilliard had created in the miniature of 1572 in the National Portrait Gallery. It certainly belongs to the group of portraits influenced

Plate 48.   Sir Francis Drake, 1581

Plate 47.   Sir Francis Drake, 1581

Plate 50.   An Unknown Man, aged
28 in 1582

Plate 49.   Called Sir Francis Drake, 1581

by his manner and it must have been painted between 1575 and 1580.[1] The latter portrait has a rounder face and should be dated *c*. 1580, or slightly later, i.e. between the Queen's image on the Saxton Atlas and that in the

[1] Goodison, *Catalogue of Cambridge Portraits*, I, 1955, No. 12, Pl. III. Auerbach *Portraits of Elizabeth I*, p. 202, pls. 33, 34.

prayer book. It is extremely close to Hilliard's style and there is, in this case, hardly any reason to doubt the traditional attribution to Hilliard. If one compares the characteristic line of the foreshortened side of her face, rising up to the forehead and seen against the tightly curled, crisp hair, with that on his *Self-Portrait*—the enlarged photograph of the miniature proves this clearly—

Plate 51. Called Sir George Carey, 1581

Plate 52. An Unknown Man, aged 25 in 1581

the identical conception is easily appreciated. The details of the dress, the rendering of jewels and accessories, and the colour scheme confirm this view.

A few portraits, dated 1581 or 1582, probably painted before the miniatures on the prayer book, remain to be discussed briefly. The charming unfinished miniatures of *An Unknown Lady* of about 1580 in the Victoria and Albert Museum (*Pl. 45*) and of *An Unknown Lady*, aged 21 in 1580, at Welbeck Abbey (*Pl. 46*) follow the lines started in Alice Hilliard's miniature. Perhaps the most important portrait of this group is that of *Sir Francis Drake* in Vienna (*Pl. 47*) from which an oil copy was made for the Archduke Ferdinand's collection. The bold inscription, in Hilliard's hand, on the oval miniature gives the sitter's age as 42 in 1581. The exact rendering of every detail helps to define clearly the personality of this great Elizabethan seafarer. Another version, smaller, and in the round, is in the Earl of Derby's possession (*Pl. 48*). Related to this picture, though not representing the same sitter, is the portrait *Called Sir Francis Drake*

Plate 53. An Unknown Man, *c.* 1582

at Greenwich (*Pl. 49*). The same forceful style can be detected in the oval miniature of *An Unknown Man*, aged 28, in 1582, at Madresfield Court (*Pl. 50*). Again two interesting miniatures in the collection of the Duke of Buccleuch, both formerly not ascribed to Hilliard, seem to belong to this group; the circular miniature, *Called Sir George Carey*, aged 51 in 1581 (*Pl. 51*), and an *Unknown Man*, aged 25 in 1581 (*Pl. 52*). In both cases the precise drawing of the features is enclosed by elaborate lettering which not only follows the curve but extends crossways over the shoulders.

A third miniature of *An Unknown Man* in the National Museum, Stockholm (*Pl. 53*) belongs to the same circle and period.

In all these portraits a three-quarter view to the left is given. A realistic conception distinguishes the face. The French influence has been assimilated and the whole concept of the portrait becomes compact and shows more subtle concentration.

IV

MATURITY

IN THE last twenty years of Queen Elizabeth's reign Hilliard's output of miniatures increased in number and quality and his style, which had reached maturity, flowered as never before. His contemporaries, both the famous and the lesser known, desired to be portrayed by him and a whole gallery of Elizabethans was represented within the small area of the

Plate 54. John Croker and his wife, *c.* 1580–5

miniature frame. Hilliard made full use of the picturesque costume of the period. The delicate faces are supported by wide radiating lace ruffs which, in their turn, rise upwards from slender shoulders and unfold like the calyx of a rose. The three-quarter faces turn to the right, almond-shaped eyes, slightly veiled

87

by the sweeping lines of the upper lids, look in the opposite direction. The foreshortened curve of the forehead is precisely drawn and corresponds with the clearly defined outline separating the fuller side of the face, turned towards us, from the lace ruff on which it seems to rest without any indication of a neck. Examples of this style are the beautiful double portrait of *John Croker and his Wife* (*Pl. 54*) in the Victoria and Albert Museum, and the portrait of

(a)   (b)

Plate 55(a). An Unknown Man, 1583, enclosed in locket; (b) Crucifixion, enamelled, on locket

An Unknown Man in Stockholm (*Pl. 55*) which is dated 1583 and has an enamelled crucifixion on the back of the locket. The latter date leads us to the important year 1584, when Hilliard's fame was so well established that he was considered—according to the draft patent mentioned earlier[1]—the only painter capable of representing the Queen's portrait in miniature. Even if this grant was never actually enrolled, it is evident that he virtually had the monopoly of limning the royal likeness and, for that matter, the images of numerous members of the Court as well. In this connection, it seems possible that he had a hand in the Mildmay Charter (*Pl. 56*),[2] recording the foundation of Emmanuel

[1] See p. 20, *ante*.   [2] Repr. J. E. Neale, *Elizabeth I and her Parliaments*, I, frontispiece.

Plate 56. Queen Elizabeth I, by Nicholas Hilliard (?), on the Mildmay Charter

College, Cambridge, which bears the date of the same year. Not only do we know that he had lately been recommended to Sir Walter Mildmay,[1] but the conception of the royal figure and face is closely related in style to that of the miniatures just discussed. In particular, the rendering of the face and ruff is much akin to that of *Mrs. Croker*. Again, evidence has now come to light that Hilliard painted miniatures which come very near in style to manuscript illuminations and might even be considered as such. We have only to think of *Elizabeth I playing the lute* at Berkeley Castle to realise that he may have even illuminated legal documents of all kinds and descriptions. In addition, the enthroned royal figure, a motif long known to us from the early tradition of the Plea Rolls, assumes at this very moment an increased importance, as it seems to anticipate the design of the second Great Seal, which Hilliard was to complete only two years later.

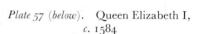

Plate 58 (left). Queen Elizabeth I, *c.* 1585

Plate 57 (below). Queen Elizabeth I, *c.* 1584

Plate 59 (above). Queen Elizabeth I, *c.* 1585

Plate 60 (right). Queen Elizabeth I, *c.* 1590

The illumination of the initial E of the Mildmay Charter is of a very high quality and shows much charm in the details of the accessories and jewellery. The square-cut partlet of the black embroidered dress, the regal coat opening

[1] Blakiston, "Nicholas Hilliard at Court", p. 17.

90

Plate 61.   Queen Elizabeth I, by Nicholas Hilliard (?), the *Ermine* portrait, 1585, oil on panel

wide in the centre over a lighter embroidered skirt give a dignity to the royal figure that rises from an especially broad basis. The Queen here almost surpasses in majesty the sovereign of the *Second Great Seal*. The whole illumination stands on a plain vellum ground and the initial E is only part of the decorative border. Whether the Mannerist figures and grotesque masks, garlands, bands, fruits, and flowers surrounding the throne are by Hilliard, his workshop or any other limner, is more difficult to decide.

Other portraits of Queen Elizabeth follow, in miniature and in oils. Amongst the former, belonging to that period, one would mention *Elizabeth I* at Madresfield Court (*Pl. 57*), the royal portrait miniature at Drumlanrig Castle (7/27), (*Pl. 58*), No. 2837 at The Hague (*Pl. 59*) and two minute circular ones of *c.* 1590 at Windsor (*Pl. 60*). They all agree closely with the life-size portrait at Hatfield House, the so-called *Ermine* portrait (*Pl. 61*), which has been traditionally ascribed to the Queen's limner. It is luckily inscribed 1585 on the handle of the sword and I think that there is a strong case in favour of Hilliard being the painter of this beautiful picture, done in the best English tradition. The decorative quality of the gold, freely applied to the sword and the jewellery, the little daisies fully but not schematically scattered over the black dress, and perhaps

Plate 62.   Henry, 8th Earl of Northumberland, 1585 (enlarged)

most remarkable, the sensitive, almost life-like rendering of the little ermine, the grasp of the rhythm of life and nature, all point to Hilliard's hand.

The same year, *Anõ Dni 1585*, is inscribed in Hilliard's cursive hand on a miniature at Belvoir Castle (No. 10), representing *Henry, 8th Earl of Northumberland (Pl. 62)*. This, though ascribed to Isaac Oliver, actually is clearly an excellent specimen of Hilliard's mature style. The beautiful gold inscription on the left is supplemented on the right by *Ætatis Suæ 54* and round a thin gold line the oval frame carries Roman letters on a grey band informing us of the identity

Plate 63.   Sir Francis Knowles, 1585

Plate 64 (below, left).   An Unknown Young Man, *c.* 1585

Plate 65.   An Unknown Young Man, *c.* 1585

of the sitter. Here is one of those extremely forceful male portraits which demonstrates with blunt realism, just as does the related *Sir Francis Drake* in Vienna; the vigorous character of an Elizabethan gentleman. The head is modelled in the round, rising from the radiating ruff, and the rendering of the

Plate 66.   (?) Anne, Lady Hunsdon, *c.* 1585

clearly outlined features, the blond moustache and beard, the blue eyes under heavy eyelids, the short grey hair, receding with age from the high, fleeting forehead, all this is done in the usual masterly manner.

Related too is *Sir Francis Knowles* (*Pl. 63*), aged 29 in 1585, at Drumlanrig Castle, with a similar three-quarter view, but painted in a lighter colouring. The same penetrating view of character emerges also from younger faces, portrayed at that period, such as those in the two enchanting miniatures at Longford Castle (*Pls. 64, 65*). Here daintiness and grace predominate. In one of these portraits, painted in delicate grey colours, the gesture of the half-hidden left hand is particularly suggestive of the aristocratic sensibility of the sitter. Again, the feminine charm of a lady, perhaps *Anne, Lady Hunsdon* (*Pl. 66*) at Welbeck Abbey is captured at approximately the same period in this mature manner. Related to the latter, supposed to represent the same sitter, is the forceful miniature in the collection of Mrs. E. H. Heckett (*Pl. 67*).

94

Probably one of the most exquisite portraits of the late eighties is that of *Sir Walter Raleigh*, formerly at Ganthorpe Hall (*Pl.* 68).[1] The beautiful expressive

Plate 67.   (?) Anne, Lady Hunsdon, *c.* 1585 (enlarged)

face is framed by a dark beard and hair, the eyes in a narrow slit look away to the right, the lovely lace ruff and an ornament in the hair indicate that the sitter

[1] Sold on 9 May 1959, now in the National Portrait Gallery. See p. 79, *ante.* It has been identified as Raleigh by comparing it with an inscribed old oil copy in Vienna.

is a courtier. Hilliard endowed the portrait of his fellow west-countryman with special grace and poise. A delicate miniature of *An Unknown Lady* at Drumlanrig Castle (*Pl. 69*) shows the same refinement. The well modelled portrait of

Plate 68. Sir Walter Raleigh, 1588

Plate 69. An Unknown Lady, 1585–90

96

A Gentleman of the family of St. John of Bletsho of 1586 at Welbeck Abbey (*Pl. 70*) combines the tangible roundness of the male portraits of 1585 with a new decorative quality which is enhanced by the brilliant gold lettering.

We now approach the series of miniatures of 1587/8, a period when a greater variety of individual works appears and when Hilliard was at the zenith of

Plate 70. A Gentleman of the family of St. John
of Bletsho, aged 24 in 1586

his power. During these two years a more psychological approach to the character of the sitter is achieved and a Mannerist reflection of fleeting feeling is often caught, accentuated by the introduction of allegorical motifs and emblems.

Thus, the wistful expression of the lovely lady at Longford Castle (*Pl. 71*) is achieved by a faint quivering of the corners of the mouth suggesting an enigmatic smile and enhanced by neatly fixed bows under the chin and one ear. Her aristocratic status is shown by the rising, unfolding lace collar that, together with the minutely drawn and carefully arranged hair, completely fills the oval. Not so much is seen of the blue background now. Throughout this period Hilliard is striving to impose on his portraits a carefully balanced pictorial composition. The capturing of the likeness itself was no longer all that was expected of his art, but what was required by a new sophisticated society with so much literary ambition was a more complex interpretation of the character of the sitter, aided by personal allusions in the form of verse and allegorical emblems. All this was in accordance with the ideals of Mannerism then in vogue in Europe with which, though in a restrained way, Hilliard thus complied.

Plate 71. An Unknown Lady

Most moving is the miniature, in different shades of white, representing *Mary Queen of Scots* (*Pl. 72*), at Welbeck Abbey, probably painted as a memorial picture after her execution in 1587. In her white widow's weeds she is seen propped against white pillows, wearing a stiff piped ruff and holding a prayer book in her hands. Merely a touch of orangy red in her hair and the binding of her book relieves the symphony of various whites and greys. Her face is an authentic likeness and conforms to the image Hilliard himself had created in his earlier portrait of the unfortunate Scottish Queen and to a beautiful miniature of her that was probably painted by François Clouet *c.* 1558, when her marriage to the later Francis II was celebrated. This French miniature is now in the Royal Collection at Windsor and was shown recently, in the Exhibition of British Portraits (1956/7), in juxtaposition to the English limner's work. While the portraits agree in the exquisite clarity of form and delightfully pure colouring, the Englishman's superior power of character interpretation, giving a true reflection of the mind and the inner life of the portrayed person, was shown incontestably.

It was during the years 1587/8 that Hilliard painted that splendid array of portraits of the elegant and glamorous gentlemen-courtiers of the Elizabethan

Plate 72. Mary Queen of Scots, *c.* 1587

Plate 73. Charles Blount,
Earl of Devonshire, 1587

Plate 74. A Man Clasping a Hand from
the Cloud, 1588

Plate 75. A Lady, called the Countess
of Essex, *c.* 1588

age. They appear before us with their curly hair, their swelling lips and short moustaches, their passionate slit-eyes, with filigree lace collars, or golden armour, and at times a pearl hanging from the ear. Whether they are called *Charles Blount, Earl of Devonshire, Fulke Greville*, or even *Robert, Earl of Essex*, or whether their identity is hidden behind that of an *Unknown Person*, they all seem strangely alike. In some cases it seems that only a minute scrutinising of every feature of their faces will distinguish one from another. A verse or word alluding to their personalities, written in flaming gold letters and curving around the blue ground, may have given an indication of their identity to their contemporaries. Now, unfortunately, the meaning of these allusions escapes us. Such sayings as *Amor Amoris Premium* or *Attici amoris ergo* for us only add to the mystery. That is why Mr. Pope-Hennessy spoke of their "tantalizing intimacy"[1] which makes such an evasive kind of contact between us who view these miniatures from the closest quarters and the vivid personality of the sitter who lies in our hand and watches us so enigmatically from that distant past. One conclusion may, however, fairly be drawn: some of these allusions are of a similarly intimate character, as are today inscriptions on photographs given by a lover to his or her beloved, and it is clear that at least some of these miniatures were kept or worn as tokens of love and affection.

One of the loveliest and earliest examples of this group is the 1587 dated *Charles Blount, Earl of Devonshire (Pl. 73)*, belonging to Col. Sir John Carew Pole, on which the expressive face rises from an almost transparent piece of golden armour covering the short bust.

Another is the famous miniature of a *Man Clasping a Hand from the Cloud (Pl. 74)*, sometimes called *Earl of Essex*, formerly at Ganthorpe Hall,[2] which is dated 1588. It is enchanting in its rhythm of lace, ornaments, curls of hair, the two elegant hands, the cloud, and the curving letters, knitted into a most intricate and refined composition. The mauve colouring shows Hilliard in harmony with the Mannerist taste of the period, that fastidious taste for unemphatic colours that belonged to the style which was the bridge between Renaissance and Baroque painting.

The same refinement of taste can be seen in the portrait of *A Lady, called the Countess of Essex (Pl. 75)*,[3] from the same collection and formerly considered to be a companion picture. Although it is $\frac{1}{8}''$ shorter and facing the same direction (not the opposite one as we would expect), it is indeed very close in manner to that of the *Man Clasping a Hand from the Cloud*. The high rising lace collar, almost filling the upper half of the oval frame, provides an intricate ornamental foil for the neatly arranged golden hair of the fair lady, whose extremely light

[1] *Lecture*, p. 23.   [2] Now Coll. Lord Wharton.   [3] Now Coll. Harry G. Sperling.

complexion is taken up by the pink shades in the sleeves and the bows decorating the black bodice. A blond curl, revealing the master's hand, steals forward from under the lace and falls on to the bare neck. The sensitive hand with the long and elegant fingers only just touch the jewel pinned to the dress. In spite of the faint colouring of the face, the likeness is interpreted with great psychological understanding.

Plate 76. An Unknown Lady, *c.* 1588

An Unknown Lady (*Pl. 76*) in the Victoria and Albert Museum must have been painted at approximately the same time. It is, however, more serious in conception, and lacks the feminine charm that distinguishes the exquisite miniature from Ganthorpe Hall.

An oil portrait of *Queen Elizabeth I* has to be considered next: the famous *Armada* picture at Woburn Abbey (*Pl. 77*). More monument than ordinary portrait, its function was to celebrate in a lasting fashion the victory over the Armada by an image of her Majesty painted on the grand scale. Again, we do not know who the painter was. Though the composition is rather rigid and formal, the colouring of the black, grey and pink shades and the detailed and precise treatment of jewels and accessory ornaments strongly suggest the influence of Hilliard's miniatures. The impression of this radiant painting is

Plate 77. Queen Elizabeth I, the *Armada* portrait, oil on panel, *c.* 1588, in the manner of Nicholas Hilliard

overwhelming both in view of its size and from the awe-inspiring, light-coloured image of the Queen which, again, may have been modelled in a stylised form on a pattern drawn by our limner. In detail it is near to *A Lady, called the Countess of Essex*, formerly at Ganthorpe Hall. In particular, the hand holding the fan on the oil painting agrees with that touching the jewel of the miniature in the elegant movement of the long fingers. Moreover, the soft pinks in the sleeves and bows attached to the lady's black bodice on the latter recur as a prominent feature on the regal attire of the Queen in the *Armada* portrait.

Reverting to the miniatures, the *Unknown Youth* in the collection of the Duke of Rutland of *c.* 1588 (*Pl. 78*), formerly ascribed to Oliver, belongs to the group of fascinating bust portraits of young courtiers discussed above. Here are the precisely circumscribed features, the full, minutely treated hair, the clear pattern of the lace collar and the enigmatic expression of the mouth depending on the sweep of the middle line, with the corners tucked up a little. A comparison with a version at Madresfield Court (*Pl. 196*), apparently copied by Oliver, shows the latter's desire to give a fuller psychological rendering of personality, with a realism that is in contrast to Hilliard's more abstract feeling. Another striking bust portrait is the miniature of the expressive *Unknown Young Man* of *c.* 1588 in the collection of Mr. J. N. Bryson (*Pl. 79*).

The full-length miniature of *An Unknown Youth* leaning against a tree among roses (*Pl. 80*), enclosed by an oval frame, of approximately the same year, has been widely held to be one of the most beautiful treasures of English art, and one that shows Hilliard at the height of his power. It is full of poetry and imagination. The love-sick attitude of the young man, swaying towards the tree's trunk on elongated legs, clad in tight white stockings, standing firmly on his left leg, across which the right leg is bent in an elegant and nonchalant pose, recall the curves and attenuations of the medieval line. The youth, while leaning against the tree, is closely interwoven with branches bearing roses, so that they grow partly behind him and partly in front, thus breaking the monotony of his long legs and the plain coat thrown over his shoulders. He and the surrounding plants, with a little of the sky overhead, have become one pictorial unit, and the natural growth of the tree and the rose bushes has been studied with the same sensitive feeling that has been bestowed on the imaginative rendering of the flexible young figure. So much about the purely aesthetic impression which everybody will appreciate today. In addition, there is the typically Elizabethan symbolism of the roses, expressing at the same time joy and pain, and the inscription *Dat poenas laudata fides* (praised faith brings sufferings or penalties) which will no doubt have been understood by the youth's contemporaries and recalled to them some event which was the cause of his wistful melancholy. The allusion is lost to us now. It has recently been suggested[1] that *An Unknown Youth* may represent the second Earl of Essex and, indeed, the whole character of this splendid miniature makes us believe that it is somehow touching on the Queen's intimate circle of friends. A portrait of Robert Devereux of 1590 by Segar, identified by Mr. Piper only a short while ago, gives us a fairly clear picture of his likeness during the period when he did not yet wear a beard. Two portrait bust miniatures, one inscribed *Anō Dni.*

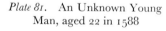

Plate 78.　An Unknown Youth,
　　　　c. 1588

Plate 79.　An Unknown Young
　　　　Man, *c.* 1588

Plate 81.　An Unknown Young
　　　　Man, aged 22 in 1588

1588 Aetatis Suæ 22—the date would fit that of Essex—in the Metropolitan Museum (*Pl. 81*), and the other at Belvoir Castle (*Pl. 82*), seem to represent the same person. The former came from Warwick Castle, probably from the

[1] Piper, *Essex*, II, pp. 300–1.

Plate 80. An Unknown Youth
Leaning against a Tree among
Roses, *c.* 1588

collection of Sir Fulke Greville, a close friend of Essex. The latter, however, is traditionally said to represent just that friend rather than Essex himself. Even the Latin inscription which, as Miss Carolyn Merion has shown, originates from Lucan,[1] does not take us any further. If the iconographical traits of the likeness on the miniatures are compared with those on Segar's oil portrait, it must be stated that, although the suggestion may be tempting, the roundness of the face

Plate 82. An Unknown Young Man, formerly
called Sir Fulke Greville, *c.* 1588 (enlarged)

and the small features of *An Unknown Youth* among roses differ greatly from the long out-drawn shape of Essex's head on his life-size portrait. He also seems to have had a much longer nose. A comparison, however, is not easy on account of the rather surprising perspective Hilliard chose for the representation of the

---

[1] *De Bello Civili*. To infer from the lines *Dat poenas laudata fides* a prophetic allusion to events that happened 13 years later, when Essex was beheaded, seems rather doubtful. See Piper, *Essex*, II, p. 303.

Plate 17.   An Unknown Man, aged 24
in 1572

Plate 102.   Mrs. Holland, 1593

Plate 83.   An Unknown Lady, aged
24 in 1589

Plate 84.   An Unknown Lady,
c. 1590

Plate 85. Queen Elizabeth I, *c.* 1590

Unknown Youth leaning against a tree, whose head is seen from well below. The impression of roundness and the illusion of a tall and slim figure are thus much increased.

Before considering the series of full-length miniature portraits of Elizabethan gentlemen initiated by the *Unknown Youth* among roses, a group of enchanting women's portraits has to be mentioned. The charming three-quarter length of *An Unknown Lady*, aged 24 in 1589 (*Pl. 83*), belonging to the Marquess of Anglesey, has all the attraction of Hilliard's style, including the lovely gold lettering curving round the top border. An almost rococo treatment of the hair, with corkscrew curls falling down onto the standing lace ruff, distinguishes the miniature of *An Unknown Lady* of *c.* 1590 in the collection of the Marchioness of Cholmondeley (*Pl. 84*). Finally, there are two portraits of Elizabeth, which belong approximately to the same period. One, in the collection of Mrs. Doris Herschhorn (*Pl. 85*), is of an excellent quality and closely related to that at Madresfield Court and the royal portraits grouped round it, though it may be dated slightly later, between 1585 and 1588. It is also near in style to the *Ermine Portrait* at Hatfield House. The radiating ruff is open in front and the expression of the face is more personal and individual than that of others in that group. It seems to be based on a fresh life-study. The other, at Longford Castle, of *c.* 1590 (*Pl. 86*), points to a later style. The more ornate rendering of the hair, jewellery and ruff, the lighter colouring and the changed proportion of the head which has now grown bigger—the single features are still given in a true-to-life fashion—herald the ostentatious portraits of the rapidly ageing Queen.

In order to appreciate the series of full-length miniature portraits Hilliard painted between 1590 and 1598, it is necessary to pause for a moment and survey briefly the development of English painting in general during that period. The Queen had now two Englishmen as her principal painters. Apart from Hilliard, her limner and goldsmith, there was George Gower, her Sergeant Painter, from 1581–96, the first holder of that office, who was a distinguished portrait painter himself.[1] Although we do not know any portraits he painted in his official capacity, we can judge from the style of those he painted in the 'seventies that he was a decorative and subtle portraitist of sound quality.

Plate 86.   Queen Elizabeth I, *c.* 1590

The general ornamental character of his pictures is somehow related to Hilliard's manner; they probably knew each other, as would appear from the draft patent of 1584; but his style is drier in detail and his portraits are lacking in that refined charm and exquisite taste which were Hilliard's. Apart from the two Englishmen there were also foreign artists active at the Elizabethan Court. They were mostly refugees from religious persecution. Amongst them were the two Marc Gheeraerts, father and son, who devoted their talent to portrait

[1] *Tudor Artists*, pp. 107 *et seq.*

Plate 87. Robert Dudley, Earl of Leicester, *c.* 1586

painting. They and others like Cornelius Ketel or Haunce Eworth in his later work, started to revive in the last quarter of the sixteenth century the pattern of the full-length standing portrait which had come into use for a short span of time in the fifteen-forties, mainly through the influence of Holbein and of another Fleming, the Court painter Guillim Scrotes.

It is possible that Hilliard was inspired in this fashion by the Flemish painters in oil. It is still more likely that he saw full-length portraits by François Clouet both in England and France. We have mentioned already a drawing of the *Duc d'Anjou* by the French Court painter.[1] There are also the two full-length portrait drawings of Elizabeth and the Earl of Leicester which Zuccaro is supposed to have made in this country in 1574. All these influences may have come together to cause him to adopt that formula. Whatever the stimulus may have been, the fact is that a series of such portraits followed the *Unknown Youth* among roses; and whilst he still preserved the oval frame in the latter, he now chose a rectangular one for each of the six or seven miniatures of that type which were to follow. He thus abandoned the portable locket-like shape and created proper independent pictures, though he painted them on vellum in a small size. (The largest limning, that of Leicester, measures $10\frac{1}{4}'' \times 7''$.) Consequently, the uniform blue background disappears too and the sitter is seen in the context of his surroundings, an open landscape or an interior. The stance that now develops is almost always the same: the weight of the body rests firmly on the left leg and foot, seen in frontal position, whereas the right leg, bent and at ease, is taken aside and represented in profile. On the *Unknown Youth* among roses a short coat gracefully cover the left arm, but on the later miniatures the left arm is visible, sharply bent, the hand pressed against the hip and the elbow pointing to the right side. The other arm is usually stretched out in a wide gesture. Such is the pose of *Leicester* (*Pl. 87*), formerly in the Currie collection, standing on the steps of a stair, supporting himself on a stick, in front of a patterned wall with a view into a garden; or of *Sir Robert Dudley* (*Pl. 88*), his natural son, now in the National Museum, Stockholm, with a table on the left and a helmet lying on it, on which Sir Robert rests his hand. Even *George Clifford, third Earl of Cumberland*, now at Greenwich (*Pl. 89*), the Queen's champion and the well-known sailor and courtier, appears in a similar attitude, holding a long spear in his right hand, his arm outstretched in an almost horizontal direction. Surrounded by his gloves, helmet, coats of arms, the Queen's glove pinned onto his helmet, he stands on a hill with a view into a distant landscape, painted in the Netherlandish manner. In all these miniatures layers of the ground are painted in characteristic striated brushstrokes, in a streaky texture, just as the plume of the helmets or the pattern

[1] See p. 74, *ante*.

Plate 88. Sir Robert Dudley, called Duke of Northumberland

Plate 89. George Clifford, 3rd Earl of Cumberland, *c.* 1590

of the wallpaper, a loose technique, yet alive, never dead or empty, and always recognisable as Hilliard's own style. This is the European Court portrait of the end of the sixteenth century transposed from the life-size scale into the Lilliputian shape of the miniature.

Plate 90. George Clifford, 3rd Earl of Cumberland, *c.* 1590

It is interesting to compare Hilliard's oval miniature of *George Clifford, third Earl of Cumberland (Pl. 90),* now in the Starr Collection, Kansas City, with his rectangular full-length version, just discussed. Both were painted at approximately the same time, in *c.* 1590. As to the actual portrait quality, the former is, without any doubt, the stronger and more effective likeness. Whereas on the full-length painting the head is relatively small and seen from slightly below, the straight-forward expression of the bare-headed Earl on the oval miniature shows the same individual features in a larger area to much greater advantage. The beautifully painted armour with all its transparency, the light sky, the emblem of the thunderbolt amidst clouds, and the inscription *Fulmen aquasque fero* (I bear lightning and water) stress the naval achievements of this great Elizabethan hero.

The full-length standing portrait of the Lord Chancellor, *Sir Christopher Hatton (Pl. 91)* is painted on the small scale of the miniature locket $(2\frac{1}{4}'' \times 1\frac{7}{8}'')$ and is most attractively placed within an interior, fitted with a carpet, a table, an armchair, and some architectural accessories, such as a window and a fireplace. The Chancellor's mace is on the table and his right hand is resting on the

Great Seal. He wears the insignia of the Garter, and this miniature was therefore painted between 1588 and 1591. It exists in two versions, one at Belvoir Castle, the other in the Victoria and Albert Museum. The latter is discussed and reproduced here. In spite of the small size the spatial view is effectively brought out by the long coat hanging to the ground and creating depth for the standing figure, and the little dog at the bottom helps to suggest space. Even the features, though small, are portrait-like, and the low forehead, mentioned by Hilliard in his *Treatise*, is hidden under the hat.

Plate 91. Sir Christopher Hatton, *c.* 1590

Plate 92. A Lady, called Anne Clifford, Countess of Pembroke, *c.* 1590

The graceful full-length standing *Lady, called Anne Clifford, Countess of Pembroke* (*Pl. 92*), an oval of the same dimensions, at Windsor Castle, has close affinities with *Sir Christopher Hatton*, and shows a similar treatment of figure, dress, accessories and the interior.

One of the most impressive full-length portraits in the larger rectangle ($9\frac{1}{4}'' \times 6\frac{7}{8}''$) is *Sir Anthony Mildmay* (*Pl. 93*). It was mentioned above when compared with a drawing by Clouet. The spacious interior of a tent, surrounding the figure in a wide span, is filled with a great number of pieces of furniture and objects bearing on the professional and personal qualities of the sitter. In spite of the untidiness the figure itself, clad in long white stockings and half covered by armour, which he is in the process of putting on or off, stands out brilliantly. So does the broad face with the curly hair, rising up wildly from the low forehead. He is seen in his white stockings against the typical striations of the dark floor and the

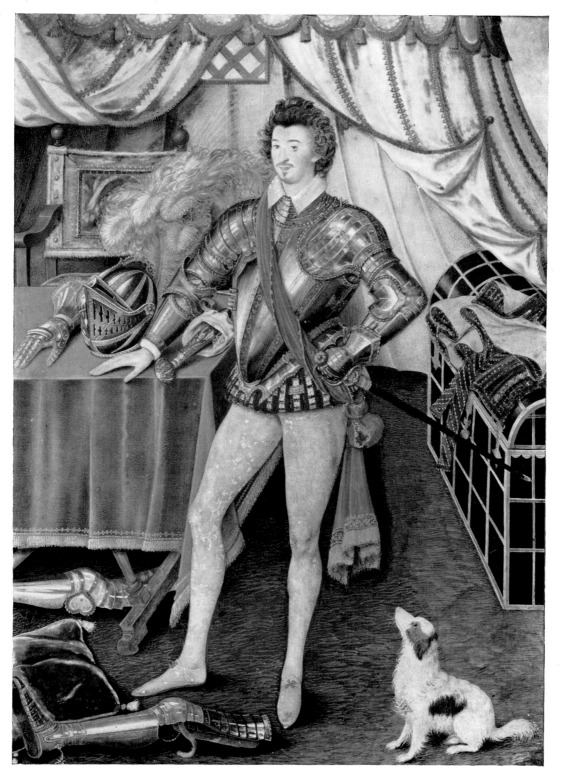

Plate 93. Sir Anthony Mildmay, *c.* 1595

Plate 94. Henry Percy, 9th Earl of Northumberland (?)

white long-haired dog in the right-hand corner looks faithfully up to his master and leads us, because of its colour, to the plume of the helmet on the table and to the light tent-like curtain in the background. Whether Hilliard paints a dog or a human being, a dead cushion or a piece of armour, a plume or a curl, he always strives to give something more than the mere features of these living or dead objects, something he has really seen, felt and experienced.

Plate 95. Henry Percy, 9th Earl of Northumberland (?)

Perhaps one of the most interesting full-length miniatures is that of *The Young Man* lying in a horizontal position on the ground of an enclosed formal garden and supporting his head in his hand, in the collection of Dr. M. E. Kronenberg, Rotterdam *(Pl. 94)*. It was probably painted between 1594 and 1598. It is remarkable that the figure lies right at the bottom of the painting and takes up the whole width of the miniature. There is a closed ochre book on the left near to the head with its ivory flesh-tints, giving the transition to the dead-white blouse he is wearing and the handkerchief he is holding in his left hand. A black hat gives the continuation of the figure to the left, two gloves emphasise the horizontal stretch to the right. The ground is painted in the same striations we noticed before. The trees rising behind the young man are planted at regular intervals, the trunks as well as the branches are painted with minute care, the foliage given in light and shade according to whether it is nearer or further away, against the pale-blue summer sky. From one of the branches hangs a ball or sphere balanced by a quill or feather, and the word *tanti* is written across. The meaning of this emblem is not quite clear, but has been interpreted as showing that the written word is as important as the world, with an allusion to the sitter who may have been a poet or a man of letters. The romantic and poetical atmosphere of this lovely limning is closely linked with that of the *Unknown Youth among roses*. The lyrical rhythm and the swaying attitude is expressed by the crossing of the legs in both paintings, and the elongated line, horizontal and vertical, predominates likewise.

As in the case of *George Clifford, third Earl of Cumberland*, another version in a smaller oval size ($2'' \times 2\frac{1}{2}''$) exists on a playing card, repeating with variations the bust portrait of the same sitter who is also seen supporting his head in his hand in a recumbent position. This version, which is of great beauty, came originally from the collection of Lord De l'Isle and Dudley and is now in the

Plate 96. Called Sir Philip Sidney, *c.* 1590

Fitzwilliam Museum (*Pl. 95*). The hand and the broadly seen face are treated in soft light colours, but a strong line gives the contours and a fine modelling suggests the movement of head, shoulders and neck. An open book with pink ribbons,

Plate 97. Sir Henry Slingsby, 1595

the trunk of a tree, pink daisies and red poppies in the pale green grass, and a buff-coloured glove are distributed round the figure, clearly encircling it, and a narrow oval golden border, apparently by Hilliard's own hand, closes the composition. This miniature is not only an abridged repetition of the rect-angular limning but a carefully finished work of art on its own that clearly shows Hilliard's superb decorative abilities.

As to the possible identification of the subject it is best to discuss both minia-tures together. The latter was exhibited as *Sir Philip Sidney* by Isaac Oliver in 1926.[1] This attribution resulted probably from a mistake over two miniatures, shown in 1862.[2] The identical portrait was actually called in the Catalogue

[1] B.F.A.C., *Late Elizabethan Art*, 1926, II (4), pl. 20.
[2] Exh. Sth. Kens. Mus., 1862, Nos. 2207 & 2212.

Henry, 9th Earl of Northumberland. There is also a water-colour copy, of the miniature in the Fitzwilliam Museum, amongst the Sutherland drawings in the
Ashmolean which is described as *Henry, 8th Earl of Northumberland*, by Hilliard,
in the possession of the Duke of Northumberland. The latter identification
cannot be possible because of the dates of the 8th Earl, and again, according to
the authentic portrait at Belvoir Castle[1] he looks completely different. The
second point proved also negative, as no variant of the two miniatures could
be found at present in the possession of the Duke of Northumberland. There is,
however, a strong and substantial case to be made for *Henry, 9th Earl of Northumberland*.[2]

Henry lived from 1564–1632. He was called the "Wizard" earl because of his
interest in science and alchemy. His personality would fit admirably the character Hilliard has painted of him in the two miniatures. He collected books from
an early age, was widely read, and was called the Maecenas of learning of his age.
When he was in the Tower, he was attended by *Three Magi*. He was an in-
tellectual, given rather to books than to speech. He is said to have preferred
"the infinite mistress, Knowledge" to the finite attractions of his hot-tempered
wife: "It (the former) produced out of conclusions perpetuall contentment, shee
in conclusion produced sadnes. . . . " His wife, whom he had married in 1594—
which, incidentally, might be a possible date for the miniatures—was Dorothy,
sister of Robert, 2nd Earl of Essex. To that type of man the emblem appearing
on the rectangular limning would have been a welcome allusion. He may even
have borrowed the idea from his brother-in-law, for a strange story is reported
in the diary of the Duke of Stettin,[3] who, in 1602, was shown in London a
long gallery with the shields and emblems of the noble Knights. Amongst
them there was a verse "used by the great and celebrated noble warrior the
Earl of Essex in several tournaments against the Lord of Borle or Burghedt, the
Queen's Secretary". As he saw that he could not achieve anything against the
latter who was his adversary, "he got a shield made with a pair of scales upon
it, and in the one scale was a big canon, in the other a writing-pen which
nevertheless outbalanced the canon with this inscription: *Et tamen vincor*".
If one replaces the cannon by a cannon ball, the emblem becomes that which
we have seen in the branches behind the *Young Man* lying in a garden.

---

[1] See pp. 92–4, *ante*.

[2] Mr. Piper has drawn my attention to this possible identification. I am greatly indebted to
Mr. G. R. Batho, who very kindly gave me all his material on the 9th Earl and also assisted
me in my search at Alnwick. See G. Batho, *The Household Accounts of Henry Percy*, 1953, p. 270,
and *History Today*, May 1956, pp. 344–51.

[3] *Transactions of the Royal Historical Society*, New Series, VI, "Diary of the Duke of Stettin's
Journey", p. 25. Miss C. Marion drew my attention to this book.

Plate 98. Robert Devereux, 2nd Earl of Essex, *c.* 1595

Maturity

The iconographical likeness is difficult to establish, as the 9th Earl used to wear a full beard in his later life. There is an interesting oil portrait at Alnwick, ascribed, though not conclusively, to van Sommer, which represents the Earl standing near a red table and dressed in a beautifully patterned gold doublet. His hands are sensitive and his features and shape of head seem somehow to conform to the likeness Hilliard created in the miniatures. The same applies to the posthumous portrait by van Dyck, on which, strangely enough, he is also seen supporting his head on his hand.

There are, however, two further points, which seem to strengthen this theory. We definitely know from the Household Accounts of the Percies (1585–1632) that Hilliard was paid 3*l.* several times for his lordship's picture. The first payment dates from autumn 1585/6. The second covers the period from 16 June 1587 to 8 July 1588 and runs: "for yor Lp: Picture to Hillyard lx*s.*" And again the third relates to "2 Mar 1594/5 to 21 Feb 1595/6" and reads as follows: "Emptions of necessaries . . . to mr Hilliard for his Lp Picture lx*s.*" Even if the first two items may refer to the miniature of the Earl's father, they show clearly that Hilliard was employed by the family. The last payment may very well apply to our miniature.

Finally, there is a reference by Vertue to pictures in the collection of the Duke of Somerset,[1] where he noticed "a Lord Percy, a limning, lying on the ground". This seems to be a definite description of the Rotterdam miniature, which, therefore, in the eighteenth century was known as a Lord Percy. In addition, the Earl of Aylesford, from whose collection this miniature came, was a descendant of the Duke of Somerset. Consequently, the case in favour of Henry, Lord Percy, 9th Earl of Northumberland, seems to be fairly conclusive.

A rectangular miniature ($5\frac{3}{8}'' \times 4\frac{1}{8}''$), sold at Sotheby's on 24 June 1948 (lot 188) as *Called Sir Philip Sidney* by Hilliard (*Pl. 96*), definitely belongs to the same period and is, because of the way in which the seated young man bends his right arm and supports his head on his hand, whilst his left arm hangs down with the hand holding a handkerchief, closely related to the Rotterdam miniature. Judging from the photograph this limning appears to bear Hilliard's characteristic traits and is an interesting addition to the varied style of his work during the fifteen-nineties. The sitter's likeness, though in some ways near to that of the Cambridge miniature, differs from it in the shape of the forehead and the curly hair. In that respect it resembles the image of the sitter on Oliver's miniature, *Called Sir Philip Sidney* at Windsor Castle. In both cases the identification with Sidney is doubtful, as Sir Philip died in 1586, almost ten years before the miniatures representing the portraits of a young man were painted.

[1] Vertue, *Notebooks*, IV., p. 152. Vertue describes the background: "in Syon Gardens".

124

Maturity

A most noble miniature (oval, $3\frac{3}{8}'' \times 2\frac{1}{2}''$), fortunately dated, and thanks to a seventeenth-century inscription at the back even identified, rounds off this interesting group: *Sir Henry Slingsby*, aged 35 in 1595, in the Fitzwilliam Museum (*Pl. 97*). Of a bigger size than usual, it shows the impressive likeness of a young man wearing a patterned grey and black doublet with a simple white collar over a tiny piece of golden lace and a tall black hat embellished with a flower in yellow and green and a scroll with the words *semper idem*. The yellow also relieves the grey black of the left sleeve. The pale face with the small moustache, the round chin, the wavy hair and the blue eyes has the strange moving expression typical of that group of portraits, brought out strongly by the curtain-like cerise background enlivened by vivid lights. The red background colour, sometimes more terracotta, sometimes more cerise, has now, in this late period, frequently replaced the blue one, almost always used on the earlier miniatures.

Another large rectangular ($9\frac{7}{8}'' \times 8''$) limning with an interesting full-length standing figure, of *c.* 1595, belonging to Lady Lucas (*Pl. 98*), could be closely studied by the public for the first time in the 1956/7 Royal Academy Exhibition of *British Portraits*. It was exhibited as *Sir Philip Sidney* (?) by Nicholas Hilliard. A very tall, youngish man, clad in gold-filigree, transparent armour, stands in front of the white and gold curtain of his tent, his right hand on his hip, his left touching a table covered with green cloth on which lies his helmet with a splendid plume of feathers. His stance is approximately the same as those described before, but seen in reverse, and slightly more unstable and elongated than usually. His servant in a black and white striped uniform holds his horse which again wears a large plume on its head. In the background there are armies gathered and tents in an open, hilly and cloudy landscape under a rising sun. In spite of the fact that the limning has been in parts retouched by a later hand, the whole conception of the slender figure, the treatment of the hands and the face with the moustache, the brown eyes, the characteristic forehead and hair, the beautifully painted armour in its transparency, wherever it is genuine, the loose and striated technique of the ground and the feathers in their double occurrence, all these elements speak certainly for Hilliard as the author of this almost heraldic miniature. Specially the groom holding the charger classifies it as belonging to the more decorative field of ornamental work as it was often carried out by the heralds. This is interesting because, as we know,[1] precisely at that period, in 1593/4, Hilliard was in close touch with two painter-stainers who were engaged on paintings for funerals under Clarenceux.

In a recent article in the *Burlington Magazine*, Mr. Piper has suggested—as I think, plausibly—that the subject may represent *Robert, 2nd Earl of Essex*.[2]

[1] See p. 27, *ante*. [2] Piper, *Essex*, II, p. 303.

There is definitely an iconographical likeness with Segar's oil portrait of him. In addition, the strange words on the swordbelt and the skirt *DVM FORMAS . . . VM EOR . . . MV* or *MY NV* may perhaps be allied to the motto *DVM FORMAS MINVIS*, which Essex is reported to have used written round a single diamond he had in the centre of his shield:[1] a diamond loses its value when fashioned into shape. What speaks against the identification with Essex, but is perhaps of minor importance because of the heraldic character of the miniature, is the fact that the figure has no insignia of the Garter. As to *Sir Philip Sidney*, he had died a long time before this miniature could have been painted.

In view of the difficult problem this ambitious miniature presents to us, it may be of some interest to quote what Vertue thought of it by the middle of the eighteenth century. A letter of 1750, from him to the owner, Mr. James West, set in the back of the frame, accepts an identification with Sidney and attributes it to Oliver. In one of his Notebooks, published by the Walpole Society,[2] he mentions the painting as being in Mr. West's collection, but "doubtful if Sir Philip Sidney". But a much fuller account of this limning appears in his unpublished manuscript collection which shows that he took some trouble to form an opinion about this interesting work.[3] The date is 26 Dec. 1750. He starts with the assumption that:

> it was calld Sr Phillip Sydney, that most famous Hero of England, I think the whole picture taken together is about his time and age, and his rich dress in armor. his horse accoutred and his Servant. his helmet with fine plumes are suitable to his Character. The face, complexion and hair, agreable to other limnings and pictures of him as I have seen in his middle ages.

He then sees in the camps in the distance and the rising sun an allusion to his "spirit and character". He continues to read the motto on the belt, as far as is visible, in the following words—also mentioned in the Catalogue of the 1956/7 Exhibition—*DVM FORMAS PRAELI/VM EORVM*. This, he says,

> alludes very well to his being ready and armed for action with his Ballalia inorder as the riseing Sun or some such like meaning may express the Subject of this representation of him or expectation of . . .

He further remarks as follows:

> But when I consider this limning in relation with art of limning or the artist that did it. I at present am of the oppinion—that it might be Hillyardes work or truely Isaac Oliver. who lived in that time and their work is most like it (their works I

---

[1] Camden, *Remaines concerning Britaine* (1605), p. 174. Mr. Roy Strong first noticed this interesting reference.

[2] Vertue, V, p. 84.

[3] B.M., Add. MSS. 23091, fols. 56 and 60.

Plate 99. An Unknown Lady, unfinished, *c.* 1590

express because) as it is said Oliver first learnt of Hillyard and from thence imitated this mode of such rich gold ornaments, in armor etc—Yet as I further do observe—that the tall and long leggs and shape of this portrait may not be his just proportion. therefore (afterwards) it might occasion Sr Philipp to put that Question to Hylliard the Limner if it was possible to represent the true linieament and proportion of any person in small so to represent the true figure justly in suche proportion as the natural person is—I think the figure or servant that holds the horse—is surely of Isaac Oliver drawing in manner. beyond dispute, this he coud draw with liberty in his own manour. and the whole limning I think is of his Early manner of Limming.

According to this passage Vertue seemed to have been firm about Sidney being the subject. It is extremely interesting that at least at that moment he was also in favour of Hilliard as the painter of the figure and it is remarkable that the long legs caused him to think of the episode, referring to Sidney, Hilliard mentioned in his *Treatise*. It is only natural that Vertue should think Oliver to be the author of the freer attitude of the servant and the horse, as nothing in that line by Hilliard is known. But the treatment of the groom's face and the armour and plume of the horse are identical with the rest of the picture and by the same hand.

A few pages further Vertue reverts to the limning and makes poignant remarks on its state of preservation:

as to the present State or case of this picture it is by time certainly decayed. some small refreshment may be usefull to be done to it by a carefull hand, and in some places where the colours are craks and is peeling off—to prevent its ore—the straining it on a new frame, would make it ly smooth and even and would show the more beautifull with a better glass also, may be necessary. . .

This may explain the retouching by a later hand. He finally considers it to be *Temp. Elisabeth* "which year can't precisely be fixd, but probably soon after he (Sidney) went abroad in the armyes".

Though this passage does not settle the problem, it is highly significant because it indicates that the celebrated *connoisseur* of the eighteenth century appreciated this rare masterpiece as a truthful picture of the Elizabethan Age.

How Hilliard actually worked on the larger full-length standing portraits can best be studied in his lovely rectangular miniature ($7\frac{1}{4}'' \times 4\frac{3}{4}''$) of *An Unknown Lady* of *c.* 1590, in the collection of Dr. L. C. G. Clarke (*Pl. 99*), which is on loan to the Fitzwilliam Museum. This miniature, formerly believed to be by Oliver and first attributed to Hilliard by Mr. Carl Winter, is unfinished. It therefore shows clearly the process Hilliard adopted when building up his composition. It is painted on a sheet of vellum attached to a board. Against an already perfectly finished crimson curtain, enlivened by vertical, horizontal

Plate 128.   Queen Elizabeth I

Plate 124.   An Unknown Lady,
1595–1600

Plate 100. An Unknown Lady, *c.* 1595 (enlarged)

and diagonal lights, the standing figure is broadly outlined by sketchy brush-strokes. A yellow line separates the floor from the curtain and adjoining wall, and a patch of the same colour in the right-hand corner marks the shadow which the farthingale throws on the ground. In the same sketchy way the general position of the left hand is indicated without detail. The main idea of the lady's pose and her surroundings have become perfectly clear, though in parts only suggested. What is exactly finished is the rendering of the features of the face—with the exception perhaps of a little colour that would be expected for the flesh tint—the headdress, the curls with one earring, the pattern of the left

Plate 102.   Mrs. Holland, 1593

Plate 101.   An Unknown Lady,
1590–5

Plate 103.   An Unknown Lady,
1597

sleeve, the radiating ruff, open in front, the two standing semicircular wires, and the stomacher sharply outlined against the curtain. Hilliard worked from the background towards the front, having always in view both the figure and its surroundings. As to detail, he tackled first the likeness as the most important part; but, at every point of the process of painting, the composition was seen as a whole and its balance preserved.

Plate 104. Called Lady Arabella Stuart, *c.* 1590

Plate 105. An Unknown Lady, called Mrs. Hilliard

Plate 106. Called Lady Arabella Stuart

Plate 107. Catherine Carey, Countess of Nottingham, 1595–1600

As to the treatment of ruffs and faces, three charming women's portraits can be grouped round the rectangular miniature: *An Unknown Lady* of *c.* 1595 in the Victoria and Albert Museum (*Pl. 100*)—one of the finest psychological interpretations of the female character Hilliard created—the more *bourgeois*, yet

Plate 108. An Unknown Man, *c.* 1590

Plate 109 (right). Leonard Darr, 1591

not less impressive, *An Unknown Lady* of *c.* 1590–95, in the Cleveland Museum of Art (*Pl. 101*); and the lovely *Mrs. Holland*, aged 26 in 1593 (*Pl. 102*), inscribed in beautiful gold letters on the blue background.

There follows, perhaps a few years later, another charming set of ladies, seen in the same three-quarter position turned to the left, the hair and ruffs elegantly arranged, and the whole expression dominated by the eloquent eyes and a bewitching smile round the corners of the mouth. *An Unknown Lady*, formerly called *Princesse de Condé*, in the Metropolitan Museum (*Pl. 103*) is dated 1597 and represents a more mature-looking type; the young *Unknown Lady*, formerly *Called Lady Arabella Stuart*, in the Museum of Fine Arts, Boston (*Pl. 104*), looks at us in a coquettish and witty way; the more gentle *An Unknown Lady, called Mrs. Hilliard*, in the National Museum, Stockholm (*Pl. 105*), and finally, nearer the end of the century, *A Lady, called Lady Arabella Stuart*, formerly in the Sotheby Collection (*Pl. 106*) and *Catherine Carey, Countess of Nottingham*, at Drumlanrig Castle (*Pl. 107*), both fascinating in their youthfulness and charm.

133

Hilliard's power of characterisation did not weaken in the last decade of Queen Elizabeth's reign; on the contrary, it became intensified. Some forceful men's portraits date from that period: *An Unknown Man* of *c.* 1590, at Longford Castle (*Pl. 108*), in a contemporary ivory box, has a moving expression, poignant and lively, against a cerise curtain. One of the most beautiful

Plate 110 (left). Henry Wriothesley, 3rd Earl of Southampton, 1594

Plate 111 (top, left). An Unknown Gentleman, called Sir Walter Raleigh, 1595

Plate 112 (above). An Unknown Young Man, aged 22 in 1596

portraits is that of *Leonard Darr* (*Pl. 109*), a Tavistock merchant, who was 37 in 1591. It is bigger in size than usual, and most exquisitely modelled in bright-red hatching lines, almost monumental in conception, with a tall black hat and the clear unfolding of the ruff against the blue background with the calligraphic lettering in gold that, because of its brilliance, stands right out and supports the whole composition. A third is the lovely *Henry Wriothesley*, aged 24 in 1594, at the Fitzwilliam (*Pl. 110*), on which the refined likeness of the young man is

134

again seen against a cerise curtain-like background. Another miniature, certainly by Hilliard and belonging to that group, I was able to identify at Chantilly, in the former collection of the Duc d'Aumale, where it is called *Sir Walter Raleigh* by an unknown painter (*Pl. 111*). It is dated 1595 and has the

Plate 113. George Clifford, 3rd Earl of
Cumberland, 1593 (?)

Plate 114. An Unknown Man,
aged 22 in 1597

Plate 115. Sir Thomas Bodley, 1598

135

inscription *In Noua fert animas* on a blue ground. It is the half-length portrait of an elegant courtier and the sitter is not unlike various oil portraits representing Raleigh, though it is difficult to say if it agrees with Hilliard's miniature of him, in the National Portrait Gallery. It was exhibited in the 1865 Exhibition at South Kensington as *An Unknown Man* by Hilliard and had been completely lost sight of ever since. *An Unknown Young Man*, aged 22 in 1596, in the National Museum, Stockholm (*Pl. 112*), is attractive and very similar in conception.

Another group of male portraits, slightly less imposing and more modest, originated at approximately the same time: A bust portrait of *George Clifford* of 1593(?) on loan to the Victoria and Albert Museum (*Pl. 113*), a most charming and colourful miniature of *An Unknown Man*, aged 22 in 1597 in the Victoria and Albert Museum (*Pl. 114*); *Sir Thomas Bodley* (*Pl. 115*), inscribed *Año Dñi 1598 Ætatis Suæ 54*, in the Bodleian, which shows Hilliard's clear modelling in short lines; the small circular bust portrait of a youngish *Unknown Man*, in the collection of the *Earl of Leicester* (*Pl. 116*), which is signed at the back in gold in

Plate 116.   An Unknown Young
Man, 1599

Plate 117.   An Unknown Gentleman,
aged 28 in 1599, in the manner of
Nicholas Hilliard

Hilliard's own hand *N. Hillyarde. fecit 1599*. This signature, a unique occurrence in his work, is written in a beautiful calligraphic style and may perhaps point to a special relationship between the artist and the sitter. Finally, there is a miniature of *An Unknown Man*, aged 28 in 1599, at Drumlanrig Castle (*Pl. 117*), which is probably, but not definitely, from Hilliard's hand and generally conforms to the style of that period.

But as to the intensity of feeling and passion brought out in the expression of the sitter, none of the miniatures discussed above can be compared with *An Unknown Man against a background of Flames,* in the Victoria and Albert

Plate 118. An Unknown Man against a
background of flames

Museum (*Pl. 118*), which must have been painted in the late fifteen-nineties. Here is a most dramatic effect, and within the small oval of the miniature a striking picture of human tragedy is given. Here, the sitter, whoever he was, does not matter, but the intense feeling which his image expresses, moves and touches us profoundly. As if it were a symbol of burning love, the card on which the parchment is pasted is the ace of hearts. The "burning" lover wears a fine linen shirt, wide open in front, a locket hangs on a long chain and he presses it with his left hand against his heart, as if it contained the picture of his beloved mistress, and, in strong contrast to the white of the garment, the noble and ecstatic face with dark hair and beard, turned to the right, looks at us with fanatical eyes. The man appears in front of the yellow golden flames like one who is suffering as a martyr for his love. Hilliard accomplishes this extraordinary effect by means of precision and accurate linear detail, without losing sight of the whole. A contemporary would, of course, have understood the allusion to the person represented and the Elizabethan symbol of the lover "burning in flames beyond all measure".[1]

[1] Winter, *Eliz. Miniatures,* p. 26.

The same firm handling of the features and their subtle modelling can be seen on a little known miniature of *George Carey, 2nd Lord Hunsdon* at Berkeley Castle (*Pl. 119*), dated 1601. The miniature of his wife (*Pl. 120*), is also impressive but not so well preserved.

Plate 119.   George Carey, 2nd Lord Hunsdon, 1601 (enlarged)

The more serious and in a way heavier trend that had started in the image of "the burning lover" developed further towards 1600 and is even found on miniatures representing women. It appears that Elizabeth's Court had, after all, grown older and its ladies had to be portrayed in a more authoritative fashion. The size of the oval becomes bigger and the half-length figure fills the miniature voluminously and projects towards us in a new realistic way. A portrait of this period is that of *Frances Howard* or *Mary Sackeville, Countess of Dorset*, as it is sometimes called, of *c*. 1600, extant in two versions, at Drumlanrig Castle (*Pl. 121*) and in the National Museum, Stockholm (*Pl. 122*). In both cases the lady wears a flowery dress, painted in light colours, but the pattern itself is different. The well-modelled hand is seen on both miniatures right in the middle of the lower frame holding, in the Stockholm version, a lovely sprig of white flowers outlined against the attractively embroidered dress. Just as in the *Man against Flames*, the head is seen, contrary to the usual manner, three-quarter to the right with the result that the foreshortened side is somewhat more strongly modelled by grey shades and strengthened by a darker line running down the neck which is picked up by the black jewel she is wearing on a thin necklace of the same colour. Corresponding to this colour scheme is also the tightly curled brown hair and her dark brown eyes looking in the opposite direction. The cerise background is again treated like a curtain with various lights and reflections. The quality of painting is excellent. It is clear that, as Sir Basil Long remarked about the miniature in the collection of the Duke of Buccleuch[1] "it resembles Isaac Oliver's work a good deal". But there cannot be any doubt that the precise lines characterising the features of the face and the pattern of the

Plate 120.   Elizabeth Spencer, Lady Hunsdon (enlarged)

dress are truly Hilliard's hand. It is interesting that, at the end of Elizabeth's reign, he succumbed slightly to the more realistic view, now expounded by his former pupil.

[1] Notes in MS. on the Buccleuch Collection.

139

Two other portraits conform to the same stylistic principle: *An Unknown Lady*, formerly called *Queen Elizabeth*, at Drumlanrig Castle (*Pl. 123*), and *An Unknown Lady*, also called *Anne Clifford, Countess of Dorset and Pembroke*, formerly in the

Plate 121. Frances Howard, Duchess of Richmond and Lennox, *c.* 1600

Plate 122. Frances Howard, Duchess of Richmond and Lennox, *c.* 1600

same collection and now in the Fitzwilliam Museum (*Pl. 124*). Both are most charming portraits, formerly ascribed to Oliver but certainly by Hilliard. The first is slightly shorter and shows somewhat less than half-length. The lady wears a beautifully patterned grey and black dress with clearly drawn arabesques in blue and gold. A pale green thistle with a mauve flower is pinned to her dress and a rosebud to her lace ruff. The background is pale blue. White flowers with touches of gold adorn her neatly arranged brown hair that terminates—as often during this period—in some falling curls. There is energy and determination in her interesting features. The Cambridge miniature appears more elongated; the sitter is more graceful and younger; the colours are kept

Plate 129.   Queen Elizabeth I, in locket

Plate 118.   An Unknown Man against a
background of flames

lighter in mauve and grey against an identical pale blue background; black bands line the sleeves and a cap of the same colour is decorated with gold. A red cherry is pinned to her dress. Lovely curls emphasise a youthful appearance.

We now come to the end of Elizabeth's reign, and here have to be mentioned some of the splendid miniatures which Hilliard painted of his royal patron during a time when—though ageing—she gained ever more prestige and admiration. Though the last image of the Queen may appear magnificent in dress, make-up and jewellery, and ever more youthful in the expression of the face, this has only been achieved by a general smoothing out of surfaces, by compressing "her face oblong" to a slightly rounder shape, and by obliterating completely the wrinkles and furrows which age had imprinted on her countenance. Her features, however, are still true to nature even on her limner's late miniatures, true, at least to the description Paul Hentzner gave of her in his *Itinerary*, in 1598:

> Nexte came the queen, very majestic . . . her eyes small, yet black and pleasant, her nose a little hooked, her lips thin, . . . She had in her ears two pearls, with very rich drops; she wore false hair, and that red; upon her head she had a small crown.

On all those miniatures there are small black eyes with heavy eyelids, the clearly outlined, hooked nose, the small, thin mouth, and the red, elaborately

Plate 123. An Unknown Lady   *Plate 124.* An Unknown Lady, 1595–1600

Plate 125. Queen Elizabeth I, *c.* 1600

Plate 126. Queen Elizabeth I,
c. 1600

Plate 127. Queen Elizabeth I,
c. 1600

Plate 128. Queen Elizabeth I

Plate 130. Queen Elizabeth I, detail from visit of Queen Elizabeth to Blackfriars, after Nicholas Hilliard, *c.* 1600, oil on canvas

10—N.H.

bejewelled wig. Her fair complexion, also mentioned in this contemporary description, suited Hilliard's transparent glazes well and was aided by the absence of heavy shading. As to accessories of costume, jewellery, pearls and diamonds, necklaces, flowers pinned to the bodice or half-hidden behind the ear, lace, silk or heavier material, he could work on them to his heart's desire. One of the most impressive and near to life portraits of Elizabeth is the miniature at Ham House (*Pl. 125*), which presents her in three-quarter length, seated, with both arms and hands visible, beautifully modelled and most elaborately ornamented with an attractive pattern in the costume and masses of jewellery. Surely, for this type of portrait the Queen must have given Hilliard a sitting which could then have enabled him to create a pattern which he could repeat and which became the standard likeness during that late period. He had, after all, been painting her for almost thirty years. The best specimens of this group of royal portraits are the miniatures in the Fitzwilliam Museum (*Pl. 126*), the Fredericton Art Gallery, New Brunswick (formerly Sotheby Collection),[1] the collection of the Earl of Derby (*Pl. 127*), and two in the Victoria and Albert Museum (*Pl. 128*), one of which is reproduced here on an enlarged scale. The other is enclosed in a beautiful locket, the lid of which is set with rubies and diamonds, and pierced through. Thus, the crimson background is partly visible and matches the colour of the rubies (*Pl. 129*).[2]

It has to be repeated that Hilliard's late miniatures represent the Queen's likeness not exactly as a mask, though modified to a more youthful appearance. Nevertheless the likeness is still there, but most oil portraits, based on his miniatures, become strongly formalised and stylised. This tendency begins *c.* 1588 and continues to the end of the reign. Taking all the evidence together, we see that Hilliard had something like a monopoly of the royal portrait, even if the draft patent was not given legal effect. Again and again, we find that his miniature style was the predominant influence on paintings in large. It matched so well the spirit of pageantry and worship of the Queen as a goddess that had then developed. This is perhaps nowhere better expressed than in the ethereal, goddess-like regal figure, clad in white and covered with sparkling jewellery, who is seated on a litter in the *Visit of Queen Elizabeth to Blackfriars* (*Pl. 130*). What a difference there is between this radiant and glorious apparition and the realistic figures of the courtiers, who may very well have been painted by Gheeraerts.

With this splendid and truly Hilliardesque representation of the Queen we may suitably close the chapter on Hilliard's greatest artistic period.

[1] Auerbach, *Portraits of Elizabeth I*, pl. 38. Repr. in colour: Cat. Sotheby's, 11 Oct. 1955, No. 73, frontispiece.   [2] Repr. in colour: Winter, Pl. IVa.

V

EVENTIDE

URING THE reign of James I documents record the special tasks
entrusted to Hilliard by the sovereign more clearly than before.
More prosaic and utilitarian than his great predecessor, the King
asked his limner to paint a great number of royal portrait miniatures, of himself and his family, which were to be distributed widely amongst
members of his own and foreign Courts and ambassadors residing abroad.[1] In
these documents the portraits specially referred to are those of the King and his
two sons, the Princes Henry and Charles. On stylistic grounds we know that
Hilliard also painted Queen Anne, Princess Elizabeth and her husband
Frederick, the Elector Palatine. But it has to be stated from the outset that the
artistic situation at the Court had shifted, to a certain degree, in favour of
Hilliard's former pupil, Isaac Oliver, who was more realistic, more cosmopolitan
and perhaps more "modern" in his manner than his teacher and therefore more
able to fulfil the requirements of a new society. It has been found recently that
Oliver had two definite appointments with the Court: in 1604 he was made
Queen Anne's "painter for the Art of Lymning" with a fee of 40l. a year, a fee
which was entered as paid in 1615,[2] and as "Mr. Isacke Paynter" he was
attached to the household of Prince Henry. He functioned as such in the list of
"artificers" following the prince's funeral on 6 November 1612.[3] However,
Hilliard was firmly established as His Majesty's limner and we already have
mentioned that in 1617 a twelve-year monopoly of royal portraits in every
possible technique was granted to him. It seems as though the older generation
at Court was more in favour of the typically English master, whereas the feminine side and the younger ones tended to patronise the more "progressive"
artist.

[1] See p. 39, *ante.*   [2] Auerbach, *Tudor Artists,* p. 179.
[3] *Ibid.,* p. 133.

147

As to the surviving material of portrait miniatures of the King and his family, Mr. Graham Reynolds has recently made a successful attempt to disentangle the vast number of such portraits and to ascribe to Hilliard on stylistic

Plate 131. King James I, *c.* 1605

grounds many which were formerly attributed to Oliver.[1] He emphasises that invariably assistants will have helped the King's limner and that it is sometimes hard to tell how much was actually finished by the hand of the master himself.

Plate 132. King James I, after 1604

Nevertheless, a quite considerable number of miniatures of a high quality can thus be assembled which are undoubtedly by Hilliard or members of his workshop and definitely differ from those by Oliver. Certain types, frequently repeated in many versions, can be clearly discerned. The first type is well

[1] See Reynolds, *Walpole Society*, pp. 14 *et seq.*

148

exemplified by a miniature of *King James I* at Windsor, which must have been painted *c.* 1604/5 (*Pl. 131*). The King's rather timid appearance is mainly due to a black hat and plume he is wearing, pushed backwards to show the forehead and some strands of hair falling on to it. The lace-edged collar falls over the light-coloured quilted doublet. The King wears the Garter ribbon twisted round a gold chain and the blue background is, as so often in Hilliard's miniatures, framed by two gold lines. The face, turned to the right, is precisely, though delicately, outlined with almost no shading. Various miniatures are based on

Plate 133. King
James I, *c.* 1604

Plate 134. King
James I, 1608

Plate 135. Anne
of Denmark

Plate 136. Anne
of Denmark

the same type, though varying as to the size of the half-length, the pattern of the doublet, the colouring of the hat and the background. On one in the Victoria and Albert Museum (P.3–1937) (*Pl. 132*) the King's right hand is shown on his hip and there is a crimson curtain in the background. The inscription, following the oval frame, reads as follows: *IACOBVS. DEI. GRAIA MAGNAE. BRI-TANIAE. FRAN ET. HIBE REX.* This particular legend was not used by

James I before November 1604, so that the miniature must have been painted after that date. There is a short half-length in Vienna (No. 215) (*Pl. 133*), on which the sitter also appears against a red curtain. Another version is at Drumlanrig Castle. What is perhaps the last appearance of that type is the portrait in the collection of the Marchioness of Cholmondeley (*Pl. 134*) which has a beautiful gold inscription on a blue ground: *Ano Dni 1608. Ætatis Suæ 42*. The collar is stiffened and slightly raised above the shoulders and, if anything, the modelling is bolder and more articulate.

Plate 137. Henry VII, 1600–10

Plate 138. Henry VIII, 1600–10

Plate 139. Edward VI, 1600–10

Plate 140. Jane Seymour, 1600–10

The same royal portrait was also used on coins and medals by James I in the years 1603/4, immediately after his accession. As we know that Hilliard was paid for medals during that period, it is plausible to suppose that he designed those or at least that they were based on the royal image he had created.[1] Even the Accession medal of 1603 is modelled on that type, and it is therefore possible that the royal limner painted the first portrait of his new patron as early as that year.

The two companion miniatures of *Anne of Denmark* in Vienna (*Pl. 135*), and in the collection of the Marchioness of Cholmondeley (*Pl. 136*), conform to that one type Hilliard is known to have created of her likeness, and the latter is of an especially fine quality.

The somewhat thin linear style of these early portraits of *King James I* and his Queen and the complete absence of any rich ornamental accessories, except the

[1] Farquhar, *Portraiture of Stuart Monarchs*, pp. 160ff. and John Pinkerton, *The Medallic History of England to the Revolution*, 1790. Reynolds, *Walpole Society, p. 16*.

little that is shown of the dress, is also evident in other miniatures of the same period. Outstanding in this respect are the small circular roundels representing *Henry VII* (*Pl. 137*), *Henry VIII* (*Pl. 138*), *Edward VI* (*Pl. 139*), and *Jane Seymour* (*Pl. 140*), at Windsor, which once belonged to Charles I, and were part of an elaborate golden jewel, now lost, which, in addition, had "at the top the outside being enamelled, the battle of Bosworth Field, . . . and at the other side the red and white roses joined together". The lovely portraits are most refined and beautifully clear and show, no doubt, the absolutely sure hand of the master during the late phase of his career. They are certainly based on

Plate 141.   Called Sir Walter Raleigh, *c.* 1605

Plate 142.   An Unknown Gentleman, by Nicholas Hilliard (?) aged 26 in 1603

oil portraits by Holbein and others and in all four of them the likeness stands out brilliantly from the background with its fine calligraphic lettering in spite of the small size.

To the same period belongs the oval miniature, *Called Sir Walter Raleigh* in the collection of Mr. A. D. R. Caröe (*Pl. 141*), which shows an expressive face under a tall hat. Again, the circular portrait of *An Unknown Gentleman*, aged 26 in 1603 (*Pl. 142*), though somehow weaker in quality, and the much faded *Sir Walter Raleigh* (No. 7/20), both at Drumlanrig Castle, may possibly be by Hilliard.

The refined half-length of *Henry Frederick*, Prince of Wales, now in Windsor Castle (*Pl. 143*), wearing armour and a lace-edged collar, a little raised above the shoulder, was probably painted *c.* 1603. It agrees closely with the charming miniature of Henry's brother, *Charles, then Duke of York*, in the Victoria and Albert Museum (*Pl. 144*), though the latter may have been painted—to judge by the age of the sitter—a few years later. He appears in a white doublet with silver stripes and the blue background with patterned vertical lines stretches high above the boy's head and makes him therefore look still younger and much more like a child. This somehow timid, linear, but exquisitely refined style Hilliard expressed in the royal portraits immediately after the accession of James I may have been prompted by his increased productivity in the field of coins and medals, and this fact may also explain his preference for the short head and shoulder portrait he mostly used during that period. The wealth of allegorical allusions or other accessories in costume or surroundings appears to have faded slowly from the miniatures he now painted for a patron who was less poetical and artistic than his predecessor.

Plate 143. Henry Frederick, Prince of Wales, *c.* 1603

Plate 144. Charles I as a boy (enlarged)

Two splendid miniatures bear the same date, that of 1605: the now identified portrait of *Charles Howard*, Baron of Effingham, formerly called *Henry Carey, 1st Baron Hunsdon*, at Greenwich (*Pl. 145*), and that of *An Unknown Lady* at Hatfield House (*Pl. 146*). Both are excellent examples of Hilliard's late style which show that at times his refined and decorative manner within the small area still expresses the charm which his skill used formerly to produce so frequently. Both have the blue background, decorated with gold letters. The faces, turned three-quarter to the left, are precisely outlined and clearly given in refined linear terms, just as in the style of the likeness of the two princes, discussed above. The black hat on the former matches black buttons on the white doublet and the blue ribbon of the Garter takes up the colour of the background. The same decorative quality is apparent on the lady's miniature in the charming repeat of three bows in terracotta-colour attached to her richly adorned and attractively low-cut bodice. The lace collars are in both cases delicately painted to suggest the transparency of several layers, falling on top of each other. It is possible that the Hatfield House miniature may represent Lady Clifford,

152

Lord Salisbury's daughter, as Hilliard was paid 10*l*. on 15 June 1611 "for 3 limned pictures which were maid for my lady Clifford".[1] But no authentic portrait of her is known.

Plate 145. Charles Howard, Baron
Howard of Effingham, 1605

A more ambitious scheme is conveyed by four women's portraits which show the sitters wearing their hair loose and falling down on to the shoulder. Here Hilliard reverts, probably at the dictate of fashion, to an earlier motif which he

Plate 146. An Unknown Lady, 1605

had successfully applied in his first portrait of *Elizabeth I in robes of state*. Three of these miniatures are among the most fascinating works he ever created and the

---

[1] Salisbury MSS, Private Estate MSS. Accounts 160/1. On the same day Oliver was also paid 6*l*. "for a picture" for the same lady.

fact that they were limned between 1605 and a few years later shows how his unsurpassed skill and psychological power of penetration had not—whenever he was really interested—declined even in his old age. The most accomplished

Plate 148.   Called Lady Arabella Stuart

Plate 147.   Lady Elizabeth Stanley,
1605–10

Plate 149.   An Unknown Lady,
1605–10

portrait of this group is that of *Lady Elizabeth Stanley* in the collection of Viscount Bearsted (*Pl. 147*). It is a relatively large oval and a good half-length figure with the right hand shown. The background is a pale-blue sky, enlivened by clouds, the sun and a heart pierced through, and an inscription that

154

runs: *facies mutabilis | sed amor stabilis | semel missa | semp fixa*. At the back it is thus inscribed: *Demitte michi deus | parce Deus*. She wears a diadem, earrings, a necklace and other jewellery. Her low-cut dress has a multicoloured pattern on a light ground; the beautifully painted hand lets the curls glide through her fingers. The fullness of her rich, wavy hair frames a lovely face in clear outline. One should only follow the characteristically round and sweeping line of the forehead in continuation of the foreshortened side of her three-quarter view, in order to realise fully Hilliard's delightful mastery in rendering form. The

Plate 150. Mrs. Mole, *c.* 1605
Plate 151. Mr. John Mole, *c.* 1605

expression of an enigmatic smile, matched by eyes turned to the onlooker and surmounted by arched brows, conveys a strange awareness and an almost sophisticated mood. This particular expression, in some ways ambiguous and hinting at more than the mere surface reveals, together with the light and fastidious colouring, the wild movement in the hair and the presence of emblems and lettering, makes this miniature a typically Mannerist work of art, perhaps more so than any other portrait Hilliard painted in earlier years. It was therefore most revealing so see this miniature together with pictures and other objects demonstrating that style in the Amsterdam Exhibition of *The Triumph of Mannerism*.[1] In spite of its small size the same spirit could be detected here as on large paintings in oil or even in pretentious works of sculpture. The decorative quality, so often shown in Hilliard's work, was best paralleled by the attractive *Triumph of Flora*[2] by the *Maître de Flore* with its lovely conception of flowers, trees, *putti* and other figures, and it is important to state in this connection that such

[1] 1955, No. 70.   [2] *Ibid.*, No. 78.

French influences, even in that late period, may have inspired much of Hilliard's style.

A much smaller miniature, also attractive, if less intense in expression, is to be found in *An Unknown Lady* called *Lady Arabella Stuart* in the Victoria and Albert Museum (*Pl. 148*). Yet *An Unknown Lady* (*Pl. 149*), formerly called *Elizabeth, Queen of Bohemia,* and attributed to Isaac Oliver, in the collection of the Earl of Derby, comes very near in poetical interpretation to that given in *Lady Elizabeth Stanley.* With the warm glowing colouring of the bodice and the vigorous movement of the long waves of the loose hair, appearing in spiral strands between the outstretched arms and the dress, it again conveys Hilliard's manner in creating restlessness surrounding a strangely calm and composed face, a technique he especially liked during that period, which, in its contrasting effects, is decisively Mannerist.

But probably the most beautiful and expressive portrait of the group is that of *Mrs. Mole* in the possession of Miss M. R. Bulkeley (*Pl. 150*). Human tragedy is reflected here in the small white face framed by the lovely golden curls of the loose hair against the crimson curtain background. No glittering jewellery distracts from the purely human conception; only black earrings and a narrow cord of the same colour ending—so we suppose—in a miniature locket comprising the picture of her husband, disappears behind the patterned low-cut bodice. And, indeed, *Mr. John Mole,* whose miniature in the same Collection (*Pl. 151*), is also of fine quality but less interesting, was, whilst travelling to Rome, imprisoned for life by the Inquisition or confined for thirty years. Hence we have good reason to read in Mrs. Mole's uneasy eyes, which, in this case, contrary to Hilliard's usual manner, are wide open, an expression of apprehension and fear.

Reverting to Hilliard's royal portraits of that period, the extremely fine *Henry Frederick, Prince of Wales* in the Royal Collection at Windsor (*Pl. 152*), should be mentioned. It is inscribed in gold letters on the crimson curtain as follows: *Ano Dni. 1607. Ætatis Suæ 14.* The young man is shown half-length wearing an exquisitely painted golden armour that testifies to the master's superb ability to represent the shimmering surface of beautiful metal. Again in the best tradition of his style is the painting of the helmet with white plumes against a black background, that is resting on a table on the left of the youthful figure. It is brought very near to the sitter, whereas the crimson curtain on the right suggests some depth, and the white of the plumes echoes the white of the standing collar and the pale flesh-tints, which in spite of the softness give a clear portrait-like image. The tenderness and delicate handling of the boyish features render this picture most attractive.

A fine miniature of *An Unknown Young Man* in Windsor Castle (*Pl. 153*) is certainly by Hilliard and of approximately the same period. He wears a black doublet and a standing plain collar; his distinguished features, framed by blond hair, are seen against the now popular cerise curtain.

Plate 152. Henry Frederick, Prince of Wales, 1607

Plate 153. An Unknown Young Man

Plate 154. King James I, *c.* 1610

The second group of Hilliard's portraits of James I, which Mr. Reynolds lists as Type II, covers the period from *c.* 1609 to 1614. The King has now discarded his hat and his head seems to have grown in proportion to the size of the miniature. His face is rounder and more protruding and, strangely enough, he is again always seen in a three-quarter turning to the right, probably in anticipation of a companion picture of his Queen. The earliest dated example is that in the collection of Mr. and Mrs. Heckett which is dated 1609. Another, at Castle Howard, in the collection of Mr. George Howard, is dated a year later and has the inscription *Ano Dni 1610 Ætatis Suæ 45*. One of the best miniatures of that type is *King James I* at Windsor Castle (*Pl. 154*), where the short half-length figure of the King is clad in a lavender blue doublet with a slightly raised lace-edged collar and the "lesser George" suspended from a blue Garter ribbon.

The usual red curtain indicates the background and a narrow gold rim frames the miniature. Though not particularly exciting, the modelling of the portrait is realistic and precise. Fortunately, in this case, an entry in Vanderdoort's Catalogue of Charles I's collection establishes Hilliard's authorship "Done by old Hilliard. Bought by the King: another of King James's of famous memory, a picture without a hat, in a bone lace falling band, in a lavender

Plate 155.   King James I, *c.* 1610

Plate 157.   Charles I as a young man, shortly after 1611

cloth suit".[1] Though the measurements do not tally, there cannot be any doubt that it is this miniature to which Vanderdoort refers.

Two further portraits of James I, conforming to that type, show more of the figure and part or the whole of one hand. One, formerly owned by H. E. Backer (*Pl. 155*), shows the King in a black doublet against the red curtain; the other, in the Scottish National Portrait Gallery (*Pl. 156*), a splendid example of decorative beauty, represents the sitter in a white doublet and hose against a blue background.

Hilliard painted two further portraits of *Charles, Duke of York*, later *Prince of Wales* and finally *King Charles I*. Both are of excellent quality. The first, in the Victoria and Albert Museum (Salting Bequest) (*Pl. 157*), must have been painted *c.* 1611, as it shows the young prince wearing the lesser George suspended from the Garter ribbon. He received the Garter in May 1611. A tall white head matches his dainty doublet and the light reflections in the red background curtain stress the dainty appearance of the refined and elegant

[1] See Reynolds, *Walpole Society*, No. A8.

figure. This miniature, with five others, is included in a black seventeenth-century frame which was once in the collection of Charles I. Still more remarkable is Hilliard's second portrait of *Charles I as Prince of Wales* at Belvoir Castle (*Pl. 158*). It is of an exceptionally large size and a most ostentatious piece of work. The prince, now 14 years of age, stands in front of us, a three-quarter length, with his left hand on his hip, in a black suit with a grey pattern, wearing

Plate 156. King James I

the lesser George hanging from the Garter ribbon. A white stiff pleated ruff, rigidly shaped, supports his beautifully modelled face with the sweeping line of the forehead and the eyes looking to the right in a three-quarter turning to the left. The background is one of the most complex compositions ever to appear on Hilliard's miniatures during the reign of James I. On the right, there is a vertically hanging crimson curtain with lighter reflections indicating long folds, and nearer to the frame there are clouds with rays of light bursting from them and underneath the Prince of Wales crown and feathers above the sickle of the moon and some stars. On the left, approximately a fifth of the width of the oval is treated like a window opening formed by the gold fringes of the curtain. Here an iris and roses are seen against mountains in the distance and a blue sky with light clouds. Every single object is painted with the most meticulous care without, however, disturbing the whole unit of the picture. The vicinity of these emblems to the sitter may be compared with a similar treatment of the objects in the background on Hilliard's *Henry Frederick, Prince of Wales*, of 1607 (*Pl. 152*). A narrow gold rim finishes up this splendid portrait of *Charles as Prince of Wales* and an inscription in Roman gold letters runs round it: *ILLVSTRISS-IMVS. ET SERENISSIMVS CAROLVS WALLIAE PRINCEPS. MAGNAE BRITANIAE MAXIMA SPES. ANNO ÆTATIS SUÆ. 14.* After the death of Prince Henry, the younger son of James I was indeed the hope of the loyal

Plate 158.   Charles I as Prince of Wales, 1614 (enlarged)

citizens of this country and Hilliard created, in this magnificent miniature, a dignified likeness of the future king.

Another excellent example of Hilliard's final phase can be seen in the closely related "Gentleman" thought to be *Henry Carey, 2nd Earl of Monmouth* at Welbeck Abbey (*Pl. 159*). Clad in a plain black doublet with a standing white collar,

Plate 159. Called Henry Carey, 2nd Earl
of Monmouth, 1616

fastened by a cord in the same colour, the elegant young man stands in front of us, a half-length against a blue background, his right hand raised and his fingers gliding through the white cords that tighten his collar. No piece of jewellery is seen, and, indeed, it has been said that the sitter may have been in mourning. Though the background is without the elaborate motifs which we have noticed in the miniature of Prince Charles, the beautiful treatment and position of the sitter is very near in style to the latter, and proves again the quality of Hilliard's style even in this last phase of his career. The pale modelling of the lovely face is yet strong enough to set it off against the standing collar, and the blue eyes look again at us, in the opposite direction to the turning of the head. The hand is treated in Hilliard's best manner. A gold inscription in the artist's usual fine calligraphic lettering runs along the top border: *Encore un* (astre) *Luit pour moj.* (Still one star shines for me.) The miniature is mounted on a card, the oval border of which is ornamented in Hilliard's fashion and bears the additional inscription in gold letters: *Quadragessimo Anô Dñi 1616 Vera Effigies Ætatis Suæ 20.*

Altogether, it is one of the finest portraits by Hilliard, and one that gives us a deep insight into human nature.

Before we discuss the final type Hilliard created of *King James I*, two more miniatures representing members of his family have to be discussed. First, a portrait of *Frederick, Elector Palatine and later King of Bohemia*, in the Victoria and Albert Museum (Salting Bequest) (*Pl. 160e*). Like the portrait of *Prince Charles* of 1611, it is framed with other miniatures of members of the royal family in a seventeenth-century frame and was formerly in the collection of Charles I. As Mr.

Plate *161*.   Elizabeth, Queen of Bohemia

Reynolds says, it is the only portrait of the Prince known to be by Hilliard's hand, and repetitions from it by Isaac and Peter Oliver exist. As the sitter wears the ribbon of the Garter and the lesser George, it was probably painted between 21 December 1612, when he was elected to the Order, and April 1613, when he left the country. The treatment of the extremely well modelled, broadly seen face, this time turned three-quarter to the right, accords well with that of *Charles as Prince of Wales*, of 1614, at Belvoir Castle. The face has grown in relationship to the size of the surround and is clearly formulated, with eyes slightly bigger and wider open than is usual in Hilliard's earlier portraits. Forehead and hair show the typically bold manner we have often noticed, and the doublet and the standing lace collar are carefully painted against the blue background. Clearly, the picture was painted from life.

The only portrait of *Elizabeth, Queen of Bohemia* (*Pl. 161*), by Hilliard is that in the Victoria and Albert Museum which was acquired as a companion picture to *King James I* (*Pl. 131*) and as representing a lady of his family. There can

Plate 160. King James I and his family: (*a*) James I. (*b*) Anne of Denmark. (*c*) Prince Henry, by Oliver. (*d*) Prince Charles (also Pl. 157). (*e*) Frederick, Elector Palatine, later King of Bohemia. (*f*) Elizabeth, Queen of Bohemia, by Oliver

be no doubt that the young girl painted here is the same sitter as in Oliver's miniature of James' daughter at Windsor (*Pl. 219*). The latter is identified as Princess Elizabeth by an entry in Vanderdoort's Catalogue.[1] Both were painted

Plate 162 (*left*). Called James I

Plate 164. King James I

when she was still very young, perhaps eight or ten years of age, and in any case a long time before 1613, when she was married. In spite of the great likeness of the features, it is evident that Hilliard renders the refined and serene face, the costume and its accessories, in a much more precise manner, whereas Oliver's portrait looks slightly blurred and the young lady has a somewhat discontented expression.

A fine portrait, *Called James I*, but certainly not representing the King, is now at the Barber Institute of Fine Arts (*Pl. 162*), and gives a welcome transition to the last type Hilliard created of his royal patron. The main factor here is the growing size of the sitter's head which is predominant in the picture and shows a new conception in a much broader treatment of the freer and softer modelling. This fine late manner is in this particular case effectively brought out by a blue background.

Two excellent miniatures of *James I*, who has now aged, represent Hilliard's last version of the image of his royal patron: one, in the Victoria and Albert Museum (Salting Bequest) (*Pl. 160a*), the other, in the Mauritshuis at The Hague (*Pl. 163*). They both have a similar pattern, with a larger head than usual, three-quarter turned to the right, with eyes wide open, looking at us, curly hair, the usual full beard, but slightly shorter. The king wears a white

[1] See Reynolds *Catalogue*, 1947, No. 88.

doublet, a high, closely fitting ruff, the Garter ribbon, and the short bust cuts off part of the lesser George. On the former, the background is subdivided into a cerise curtain on the left and a window opening on the right showing an iris against hills in the distance and the sky, a motif—it may be recalled—which, in a larger size, resembles exactly that used on the portrait of *Charles as Prince of Wales*, at Belvoir Castle, dated 1614. The latter miniature has the shape of a heart, and the cerise curtain takes up the whole area of what is visible of the background. It is interesting to compare *James I* of the Salting Bequest, mounted as it is with five other miniatures in a seventeenth-century frame, with *Prince Henry* by Oliver which hangs immediately beneath it. Even at this late stage Hilliard remains faithful to his own crystal-clear and precise linear style, in contrast to that of his former pupil, whose soft tone and full shading, a new distinction of darkness and light, namely an Italianate conception heralding the Baroque atmosphere of the seventeenth century, must have gained a particular appeal in the fashionable circles of the Jacobean Court.

A smaller portrait of *James I* at Windsor Castle (*Pl. 164*) belongs to the same type. On the back of the playing card on which this miniature is painted there

Plate 163. King James I

appears, according to Mr. Reynolds, in gold figures the date 1614 in Hilliard's own hand. Double evidence is thus available showing that the 'Salting Bequest' portrait was painted in that year. A still smaller *King James I* at Windsor (No. 50) shows a similar type in general, though it is of inferior quality.

165

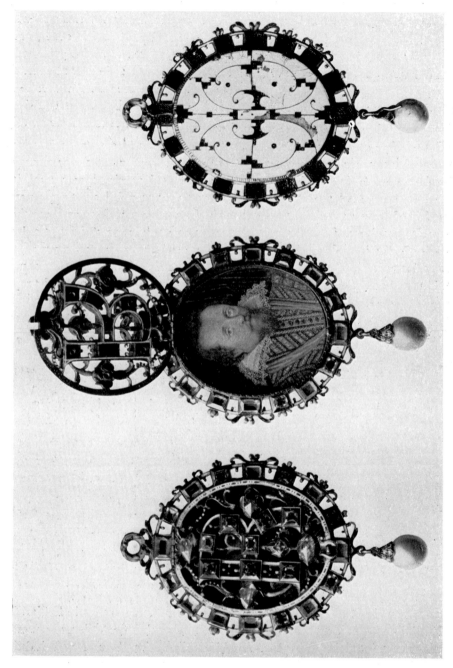

Plate 165. King James I, in the Lyte Jewel

To complete this account of Hilliard's portraits of James I and his Queen, two miniatures must be mentioned, which fortunately are preserved in their elaborate jewelled cases. The first is that contained in the beautiful 'Lyte'

Plate 166. Anne of Denmark

jewel in the British Museum[1] (*Pl. 165*). Like the others, it is generally attributed to Oliver, but, in view of the foregoing survey of Hilliard's work for the royal family, is certainly from the hand of our limner and goldsmith. It comes nearest to the last type of the king's likeness but may have been painted slightly earlier. His beard is a little longer and he is wearing a standing collar. He is again seen against a crimson background. This jewel is said to have been given to Mr. Thomas Lyte by James I on 12 July 1610 when the former presented the king with a beautifully illuminated pedigree. It is thus clear that the miniature was painted before that date. We have therefore an early example of the third

[1] Waddesdon Bequest, No. 167. See Sir H. Maxwell Lyte, "The Lytes of Lytescary", *Proceedings of the Somersetshire Archaeological & Natural History Society 1892*, II, pp. 59ff. Joan Evans, *A History of Jewellery, 1100–1870*, (1951) p. 146, pl. 107a, and *English Jewellery*, p. 120.

type, if not the transitional specimen from the second to the last pattern. When the case is closed and the lovely lid with its open grille of gold covers the miniature, the red background is still visible in parts through the filigree work and matches perfectly the colour of the rubies decorating the locket. For that reason Hilliard must have chosen the cerise curtain motif in his later miniatures in preference to the earlier blue background.

The second is the miniature of *Anne of Denmark* kept in an enamelled and jewelled case of *c.* 1610 and probably also painted at that time, in the Fitzwilliam Museum, Cambridge (*Pl. 166*). It is a most refined and impressive portrait, showing the half-length figure, touching with one hand the front of the low-cut buff-coloured dress. She is seen against a blue curtain with darker indications of folds, a motif not otherwise used by Hilliard. Most attractive are the hair, the open standing lace collar, the elegant features of the clearly drawn face, the well-modelled hand, and the pink bows in the dress and the hair, decoratively harmonising with the light blue shades distributed over the miniature.

The two jewelled lockets that contain these miniatures will be discussed in the following chapter in which Hilliard's work as a goldsmith will be considered.

VI

NICHOLAS HILLIARD AS A GOLDSMITH

IT HAS ALWAYS been a matter of conjecture whether Hilliard actually made pieces of jewellery himself and particularly whether the often beautiful and elaborate lockets enclosing his miniatures could be ascribed to his hand. These questions have been asked frequently by scholars at the beginning of the twentieth century[1] and a more or less tentative attribution of various sixteenth-century jewels to the Queen's "goldsmith, engraver and limner" has been made. Though it was known that he had designed her Majesty's Second Great Seal, our knowledge that he also engraved it is only due to recent research.[2] Whilst we still cannot be absolutely sure about Hilliard's authorship in individual works, the general appreciation of his activities as a goldsmith is now put on a much safer footing by the study of the Minute Books of the Goldsmiths' Company, an invaluable source which was hitherto almost entirely unknown. Reference has already been made to this new source in the first chapter, where it was used to show that throughout most of his career Hilliard was in much closer contact with the Company than had commonly been thought. The various references to goldsmith's work executed by Hilliard are examined in the following.

Shortly after he became a Freeman of the Company, on 6 April 1571, a "Jewell of gold" is mentioned, apart from 4 little rings, which came from the hands of Hilliard and his brother John.[3] It is described as a rose made of enamelled gold with a diamond on it and a pearl suspended from it. This is just what an Elizabethan jewel very often was like, and it proves that owing to his training Hilliard was familiar with the technique of gold enamelling that was much in vogue during that period.

[1] Farquhar, *Nicholas Hilliard*, pp. 324ff.
[2] Blakiston, *Nicholas Hilliard and Queen Elizabeth's Third Great Seal*, pp. 187–9.
[3] See p. 7, *ante*.

Again, on 15 June 1578, when in France, he was engaged on finishing a jewel for the Earl of Hertford,[1] a commission which apparently worried him considerably; he stated that he hoped to complete it within the next three weeks.

From 1584 to 1586 he was working on designing and engraving the Second Great Seal,[2] and *c.* 1588 a workman called "Abell Feckemann" was especially employed by Hilliard in engraving goldsmiths' work.[3]

With the beginning of the reign of James I more detailed payments for individual work were received and goldsmiths' work was much in the foreground. In 1604 he was paid for 12 medallions in gold[4] and in 1611 he had to make two gold tablets.[5] On 30 September 1610, he was paid 20*l.* "for Christall sett upon twoe pictures in a George" for Lord Salisbury.[6] This payment of a rather large sum and the wording clearly points to the fact that he made a richly adorned case for the miniatures. On 3 November 1613 he received 12*l.* for one engraved gold tablet which was enamelled in blue and contained the miniature of the Prince.[7] In 1614/5 a "riche christall" is referred to as frame for a portrait, and in 1615 he was paid 35*l.* for garnishing the case of a picture of James I with diamonds.[8] To these references Vanderdoort's description of the famous jewel containing the portraits of *Henry VII, Henry VIII, Edward VI* and *Jane Seymour* has to be added:[9] he states that it was of gold with a pendant pearl hanging from it; the four miniatures had separate cases; at the top there were pictorial engravings in enamel work. If we supplement this list of references to individual works made in the goldsmiths' craft by recalling the great number of apprentices Hilliard had engaged over so many years, and the various contacts, friendly or otherwise, he constantly maintained with his fellow-craftsmen, his career as a goldsmith assumes a new importance and the whole field of this side of his activities has to be reviewed.[10]

From many old inventories we know that during Elizabethan times and at the beginning of the seventeenth century jewellery played an important part

---

[1] See pp. 12/3, *ante.*   [2] See pp. 20 *et seq., ante.*

[3] See pp. 26/7, *ante.*   [4] See p. 38, *ante.*

[5] See *ibid.*   [6] Salisbury MSS., Accounts 160/1.

[7] See p. 38, *ante.*   [8] See *ibid.*

[9] See p. 151, *ante.*

[10] Mr. J. G. Philip of the Bodleian Library has kindly drawn my attention to a reference (MS. Tanner 78, f. 105-106) which may or may not refer to Hilliard's work as a goldsmith. Stephen Powle wrote a letter to Burghley on 12 January 1587 from London. He has been in Germany during the years 1585 and 1586. The heading of this letter reads as follows:

To my Lord Treasorer: With the picture in sylver curiously painted by Hilliard in an yvoyry box, and perfumed imbrodred velvet purse.

The description that follows leaves the matter rather ambiguous.

at Court and in society. For instance, from depositions in Chancery proceedings, we learn of a list of jewels that once belonged to Sir Henry Lee, who then—in the year 1615—was deceased.[1] There is mention of "two other juells or Tablettes of gould": the "one sett with the picture of the late Queene the other with the picture of Mrs. Fynch." There was "an other Juell of gould with his owne picture . . . ", and one "wth the picture of the Earle of Essex and the said Sr Henry nowe deceased runninge at Tylte and a booke of goulde". It is clear that in every case the likeness painted in miniature was considered an inseparable part of the jewellery. Other jewels had strange imaginative names, such as "the Gloabe", "the Robyn Redbrest", "the Lynnett", "the Raven" and "the Butterflye". There was also "an Aggett sett in gould" and one jewel "called the Queenes Picture". This is only one account of the wealth of jewellery owned by an Elizabethan gentleman. One has to assume that many a rich courtier of that period had an equally varied collection of ornamental goldsmiths' work. What a wonderful opportunity this fashion gave to the skilful craftsmen, English or foreign, residing in London and trained according to the ordinances of the Goldsmiths' Company! No wonder that the Minute-Books are full of names of masters and their apprentices, of Freemen and members of the Livery, of many famous artists and men of considerable wealth and substance! No wonder, too, that the importance and influence of the Company was steadily growing and that the part it played in the life of the City and the country was ever-increasing!

But even before the reign of Elizabeth, during that of Henry VIII, a strong and healthy activity developed in the field of this craft. It is widely known that the arrival of Holbein in this country meant a great deal for the promotion of goldsmiths' work. Many designs by his hand, preserved to-day in the British Museum, testify to his importance in this field, as these drawings were specially made for ornaments and pieces of jewellery. It was largely through the medium of these sketches that a wealth of Renaissance motifs penetrated into the stock-in-trade of the native craftsmen. Again, the Minute Books of the Goldsmiths' Company reflect lively activities of its skilful members at that time. Amongst the foreign craftsmen who took up residence in this country, "John van Andwerpe" may be mentioned, as we know him to have been Holbein's friend. On 9 April 1537 a letter in favour of him by "Thomas Crumwell" is read to the assembled Wardens and their assistants: it is stated that John seeks the liberty of the town, but thinks it would be better to be first admitted a member of the Company in view of his long abode here,

---

[1] I am indebted to Mr John T. Feil who kindly drew my attention to this document. C. 24/ 418/53.

namely for 26 years, and because he is married to an Englishwoman, has many children and proposes to live here for the rest of his life. He is then made a Freeman of the Company.[1] Here is the case of a foreign craftsman becoming completely anglicised. But also many English names appear in these records, or at least names that sound as if the owners were of English origin. Morgan Wolf, Henry Goldwell, both the king's goldsmiths, of whom we know that they were engaged on work in connection with the royal seals, were ardent and active members of the Company.[2]

Though we thus have quite a good documentary knowledge of the state of jewellery produced in this country during the Early Tudor period, not much of the actual work has survived. It is therefore most fortunate that the British Museum acquired recently, on two different occasions, important jewels belonging to the reign of Henry VIII and forming, together with some additional specimens, something like an English group.[3] The first is a small round

Plate 167. Tudor Hat badge, the Samaritan at
the Well, by an unknown English goldsmith

hat badge, a gold-enamelled jewel with figures, representing the *Samaritan at the Well* (Pl. 167). In the centre, the architectural well is enamelled in black, white and blue, and an English inscription in uneven Roman letters runs round it: *OF . A . TREWTHE . THOW . ART . THE . TREW . MESSIAS*. The Samaritan, on the left, appears in blue and gold, and the young woman,

[1] Book F, p. 61.

[2] See *Tudor Artists*, pp. 62, 93, 165.

[3] I am indebted to Mr. G. H. Tait of the British Museum for letting me read in manuscript a paper he read to the Society of Antiquaries: "Tudor Jewellery", shortly to be published.

on the right, with the jugs to fill in her hands, in a lovely red dress with a gold bodice which is separately enamelled and properly fixed later. As usual in this type of encrusted enamelling technique, the back of the badge shows slits, clips, hooks and punches to fasten the different parts of the figure work in its high-relief. The protruding rim round the pictorial representation is also of enamelled gold. There is a certain Renaissance-inspired elegance in the figures and ornaments. Apart from the English inscription which certainly points to an Englishman as the patron, the style too is different from the Continental one and there is good reason to assume that the author was a native craftsman. The liveliness of the figures in their movements and exaggerated expressions recurs on the second jewel, a historiated pendant with the subject *Joseph in the Well* (*Pl. 168*a). There is no doubt that both jewels are by the same hand. Here, the figures are crowding together more closely than on the hat badge; the enamelling is achieved on one sheet and the ground is likewise enamelled. The frame with its heavy scrolls, studded with five diamonds, is reminiscent of the last phase of Holbein's manner. The back (*Pl. 168*b) shows a beautiful translucent enamel design of grotesques and birds, recalling the style of Du Cerceau, and the date is probably the early forties of the sixteenth century, whereas the badge must have been made in *c*. 1537. As to our present subject, it is interesting to point out that, even at that early period, this particular enamelling technique, later on so often used on miniature lockets, was known in this country.

If we now come nearer to Hilliard's period, there was, in another field, a growing demand arising for the activities of the goldsmith. This was the effect which the Reformation had on the creation of Church plate. Mr. Oman[1] has stated that in 1548 the first pieces of plate were expressly made for Protestant use and that this led to the introduction of the "Communion cup". After Mary's attempt to revive the "chalice", Elizabeth's early proclamation to restore the cup was followed in December 1559 by the joint decision of the Archbishop of Canterbury and the Bishop of London that every church must have its chalice converted into a communion cup. This ruling gave an enormous impetus to the goldsmiths who then worked for the churches. It spread all over the country and was one of the reasons why, for instance, this craft flowered so much in Devon. Here, it may be recalled, commissioners from London had to examine the work of the goldsmiths of Exeter and Barnstaple in 1571 and shortly afterwards the compulsory conversion into the Communion cup must have started. Two such cups bear Richard Hilliard's initials. The beautiful Communion cup of *c*. 1570 made for St. Sidwell's, Exeter, is reproduced here (*Pl. 169*) and gives an excellent impression of Richard's fine craftsmanship.

[1] Oman, *Church Plate* (1957), pp. 129ff.

Plate 168 (a). Tudor Pendant, Joseph in the Well, by an unknown English goldsmith, *c.* 1542　　　　*(b)* The reverse, gold and enamel

Plate 169. Communion Cup, by Richard Hilliard, *c.* 1570

The foot and knob show richly ornamented bands and the inverted bell-shaped bowl is crowned by an early example of the "Exeter lip" which has an engraved band below which the monogram appears. Two further marked examples Richard made for church and domestic purposes, namely for table use: the

Plate 170. Font-shaped standing dish, by Richard Hilliard, 1560–5

charming Font-shaped Standing dish of 1560–65 (*Pl. 170*)[1] called *The Colaton Raleigh Cup*, is the earliest marked Exeter piece that has survived. It shows an excellent feeling for proportion, is architecturally well built up and the decoration

[1] See Cat. Devon Festival, 1957, Exeter, Silversmith Domestic Silver, of the sixteenth to eighteenth centuries, arranged by R. C. Blackie, Nos. 43 and 66. N. M. Penzer, "Tudor Font-shaped Cups—III", *Apollo*, March 1958, pp. 82–6, Figs. II and III: it formerly belonged to St. Michael's Chapel within the Deanery House to the Church of Colaton Raleigh.

Plate 171. Seal-topped Spoon, by Richard Hilliard

is applied with much taste. The same qualities can be seen in the firmly constructed second example, the *Seal-topped Spoon* of *c.* 1570, now in the Royal Albert Memorial Museum, Exeter (*Pl. 171*). Richard's skill as it is shown by his ecclesiastical and domestic plate must have been well known to Nicholas, though by that time he already had left his home town for London.

At the time when Hilliard started his training with Robert Brandon, a Dutch medallist of great abilities worked and resided in this country. He is

Plate 172. Edmund Withipoll, 1562, medallion by Steven Van Harwick

Plate 173. Maria Dimock, medallion, by Steven Van Harwick, 1562

known as Steven van Harwick or Hartwick and, according to his will, died in London in 1566.[1] Several signed portrait medals of an excellent quality which were made by him in silver are preserved in the British Museum. According to their legends they are mostly dated 1562. Though the sitter is usually seen in profile, he is also occasionally represented in a three-quarter view. Such a medal is that representing *Edmund Withipoll*, son of Paul, a merchant tailor, who was granted the Manor of Walthamstow in 1545 (Med. Ill. Elizabeth, No. 34) (*Pl. 172*). It is a most beautifully modelled bust, turned three-quarter to the left, with a pointed beard, a small, piped ruff, an excellent likeness in a fairly high relief, and clear Roman lettering, following the round, but intersected on top by the figure. It is cast and chased, and the concave reverse has no pictorial subject. Another of these medals represents *Maria Dimock*, the lovely daughter of the mercer Clement Newce (Med. Ill. Elizabeth, No. 36) (*Pl. 173*); she wears a gown with a stiff collar and a close fitting ruff rendered in detail,

[1] C.P.C. 8 Stonarde, 1566. Reynolds, *Miniatures*, p. 8; Auerbach, *Tudor Artists*, p. 166.

and the reverse shows a charming female figure of a classic appearance, putting her arm round the neck of a stag. The legend *SICVT . CERV . AD . FŌTES . AQVARV .* (as the hart panteth after the water brooks), stresses the Renaissance element. Such medals must have been known to Hilliard and probably inspired his own work on medallic portraits and his miniatures, the compositions of which show a certain resemblance to those of Steven's medals. A similar affinity between miniatures and medals was already noted when the influence which Germain Pilon exercised on our limner during his stay in France was discussed.

Just as in the case of oil paintings, we can, as a rule, merely make tentative suggestions about Hilliard's surviving goldsmith's work. There is, however, one absolutely clear fact, viz. that he designed and made the Second Great Seal. This fact, together with the dated miniatures, gives us opportunities of comparison which will help to establish at least a group of more or less authentic jewelled ornaments by his hand.

The most important early example of these jewels is the *Phoenix Badge* (Med. Ill. Elizabeth, No. 70). A silver impression is in the British Museum, and it is most likely that it was worn by people personally attached to the Queen. On the reverse of one version the date 1574 has been roughly engraved, apparently by a later hand. But more conclusive is the *Phoenix Jewel (Pl. 174a)*, a golden ornament—close to the medal but not identical—surrounded by a beautifully enamelled wreath of Tudor roses in various colours and gold. It was bequeathed to the British Museum by Sir Hans Sloane in 1753. The Queen's bust in profile is facing left; her features are clearly modelled, her hair is elegantly arranged; she wears a closely fitting ruff, a partlet and a *chemise* in the just visible square cutting of the bodice; pearls and jewels decorate the hair and the dress. The reverse *(Pl. 174b)* shows the phoenix amid flames, surmounted by the crowned royal cypher. Otherwise there is no legend on the jewel. The inscription on the medal suggests a grief about the celibacy of the Queen and that such a wonderful English phoenix has the unhappy fate to be the last in this country. The craftsmanship of both sides is of the finest quality. Elizabeth's age, her costume and the precise style of every minute detail is closely linked with Hilliard's miniature of the Queen of 1572 in the National Portrait Gallery. There is also a similar cutting of the bust and the rose is a predominating feature of the decoration. It may be recalled that the wreath of parti-coloured Tudor roses and green leaves also frames the miniatures of *Elizabeth* and the *Duc d'Alençon* on the pages of the famous prayer-book. The rose, incidentally, that hangs right on top of the Queen's head from the circular wreath, emphasises the middle line and may be compared with a motif Hilliard used on his

Great Seal: the clouds forming a niche for Elizabeth's crown and overlapping the band bearing the lettering, a motif which, so far as I know, was never applied to any Great Seal before. It serves in both cases to give stability and importance to the dominating figure of Her Majesty. According to the costume and age of the sitter, especially if considered in comparison with the definitely later bust on the *Armada Jewel*, the *Phoenix Jewel* is probably rightly dated between 1572 and 1574.

(a)   (b)

Plate 174 (a).   Queen Elizabeth I, the *Phoenix Jewel, c.* 1574; (b) The reverse of
the *Phoenix Jewel*, the Phoenix amid flames

That Hilliard was "graving" during this period, if not on metal but on wood, emerges from a richly adorned title border bearing his initials N H and the date 1574, which is reproduced by McKerrow and Ferguson.[1] The style and feeling come very close to his manner, especially to his *Duke and Duchess of Nevers* portrayed in the same medium. The treatment of the vine leaves against the stone background of the twisted columns on the architecturally constructed title-border reminds us of his own typical technique of letting minutely rendered ornaments stand out in relief against a darker tone achieved by short crisp lines— a technique which, as on the *Phoenix Jewel*, is at the same time detailed and full but not fussy. In addition, the lamb with legs bound and a knife at its throat, which appears at the top of the border within a circular frame, not only

[1] *Title-page Borders used in England and Scotland, 1485–1640* (1932), pl. 148. Auerbach, *More Light on Nicholas Hilliard*, p. 167.

suggests the shape of the miniature locket, but also reveals the sensitive feeling Hilliard shows in his conception of animals and flowers.

With Elizabeth's *Second Great Seal (Pl. 175a)* we come at last to an authentic work by Hilliard in the field of the goldsmiths' craft. Ample documentation as to his designing and graving of this highly accomplished work of art has survived and has been discussed before.[1] It may be recalled that the original order was issued to him and Dericke Anthony in 1584. The importance of this task, so beautifully solved, is that stylistically it introduces a new phase in the evolution of a more consolidated, formal, clear and dignified style in English art. This fact emerges clearly when the Queen's *Second Great Seal* is compared with her *First Great Seal* on which a rather small, young figure with her hair falling loose on to her shoulders seems almost lost within the framing circle; here too, much space is reserved for the canopied throne and the arrangement of the gartered and crowned Arms of France and England on either side is haphazard. On her *Second Great Seal*, the Queen of a more mature age, and conceived realistically as a human being, seated on a throne of Renaissance construction, of which merely four knobs are visible, fills the height completely from the bottom to the top, breaking through the circular legend to gain weight and protruding in spite of the relatively low relief. The wheel ruff curves up to support the full face, the crown surmounts the neatly arranged curls, the arms are rounded and the hands, holding the royal insignia, are placed on either side of the middle line near to each other. The stomacher is precisely defined, the farthingale swings out broadly and the feet rest on a square cushion. The remainder of the space within the circle is tightly packed with scrolls topping the balls of the back posts of the throne, mysterious arms emanating from clouds and hands drawing the royal coat apart, the large coats of arms, gartered and crowned, the thick folds of the full skirt, and the tassels of the various cushions. All these objects crowd in the principal figure from both sides without allowing any breathing space to develop and thus push it forward into a dominating position, true to the Mannerist expression of movement and conflict combined with the Renaissance feeling for symmetry. Only once before, in the *Third Great Seal of Henry VIII*, has such an impressive representation of awe-inspiring majesty been achieved.

The reverse *(Pl. 175b)* shows the heavy figure of the Queen, dressed in the same habit, riding on horseback. This time, the horse, seen in profile, takes up the whole width of the circle. Grass and flowers on the ground, Tudor roses, the mane and tail of the horse show Hilliard's sensitive hand.

His conception of the Queen's iconic portrait is, of course, based on a long

[1] See p. 20, *ante. Tudor Artists*, pp. 128ff.

tradition and the image of the sovereign, enthroned and holding the royal insignia, was the usual feature on any Great Seal. It was indeed a tradition, widely applied to various branches of art. Not only did it occur on early oil portraits, such as that of Richard II in Westminster Abbey, but it also had—as

Plate 175 (a).   The Second Great Seal of Queen Elizabeth I, obverse,
the Queen enthroned

we have seen before—a long and unbroken sequence of appearances on the Great Letters of manuscripts and legal documents. It was in that kind of art, in the field of illumination, that Hilliard became acquainted with this formula. Already his early portrait of *Elizabeth I in robes of state*, at Welbeck Abbey, it may be recalled, reveals his knowledge of the iconic type of the royal likeness. There was often a close connection between the royal image appearing in the initials of documents and that on the seals. Thus, the early illuminations on Plea Rolls representing Elizabeth's youthful figure, often with flowing loose

Plate 175 (b). The reverse, the Queen on horseback,
1584–6

hair, sitting on a canopied and curtained throne, conform to the young Queen's image on her *First Great Seal*. Later, beginning with the type on the Easter Roll 1584, and standardised on the Michaelmas Roll 1585, a likeness of the Queen came into being which was to remain the principal image until

183

the end of her reign. It is closely related to, if not based on, the type Hilliard was engraving on the new Great Seal at exactly that moment.[1] Hence, not only in the field of manuscript illumination, but also in that of oil painting and elsewhere, a more formalised conception of the royal portrait became widely accepted as the most adequate and favourite likeness of the ageing sovereign. In that development, Hilliard's *Second Great Seal* played a decisive part. One can also recognise the stages in which he prepared the way for his final achieve-

Plate 177.   Queen Elizabeth I, drawing, designed for the obverse of (?) Third Great Seal

ment in the royal likeness on the Saxton Atlas and the Mildmay Charter, in the creation of both of which he probably had a hand.

The clearly-modelled style of Elizabeth's *Second Great Seal* can only have been accomplished by developing it from some very precise drawings and the lovely

[1] *Tudor Artists*, p. 130, pls. 44 and 45.

184

Plate 176. An Elizabethan Lady, drawing

Elizabethan Lady in court costume in the Victoria and Albert Museum (*Pl. 176*), drawn in pen, ink and pencil, gives us a glimpse of the high quality achieved by Hilliard in this medium. It is closely related to the seal and the costume and manner of treatment point to the early fifteen-eighties as the likely date. Here is the ruff of the same shape; the refined linear pattern in the dress, the bows, the curls of the hair, the spidery fingers, the feathers of the fan, the locket, the striations on the ground, also behind the figure, and above all, the dainty, yet crystal-clear face, all these features reveal Hilliard's delightful style.

Another beautiful drawing, this time the proper design for the obverse of a Great Seal of Queen Elizabeth by Nicholas Hilliard, has survived and is now in the Print Room of the British Museum (*Pl. 177*). This is a most accomplished drawing of first-rate quality. Pen and ink and wash over pencil produce shades to make the figure itself stand out clearly, with curved arms and protruding knees, in a three-dimensional view. The design seems to be of a somewhat later date than the obverse of the *Second Great Seal*. This is indicated by the costume, especially by the standing lace ruff, which is now open in front. The whole composition is less crowded and more modified in spite of the close similarity to the executed Seal. The scrolls on the latter, resting on the balls of the throne, are now replaced by a symmetrical, classic architecture of three semicircular arches supported by brackets in the Renaissance fashion. Cartouches appear instead of the heavier arms and the whole atmosphere is calmer and more serene. Two essentially Irish emblems, the harp and the three crowns, have been lightly drawn in and this drawing has therefore been acclaimed as a design for the Great Seal of Ireland.[1] However, it may easily be one of the designs for a *Third Great Seal* mentioned in the accounts of Charles Anthony,[2] especially as the Irish emblems could have been drawn in later and an Irish Great Seal of that description was never executed. On the drawing the Queen looks younger than ever, and it is quite possible that she herself stipulated this kind of alteration of her *Second Great Seal* and that Hilliard followed her suggestion by making such a drawing as this. It seems a great pity that more drawings of that quality by Elizabeth's limner and goldsmith have not come down to us.

Returning to the jewels, we have to consider the *Drake Pendant* (*Pls. 178a, b*) which may or may not be by Hilliard but which encloses a miniature of Elizabeth by his hand. The gold jewel, of beautiful workmanship, has a cameo in oriental sardonyx with a classical head in a white layer behind a darker negro profile bust. The elaborate border is enamelled and set with rubies, diamonds

[1] Reynolds *Catalogue, 1947*, No. 107.
[2] Blakiston, *Nicholas Hilliard and Queen Elizabeth's Third Great Seal*, p. 107. Hilliard recommended Charles Anthony to Sir Robert Cecil in his letter of 2 June 1599 (Cecil Pap. 70, 76. Cal. IX, 191).

(a) (b)

Plate 178 (a). The Drake Pendant, by Nicholas Hilliard (?) (*b*) Queen Elizabeth, within the locket

187

and pearls. The design consists of interesting scrolls and flowers in a typically English pattern and somehow anticipates the ornaments on the obverse of Hilliard's Great Seal. Hanging from the jewel is a bunch of pearls looking like a cluster of grapes and one large pearl. Behind the cameo is the miniature of Elizabeth, dated *Ano dmni 1575* (*sic*) and *Regni 20*. Judging from style and costume, the latter date, namely 1578, is far more plausible. It must have been painted before 1579, when it was presented to Sir Francis Drake by the Queen. The jewel can be seen worn by Sir Francis on his oil portrait of 1591 at the National Maritime Museum, Greenwich. The lid, covering the miniature, shows the enamelled drawing of the phoenix, which is much akin to that on the *Phoenix Jewel*, thus leading us back to the group of goldsmith's work closely connected with Hilliard.

Related too is the *Barbor Pendant* (*Pl. 179*), said to have been made for William Barbor, to commemorate his deliverance from death through Elizabeth coming to the throne. Here is a small cameo portrait of Elizabeth in the centre, surrounded by an enamelled border in the same fashion, set with square stones and surmounted by a crown. Here, too, a cluster of small pearls is hanging down. In this connection it is interesting to refer to *Barbor's portrait miniature* by Hilliard (*Pl. 180*), preserved in its contemporary ivory box in the Victoria and Albert Museum, which must have been painted in the early fifteen-eighties. It is one of the very few portraits for which Hilliard chose the profile view. This fact may have had a bearing on the style of the jewel with its cameo centre. The beautiful treatment of hair, beard, lace and profile speaks undoubtedly for Hilliard's authorship.

One of the most beautiful jewels of Elizabethan times, and most probably by Nicholas Hilliard, is the *Armada Jewel* (*Pl. 181*), which has now found a home in the Victoria and Albert Museum. After the defeat of the Armada Elizabeth is said to have given it to Sir Thomas Heneage who stood in great favour with her and was responsible for the armies levied to resist the Spanish invasion. It therefore must have been made in or before 1588. In the centre appears the impressive gold profile bust of the Queen, medallion-like, mounted on a ground of deep blue enamel of great translucency, which is evidently taken— it is almost identical—from the Garter Badge of 1582 (Med. Ill. I, p. 132, No. 85). The legend reads: *ELIZABETH. DE. G. ANG. FRA. ET. HIB. REGINA.* and comes in style and lettering very near to that on the obverse of Elizabeth's *Second Great Seal*. Compared with the *Phoenix Jewel* to which it is related in style the queen's bust shows the image of an older woman and the more elaborate ruff, now approaching the wheel shape, and what is seen of the costume, confirms this impression. Though the features are fundamentally the same, they have become more pronounced on the *Armada Jewel.* The treatment of the slashed dress with the ribbon ornament in the sleeves, the minute rendering of the jewellery, is again akin to that on the *Phoenix Jewel,* and undoubtedly in Hilliard's accomplished manner. The medallion is surrounded by a border, standing a little away from it, which is enamelled in white,

Plate 180. William Barbor, *c.* 1585

Plate 179. The Barbor Jewel, perhaps by Nicholas Hilliard

red, and green, and set with squarely framed rubies and diamonds. The design of the ornamental decoration of this rim is comparable with that of the *Barbor Jewel* and is clearly of English workmanship. The back (*Pl. 181b*) is engraved with an emblem of the ark sailing calmly through stormy waves in translucent enamel and surrounded by the legend: *SAEVAS . TRANQVILLA . PER . VNDAS.* (calm through the savage waves). This lid lifts up and a much restored miniature portrait of the Queen (*Pl. 181c*), dated 1580, by Hilliard appears. The inside of the lid is adorned with a Tudor rose within a wreath of rose leaves in colourful enamel and the motto *Hei. mihi quod tanto virtutis perfuse decore non habet eternos inviolata dies.* (Alas! that virtue endued with so much beauty should not uninjured enjoy perpetual life.) This motto also appeared on the *Phoenix Badge* of *c.* 1574. Altogether, the *Armada Jewel* is exquisite in design and workmanship, purposefully thought out and carefully planned. Its decorative quality is what one would expect from the hand of Hilliard.

189

Plate 181 (a). Armada
Jewel, after 1588

Plate 181 (a) and (b). The
reverse

The additional links with the *Phoenix Jewel* and the style of his miniatures help to establish his claim to authorship.

We come now to the *Dangers Averted* or *Armada Badge* (*Pls. 182a, b*), and the closely connected *Dangers Averted Medal*, in the Fitzwilliam Museum, Cambridge (*Pl. 183*), both *c.* 1588. The gold badge in the British Museum was

Plate 181 (c). The miniature

possibly a naval reward in commemoration of the destruction of the Armada. The Queen's portrait has much in common with that on the *Armada Jewel*, especially in the dainty execution of the hair, crown, and the ornaments of dress and ruff. Elizabeth's face is seen three-quarter to the left, well modelled, framed by richly arranged hair with some curls falling down loosely, and rising from a delicate lace ruff, standing high up and being open in front. In spite of the low relief, different degrees of depth are achieved. The legend: *DITIOR . IN . TOTO . NON . ALTER . CIRCVLVS . ORBE.* (No richer circle in the whole world than this) refers to the power of the Queen's crown which, after

(a)   (b)

Plate 182 (a). Armada Badge or Dangers Averted Badge, gold, by Nicholas Hilliard (?), obverse, Queen Elizabeth I; (*b*) Reverse, a bay tree on an island

Plate 183. Dangers Averted Medal, gold,
after 1588

the defeat of the Armada, was equal to any crown in Europe. On the reverse there is a bay-tree growing on an island, surrounded by the waves of the sea, bearing some small ships near the horizon. Clouds are gathered round the top of the rim and rays emanate from them. The drawing of the waves resembles that on the lid of the *Armada Jewel* and that of the clouds is like that used on the *Second Great Seal*. The inscription on the island reads as follows: *NON . IPSA . PERICVLA . TANGVNT*. (Not even dangers affect it.) The bay-tree was supposed to be incapable of injury, even from lightning.

Although the *Dangers Averted Medal* in Cambridge has the same device on the reverse and a similar legend round the front, it is larger in size and has a slightly different likeness. It is again of gold, cast and chased, of an excellent workmanship and must have been executed at approximately the same time, *c.* 1588. The Queen's face is now turned to a full frontal position and if any- thing, she looks slightly older. Her right hand holding the sceptre and the left touching the orb from below are partly visible at the bottom of the medal's rim. Hair, jewellery, the lace ruff, the pattern of the dress with the bulky sleeves and shoulders are most carefully studied and rendered in accurate detail. The whole figure, including the much pronounced and protruding head, is of an imposing weight. The height of the medal is completely filled by the vigorous image of the Queen and it conveys the same awe-inspiring impression of majesty which is the predominating feature of the *Second Great Seal*. It is in the latter that the nearest parallel can be discerned. It is, in fact, so close to it, also in the surprisingly plastic treatment of the relief, the figure type and the detail, that it must be ascribed to the same artist. This lovely medal can therefore be attributed to Hilliard with some confidence. The more so, as we know[1] that a capable workman, one 'Abell Feckeman', was in Hilliard's employment at exactly that period, when our limner was busily engraving goldsmiths' work. Thus, a small, but important, group of jewellery, beginning with the *Phoenix Jewel* and ending with the *Dangers Averted Medal*, from *c.* 1574 to *c.* 1588, can be established as a nucleus of Hilliard's surviving work in this branch of art.

The graceful, flat, and slightly more schematical gold medal of the Queen of 1602, at Windsor, seems to be by a different hand and may conceivably be the work of Charles Anthony.[2]

The first medal that was made for Elizabeth's successor, the *Accession Medal* of 1603 (Med. Ill. Pl. XIV, No. 1) already bears the King's likeness—though in the guise of a Roman Emperor and wearing a laurel wreath—which Hilliard used in the first portrait type he limned for his new royal patron.[3] The most illuminating medal is, however, the beautiful gold *Peace with Spain* medal of 1604 (Med. Ill. Pl. XLV, Nos. 14 and 15) (*Pl. 184a*). It has been ascribed to Hilliard by John Pinkerton[4] and Miss Helen Farquhar accepts this view as plausible.[5] The King's bust faces three-quarter to the right. He wears the

---

[1] See pp. 26/7, *ante*. [2] Auerbach, *Portraits of Elizabeth I*, p. 205, Note 48.
[3] See p. 149, *ante*. [4] *The Medallic History of England to the Revolution* (1790).
[5] *Portraiture of Stuart Monarchs*, pp. 160ff.

full beard that usually is seen in his early portraits. A tall hat, crowned and plumed, pushes high up and through the letters of the legend, touching the outer rim. It may be recalled that this motif, emphasising the height of the figure, was often applied on numismatic work acribed to Hilliard. The legend reads: *JACOBVS . D'. G'. ANG'. SCO' . FR' . ET . HIB' . REX* and is engraved in bold roman type. A big, rather bulky, jewel is attached to the hat under its brim and the slashed doublet is detailed and rendered with care.

(a)   *(b)*

Plate 184 (a). King James I, Peace with Spain Medal, obverse, by Nicholas Hilliard (?), 1604, gold; *(b)* The reverse, Peace and Religion, two classical figures

The reverse (*Pl. 184b*) shows the beautifully composed representation of two graceful classical figures, "Peace" holding a palm branch and a cornucopia, and "Religion" standing opposite. It is remarkable how the fine roman lettering of *HINC . PAX . COPIA . CLARAQ . RELIGIO. A'1604* corresponds to the dainty relief of the figure work. The bold modelling of the king's features on the obverse is closely related to that on the *Dangers Averted Medal* and the *Second Great Seal*. The treatment of the short doublet, which has the same cutting as that on many of Hilliard's miniatures, is also very similar to the rendering of the dress and its ornaments on the *Armada Badge* and other work connected with it. These stylistic similarities confirm the view that this medal has to be ascribed to Hilliard. Two other medals bear the same likeness of the king, the *Attempted Union Medal*, 1604 (Med. Ill. Pl. XIV, No. 17) and the *Badge* (Med Ill. Pl. XIV), but the workmanship of both definitely shows another hand. The latter has at the back the *Armada Jewel* motif of the Ark sailing through troubled waters. However, it is extremely difficult to ascribe more numismatic work to Hilliard during the reign of James I. Though we know from documents that he executed gold medals for the king, there are just as many, if not more, references to Charles Anthony's work. It must therefore be assumed that in that period Anthony, "Graver of the Mint", played an important part in the production of medals and other goldsmiths' work.

The beautiful enamelled and open work of the *Lyte Jewel* containing James' portrait, ascribed to Hilliard,[1] has, however, great likeness to the design and

Plate 185. A Queen with a little boy, by Nicholas Hilliard (?) drawing

execution of the locket of the *Armada Jewel.* Here are also the little scrolls and arabesques, often set with tiny rubies, framing the square diamonds. In addition the red in the filigree pattern of the lid matches, as we have seen, the background

[1] See pp. 167/8, *ante.* Another possibility is that the case of the jewel was made by Heriot, but the design speaks for Hilliard.

195

colour of the miniature comprised therein. Related, of course, is the equally exquisite lid of the locket with the miniature of *Queen Anne* at Cambridge, but in view of the difference in design it is less likely that it is a work by Hilliard.

Plate 186. Queen Elizabeth I, engraved by Francis Delaram after Nicholas Hilliard, 1617–19

As to Hilliard's drawn and engraved work, it remains to mention a curious drawing in the Print Room of the British Museum (*Pl. 185*), which bears the initials *NH* in the left-hand corner. It shows the full-length figure of a queen

196

handing over the sceptre to a little boy, who is standing on a stool, in front of her. The child wears a crown and a small orb is seen in his left hand. But who actually this queen represents is difficult to establish. The features come near to those of Elizabeth I, but it does not appear to make sense that she should be portrayed as passing over her realm to Mary Stuart's son, unless one looks upon it as a purely allegorical or imaginative representation. Again, from the drawing one would infer that the figures represent mother and child. According to another suggestion, the queen is supposed to be *Elizabeth of Bohemia*, James I's daughter, whose son was at one time—after Prince Henry's death and during a spell of bad health of Charles, the Prince of Wales—considered as a likely successor to his grandfather. But her likeness is completely different from that on the drawing. With that the matter of identification must rest. As to the style, it is definitely made for an engraving. Much in the composition and the distribution of shade and light is achieved by crosshatching and supplemented by a line, sometimes fine and thin and at times strong and striking; this recalls Hilliard's technique used on his drawing of the (*?*) *Third Great Seal*.

It is important to compare this drawing with Delaram's *Queen Elizabeth I* in the Print Room of the British Museum (*Pl. 186*); the only surviving engraving on which is printed *NIC: HILLYARD DELIN: ET EXCUD: CUM PRIUI-LEGIO MAIEST:* it thus bears witness to the validity of the monopoly Hilliard was granted in 1617 for the production of royal portraits. It is a posthumous image of the Queen, based on the type Hilliard had created in his miniatures of about 1600, and could have been only published with his permission. Something like the style of this engraving may have been the aim of the curious drawing of *A Queen and her Son*. Perhaps Delaram had a hand in it as preparation for a work he intended to engrave but never completed. The Queen's figure and dress would confirm this view, but the handling of the child's dress and the architectural surroundings, in addition to the monogram, connect it more closely with Hilliard's drawing for the (*?*) *Third Great Seal* and make the attribution to him almost convincing.

VII

NICHOLAS HILLIARD AS A WRITER

ILLIARD'S *Treatise on the Arte of Limninge*, preserved only in one manuscript copy of 1624 at Edinburgh University, is a document of the greatest importance. Though Hilliard is not named anywhere in the text as the author, there is much internal evidence to point to his authorship. The most important item in the series of conclusive links is the well-known remark by Richard Haydocke—set out in the Preface to the Reader in his translation of Giovanni Paolo Lomazzo's *Tracte* (1598)[1] that he asked Hilliard to write down his views on miniature painting, based on his own practice, for everybody to read, and that he was happy to receive the artist's promise to do this with great speed. So strong was Haydocke's admiration for Hilliard's work that he could not think of any other means of describing his theories than to persuade him "to doe it himselfe, to the view of all men by his pen; as hee had before vnto very many, by his learned pencell". Here, the appreciation of the efficient teacher and master is noticeable. That the *Treatise* is actually that prose essay mentioned by Haydocke as being from Hilliard's pen is corroborated by the fact that it contains various references to Lomazzo whose *Tracte* was very well known to the author. Again, the time when it was composed agrees with the date one would assume as correct from Haydocke's indications. Queen Elizabeth, so often mentioned in the *Treatise*, was then still alive, so it must have been written before 1603. From a reference in the text to Sir Christopher Hatton, it appears that he was then dead, and we know he died on 20 November 1591. Again, another remark points to Sir John Harington's *Orlando Furioso*[2] Ariosto which was published in the same year 1591. According to Haydocke's Preface, Lomazzo's *Tracte*, appearing in 1584, remained untranslated for 13 years, which brings us to 1597, the year in which

[1] Address to the *Ingenious Reader*.   [2] See p. 44, *ante*.

198

he completed his translation and in which he probably also conferred with Hilliard about his writing an essay on the art of limning. Thus the gap is narrowed and the *Treatise* was written between 1597 and 1603.

Apart from this evidence, who else could have given such an exact account of a style and technique conforming in every detail to that of Hilliard's miniatures? The wording and style of writing bear the closest affinity to Hilliard's letters. The same rambling flow of words, sometimes rather slow and slightly involved, at other times carried forward by emotion and quickening in its pace, often repeated, frequently awkward or even ungrammatical, but always touching in its simplicity and naïve feeling, a strange mixture of sophistication in the sense of the Elizabethan Age and delight in the perfect handling of the craft, in which the humble and devoted craftsman was trained.

The manuscript itself is written in a rather untidy hand, which has not the slightest resemblance to that of Hilliard himself, and has at the end the words denoting date and place: "the 18 of March 1624 Londres". Apart from a short appendix in a different writing, the main text is nowhere divided into paragraphs, which makes it difficult to read. This may have been the reason why it was broken into paragraphs when published and edited in 1912 by Philip Norman for the Walpole Society.[1] In addition to the subdivision which on occasion is arbitrary, the punctuation was completely changed and consequently the meaning is sometimes lost, though the actual transcription of every single word is correct. In the following consideration of the *Treatise* I shall therefore quote from the manuscript copy and not from the printed transcript.

The importance of the *Treatise* is considerable for three reasons: it gives valuable information about Hilliard's life and personality; it clarifies his style, technique and working methods as a craftsman; and finally, it reveals his position against the contemporary background of the fine arts in this country and on the Continent. The importance of the latter aspect was emphasised by Mr. Pope-Hennessy;[2] much of what I am going to outline on this particular subject is based on his lucid article. It remains to be stated that the manuscript copy was once the property of Vertue, who added the title and various comments and marginal notes in his well-known hand.

In spite of the continuous flow of words there appears to be a logical development of thought in Hilliard's *Treatise*. He begins with a reference to "Paolo Lomatzo" and states that the latter's theory of painting is well known

[1] *Walpole Society* (1911–12), Vol. I.
[2] "Nicholas Hilliard and Mannerist Art Theory", *Journal of the Warburg and Courtauld Institutes*, VI (1943), pp. 89–100.

to the learned, and he, Hilliard, therefore intends to teach the art of limning only and to show who are "fittest to be practisers". Already the ancient Romans postulated that "gentlemen" alone should be allowed to be taught the art of painting because only artists who are free of worries and have sufficient means not to be subject to the "comon cares of the world for food and garment" would have enough patience and do their best in producing a really good work by correcting it again and again and defacing it rather than leaving it in an imperfect state, in order to create something really precious which might be "worthy of some comendations". This theory is based on Haydock's translation of Lomazzo's *Tracte* and Baldassare Castiglione's *Cortegiano*;[1] but the reasons Hilliard gives for the justification of such a ruling are personal and gained by his own experience. Hilliard's reasons are reinforced by the exigencies of his personal life:

> now therfor I wish it weare so that none should medle with limning but gentelmen alone, for that it is a kind of gentill painting of lesse subiection then any other for one may leaue when hee will his coullers nor his work taketh any harme by it.

From these lines we may imagine that Hilliard, the courtier, the friend of so many, the husband, the father of a big family, had time for all and was quite prepared to be called away in the middle of his work.

In the eyes of Hilliard miniature painting is the finest example of pure art, as contrasted to applied art for decorative purposes:

> it is sweet and cleanly to vsse, and it is a thing apart from all other *Painting* or *Drawing* and tendeth not to comon mens vsse, either for furnishing of Howsses, or any patterns for tapistries, or *Building*, or any other worke whatsoever, and yet it excelleth all other *Painting* whatsoeuer in sondry points, in giuing the true lustur to pearle and precious stone, and worketh the metals Gold or Siluer with themselfes which so enricheth and innobleth the worke that it seemeth to be the thinge it selfe euen the worke of God and not of man, benning fittest for the deckin of princes bookes or to put in Jeuuells of gould and for the imita . . . of the purest flowers and most beautifull creatures in the finest and purest coullers which are chargable and is for the seruice of the noble persons very meet in small voloms in priuat maner for theem to haue the Portraits and pictures of themselves their peers, or any other forraine . . .

Here the manuscript is mutilated.

In the foregoing lines Hilliard gives his theory of the aim and purpose of limning in a nutshell. He distinguishes it from other painting as having small appeal to the man in the street, yet as excelling in that it can give the true brightness of pearls and precious stones, and can make good use of gold and

[1] See Pope-Hennessy, *Treatise*, p. 91.

silver. Thus it is best applied to the embellishment of "princes bookes" or to the decoration of golden lockets or other pieces of jewellery, which may hold the portraits and pictures of the loveliest creatures painted in the purest colours and destined to be worn by noble persons. Here speaks the goldsmith and the artist trained in the tradition of medieval manuscript illumination, as well as the experienced painter of portraits in miniature. It is clear that Hilliard considered the independent portrait "in little" as originating from, and closely related to, the decorated page of a manuscript.

After a partly mutilated and therefore not quite understandable reference to passages of the Bible and foreign princes, Hilliard again returns to the doctrine that this branch of art is most suitable to be "practiced by Gentlemen". But in that passage he only refers to those who have been granted by God the talent to paint "after the liffe" and who are blessed with such a wonderful gift that they should always remember it in "humble thankfulness". Therefore, he continues, they should live accordingly and be "temperat in diet and other goverment, least it be son taken from them againe by some sudaine mischance, or by their evell coustomes, theire sight, or stedines of hand decay . . . ". By moderation in his habits of life the gifted artist can protect himself from losing his ability to paint. Apart from this warning Hilliard raises a second point to encourage the workman: Talent alone is not enough. Unless he is industrious, he will not be able to achieve anything really good. He has to "put his whole uttermost and best endeavors to exceell all other" and even the strong man needs "the same diligence, or rather more, to effect and performe his worke . . . ". Nobody can say

> that a man be he never so cunning by teaching or naturall Inclination, yet it will growe out of him as haire out of the head, or fall from him whether he will or no, but with great labour, and this comfort shall he haue then, aboue others, euen an heauen of Joy in his hart to behould his own well doings remaining to his credit for euer. . . .

What follows now is the description of the purest pleasure the artist experiences from the creation of his work: an idea well known to, and discussed by Lomazzo,[1] but yet again expressed by Hilliard in his own personal style with great sincerity:

> yea, if men of worth did knowe what delight it breadeth, how it remoueth mallancoly. avodeth evell occasions, putteth passions of sorrowe or greefe awaye, cureth rage, and shortneth the time, they would neuer leave till they had attained in some good meassur, A more then comfort maie he haue, both praysse and euen honor in the sight of men liuing, and fame for euer after,

---

[1] Pope-Hennessy, *Treatise*, p. 91; Haydocke, p. 14.

The blessing derived from his painting as a protection against the human emotions which he probably had to endure more often than was agreeable to him, leads him to the discussion of the vital question of noble patronage:

> And *Princes* comonly give them competent meanes, by which not the workmen soe much as themselves ar eternized, and famously remembred as the nuresses of vertue and Arts, wherfor it is truly written *Honos alit Artes*, and many noble and honorable perssons haue bine practizers themselves of the art of painting, as *Lomatius* very learnedly and truly hath in order repeated and some haue counted themselves the greater therby as the famous and victorious *Roman Quintus* added it as an honnore unto his tytle to be called Quintus *Fabius Pictor, /.*

The latter was according to a Roman source (Pamitius is mentioned) the principal painter to the Emperor Marcus Aurelius.

> Nevertheless if a man be so indued by nature and liue in time of trouble, and vnder a savage goverment: wherin arts be not esteemed, and himselfe but of small meanes: woe be vnto him as vnto an vntimly Birth:

He continues to tell us about "the most rare *Englishe Drawer of Story Works* in black and white, *John Bossam*",[1] who had so much skill that he could have been Sergeant Painter to any king or emperor. He enjoyed no encouragement in his art and was therefore driven to give up painting and become a clergyman. This happened when Queen Elizabeth came to the throne. It is therefore clear that Hilliard thinks of the reigns of Edward VI and Mary when he continues in the following words:

> only vnfortunat becasse he was english borne, for euen the strangers would otherwisse haue set him vpp,

This statement does not throw a favourable light on royal patronage in the early days of the Tudor period, and Hilliard hastens to exempt Henry VIII from this verdict:

> Heer must I needs incert a word or two in honore and praisse of the renowned and mighty King Henry the eight a Prince of exquisit Jugment . . . and Royal bounty, for that of cuning Stranger euen the best resorted vnto him, and remoued from other Courts to his Amongst whom came the most excelent painter and limner *Haunce Holbean*, the greatest Master truly in both thosse Arts after the liffe that euer was, so cuning in both to gether, and the neatest, and thewithall a good inventor soe compleat for all three, as I neuer hard of any better then hee yet had the King in wages for Limning diuers others, but Holbeans maner of Limning I have euer Imitated, and howld it for the best,

This passage is not only important because of the tribute Hilliard pays to Henry VIII as patron of the fine arts,[2] but also because of his own appreciation of Holbein's skill. He admires him as a great artist, both as a painter and as a

---

[1] *Tudor Artists*, pp. 95–6.   [2] *Ibid.*, p. 6.

limner. It further is interesting that he draws the line sharply between painting and limning, a difference he often discusses both generally and technically, in his *Treatise*. What he admires most in Holbein's skill in mastering both these arts "after the liffe", is the neatness of his manner; we can judge from Hilliard's miniatures how much he was inspired by the great German master's clear-cut and economical style of portraiture. In addition, he also considers him a good "inventor", whatever that means, whether the designing of oil portraits and religious paintings or of miniatures and goldsmiths' work. In conclusion he states that, though Henry VIII had some other limners in his service, he, Hilliard, has always followed Holbein's "maner of Limning", because he is convinced that it is the best. This important statement shows that Hilliard was fully aware of the artistic situation at the early Tudor Court and that he was certainly acquainted with the miniatures limned by the Flemings Luke Horenbout and Levina Teerlinc.[1] That he definitely referred to these foreign artists emerges from the immediately following passage:

> by Reason that of truth all the rare sciences, especially the arts of *Caruing, Painting, Gouldsmiths, Imbroiderors,* together with the most of all the liberall siences came first vnto vs from the Strangers, and generally they are the best, and most in number,

It is quite remarkable that he includes in this list of foreign craftsmen also the goldsmiths. But he has also a good word for the indigenous artist.

> I hard Kimsard (Ronsard) the great french poet on a time say, that the Ilands indeed seldome bring forth any cunning Man, but when they doe, it is in high perfection so then I hope there maie come out of this ower land such a one, this being the greatest and most famous Iland of Europe:

He then proceeds somewhat abruptly, to the consideration of the most excellent artist *Albrecht Dürer*, who was born in Germany, "a part of the greatest Mainland of Europe, that brings forth more than a hundred workmen for one in this country". What he likes best is his excellent and perfect "Grauing on Copper", the best since the world began, as it appears from many extant specimens of his work. This remark makes it clear that Hilliard knew Dürer's graphic work well. The second merit of Dürer, according to Hilliard, is "that he hath written the best and most rulles of and for painting and grauing hetherunto of any maister vntill *Paulo Lomatio*", but here again, he emphasises that most of these rules are not of interest to the limner and rather "tedious":

> which Rulles of Albert for the most part ar hard to be remembred, and tedious to be foloued of Painters, being so ful of diuisions, but very fittable for caruers and masons, for architects and fortifications, and all which drawing is the entrance the very high waye and foundation

[1] See pp. 49 *et seq., ante.*

He states that Dürer himself hoped for better work to come, and as a matter of fact there have been several excellent Germans, Italians, French, "and the lowe countries also", who were good engravers, amongst them

> *Hendrick Goltzius*, aproched Albertus very neer, most admirably imitating him, and *Lucas of Leydon*, also, in their seuerall handling the grauer, which he hath done in sertaine peces to showe what he could doe if he list, but he afecteth an other maner of line, which is swifter acording to his spirit, and doubtles very exclent, and most folowed, . . . Albertus Dure was both inventor and grauer as few of the rest of the grauers are, a double honnor to him,

Here we see that Hilliard was well versed in the contemporary range of engravings, and as we already have mentioned that he practised wood engraving himself, we thus gain an idea about the formation of his style in that medium. Especially, the technique of the contemporary Goltzius must have influenced him strongly. Again, as in the case of Holbein, he points to the praiseworthy fact that Dürer also designed his graphic work, which was rare but surely the case with his own engravings, whether in wood or metal. He then reverts to the question of the usefulness of Dürer's theory of proportions, a question much in his mind, and one he solves in his own way, by stating that Dürer's ideas were actually superseded by Lomazzo:[1]

> nowe the reasson why the rules of Alberte, serue mor the caruer then the *Painter* is becausse he discribeth and deuideth the propeortion or of parts of men, like as of pillors or such other things, by measures of inches in length, breadth, thiknes, and circumference, which measure serue not, nor can howld in painting,

This idea is linked with that of perspective, and he continues as follows:

> for as Lamatzo truly speaketh in the eleuenth chapter of *Opticio*, you cannot measure any part of the pictures by his true superficions, Because painting perspectiue, and forshortening of lines with due shadoing acording to the rule of the eye, by falshood to express truth in very cunning of line, and true obseruation of shadoing, especially in human shapes, as the figure, lieth, boweth, or standeth, and is situated, or is, and aptly shalbe placed to deceaue the eye, for perspectiue, to define it brefly, is an art taken from, or by, the efect, or Jugment of the eye, for a man to express any thing in shortned lines, and shadowes, to deseaue bothe the vnderstanding and the eye, this cassed the famous and eloquent Cissero to say, O how many things doe painters see in highning or lightning, and shadowing which wee deserne not,

The artist's experience is reflected in these lines. They indicate that Hilliard attached great importance to the illusionary effect of perspective on the onlooker and that he was aware of the fact that foreshortening lines in themselves do not exist in painting unless seen in relationship to the whole visual appearance. The same idea was already stated by Lomazzo—and this passage is

[1] Pope-Hennessy, *Treatise*, p. 94.

204

quoted by Hilliard—in Haydocke's translation: "No painter or carver ought in his workes to imitate the proper and naturall proportion of things, but the visuall proportion . . . ".[1] The writer of the *Treatise* expresses that theory even more strongly and—as Mr. Pope-Hennessy has suggested[2]—"In these sentences mannerist art theory merges imperceptibly into the naturalism of the 17th century!" It is a trend of thought that in contemporary literature emphasises the empirical view in contrast to the consideration of the theory of proportion as such. This idea, according to Mr. Pope-Hennessy, is the most striking feature of Bacon's essay on *Beauty*, which was first published in 1597: "There is no excellent beauty that hath not some strangeness in the proportion." When Sir Francis Bacon later mentions the blissfulness in which the painter should perform his work, we can truly imagine the Queen's limner, who always, in devotion to beauty, relies purely on the strength of his eye and follows steadfastly the impression of the appearance he has before him without thinking of any rules or theories.

That Hilliard was, however, *au fait* with the aesthetic theories of his age, is shown by the next question he poses, namely whether painting or carving is the worthier art. Though deciding at once in favour of painting, he brushes the problem aside and postpones it for "the last leafe", on which it may or may not have appeared. In the version of the Edinburgh manuscript the last page seems to contain only some remarks written down at random and finishes off rather abruptly.[3]

He then reverts to Albrecht Dürer and qualifies the criticism which he has expressed on his theoretical concept by adding that he is such an excellent man, "the most exquisite man that euer leaft vs lines to vieue for true delination, the most perfect shadower that euer graued in metall, for true shadowes, and one of the best and truest in his perspective", Hilliard attributes the shortcomings of Dürer's theoretical concept to lack of contact with the Italian school; he says of Dürer that he did not travel much and did not see those beautiful creatures that the Italian artists, such as Rosso and Raphael, had seen and also "Lambertus Suauius". Hilliard clearly did not know that Dürer had, in fact, visited Venice, or he may have considered Rome and Florence as the only important centres of Italian art. Should the latter be the case, it is possible—as Mr. Pope-Hennessy pointed out—that in this statement he followed van Mander.

[1] Haydocke, pp. 181 and 205.

[2] Pope-Hennessy, *Treatise*, p. 94.

[3] *Ibid.*, p. 91; Frederick Hard, "Richard Haydocke and Alexander Browne: Two half-forgotten writers on the Art of Painting", *Publications of the Modern Language Association of America*, Vol. LV, 1940, No. 3 (September), p. 735.

Having expressed his views on the beauty of Italian women and men, Hilliard at once pays a compliment to his own patrons. He asserts that rare beauties are likewise to be found in this country, and not only the face, "but euery part, for euen the hand, and fooet, excelleth all pictures, I euer sawe". Therefore a certain Pope had asserted that the word *Anglia* was derived from *Angeli* and denoted the country of Angels. How truly Elizabethan that statement sounds!

When in the subsequent passages he discusses the practical process of limning, we seem to hear the Master himself giving advice to his pupils, just as Haydocke had wished him to do. Here, his heart warms and the perfect teacher speaks, eager to pass on his own skill and experience to his charges. He tells them that it is, first of all, necessary—and here he repeats what he had said before—to be moderate in habits of life:

> I meane sleepe not much, wacth not much, eat not much, sit not long, vsse not violent excersize in sports, nor earnest for yr recreation/ but dancing or bowling, or littel of either,/

What a delightful description of the Elizabethan courtier's recreation this is! As to limning itself, the most important precept he gives "is cleanlynes" and for that reason, he repeats, it is "fittest for gentlemen". Every single tool that is used has to be clean, and he gives details about the best kind and their use. The artist must grind his colours in a place "wher ther is neither dust nor smoake", the water must be pure, "as the watter distilled frome the watter of some clear spring, or frome black cherize which is the Cleanest that euer I could find, and keepeth longest sweet and cleare". The "Goume Aarabeeke" has to be white and broken into a powder on a clear grinding stone. The "suger candy" is to be kept in ivory boxes. The grinding stone should be of fine cristal, "Serpantine", etc., and, in addition to this, the gentleman must be dressed properly :

> at the least let yr aparell be silke, such as sheadeth lest dust Dust or haires weare nothing straight, beware ye tuch not yr worke with yr fingers, or any hard thing, but with a cleane pencel brush it, or with a whit feather, neither breath one it, especially in could weather, take heed of the Dandrawe of the head sheading from the haire, and of speeking ouer yr worke for sparkling, for the least sparkling of spettel, will neuer be holpen if it light in the face or any part of the naked,

He then describes the best working condition which sheds an interesting light on his own workshop in Gutter Lane. The best light is that coming from the north a little towards the east, as there is not much sunshine. There should be only one big light:

and faire let it be, and without inpeachment, or reflections, of walls, or trees, a free sky light the dieper the window and farer, the better, and no by window, but a cleare story in a place wher neither Dust, smoak, noisse, nor steanche may ofend,

When he continues to speak of the painter's sensibility, he again gives us his self-portrait:

a good painter hath tender sences, quiet and apt, amd the culers them sellues may not endure some ayers, especially in the sulfirous ayre of seacole, and the guilding of Gowldsmithes, sweet odors comforteth the braine and openeth the vnderstanding, augmenting the delight in *Limning*, *Discret* talke or reading, quiet merth or musike ofendeth not, but shortneth the time, and quickneth the sperit both in the Drawer, and he which is drawne, also in any wisse avoyd anger, shut out questioners or busy fingers, all theesse things may be hadd, and this authority may best be vssed by gentelmen, therfor in truth the Art fitteth for them,

The pleasant atmosphere he describes in these lines must have prevailed when he painted his happiest miniatures.

Hilliard then discusses the aim of painting in general, of which he states that it is the imitation of life. The painter of "story worke" can always rely on his memory and skill to express this. The highest purpose, however, is to imitate "the face of man kind", which is also the most rewarding. Nobody should attempt such a difficult task before he can manage "story worke" after the life. Nothing gives us so much pleasure and "feedeth soe wonderful ower afection" as to bring out well the likeness of a face. Three points have to be observed:

the first and least is the faire and beautiful couler or complection which euen a fare of, as neare is pleassing greatly all behoulders, the next and greater part is the good proportion sometime called fauore, wherof ouer deuine part vppon nearer view, by an admirable instint of nature, Jugeth generally both in wisse, and foolish young, or owld, learned, and simpel, and knoweth by nature without rule or reasson for it, whoe is well proportioned or well fauered, but the third part, the greatest of all is the grace in countenance, by which the afections apeare, which can neither be well vssed nor Juged of but of the wisser sort and this principall part of the beauty a good painter hath skill of and should diligently noet, wherfor it behoueth that he be in hart wisse, as it will hardly faill that he shalbe amorous, (and therfore fittest for gent:)

The three points he discusses here, as being important for the expression of likeness, he considers again later on. It has to be noted that he explains the word "fauore" in this connection as good proportion. The third point is the most interesting one. "The grace in countenance" or the face as the mirror of the soul and reflecting emotions and affections can only be interpreted properly by the wise artist who has enough experience and skill. He cannot fail to be "amorous". If he wants to represent perfect beauty, he has to fall in love with those "beautiful creatures". He identifies his own emotions with those of his sitter. How true this is and how much does it explain the attraction and charm of Hilliard's best miniatures, that seem to convey to us his own affectionate feelings towards the lovely faces he created within the compass of the locket. This is the secret of the typically Elizabethan, lyrical and poetical quality of his miniatures. It also clearly distinguishes their spirit from that of Holbein's portraits, which appear to be conceived in a wholly detached manner. The artist of the late sixteenth century, living at a sophisticated Court, expresses more complex experiences than the painter of the beginning of the century who is satisfied with stating merely facts.

In the following passage he amplifies the sentiment of the artist:

> for whoe seeth an exelent precious stone, or diserneth an exelent peece of musike with skill indeede, and is not moued aboue others with an amorous Joye and contentment then the vulger, howbeit gent or vulgar wee are all generally commanded to turne awaye ouer eyes frome beauty of humayne shape, least it inflame the mind, howe then the curious drawer watch, and as it catch thesse louely graces wittye smilings, and thesse stolne glances wch sudainely like lighting passe and another Countenance taketh place except hee behould, and very well noate, and conceit to lyke, soe that he can hardly take them truly, and expresse them well, wthout an affectionate good Jugment, and without blasting his younge and simpel hart, although (in pleassing admiration) he be very serious, bussied, so hard a matter he hath in hand calling thesse graces one by one to theire due places, notinge howe in smilling howe the eye changeth and narroweth, houlding the sight just between the lides as a center, howe the mouth alitel extendeth both ends of the line vpwards, the Cheekes rayse themselues to the eyewards, the nosterels play and are more open, the vaines in the tempel appeare more, and the cullour by degrees increaseth, the necke comonly erecteth itselfe, the eye browes make the straighter arches, and the forhead casteth it selfe in to a plaine as it wear for peace and loue to walke vppon, in like sort countenances of wroth, of feare, or of sorowe, haue their seuerall alterance of the face, and fare according to the mind is affected, maybe many faces, some lovly, some loathsom, some graue and wisse, some foolish and wanton, some proude and audatious, some poore and courardly, wherfor it would be longe to handel euery seuerall countenance,

All this the drawer may note and he should also read his Lomazzo's "second book on Actions and Gestures". In spite of the reference to the latter this passage is characteristic of Hilliard and, in fact, one of the most beautiful descriptions in the *Treatise*. It does not only express what Hilliard felt and observed when painting a miniature portrait, but it also shows his literary talent. The lucid account of the change in a face that is smiling and the delight the painter experiences while trying to reproduce that change, agrees with the formula which Hilliard applied to his miniatures: the narrowing of the eyes, the ends of the mouth turning upwards, the cheeks rising towards the eyes, the nostrils sensitively playing, the veins appearing in the temples, the eyebrows taking on straighter arches, the neck straightening itself, and above all, the forehead becoming "a plaine as it wear for peace and loue to walke vppon", all these features are characteristic of Hilliard's most accomplished miniatures. That he was also able to write about his visual experience reflects his refined and cultured personality.

In the following lines he discusses, in more detail, the function every part of the face plays in the view of the painter who wishes to create the best likeness:

> So Chiefly the Drawer should obserue the eys in his pictures, making them so like one to an other, as nature doeth, giuing life to his worke for the eye is the life of the picture,

Now follow some practical hints of great importance to the painter—hints which he himself applied widely:

> and be sure likewisse that the sircel of the sight be perfect round, (for so much therof as appeareth.) the senter truly placed in the midest therof, the reflection of the light which apeareth like a whit spek, must be placed according to the light, this seemeth but a slight thing, howbeit the most fayleth therin and noet this as the position is, or the Drawer placed acording to art, the furthest eye from the Drawer must be a littel higer then the hethermost becausse of the perspectiue if the Drawer sit any deall higer then the party drawne, but if lower, then the further eye must be a littel lower, if leauel then to be of one hight . . . for of all the features in the face of a picture, the eye showeth most life,

He then considers the other parts of the face:

> the nosse the most fauor, and the mouth the most liknes, although [he hastens to add] liknes is contained in euery part, euen in euery feature, and in the cheekes, chinne, and forhead, with the compasse of the face, but yet cheefly in the mouth,

He repeats the three points he had stated before, Complection, Proportion, being the "fauore" and Countenance and subsequently he sums up the foregoing lines in the statement that the goodness of a picture after the life depends chiefly on three points:

1	Liffe		Eye
2	Fauor	wch chiefly consist in thesse three features	Nose
3	Liknes		mouth

This is followed by a further definition of the word "fauor":

> fauor and liknes are both one in some sence, as one would say of a picture after the liffe, that it hath the very fauore of the party or the very liknes of the party, both is one thinge, but when one sayeth it is a welfauored picture, and a well like picture, theese differ; so meane I that the nosse giueth cheefe fauor, for one shall neuer see an Ill fauored face, that hath a weel proportioned nosse

Hilliard distinguishes here between two meanings of the word "fauor". He uses it in a limited sense, meaning the proportion and in the general sense of denoting likeness or appearance.[1] If a picture has "the very fauore" of a sitter, it gives an excellent likeness of him. A "welfauored" picture, however, means a picture which reproduces a well-proportioned face, a face that has good features and good proportions, and this build-up of the face is best represented in the true shape of the nose. Both meanings of the term "fauor" were known in Elizabethan England, and Bacon, for instance, used it in the limited sense and lists the three important points of beauty as colour, favour, and motion. This is related to Hilliard's definitions of complexion, proportion or favour, and countenance.

Hilliard then continues that artists "after the life" frequently fail to give the right proportions because of want of rules or judgment. He has noticed that some drawers who neglect the rules and work "out of their owne head" are unsuccessful in that respect and he thinks that the reason for this is "the ill setting of the party drawne". Here he adds some wise remarks which, to the present day, are important to the painter:

> I amonish yo of that fault both Sitter and Drawer, wch is the greatest cause of loosing the liknes in pictures, Marke weel I saye, therfore when yor worke is remoued neuer so littel, recall him to his right waye or place or proceed not, And to preuent this error, yor marke shalbe yr first lyne wch yo drawe, but that must be most truly drawne, for that lyne must be a scalle to all the rest/ and let that yor first lyne be the forehead stroake.

The importance of the typical forehead curve on most of Hilliard's miniatures, which we have often noticed, finds thus a welcome explanation. That line, the first to be put down, gave him the proper measurement for the rest of the face, and it was never to be lost and had to be remembered and marked, always in its right position.

Hilliard then mentions Dürer's rule:

> that comonly all faces howld one measure and true proportion (how differing soever they be of fauor) that the forhead is of the lenght of the nose, and the nose as long as from the nose to the chinne, if it differ in this it is Deformety (by this rule)

But Hilliard does not agree with that rule. He states that he has known people who were considered as having good features, although they did not conform to this theory of proportion:

> I wilbe bould to remember me of one namly *Sr Christopher Hatton*: some time lorde Chancellor of England a man generally knowne and respected of all men amongst the best fauours, and to be one of the goodlyest personages of England, yet had he a very low forhead, not answerable to that good proportion of a third part of his face,

[1] Pope-Hennessy, *Treatise*, p. 95.

On the other hand, there are very many faces which conform to Dürer's rule on proportion but are not pleasing or good-looking. The mention of Sir Christopher Hatton, who died in 1591, is, of course, interesting, since we know that Hilliard painted him and we can compare this statement with the extant miniature. This statement is valuable intrinsic evidence of Hilliard's authorship of the *Treatise*.

He then observes that Dürer's rule of proportion cannot be applied to old people, as their noses grow a little longer, and the nose of a child is "of no length answerable either to the forhead or distance from the nose downwards", so that the rule does not hold for children either. To this problem of proportion he adds a further remark:

> Yet one wourd more in remembrance of an excelent man namly *Sr Philip Sidney*, that noble and most valiant knight that great scoller, and excelent Poet, great louer of all vertu and cunninge,

This tribute to a great man was based on personal acquaintance, if not friendship, for

> he once Demanded of me the question, whether it weare possible in one scantling, as in the length of six inches of a littel or short man, and also of a mighty bige and taulle man in the same scantling, and that one might weel and apparently see which was the taule man, and which the littel, the picture being just of one lenght,[1]

Hilliard's answer to this problem is interesting: He showed Sir Philip that this can be done easily, as the eye is able to see these differences, even without any rules "as littel lads speake their vulger tonge with-out gramour Rulls". Nevertheless he gave him some points to observe. It all depends on the proportion of the head in relationship to the whole figure, as the short man's face may be of the same size as that of the tall man, but everything else, such as legs, feet, hands, the upper part of the body, etc., will differ. A child's body is only four times the length of his head. Often in a picture the neatness of execution and colouring is most deceptive, but

> knowe it yo for atruth, that the cheefest mastery and skill consisteth in the true proportion and line, and a tall mans picture exactly drawne but in the length of six Inches, shall shewe to be a taller mans picture, then a littel mans picture drawne at the lenght of fowre and twenty inches, or in his owne full hight, if his true shape be obserued,

The authority he then quotes, is, of course, Lomazzo with his various tables and drawings.[2]

He goes on to discuss the importance of the line, that plays the principal part in any painting or drawing after the life. Without mentioning the name of

---

[1] See p. 128, *ante*.   [2] Pope-Hennessy, *Treatise*, p. 96.

Sir John Harington, he refers here to his remark, that he has seen the Queen's portrait rendered in an excellent likeness by only four lines. It may be recalled that this reference to a drawing of Elizabeth's face was actually based on a portrait drawn by Hilliard himself.[1] The latter explains in the *Treatise* the meaning of the "fower lynes" by describing them as plain lines without shadowing.

> for the lyne wthout shadowe showeth all to a good Jugment, but the shadowe without lyne showeth nothing,

As an example he refers to the shadow thrown by a man standing in front of a white wall. The likeness, even in this case is only brought out by the line defining the shadow and if the latter were taken away and the contour alone remained, "it will resembel better then before". The line gives the expression, line *and* colour the likeness and shadow the roundness and "the effect or defect of the light wherein the picture was drawne". The story of the man standing against a white wall and drawing the outline of his own shadow with charcoal to which the foregoing passage refers, is based on an incident from Pliny, mentioned by G. B. Armenini, the Italian Mannerist writer on the Theory of Art, which was published in Ravenna in 1586 and was certainly well known to Haydocke and through him probably also to Hilliard.[2] It has often been noted that the importance of the line, which Hilliard emphasises here and elsewhere in the *Treatise*, conforms to the Italian view expressed by the word "disegno" in the writings on painting by the Mannerists Armenini and Federico Zuccaro.[3] The latter considers the line as the purest form, an absolute rendering of shapes and features. The transcendental meaning of this word, often stressed in those theoretical essays, is completely absent in the *Treatise*. Hilliard's view, though paying lip service to contemporary art theory, is founded on his own visual experience, gained from his training in the tradition of manuscript illumination and his admiration of the economical use of the line evident in Holbein's miniatures.

We now approach the important passage in the *Treatise*, often quoted, when Hilliard refers to a remark of the Queen, "when first I came in her highnes presence to drawe" which was probably at some time between 1569 and 1572. The Queen had noticed

> great difference of shadowing in the works and diuersity of Drawers of sundry nations, and that the Italians who had the name to be cunningest, and to drawe

---

[1] See p. 44, *ante*.

[2] *De Veri Precetti della Pittura* libri III, Ravenna, 1587, pp. 42, 81–2. Pope-Hennessy, *Treatise*, p. 96, n. 10.

[3] Karl Birch-Hirschfeld, *Die Lehre von der Malerei im Cinquecento*, Rome, 1912, p. 49.

best, shadowed not, Requiring of me the reason of it, seeing that best to showe ones selfe, nedeth no shadow of place but rather the oppen light/

Hilliard wholeheartedly agreed to this. It may be assumed that Elizabeth's reference to Italians who did not shadow was an allusion to Zuccaro, who at approximately that time, *c.* 1574, made a portrait drawing of the Queen, which was beautifully clear in its linear style. Hilliard, in reply to his patron's remark, affirmed that the presence of a shadow in pictures was due to the shadow of the place at which the painting was made. Some artists preferred the light from one direction only or from a small or high window which would give them "a grosserlyne", because that line would be more easily detected, would achieve a good relief and would show off well from the distance:

which to *Liming* work nedeth not, because it is to be weewed of nesesity in hand neare vnto the eye, heer her Ma[tie] conseued the reason, and therfor chosse her place to sit in for that porposse in the open ally of a goodly garden, where no tree was neere, nor any shadowe at all, saue that as the heauen is lighter then the earthe, soe must that littel shadowe that was from the earthe, this her Ma[tie] curiouse demaund hath greatly bettered my Jugment besids diuers other like questions in *Art* by her most excelent Ma[tie] which to speake or writ of, weare fitter for some better clarke,

That Hilliard makes allowances for shadow to be used in paintings on a large scale and to be seen from afar, but not in miniatures to be held in the hand and viewed from near, is highly significant. He himself may have applied more pronounced shadows, when painting pictures "in greate". He had discussed artistic problems with the Queen herself, who expressed her desire to sit in the open without any surrounding of shadows. The credit which Hilliard gives to Elizabeth for her understanding of art reveals her as a sensitive patron. Her taste must have appealed to his personal style of clarity of line.

Hilliard refers to the difference of treatment of miniatures and large pictures again when discussing the question of light. Large pictures as well as "story worke" require hard shadows. But this is not necessary in portrait miniatures,

for beauty and good fauor is like cleare truth, which is not shamed with, the light, nor neede to bee obscured,

Hilliard adds that it would be a disgrace to bring out the roundness by darkening and smutting it, as if truth were "ill towld". It is only permissible to make use of much shadow if a person were not good looking, for in that case to be placed in shadow, would be favourable to the sitter:

knowe this also that to shadowe (sweetly as wee weell calle it) and round well, is a fare greater cuning then shadowing hard or dark, for to round a worke well canot be without some shadowe, but so to shadowe as if it weare not at all shadowed, is best shadowed, for a round ball is a round ball in the oppen light, where the light cometh euery way, as weel as in a seller, wher it cometh in at a littel gratt,

This gradual modelling of the roundness of the face, sometimes hardly visible in Hilliard's miniatures, is clearly related to Zuccaro's view, who compares this method with the receding surface of a column.[1] The light in a cellar and any kind of strange light, such as that coming from a candle or torch, is sometimes required for "story worke", and Hilliard even recommends it for certain scenes supposed to have happened by night. But otherwise he fully accepts Lomazzo's view, that shadow is "but the defeet of lighting". To quote this passage in Haydock's translation:

> shaddowes are as it were the tayle of Light, insomuch as there can bee nothing more base and abiect then they, being of so melancholye and heavie a Nature, that the verie Kinge of shadowes and darkenesse beneath in the center of the earth, disdaines them, and cannot abide them.[2]

What follows then in the *Treatise* is a discussion of colours which is couched in technical and specialised language, adopted by generations of limners after Hilliard's death. Only a few points are of general interest. Thus, Hilliard states that all odorous and badly tasting colours have to be avoided in limning. Most have to be washed and ground. He then gives a list of the colours and begins with white and black. The well graven portraits by Dürer and Goltzius show that everything can be expressed in this medium, as white and black really stand for light and darkness, "in what couller soeuer it be". He therefore considers these two colours the worthiest to be mentioned first, especially as they are most frequently used.

The list of the Whites is headed by "whitlead", which should be ground, dried, ground again, mixed with gum arabic, and will then be a good white for limning. He also speaks of a fine satin white and a coarser one that may be used for flesh colour which should always be dull and never have any glistening.

As to the 'Blacks' he first mentions "veluet blacke". He tells us that it is made of ivory burnt. But he warns us that velvet black, after it has become dry in the shell, does not work so well as at the first grinding and tempering. For that reason he always has a little in powder form ready in store and tempers it on his grinding stone "for principall workes, and euen for the Centor of the eye, being but a littel tytle".

In addition to white and black Hilliard lists five principal colours which are perfect in themselves and cannot be obtained by any mixtures: the total

---

[1] Pope-Hennessy, *Lecture*, p. 20. Birch-Hirschfeld, p. 49. Pope-Hennessy, *Treatise*, p. 97. Bisagno, *Trattato della Pittura*, 1642, p.61.
[2] Haydocke, p. 176.

number of simple colours is seven. The listing of seven basic colours agrees with the number generally accepted by Mannerist art theory;[1] in Haydocke's *Lomazzo* we also find "7 sortes of simple colours, from which all the rest arise".[2] For Hilliard the five principal colours are "Murreys, Redds, Blewes, Greens, and Yellows". Murrey can be gained from "lake of murrey"—the best comes from Venice or Antwerp—and it has to be ground with gum water only. As to the reds, he recommends "lake of India", which breaks off into a scarlet colour. The best of the "blews" is "Vltermaryne of Venice" which is very expensive. The "blews" most conveniently used for shadowing are "litmouse, Indy blewe and flory". Of the greens he considers "Ceder greene" best and also "verditer" and "pinke". The best yellow is "masticot", also yellow "ocker" or "ocker de Rouse" for shadowing.

In the middle of these highly technical prescriptions there appear various generally interesting remarks, such as one on the making of rubies and stones which must appear like real precious stones. He admits that this is no part of the actual limning. It pertains to another art, though he uses it in his limning, just as a mason or joiner, after he has finished his job, paints and gilds his friezes and other parts of the woodwork.

The next important advice he gives is that a painter should never change the light in which he has started to work, but should try to create exactly the same conditions in which he had begun.

Another of these disjointed remarks refers to the best material on which the miniature should be painted:

> virgine Parchment, such as neuer bore haire, but younge things found in the dames bellye, some calle it vellym, some Abertiue deriued from the word Abhortiue for vntimly birthe. It must be most finly drest, as smothe as any sattine, and pasted with starch well strained one pastbourd well burnished, that it maye be pure without speckes or Staynes, very smoothe and white.

Hilliard continues to speak about the flesh colour which has to be laid on the vellum: "Must you laye your carnation flowing and not thine driven as ane oyle cullore." Here, again, he distinguishes between limning and oil painting. It is important that the ground colour chosen be as fair as possible. It is easy to limn the browner shades on a fair ground, but one can never do it the other way. All the shadows have to be of the same colour as that laid on the card. For the same reason one has to think twice before drawing a line and one will have to use a very small "pensile" dipped in a thinly mixed carnation colour with a little lake! At first it will hardly be noticed, until one is quite sure, and then the

---

[1] Pope-Hennessy, *Treatise*, p. 97.
[2] *Ibid.*, p. 98.

line can be strengthened. In shadowing one should proceed in the same slow and careful way: "by littel and littel at the first" and one should never listen to what the ignorant people say, as the latter would always like to teach. If the face is only slightly too red or brown, it cannot be corrected afterwards. The same applies to the height of the forehead: if it is too low, one cannot get exactly the same carnation colour to make it higher. Therefore, the forehead should be rather a little too high at first, for it can then be easily lowered, if necessary. We notice that even in Hilliard's technical writing he emphasises the importance of that part of the face, which figures so prominently in his executed miniatures.

While working one should not listen to anybody's word, he repeats, and records his experiences with various sitters: "the better and wiser sort" have great patience and will only venture an opinion afterwards and in a modest tone. But the "Ignoranter and basser sort" will not only be bold to give their criticism, but also get into a temper and "vehemently sweare that it is thus or soe" that this volume would not be big enough to relate this. The artist, however, should just proceed with his work, and have pity on their ignorance.

He returns to technical points and recommends tempering the colours with the ring finger, when they have become dry in the shells. Liquid gold and silver should not be touched with the finger, but only with a brush and with very little gum. One may burnish gold and silver when required, and he adds quite a detailed and generous prescription for the making of diamonds, pearls, and other stones.

In these last pages of the *Treatise*, Hilliard repeats himself frequently and tries to get in as much detailed advice as he can think of. The technique of shadowing in limning occupies him again; it

> must not be driuen with the flat of the pensel as in Oyle worke, distemper, or washing, but with the pointe of the Pencell by littel light touches with cullor very thine, and like hatches as wee call it with the pen,

One should not touch too long in one place, as it should not glisten, and one would do better to wait for an hour and let it dry first and deepen the shadow later. The technique itself should be copied from Dürer's engraved portraits, and until one is able to make an exact copy from the print, one should not start on limning.

> This is the true order and principall Secret in Limning, which that it maye be the better remembred, I end with it.

This, however, is not the end. The manuscript copy in the Edinburgh University Library then contains a strange essay on the links between colour and precious stones. This passage shows that Hilliard never forgot that he was a goldsmith. He intends to discourse on precious stones,

> which wilbe meet for gentelmen to vnderstand, and some gouldsmithes wilbe glad to see it for their better Instruction.

This essay is thus also addressed to his fellow-goldsmiths and not only to limners. Apart from black and white he equates the five principal colours with five bright and transparent stones, each bearing one of those colours. "Ammatist orient" stands for "Murrey", "Rubie" for red, "Saphire" for blewe, "Emrod" for greene, and "hard Orient Topies" for yellowe. The true beauty of these five colours, Hilliard writes, is best expressed by these stones, when they are perfectly hard and fully transparent. He then discusses the beauty of these stones in some delightful passages which show his wide knowledge of every kind of gem. It is interesting to read of the perfect red in a ruby, especially in candle light, which affects the eye like "fyer". The sapphire is the brightest and hardest stone with the exception of the diamond, but it can be well cut and it will then match the diamond in brightness. He rejects bad, shoddy workmanship in the following passage:

> as the bade workman spoiles many a good Juell both in cutting, pulishing, and also in the setting, Soe an excelent workman cann grace them aboue that which nature giue them both in cutting, setting and making them in valewe double of that they weare before; therfor he is better worthy of fowerfolde better payment then any other, though paradventure he doe it much soner, but commanly they are indeed longer about theire worke, which maketh that they are poorer then the bunglers. For while the good workman taketh pleasure to shewe his art and Cuning aboue other men in one peece (in what art soeuer), the botcher dispatches six or seauen, and giues it a good word or a boaste, keeping his promise within his time, which greatly pleaseth most men, for indeed the tyme is all in most matters, as sayeth one. A thing well done out of due time is ill done, and soe hee getteth credit and custome which keepeth time, wherby he is able to set many other at work, which though they be all bungler and Spoilers, yet please in respect of good cheapnes and keeping of promise and so growe rich.

This rings perfectly true, and when he continues to speak about the good workmen, it again reads like a paragraph of an autobiography:[1]

> They are generally given to travel, and to Confere with wise men, to fare meetly well, and to serve their fantasies, having commonly many childeren if they be maryed; all which are causes of impoverishment, if they be not stockt to receave thereupon some profit by other trade, or that they be, as in other countries, by pencion or reward of princes otherwise uphelde and competently mayntained, although they be never soe quicke nor soe cuninge in their professions, depending but one theire owne hand helpe . . . they will spend still if they cann come buy it,

[1] See p. 26, *ante*, where the beginning of this passage is quoted.

soe that I thinke they haue the liberall Sciences, and it is a vertue in them, and becometh them like men of vnderstanding. If a man bring them a rare peece of worke, they will giue more for it, then most men of tenne times their abilitye,

In other countries, he adds with sadness, they are mostly wealthy men, and it is a great pity that this is not the case in this country. Everybody concerned may find the reason for this himself. This question is so near to his heart that Hilliard even interrupted the discussion of the precious stones to which he reverts now with the consideration of the "emerod", the most perfect green on earth growing naturally. He compares these five stones with human beings, who at first may all appear to be excellent and valuable members of society, but whose shortcomings will be discovered soon. After having appreciated the "topas" as the perfect yellow, Hilliard considers that the most beautiful stone which has two perfect and distinct colours, a transparent white and black, is the diamond. It is of a clear water or air colour.

With a few remarks, jotted down at random, this essay trails off: questions are posed but not answered, such as "how one can paint the eyes of a sitter, so that they follow you round", or "wherof the carnations are to be made", etc.

The work concludes with a last admonition: in drawing after the life sit not nearer than two yards from the sitter. If you draw a full-length portrait, the sitter should be at a distance of at least six yards. Watch the hands and draw them quickly, as soon as you see a graceful movement, but do not tell the sitter that you are painting the hands, otherwise they will become affected. After this last observation the following words appear:

the 18 March 1624 Londres.

The appendix, written in a different but contemporary hand, is described as "A more compendious discourse conserning ye art of limning, the natture and Properties of the coullers." It mainly deals with technical questions and is essentially supplementary to the main text. Such various points as "how to make sattin", how to choose your "pencills", how to prepare your "table or carde", to lay your ground, to temper your colours, to work your first colours, and to make armour in silver and gold, are fully discussed. Hilliard's authorship of this supplement has not been undisputedly accepted. Though P. Norman in his introduction to the *Treatise* was in favour of the theory that Hilliard had also written the appendix, M. Hardie, the editor of Norgate's *Miniatura*, assumed Norgate to be the author. The conception and style of the supplement conforms, however, to the general tone of the whole essay. The technical points agree fully with the manner in which the surviving miniatures by Hilliard are executed. Moreover, in one instance at least, when discussing the application of gold, Norgate, in his *Miniatura*,[1] repeats in essence the relevant passage from the Appendix to the *Treatise* and expressly mentions in this connection Hilliard's name.[2]

It remains to consider Hilliard's *Treatise* as a whole, its sources, and its influence on later generations of painters. As far as the former are concerned the close link with contemporary Italian Mannerist theories has already been discussed and the inspiration from Haydocke's *Lomazzo*, Zuccaro, and others, has been noted. There were, however, some technical essays in existence which must have been known to the Queen's limner. Some of these practical manuals have been already mentioned by Mr. Pope-Hennessy,[3] e.g. the *Tractatus de Coloribus Illuminatorum seu Pictorum* of the fifteenth century in the British Museum. In addition, Hilliard certainly must have known a small printed pamphlet on *The Arte of Limning* by an anonymous author, which was published in 1572.[4] This short tract has no other aim than to set out the different colours used in the traditional illumination of manuscripts and the manner in which they are applied. In general, much of what is outlined there on the use of paint is still in harmony with the method applied by our miniaturist to his portrait miniatures. *The Arte of Limning* mentions the usual recipes of how to make "syse", to "laye or settle silver or goulde vppon" or "to make gumme water to temper colours with all". The anonymous author's prescriptions for making a pure white or sable black for arms, or an excellent velvet black, have much in common with Hilliard's technique, which, however, is more refined and perfected by personal experience. The view expressed earlier in this work that the style of Hilliard's miniatures originates in manuscript illuminations is thus not only supported by stylistic evidence, but also by theoretical writings.

The *Treatise* and the Appendix had a considerable influence on posterity. Various manuscripts and books on the art of limning written approximately in the middle of the seventeenth century incorporate many passages from them, particularly from the Appendix. Only the most important of those manuals can be discussed here.

Paramount amongst them is Edward Norgate's *Miniatura or the Art of Limning* (about 1646), a manuscript in the Bodleian Library, which was edited and published in 1919 by Martin Hardie. An earlier, shorter draft of it is in a manuscript in the British Museum (Harleian 6000). Many passages from the *Miniatura* were freely copied in the seventeenth century and finally, in 1658, they appeared in print, plagiarised under the name of Sanderson's *Graphice*.

---

[1] See p. 220, *post*.   [2] Norgate, p. 40.   [3] *Treatise*, p. 89.
[4] Published by Richard Tottill, London, 1573. Reproduced in Facsimile, Michigan Facsimile Series, No. 3. Further editions, 1581, 1583, 1588, 1596, 1605 or 1615.

In Norgate's *Miniatura* a number of references to Hilliard occur. They concern passages from the main text and also from the Appendix. The first of Norgate's allusions to our limner concerns "gum Arabique" with which colours for limning have to be mixed.[1] This may be broken into white powder "very fine and kept in a neat box of ivory or such like. And when you temper any colour mix a little of this powder with faire water, and you will finde it to dissolve instantly." He then continues: "And this later was Mr. Hilliard's way, an excellent man, and very ingenious and in his time a great Master in this Arte."[2]

The second reference applies to ivory black which when burned gives an excellent velvet black, "much used by Mr. Hilliard".[3]

The next of Norgate's references to Hilliard is preceded by an interesting remark. He states that the English are the best limners

> but the English, as they are incomparably the best Lymners in Europe, soe is their way more excellent, and Masterlike Painting upon solid and substanciall body of Colour much more worthy Imitation than the other slight and washy way.

He thus fully appreciates the effect of applying a substantial body of colour rather than ordinary transparent water-colour as used in sketches in wash and ink. He continues to refer to the preparation of playing cards—mentioned in the text of the *Treatise* and in the Appendix—in the following:[4]

> The best course therefore for you is according as Mr. Hillyard and his rare disciple, Mr. Isaac Olivier were wont to doe, which was to have in a readiness a dozen or more cards ready prepared.

Further revealing is his remark on the choice of the background. He states that it is usually blue but adds that it is "sometimes of crimson, like sattin or velvet curtaines, much in request with Mr. Hillyard . . . ".[5] Here Hilliard's crimson background is interpreted as representing a material.

The next passage, already mentioned, refers to a recipe from the Appendix and deals with laying on a liquid gold ground or using pure gold. "The Manner of working I shall tell you within a few leaves as I had it from old Mr. Hillyard."[6]

Another remark applies to "pencilwork", the use of crayons or "dry colours"; Norgate lists a few artists who were competent in this technique:[7]

> Hans Holbein, Mr Nicholas Hilliard and Mr. Rowland Lockey his Disciple, Mr Isaec and Mr Peter Olivier, father and son, Hoskins, etc. . . .[7]

At the end of his book Norgate gives a few recipes for the preparation of

---

[1] Norgate, p. 11. [2] *Ibid.*
[3] *Ibid.*, p. 15. [4] *Ibid.*, p. 20.
[5] *Ibid.*, p. 33/4. [6] *Ibid.*, p. 40.
[7] *Ibid.*, p. 72.

paint. This list is headed: "To prepare Ceruse, Mr. Hillyards way." It refers to Hilliard's process, as mentioned in the text of his *Treatise*, namely to divide the water into three parts:[1]

> The first parte of this water Mr. Hillyard calls his satine white, the second his lynnen white, the last shines not at all but is reserved for carnations and complexions for pictures by the Life, the first shines most the second lesse so.

There is thus evidence that Norgate had first-hand knowledge of the techniques applied in Hilliard's workshop.

The next work to which reference should be made is Alexander Browne's *The Whole Art of Drawing, Painting, Limning and Etching*,[2] published in 1660. Browne was a miniature painter, and he describes himself as "Practitioner";[3] he states that the text is "collected out of the choicest Italian and German Authors". He also mentions rules of proportion written by the "famous Painter *Odoardo Fialetti*, Painter of Boloign". In his *Ars Pictoria*, published in 1669, Browne gives an enlarged edition of the earlier *Whole Art*. In both editions Hilliard is mentioned twice by name, and though on one occasion reference is made to the early part of the text, usually passages from the Appendix are adopted, though their wording is closer to Norgate's *Miniatura* than to Hilliard's original text. Like Norgate before him, Browne speaks of velvet black, which may be tempered with a little white, Indian Lake, and Indigo, heightened with a lighter mixture, and deepened with Ivory black, "this was Hilliards way".[4] The other is a more general remark, following a recipe for "Rockcandy". It reads thus: *Additional Observations out of a Manuscript of Mr. Hilliards touching Miniature*.[5] The paragraph to which this remark may refer concerns the mixing of colours that Hilliard had often recommended: "When you begin to Paint temper all your colours afresh with your finger, in your shell or on your paller." When speaking of laying the ground for the painting of the face,[6] Browne mentions "a pretty large Pallet of Ivory" on which several heaps of shadows should be mixed with the finger. Even the wording is here almost identical with a passage from the Appendix of the *Treatise*. Norgate's version is somewhere between Hilliard's original text and Browne's adaptation. A similar remark occurs likewise in the first part of Hilliard's *Treatise*. Since Browne in the first part of his book—as Mr. Hard has shown[7]—copied "most of his material verbatim from Haydocke's work" and, in addition, took—as we have seen—

---

[1] Norgate, p. 90.   [2] See Hard, *loc. cit.* pp. 727–741.   [3] *Ibid.*
[4] *The Whole Art*, p. 11. *Ars Pictoria*, p. 80. For Norgate see p. 220, *ante*.
[5] *The Whole Art*, p. 24. *Ars Pictoria*, p. 93.
[6] *Ars Pictoria*, p. 82. Norgate, p. 22. *Treatise*, Walpole Society, p. 34.
[7] p. 730.

much from Norgate's *Miniatura*, it is remarkable that he acknowledged his debt to Hilliard.

In another anonymous publication[1] of the second half of the seventeenth century this debt to Hilliard and, for that matter, his authorship, are not acknowledged. Within the pages of a printed drawing book, which has no title page, nor does it bear the name of the author, there appears, on ten pages starting with page 31, a new chapter called:

> The Art of Limning, wherein the Colours, and their uses, are really described by Mr. Garrat, Master in that Art, and Painter to Her Sacred Majesty Queen Elizabeth, of Famous Memory, being taken from his own Mannuscripts, and now Published for the good of all Gentlemen, and other Lovers of that excellent Practice.

The reference in that passage to "Garrat" can be to nobody else but Marcus Gheeraerts. The passages that are ascribed to him by the anonymous compiler are selected at random from the text of Hilliard's *Treatise* and are identical with it, but with a different spelling and without the personal allusions. We find, for instance, "The First, and chief Precept which I give, is cleanliness", that we know from the *Treatise*, but in the latter the remark is added: "and therfor fittest for gentelmen". The various references to "gentlemen", personal allusions to Queen Elizabeth, Sir Christopher Hatton, Sir Philip Sidney, and others are invariably omitted, but technical topics are copied in full, though in modernised spelling. Occasionally a paragraph is completely left out and the correct sequence is never quite maintained. But precepts such as for place, light and shadowing, the beauty of the face being due to the colouring, the "good proportion, called Favours" and "the grace in countenance" are—subject to the above mentioned reservations—identical with the corresponding passages from the text of the *Treatise*. This is, therefore, though under a different name, the only printed version of parts of the *Treatise*, published or at least intended to be published, in the second half of the seventeenth century, in fact the only one in existence before Norman published the full *Treatise* in the first volume of the Walpole Society in 1911/12.

A second copy of this publication in the Bodleian Library,[2] bound with another drawing book, has a title page. The compiler remains anonymous, but included in the title page we find the following reference to the chapter on limning:

> In the limning part, you have here a manuscript which came happily to hand out of the collection of Mr. Garrat, limner to Queen Elizabeth, . . .

[1] In the possession of Mr. J. Campbell.
[2] Identified by Mr. Campbell. The shelf mark is L.3.12. Jur.

It follows that Gheeraerts was in possession of at least part of the *Treatise*, but not that he was the author. This fact was, however—as stated above— disregarded by the compiler in the text of the book.

The volume in the possession of Mr. Campbell contains actually three books of different sizes bound together; the first contains engravings of architecture and was printed in Holland; the second represents architectural ornaments and seems to have been printed in 1599 in Germany, and the third book bears the running title *A Drawing Book or the Pencil improved*. It begins with thirty pages of script and about a dozen engraved drawings of faces, hands, arms, taken from "Fiolet", "Master J. Cozine", and "Bloemaert". On page 31 the new chapter on "Limning", quoted earlier, begins, and ends on page 41. On the latter, right at the end, we find the only clue to its printing, viz.:

[impri] *matur Tho: Grigg R. in Christo P. D. Hum. Episc. Lond. a Sac. Dom.*

Thomas Grigg was chaplain to Dr. Henchman, Bishop of London, in 1665–6, Canon of St. Paul's in 1666, and died in September 1670. On the title page of the Bodleian copy the date of publication is given as 1664, and it was printed by Tho. Johnson for John Ruddiard. There is, however, no other trace of this book, under any related title, among the permits for printing granted by the Stationers' Company in their Registers from 1660 to 1670. Even an extensive search among the bibliographic material of the British Museum did not reveal any further copy. It is possible that, in view of economic difficulties due to the Great Fire, or for other reasons, the book was never published and that we have only the first proofs in these two rare copies before us. That Gheeraerts[1] is mentioned as the author may prompt the conclusion that the compiler was fully acquainted with the Flemish circle of artists but not so much with the English School. In any event, the first book of the composite volume in the possession of Mr. Campbell must have been known to some of the foreign limners of the period, since one of the architectural engravings was exactly copied by Isaac Oliver in the background to his famous miniature called "Sir Philip Sidney" in Windsor Castle. As to Hilliard's *Treatise*, it is highly significant that, whoever the compiler of this volume was, part of Hilliard's manuscript was already sufficiently known in *c.* 1660 to be plagiarised, an indirect tribute to his skill, which had hitherto only been given to Norgate's manuscript.

[1] Vertue (I, 93) mentions one "Gerhard", of "Bruges" as part-author of an introduction to the General Art of Drawing and Limning in conjunction with W. Gore; but this book was translated into English and published only in 1674 and has nothing to do with the *Treatise.*

VIII

HILLIARD'S CONTEMPORARIES,
FOLLOWERS AND PUPILS

LAURENCE HILLIARD

FROM LETTERS written by Hilliard to Sir Robert Cecil[1] we learn that he bestowed his loving care on his son Laurence, apparently the only one of his children who inherited his artistic ability. It may be recalled that he was proud of his son, because he had a good knowledge of the Spanish language, of writing and drawing, and because Laurence had served the King well in painting miniatures and making gold medals.

Laurence, the fourth of the children of Alice and Nicholas, was baptised on 5 March 1582. He must have entered his father's workshop in about 1597. His training as a goldsmith was perfected on 7 June 1605, when he was declared freeman of the Goldsmiths' Company.[2] On 13 October 1608 he received the office of "his Majesty's limner" in reversion after the death of his father. In his patent it was stated that he had been trained and instructed well by Nicholas and that he had acquired perfection and skill in the art of limning.[3] Laurence appears to have played an active part in the proceedings of the Goldsmiths' Company and on 28 August 1611 was one of the "batchelors" asked "to wear suitable apparel for Lord Major's show and to serve". On 28 October he is actually listed as one of the "Budg Batchelors", that it to say, he was wearing fur. One year later, he was called upon to "wait at the Renters feast".[4]

On 10 February 1612/13, the Wardens and a Finance Committee conferred with "Laurence Hillyard for the renewing of the lease of his tenementes in gutter lane" for which he had offered a fine of forty pounds. It was, however,

---

[1] See p. 38, *ante.*   [2] See p. 40, *ante.*
[3] *Tudor Artists*, pp. 133-4.   [4] Book P, pt. 1, pp. 9, 42 and 104.

agreed that he should pay the full sum of sixty pounds without any deduction.[1] On 7 May 1613 a lease was made to Laurence for "his tenement in Gutter Lane from Midsomer next for 21 years for 60*l*. fine . . . "[2] and on 18th June of the same year the lease was finally sealed. According to the Rentbook[3] his new lease was dated Michaelmas 1613 and by that time he was not only the occupier of his own house, but most probably also of that of his father, whose name then disappeared from the page of the Goldsmiths' Company Rentbook. And, indeed, he had apparently more than he needed, for on 4 March 1613/14 he is authorised to assign his lease of certain "tenementes in Goodrom lane to Mr. Humfrey Westwood",[4] probably also a goldsmith.

Of interest are further two indentures on the Close Rolls: according to the first of 29 October 1614[5] (when Nicholas still was alive) Arthur Michelborne, of London, who had to travel abroad, of one part, and various people of the other, made Laurence a "perfect and sole tenant of the Manor of Tythehurste, *alias* Tysehurste, Sussex, parcels belonging sometimes to Bishopric of Chistester." According to the second Indenture[6] Laurence was granted by Sir Richard Hoghton, of Hoghton Tower in the County of Lancaster, property near Whitingham in Lancaster for a payment of the considerable sum of 500*l*.

That he actually lived in his house in Fleet Street in 1623 emerges from a case in Star Chamber. At a meeting of that court on 6 May 1623,[7] the Attorney General accused four "turbulent" people who, unlawfully armed, assembled in the Parish of St. Andrew in Holborn at a certain place "there called the upper end of Field Lane *alias* Saphron Hill on 18 June last" in the evening with the intention of attacking the first man who would come their way. It happened that that man was Laurence Hilliard, on his way to his dwelling house in Fleet Street; he was viciously attacked, barbarously wounded, and his life was even endangered. In spite of the best help that "Surgery and Phisicke" could afford him, he had not then completely recovered and

> shalbe also for ever disabled to doe yor Ma[tie] service, and to gett his maintenance and living in the arte and profession of lumninge wch hee then vsed, [for he also received a wound on his right hand], whereby hee hath vtterly lost and is depriued of the use of one of the forefingers of his said right hand, and by that meanes is not able to worke so exactly in the said arte as formerly he was used and accustomed to doe.

Laurence's name appears frequently in the Accounts. In 1599, at Christmas, his father's pension was paid into his hands.[8] His own annuities, due to him

---

[1] Book P, pt. 1, p. 112.
[2] *Ibid.*, pp. 118 and 121.
[3] See p. 30, *ante*.
[4] Book P, pt. 1, p. 153.
[5] C. 54/2224.
[6] C. 54/2403 (10 April 1619).
[7] St. Ch. 8/33/11.
[8] E. 403/2284, f. 11.

after Nicholas's death, were regularly recorded in the lists of James I's pay-ments.[1] He also received 40*l*. as "the Kings Lymner".

Several warrants for payments to Laurence have survived and give us an idea of the work commissioned from him. In 1624 (the date of the warrant is 17 April), he received 40*l*. for five pictures, "by him drawn". In view of the price, viz. 8*l*. for each, there is no doubt that these were miniatures.[2] Another recorded payment to him is of still greater interest. In 1626/7 the following entry appears:[3]

> To Lawrence Hilliarde his Ma^tes Lymmer vpon the Councells warraunte dated the 30th Jan. 1626 For delivering by his Ma^tes Command a picture of the late Queene Elizabeth for his Ma^tes vse vnto Abraham Vanderdoort Keeper of his Ma^tes Pictures ——   74*l*.

Here he is paid quite a considerable sum for delivering a picture into the hands of the Keeper of the King's pictures for his Majesty's use. There is no reference to Laurence as the author of this painted portrait of Queen Elizabeth, as before, when the five pictures were mentioned as "by him drawn". It seems feasible that the painting in question was an oil portrait of the late Queen by Nicholas, and that it was bought by James I from young Hilliard. The high amount paid for it speaks for a full-length lifesize picture, a further indication of Nicholas' activity in painting royal portraits on a large scale.

Laurence was also in the service of the 2nd Earl of Salisbury, though according to an account of 1622 and 1624 he only did decorative work of a heraldic nature.[4]

Some more details of Laurence Hilliard's life are known. In November 1626 judgment was given against him in favour of one Francis Sympson, gold-smith, for payment of a debt.[5] Quite revealing is a letter Laurence wrote on 14 September 1631 to his son Brandon who followed his father's calling. Laurence commends him for being careful and sending him money. He is interested to get some news about Lord Swinerton and Mr. Dunsterval, and continues: "But now direct your letters to my sister Parkers at St. Edmonds Bury where we propose to be to-morrow." This sister of Laurence could only be "Lettice" or "Penelope".[6] He informs Brandon that his mother, sister and he himself are in good health, and then, after a fatherly blessing, follows Laurence's beautiful caligraphic signature which has so much in common with that of Nicholas, while the text is otherwise written in a completely different and rather careless hand. He adds a kind afterthought as a postscript: "Yf yor want monn'

---

[1] E. 304/2371.
[2] E. 351/544, m. 164.
[3] *Ibid.*, m. 222.
[4] Cecil Pap., Accounts 160/6.
[5] Long, p. 206.
[6] See p. 19, *ante.*

for yorself comend me . . . Bell and praye her to lend you twoo or three shillings."[1]

By far the most striking document that has survived is, however, Laurence Hilliard's will,[2] which has so far been overlooked by scholars. It is at Somerset House, both in the original and in the Register of the Canterbury Prerogative Court. In the following I am transcribing the original:

> I doe giue by waye of Leagacey to my dafter Lauranc An Excelent Limd pece of a gentlman dun In mourning One Mr Hearne by nayme wch I vallue at thirty pound. Itt I doo giue to my Sun Brandon my booke of Drauings of seural Masters hands/ It I doo giue him the Earl of Lestars picture in a yet box draune in his Cloake wth a Cap and Fethar. Allso I doo giue him all my Euedence and riting belonginge to my house and land in Sat. Jons of Gerusaleme. Item I doo giue to my Sun Thomas by waye of Leagacey my ᵍʳᵃⁿ Fathar[s] [pic] Hillyard his picture in an Ivrey box wth a Cristall vppon it/ Allso I giue hym a pece of Younecorns horne waing one ounce &$\frac{1}{2}$. Item I doo allso giue my Sun Thomas a book of portrature in a Ruset Forrell wth Strings. . . Itt I doe giue my Sun Brandon a picture off Queene Elisabeths Draune From hed to Foot in a small Vollume and in a yet box. . . Itt I doe allso giue him my oune picture draune when I waus a yong man in an Ivrey box . . . all these thinges aboue writtene I freely give in Wittness where of I haue sete to my hand . . And my mynd and will is that my most Loving wiff Jane Hillyard shall be my sole and absolute Execcutrix and that that third of my personable estate wch by law and the custom of the Citie is in my powre to giue where I list/ I most freely geve it to my Loving wiffe afore namd (whome) Lastly I charge by all loue and kyndness that hath ever bin betwixt vs that shee shewth more loue and kyndness to myne and her Daughter Lawrence whom eu' I pray God to Bless
>
> Laurance Hillyard
>
> February the 21th 1640.
> In witnes I set my hand
>
> Thomas Hillyard.

On 8 March 1647/8 probate was granted to Thomas Hilliard, son of Laurence Hilliard in St. Bridget, alias Brides, Fleetstreat, as Jane Hilliard who is mentioned as executrix does not want to enter it.

According to the probate of this will Laurence died much later than one had generally assumed, namely approximately at the end of 1647 or the beginning of 1648. We learn a good many details about Laurence's family. He had the most tender love for his only daughter Lawrence—it may be recalled that her father and her grandmother Hilliard were called by the same name—his affectionate feelings for her were already evident in the letter he wrote to his son Brandon.[3] In his will the legacy to her is the starting point, as if it were

[1] S.P. 16/199, No. 42.   [2] C.P.C., 45 Essex.
[3] See p. 226, *ante*.

the most important bequest he made, and at the end he recommended her especially to the loving care of his wife. She appears in later documents as Lawrence Rich. Nicholas' eldest grandson Brandon was a member of the Goldsmiths' Company and his will was proved on 7 March 1671.[1] His wife, Elizabeth, survived him and he had one daughter Jane, the wife of Mr. Owen Price. Laurence had another goldsmith son, called Charles, whose will was proved on 17 February 1675 and who bequeathed large sums to the Goldsmiths' Company.[2] This grandson of Nicholas was, however, not mentioned in his father's will. The third son, Thomas, followed his father's and grandfather's calling. He was a painter-stainer, had a house in St. Brides and was married on 20 January 1623/4 to Anne Baker, Spinster, . . . at St. Andrew in the Wardrobe.[3]

The will of Laurence Hilliard is a most enlightening instrument. It has not the usual preamble and arrangements as to the funeral and bequests for charity. On the other hand it does not look as if any part of the will has been lost. It therefore appears as though Laurence had these personal legacies very much at heart. The pictures and limnings which he lists are nowhere mentioned as being by his own hand. It is therefore possible that some of the miniatures bequeathed by Laurence to his children were the work of his famous father, although he does not refer to Nicholas by name. The identification as Nicholas's work can, however, in some cases be implied from the descriptions of the pictures on the list. That would explain why he was so anxious to distribute these family "heirlooms" fairly amongst his children. But before a final identification of these works can be established, further research will be necessary.

However, the item "my Fathers pic", later altered into "my gran Father Hillyard his picture in an Ivrey box with a Cristall vpon it" appears to be identical with Hilliard's miniatures of himself and his father in the Victoria and Albert Museum, at that time still in the possession of the Hilliard family[4] and, further, the portrait of Laurence himself, bequeathed to Brandon, and described as "my oune picture drawne when I was a yong man in an Ivrey box" probably was a portrait by Nicholas.[5] I want to mention only briefly the "excellent limning of a gentleman in mourning", one Mr. Hearne, and the "Earl of Lestar's picture in a yet box draune in his Cloake with a Cap and

[1] P.C.C., Eure, Folio 30. [2] P.C.C., 17 Bruce.

[3] Marriage Licences issued by the Bishop of London, 1611–1828, *The Publications of the Harleian Society*, Vol. 26., p. 134.

[4] In 1706 described by de Piles as having circular borders with Latin inscriptions. Before 1744 owned by Jocelyn Sydney, Earl of Leicester, when they were in the lid of a snuff box.

[5] According to the age of the sitter the *Unknown Young Man* of 1599 in the collection of the Earl of Leicester is perhaps a portrait of Laurence. That would explain the exceptionally fine signature in gold at the back.

Fether". With respect to the first picture one may think of the limning called *Henry Carey, 2nd Earl of Monmouth*, at Welbeck Abbey, which represents a gentleman in mourning[1] and the identification of which with the 2nd Earl

Plate 188. A Lady wearing a wide-brimmed Hat, by Laurence Hilliard

Plate 187. An Unknown Man, by Laurence Hilliard, 1640

Plate 189. A Lady wearing a velvet cap, by Laurence Hilliard

of Monmouth is not an indisputable fact, whilst the *Earl of Leicester* miniature, which is known to have survived, reminds one to a certain extent of the full-length miniature of Leicester, formerly in the Currie collection, although here the Earl wears a feather in his cap but not a cloak.[2] The picture of "Queene

[1] Goulding, No. 14
[2] See p. 281, *post.*

Elisabethe Draune From hed to Foot in a small Vollume and in a yet box", bequeathed to Brandon, can surely be assumed to represent a miniature by Nicholas, though it is doubtful if this particular one has survived. One thinks of de Piles' remark that Hilliard "made a whole-length of her [Queen Elizabeth] sitting in her Throne, which was deserv'dly estem'd".

Interesting are also the two drawing books. The one of "sevral Masters hands" bequeathed to Thomas Hilliard may have contained drawings by many famous masters of that time and earlier—perhaps Holbein's drawings were amongst them—and the same applies to the "book of portraiture in a Ruset Forrell wth strings". In any event this testament will stimulate further research.

Plate 190. An Unknown Man, aged 26 in 1622, by Laurence Hilliard   *Plate 192.* An Unknown Man, aged 37 in 1636, by Laurence Hilliard

There are only about half a dozen surviving miniatures bearing Laurence's signature, a Roman monogram : LH or HL. The composition is usually not very ambitious and keeps to the bust portrait without hands. The three-quarter view—on men's portraits turned to the left from the onlooker, on women's to the right—with eyes looking into the opposite direction, is familiar to us from many miniatures by his father. There is also the blue and cerise curtain background, a related treatment of the features of the face, of the hair, and of the style of the inscription. But the quality cannot compare with the inspired conception of his father's works. There is, however, on Laurence's best miniatures, such as *An Unknown Man* of 1640, in the Fitzwilliam Museum, Cambridge (*Pl. 187*), *A Lady wearing a wide-brimmed Hat* in the Victoria and Albert Museum (*Pl. 188*), and Portrait of *A Lady wearing a velvet cap* in the same collection (*Pl. 189*), a broad decorative touch which reveals a free

(b)

(a)

Plate 191 (a). An Unknown Man, by Laurence Hilliard; (b) Locket containing the miniature

handling of the brush and anticipates the style of a later period. In the Sotheby Collection there was an interesting miniature of an *Unknown Man*, who was 26 in 1622 (*Pl. 190*), and of a later period is the attractive locket in the National Museum at Stockholm (*Pls. 191a, b*). In the latter we have an excellent example of his goldsmith's work. Two lively portraits at Madresfield Court

Plate 193. An Unknown Man, aged 31 in 1638, by Laurence Hilliard
Plate 194. An Unknown Man, aged 30 in 1612, by Laurence Hilliard (?)

(*Pls. 192, 193*), round off the idea we get of the talent of this artist who is more interesting to us as the son of his father than as a master in his own right. Two portraits in the Buccleuch Collection may or may not be by his hand, Nos. 9/10 (*Pl 194*), and 9/3. They are earlier in date, one of 1611 and the other of 1612, but they are weaker than the signed examples of his work.

ISAAC OLIVER

From an artistic point of view the most important pupil of Hilliard was Isaac Oliver. He was born in France, at Rouen, the son of a goldsmith and pewterer who, a Huguenot, came to this country in 1568. The exact date of his birth is not known. It seems likely that he was only three or four years old when his father brought him to London, or even still younger. But Vertue assumed that he was born about ten years earlier. Considering, however, the average number of years, seven or thereabouts, which a young man spent in apprenticeship, the age when he entered it—being 13 to 15 years—and the approximate date of Oliver's earliest signed and independent miniatures which fall in the late 'eighties, the date of his birth comes nearer to 1565.

Hilliard's Contemporaries, Followers and Pupils

Very little has been found that would shed new light on his life by looking through the documents which yielded so much new evidence of Hilliard's career. No trace of him or of his father could be discovered in the Minutes of the Goldsmiths' Company. No indenture of Isaac entering Hilliard's workshop as an apprentice has survived. Yet there is indisputable evidence to be gleaned from Haydocke,[1] that "Mr. Isaac Oliver" was Hilliard's "scholar for limming" and mirrored his master's "true and lively Image". Isaac's style, too, especially in his earlier works, corroborates this theory. But in Oliver's case this only concerns the miniatures, and from the absence of his name in the documents of the Goldsmiths' Company it may be inferred that he did not train as a goldsmith. His style is founded rather on the technique and manner of painting in large and it does not seem to appear difficult to imagine, as Vertue assumed, that he also painted oil portraits. He, too, attained great fame and in many contemporary writings he is praised and mentioned together with his master.[2]

All his life Oliver remained proud of his French nationality and only well on in his career did he become a British subject, namely at the end of 1606. From inscriptions on two of his miniatures it can be learned that he was abroad: a Dutch inscription round the *Unknown Man*, aged 59 in 1588, in the collection of the Queen of the Netherlands, leads to the conclusion that he was in the Netherlands at that time, and on the back of *Sir Arundell Talbot* it is recorded that he was in Venice in 1596. Both visits were of the greatest importance for the development of his style.

What is known about his official status as limner and what payments by the Crown to him are recorded in the Accounts can be summed up as follows.

Already during the last ten years of Queen Elizabeth's reign his miniatures became more and more popular. We know one miniature of the Queen which, though unfinished, shows a most realistic representation of her Majesty, which surely was not approved by her. But payments to Oliver are only recorded during the reign of James I. Hilliard remained the King's limner and Laurence was to follow him after his death. As a way out and to please a fancy of the Court, Isaac was attached in 1604 to Queen Anne's household and appointed "her Ma^tes painter for the Art of Lymning" with a fee of 40*l.*[3] "Mr Isacke Paynter" was moreover a member of Prince Henry's household and enjoyed the patronage of the art-loving prince. On 7 December 1612 he was present at his funeral.[4] There was so much work to be done in limning that each member of the royal family could favour his or her own artist. This ingenious

---

[1] See p. 46, *ante.*
[2] See pp. 46–7, *ante.*
[3] E. 101/437/8.
[4] *Tudor Artists*, pp. 133 and 179.

arrangement also explains—as far as I know—the complete absence of any miniature of the King by the hand of Oliver, and the profusion of his superb portraits of the Queen, the Princes and Princess Elizabeth.

Further payments to him are not as numerous as they were to Hilliard during the same period. In 1608/9 he was paid for three portraits of Prince Henry and in 1610/12 payments are recorded for several little and 'greate pictures'.[1] The last item is interesting, as it either refers to limnings of a large size or perhaps even to oil pictures. The sums he received would seem to confirm the latter suggestion: the wording of the document runs as follows:

> Mr. Isacke for three Pictures 32*l*. one greate Picture 34*l*. three other Pictures 30*l*. one greate and two little pictures 40*l*.

The usual fee Oliver had for a miniature was, according to the size, between 5*l*. 10*s*. and 10*l*. and if he received for "one greate Picture" 34*l*., the word "greate" surely means what it says and refers to an oil portrait. Further, if he was paid 40*l*. for one great and two little pictures, he probably got again payment of about 30*l*. for the painting in large and the 10*l*. served to settle his bill for two miniatures. Already Vertue was convinced that Oliver had painted oil portraits and with the evidence of the document just mentioned any doubt that might still linger is dispelled.

There are various Exchequer books stating accounts of money disbursed by Sir David Murray for the use of Prince Henry's "Privie Purse" in which Oliver's name is mentioned. One, e.g., from 24 June 1608 to 29 September 1609, lists payments to "Izak the paynter" for Prince Henry's picture for which he received in each case 5*l*. 10*s*.[2] There is also money due to Oliver for a portrait miniature he painted in 1612/13 of Princess Elizabeth, as appears from Lord Harrington's account book.[3] In 1617 he was paid for four pictures drawn for Prince Charles and after his death, on 25 February 1618, his widow received 40*l*. for "three pictures by him made and delivered to the Prince".[4]

Of his private life we do not know much, though we have a pretty clear idea who were his friends. When his father came over to this country in 1568, Isaac, as a child, resided with his parents in "Mr. Harrison's house" in "Fletlane".[5] In 1597 he was assessed at 4*l*., when he resided in Cornhill Ward and in the Parish of St Peter and St Michael's.[6] According to his will he lived at the end of his life in the parish of St Anne's, Blackfriars.

Isaac Oliver married apparently three times, and what we know about his wives and relations points to his close connection with a circle of mainly Flemish

---

[1] E. 351/2794.
[2] E. 101/433/8.
[3] E. 407/57(2)
[4] *Tudor Artists*, p. 180.
[5] Hug. Soc., II, 425.
[6] E. 199/146/372.

artists residing in this country and having frequently intermarried. They were painters of great renown and had to fulfil tasks of importance for the Crown: the Gheeraerts, father and son, John de Critz the elder, and Robert Peake the elder and his son, who were probably Englishmen. With these artists Oliver joined hands, and though none of them seems actually to have painted miniatures, their portraits on a life-size scale appear fairly alike. We do not know the name of Oliver's first wife, but she was the mother of his gifted son Peter, who was born about 1594, and also reached great fame as a miniaturist. In 1602 Isaac married, as his second wife, Sara Gheeraerts, the daughter of Susanna de Critz and the elder Gheeraerts. A third wife, called Elizabeth, survived him, and she may have been somehow acquainted with or related to Nicasius Russell, a goldsmith, whose wife was the sister of Cornelius Jonson, yet another famous painter of Flemish origin. When in 1616 Jonson's son was born Oliver stood godfather to him, and in 1618 his widow was god-mother to another son of this family.[1]

In his will of 4 June 1617[2] he divided his goods into two parts

> except all my drawings allready finished and unfinished and lymning pictures, be they historyes, storyes, or any thing of lymning whatsoever of my owne hande worke as yet unfinished; all which I give and bequeathe to my eldest sonne Peter, yf he shall live and exercise that arte or science which he and I nowe doe. . .

Amongst his own limnings, clearly indicated as such, he also mentions stories and historical subjects, and Oliver had thus, as we shall see later, innovated a new kind of limning that, continued by his son, found great favour with Charles I. With pictures he deals differently; he directs in his will:

> that my sayed sonne Peter shall have the first proffer of the sale of my pictures that shalbe soulde and fyve shillinges in a pound cheaper then any will give for them.

Though Oliver did not classify the pictures as by his own hand, he assumed that they were of special interest to his eldest son and he clearly distinguished them from his miniatures. He was buried on 2 October 1617 in St Anne's and his will was proved on 30 October 1617.

In appreciating Oliver's career as a miniaturist, it is best to follow Mr. Reynolds' suggestion of a division into three phases.[3] The first period would reach to the year 1596, when Oliver visited Venice. The style of miniatures dating from those early years is dominated by Hilliard's influence combined with a strongly Flemish flavour. The second period starts with his stay in Italy in 1596,[4] and the third begins with his return to England.

Up to now the earliest dated and signed Oliver had been held to be an

---

[1] Reynolds, *Catalogue*, 1947, p. 12.   [2] P.C.C., 93 Weldon.
[3] Reynolds, *Miniatures*, p. 24ff.   [4] See p. 233, *ante*.

Unknown Man, aged 59 in 1588, in the collection of the Queen of the Nether-lands. But, recently, a most charming miniature of an *Unknown Girl (Pl. 195),* aged 20 in 1587, has been discovered in a drawer at Drumlanrig Castle, which had escaped even Sir Basil Long's attention. The oval portrait, rather big in size, is signed with the usual monogram Ⓞ in gold on a blue ground and is framed by a contemporary black frame. The three-quarter length of the slender young figure allows both hands to be shown: one is resting on the hip, the other holding a glove; the arm, hanging down, is slightly cut off by the frame. The hands are small but well modelled and in this as in various other respects, in composition, type, and modelling, it comes nearest to the two *Unknown Girls* dated 1590, in the Victoria and Albert Museum. They were first attributed to Oliver by Mr. Winter, and though unsigned, are undoubtedly by him. As often in this early group, the gold lettering, not quite so flourished and elegant as that by Hilliard, gives a decorative paraphrase of the oval surround. The position of the dainty face, turned three-quarter to the left with eyes looking in the opposite direction, the minute detail of the costume, the ruff and chemise are of a lovely pale grey contrasting with the dark colouring of the dress; all this accords with the style of his master. But the detailed rendering of the face, extremely small in proportion, already reveals the different approach of this still young but realistic painter. The round face is set off from the neck by two short dark strokes on either side, and the continuous clear middle line of the mouth, that invariably appears on Hilliard's miniatures, is here also replaced by one strong dab of colour to emphasise the left end of the mouth and to give a more lively expression. The same applies to the touch of shade under the nose and the eyes. Altogether, the costume, the figure itself and the more rounded, protruding, less abstract and decorative appearance is decidedly Flemish. The fact is that it becomes clear, right from the outset of Oliver's career, that his conception of art, though schooled by the Queen's limner, does not derive from manuscript illumination and goldsmith's work, but from painting in large in the more realistic Flemish style.

This contrast between the two masters is still better exemplified by comparing the *Unknown Youth* of *c.* 1588, at Madresfield Court *(Pl. 196)* with the portrait of the same sitter at Belvoir Castle[1] *(Pl. 78).* The former is probably a copy Oliver made of the latter miniature by Hilliard and the same traits of distinc-tion again become visible: one needs only compare the rendering of the mouth and the eyes or the treatment of the hair on both portraits and one realises that Oliver, in spite of all similarities with his master, prefers soft tone, where Hilliard had put down a clear, continuous line.

[1] See p. 103, *ante.* Reynolds, *Catalogue,* 1947, Nos. 123 and 33.

Plate 195. An Unknown Girl, aged 20 in 1587, by Isaac Oliver

Returning to the *Unknown Girl*, aged 20 in 1587, at Drumlanrig Castle, the *Unknown Woman* in the collection of the Queen of the Netherlands[1] is very near in style and seems even to represent the same person, though she appears on this miniature slightly older. Again, the signed and dated *Unknown Man*, aged 59 in 1588 (*Pl. 197*), in the same collection, clearly represents Oliver's style of that early period. The well modelled head, topped by a high black

Plate 196.   An Unknown Youth, by
Isaac Oliver (?), *c.* 1588

Plate 198.   An Unknown Man, formerly
wrongly called Self-Portrait by Isaac
Oliver

hat, is solidly built up, resting on the precisely defined ruff, and the foreshortened side of the face, turned three-quarter to the right, is covered by a darker shade and tone, in contrast to a lighter blue background, which brings the head forward in a definite and rounded manner. This type of modelling can also be seen on the impressive formerly wrongly called *Self-Portrait* (*Pl. 198*), again in the same collection, which according to costume and style must have been painted between 1588 and 1590.[2] Similar too is *An Unknown Man* aged 27 in 1590 (*Pl. 199*) in the Victoria and Albert Museum.[3] In this portrait one clearly formed hand is seen, just as both hands appear in the portraits of the *Unknown Girl*, aged 5, and the *Unknown Girl*, aged 4 (*Pl. 200*), of the same year. All have a splendid gold lettering running round the figures, as is usual on the miniatures of that period.

[1] Frits Lugt, *Le Portrait-miniature*, . . . 1917, Fig. 6. Reynolds, *Catalogue*, 1947, No. 122.
[2] Reynolds, *Catalogue*, 1947, No. 134.
[3] Winter, *Eliz. Miniatures*, Pl. No. IX, Reynolds, *Catalogue*, 1947, No. 131.

Two Self-Portraits, one in the collection of the Earl of Derby, the other in the Royal Collection at Windsor Castle, belong to the same period, that is

Plate 197. An Unknown Man, aged 59
in 1588, by Isaac Oliver

Plate 199. An Unknown Man, aged 27 in 1590, by Isaac Oliver
Plate 200. An Unknown Girl, aged 4 in 1590, by Isaac Oliver

to say, between 1590 and 1595.[1] By comparing them with a drawing in the Fitzwilliam Museum, which clearly represents a *Self-Portrait* (*Pl. 201*), the identity of the miniatures seems established without doubt.

[1] Reynolds, *Catalogue*, 1947, Nos. 135 and 136.

Plate 201. Self-Portrait by Isaac Oliver, drawing

One of the most important larger miniatures also belongs to the period round the year 1590.[1] It is said to be *Sir Philip Sidney* (*Pl. 202*), but age and costume make this not very likely. It is beautifully painted and represents

[1] Reynolds, *Catalogue*, 1947, No. 124. Winter, *ibid.*, Pl. VIII.

the full-length figure of a young man, sitting at the foot of a tree, against which he is leaning in an open landscape. The colouring is light and varied and the fluent touch of the modelling of the face is similar to that which Oliver applied

Plate 202. An Unknown Man, formerly called Sir Philip Sidney, by Isaac Oliver, *c.* 1590

to such portraits as the *Supposed Self-Portrait*. Figure and landscape again reveal a strong Flemish character. The scenery has been described as representing either Wilton or Penshurst, but neither can be recognised. It is, in fact, a purely imaginary landscape, which is clearly based on and copied from an engraving appearing in one of those Flemish pattern books that circulated in this country.[1]

An Elizabethan Hunting Party in the collection of Count Holstein-Ledreborg, a miniature of a large rectangular size, belongs to the same period of approxi-

Plate *203*. An Unknown
Lady by Isaac Oliver

Plate *204*. Called Mrs.
Holland by Isaac Oliver

Plate *205*. An Unknown Woman
by Isaac Oliver, 1585–95

mately 1590. It is again Flemish-inspired and the scheme of the landscape background, filled with a great number of figures, in smaller and larger sizes, is crowded together and interspersed with small genre-like scenes describing a boar-hunt and such-like events; this miniature can best be linked with similar figure- and landscape paintings by Gillis van Coninxloo. It is of an exceedingly

[1] See p. 223, *ante.*

fresh conception, in the foreground portrait-like, and toning in very well with the general style of Oliver's other miniatures.

There are some delightful miniatures by Oliver, painted between 1590 and 1596: some charming portraits of women, such as an *Unknown Lady* at Windsor, and the still more lively *Unknown Lady* in the Fitzwilliam Museum (*Pl. 203*), both very much alike, wearing tall hats, and again resembling the Flemish type of the *Young Girl* in 1587, and further, *Called Mrs. Holland* (*Pl. 204*), formerly in the Sotheby

Plate 206. Called George Clifford, 3rd Earl of Cumberland, by Isaac Oliver, *c.* 1595

Plate 207. An Unknown Man by Isaac Oliver, c. 1595

Plate 208. Robert Devereux, 2nd Earl of Essex, by Isaac Oliver

Collection, and the *Unknown Woman* (*Pl. 205*) in the collection of the queen of the Netherlands, which clearly shows Oliver's mature style of characterisation.

Some portraits of men, while still being influenced by Hilliard's technique, grow gradually more sensitive and delicate, as can be seen on the two signed portraits of *George Clifford*, one wearing a hat (*Pl. 206*), and one without, in Stockholm[1], and finally the two excellent miniatures of *An Unknown Man* in the Fitzwilliam (*Pl. 207*), and the bearded *Essex* at Windsor (*Pl. 208*).

[1] Repr. Reynolds, *Conn. Guide*, Pl. 75 B.

The excellent portrait of *Sir Arundel Talbot* (*Pl. 209*), of 1596, dated and inscribed by the artist at the back as follows: "*adi. 13. Magio. 1596. In Venetia. Fecit m. Isacq oliuiero Francese 10.*", is the culminating work of the vital and realistic period. Oliver's stay in Venice, which is thus documented, starts a more mellow-toned phase of his development.

Plate 209.   Sir Arundel Talbot by Isaac Oliver, 1596

Owing to the Venetian influence, this second period shows a new trend in Oliver's work: his miniatures are further away from Hilliard and the realistic Flemish conception and the scale of tone and colour is more adapted to what he had seen in the city surrounded by water and light. His way of characterisation too shows that he had absorbed a more subdued and subtle method. Grey backgrounds are often used and thus a different approach to tone is achieved.

In three portraits of women, the three-quarter turning to the left, with eyes looking in the opposite direction, still remains, just as his characteristic rendering of the mouth with the emphasis laid on the raising of the corners. They are *Catherine Knevet*, Countess of Suffolk, in the collection of the Duke of Buccleuch (*Pl. 210*); *An Unknown Lady*, called Frances Walsingham, Countess of Essex, in the same collection (No. IX/38)[1], and the slightly more linear *Called Elizabeth Bruges*, Lady Kennedy (*Pl. 211*), at Welbeck Abbey. All three were painted *c.* 1600. The unfinished, surprisingly realistic *Elizabeth I* in the

[1] Reynolds, *Catalogue*, 1947, No. 162, repr. pl. XXXIV.

Victoria and Albert Museum (*Pl. 212*) fits in well with this group. There are also, dating from the opening years of the seventeenth century, some interesting portraits of male personalities, such as one called *Robert Devereux*

Plate 210.   Catherine Knevet, Countess of Suffolk, by Isaac Oliver, *c.* 1600
Plate 211.   Called Elizabeth Bruges, Lady Kennedy, by Isaac Oliver, *c.* 1600

Plate 212.   Queen Elizabeth I, by Isaac Oliver, *c.* 1600

245

Earl of Essex (*Pl. 213*), in the Mauritshuis, or the signed *An Unknown Man*, in the Fitzwilliam Museum (*Pl. 214*), which perhaps represents the 9th Earl of

Plate 213. Robert Devereux, 2nd Earl of Essex, by Isaac Oliver

Plate 214. An Unknown Man, perhaps the 9th Earl of Northumberland, by Isaac Oliver

Plate 215. Called a Member of the Fanshawe Family of Ware Park, aged 43 in 1608, by Isaac Oliver

Northumberland. In addition, there is the even more softly treated portrait *Called a Member of the Fanshawe Family of Ware Park* (*Pl. 215*), aged 43 in 1608, in the collection of Mr. Brinsley Ford.

Plate 216. Lucy Harington, Countess of
Bedford, by Isaac Oliver,
c. 1605

The mature style of Isaac Oliver, as it appears in this period, is best illustrated by two splendid circular miniatures, five inches in diameter, representing well-known ladies of the Court: *Lucy Harington*, Countess of Bedford, in the Fitzwilliam Museum (*Pl. 216*), and *Frances Howard*, Countess of Essex and Som-

Plate 217. Anne of Denmark by Isaac Oliver, *c.* 1610

Plate 218. Henry Frederick, Prince of Wales, by Isaac Oliver

erset, in the collection of the Earl of Derby. In these two lovely miniature portraits, on a slightly bigger scale, Oliver has found his own personal solution of the Mannerist style. Without actually copying anything Italian, he gives two typically English portraits and reacts to the spirit of the age by choosing a sophisticated in-between colour scheme, by emphasising the fleeting moment in the expression of the face, by bringing plenty of movement into the whirling sweep of veils and other parts of the garment, and by letting the hands move in the typically Mannerist gestures. This, his personal interpretation, can only be compared with Hilliard's *Lady Elizabeth Stanley*, in which the older Master had also expressed his conception of the contemporary movement.

The last decade of Oliver's life was mainly devoted to the exacting task of working for Queen Anne of Denmark and her children, especially for the young, only short-lived, patron of the arts, Prince Henry Frederick. Innumerable portraits of the royal family by Oliver have come down to us and only a few can be mentioned in this connection: there are the two profile portraits, of

Plate 219. Elizabeth of Bohemia, by Isaac Oliver

Plate 220. Anne of Denmark, by Isaac Oliver, *c.* 1610

Prince Henry Frederick, wearing a Roman costume, at Cambridge[1] and *Anne of Denmark*, in a masque costume, as it may have been designed by Inigo Jones for the Court revels at Windsor (*Pl. 217*). They testify to Oliver's more ambitious rendering of the portrait, reflecting the classic tradition of entertainment at the Jacobean Court. Further, most ambitious of all, the rectangular *Prince Henry Frederick*, in armour, standing in front of a curtain, opening on to a landscape view with tents and soldiers on the right, at Windsor, and the very lively smaller portrait of the same sitter, also in the Royal Collection (*Pl. 218*). The latter is an excellent example of Oliver's superior ability to model a face in the round. There is also the lovely signed bust portrait of *Elizabeth of Bohemia*, at Windsor (*Pl. 219*), and finally, the dignified and perhaps grandest likeness of *Anne of Denmark*, formerly in the Sotheby Collection and now in the National Portrait Gallery (*Pl. 220*). The precision of detail, as taught by Hilliard, combined with the more European modelling, the complexity of movement in the hand, and the tonal treatment of the hair and the lace are admirable.

[1] Repr. in colour, Winter, *Eliz. Miniatures*, pl. XIVa. Reynolds, *Catalogue* 1947, No. 180.

Plate 221.   An Unknown Man, by Isaac
Oliver *c.* 1610

Plate 222.   Dr. Donne, by Isaac Oliver, 1616

Plate 223.   Richard Sackville, 3rd Earl of Dorset, by Isaac Oliver

Gradually Oliver's male portraits become more poignant and freer in treatment: *An Unknown Man* with his curly hair in the Fitzwilliam Museum (*Pl. 221*) is a good example of this late style. Most impressive too is the concentrated and serious *Dr. Donne* signed and dated 1616 (*Pl. 222*), at Windsor, and the bust portrait of *Richard Sackville*, 3rd Earl of Dorset, at Cambridge (*Pl. 223*). The latter leads to the grand rectangular miniature full-length portrait of the same sitter in the Victoria and Albert Museum,[1] standing in an interior and thus reflecting contemporary taste. The latter, like the magnificent, rectangular *Edward Herbert*, 1st Baron Herbert of Cherbury (*Pl. 224*), in the collection of the Earl of Powis, reposing in a wooded landscape populated with soldiers and

Plate 226. The Prodigal Son, by Isaac Oliver

horses, bridges over to the concept of the Flemish painters in oils, who were residing in this country and were connected with the name of Marcus Gheeraerts the Younger, who happened to be Oliver's brother-in-law.

It remains to say a few words about Oliver's more Italian and definitely Parmiggianesque manner that is evident in his last productions, especially in his more historical limnings. Though the famous *The Burial of Christ* has disappeared, two drawings, one in the British Museum and one in the Fitzwilliam Museum, testify to this influence. A signed sheet of drawn studies in the Fitzwilliam Museum (*Pl. 225*) confirms this impression. Such miniatures as the *Prodigal Son* (*Pl. 226*) at Welbeck Abbey or *The Head of Christ* in the Victoria and

[1] Repr. in colour. Winter, *Eliz. Miniatures*, pl. XV. Reynolds, *Catalogue*, 1947, No. 195.

Plate 224.   Edward Herbert, 1st Baron Herbert of Cherbury, by Isaac Oliver

Plate 225. Sheet of Sketches, by Isaac Oliver, drawing

Albert Museum are definitely related to contemporary Italian Mannerist paintings of a religious order and have nothing to do any more with the portrait limnings of the Hilliard tradition.

ROWLAND LOCKEY

As a young boy, Rowland Lockey became, as we have seen,[1] apprenticed to Nicholas Hilliard for the term of eight years from Michaelmas 1581. This term would bring us to 1589 and, unfortunately, just at this period a gap occurs in the Minutes of the Goldsmiths' Company. In the absence of evidence to the contrary, it may be assumed that Lockey's apprenticeship took its normal course and that he became a freeman with the Company at about that time. His father, Leonard Lockey, was a crossbow-maker and had a house in Fleet Street, in the Parish of St. Bride's. There is documentary proof that Rowland was a freeman by 1600. In the Apprentice Book of the Goldsmiths' Company (1578–1648)[2] it is stated that his brother Nicholas became his apprentice:

> Memorandum that I Nickholas Locky, sonne of Lennarde Lockey of Lonndonne, armerar put myself prentis to Rollaunde Lockey for 8 years beginning Midsummer 1600.

About the relationship between Rowland and Nicholas, as indeed about both their artistic activities and the data of their lives, we were completely in the dark until quite recently, when contemporary evidence and other documentary material has been found which shed a new light on artists who were so far only known by name.[3] A short review of the new details which have come to light is given here.

It appears that by 1592 Rowland was still in close contact with Hilliard, for both their names are strangely coupled in an account book of Elizabeth, Countess of Shrewsbury, for the years 1591 to 1597.[4] Mention is made of three "pictures" which, according to the price, must be assumed to have been miniatures, two of a bigger size and one of smaller dimensions. The clerk who drew up the account was apparently not quite clear about the authorship of these two artists with regards to those miniatures and I therefore give the quotation with the corrections, the crossed out words being in brackets:

---

[1] See p. 18, *ante*.

[2] P. 131.

[3] See Otto Kurz, "Rowland Locky", *Burl. Mag.*, XCIX (1957), pp. 13–16; and two letters by Professor Waterhouse and myself, *ibid.*, p. 60.

[4] MS. 7, fol. 30. Mr. T. S. Wragge kindly drew my attention to these documents.

July 24th 1592.
Itm geven the XXVII th of Julye To one Mr Hilliard for the drawing of one
[Twoe] Pictur[s] [a gratter and a Lesser fortye shillng]   40s.
Itm geven vnto the same Mr Hilliard twentie shillinges   20s.
Itm more vnto one Rowland for the drawinge of one other [twoe] pictur[s] fortye
shilling   40s.

It is evident that Hilliard thus introduced his former apprentice and pupil
to Bess of Hardwick and established a connection for Rowland Lockey
which later on became highly lucrative.

In an account book of Sir William Cavendish, 2nd husband of Bess of
Hardwick, covering the years 1608 to 1613,[1] Rowland Lockey is constantly
mentioned, and I here give these records of payments in full:

Aug. 1609. (fol. 73)
To Mr Lockey in parte for makinge the pictures   3l. 6s. 8d.
3 Aug. 1609. (fol. 96)
for 12 ells of Canvas for pictures at 3s. 4d. ye elle   40s.
to Mr Rowland Lockey in parte for drawinge 15 pictures accordinge to his note
under his hand   10l.
Sept. 1609. (fol. 142)
for carriage of twoe venison pasties to Mrs Lockey   7s. 10d.
31 Oct. 1609. (fol. 143)
to Mr Lockey in full for drawinge 16 pictures besides 15l. paid by mee [Henry
Travice] heere [i.e., London]+3l. 6s. 8d. to him in the Contrey   15l.
Sept. 1609. (fol. 145)
To the Paynter boy that brought Mr John's Picture   1s.
Given by my Lo: to Mr Lockey's man   1s.
Sept. 1609. (fol. 146)
Thre Porters that broughte pictures from Mr. Lockey   1s. 6d.
do. (fol. 147)
Given by my Lord to Three Paynters 10s. to Richard Potter a joyner for 18 frames
for Pictures and for hinges as by his bill   3l. 16s. 5d.
To Mr Lockey for Mr Cavendishes Picture, my La: Grace, my Lo: firste wife, for
Canvas and for gildinge all the frames of the Pictures made at Hardwicke accord-
inge to his bill   8l.
Jan. 1609/10. (fol. 149)
To Mr Lockeyes man for goinge wth the Queene of Scotts Picture to my Lo: of
Arundells and twoe Porters to carry it   3s.
Dec. 1612. (fol. 307)
For three ells vj of watchett taffyty sarcenett to cover pictures at 8s. ye ell   1l. 8s.
do.
To Mr Lockey For draweing Sr Willm Maynard and his wives pictures and given
to his men—12d.   7l. 1s.

[1] Vol. 29.

c. 21 June 1613. (fol. 320)

To Mr Lockey's men that brought the Scotche queenes picture   2*s.*
do.

To Mr Lockey for the Scotche Queenes picture presented to my lord privy seale
nyne pounds   9*l.*

For the frame and guilding it   10*s.*

Though it is perhaps too early, in the present state of our knowledge, to attempt an identification of certain portraits at Hardwick with those mentioned in this account, it is interesting to be thus faced with the commission, entrusted to one painter alone, to produce what amounts more or less to a complete Portrait Gallery of the family of Bess of Hardwick, which had to be housed in the specially built Picture Gallery in the Hall. There can be no doubt that the payments, though relatively small, are made for oil paintings in large, otherwise canvas or frames or heavy carriages would not be listed. It is quite probable that less was to be paid for the single picture because of the enormous number of portraits that had to be manufactured and it seems that in some cases, as perhaps in the portrait of *Mary, Queen of Scots*, the pattern of a likeness by another painter was adopted and even copied. There is then documentary proof that Lockey painted miniatures in 1592 and oils between 1608 and 1613 for Hardwick Hall.

Apart from being a miniaturist and a painter of life-size pictures, Rowland Lockey was a practising goldsmith and an active member of the Goldsmiths' Company. On 23 September 1611[1] he and "five of the yeomanrie" were appointed by the Wardens

> to attend wth others in gownes at the Guildhall on the Lord Maiors daye for the serving up of the Dynner, to be of them in all 24.

On 28 October in the same year he is mentioned as one of the "Rich Batchellers".[2] On 18 December 1612 Rowland Lockey presented one "Raphe Blackmore" as his apprentice.[3] On 24 January 1613/14 Lockey and other members of the Company were "though fitt to be receaved into the clothing they refused to accept thereof but desired to be spared".[4] However, three weeks later Lockey is mentioned amongst 42 freemen, "that were to be taken into the clothing" and their places were appointed.[5] But Rowland's life drew to a close and soon afterwards, on 21 June 1616, "Giles Allen delivered a beere boule of 18 oz: 2d wt of the guift of Rowland Lockey deceased, late one of the clothing of this Companie."[6] One John Langton, who had become Lockey's apprentice

---

[1] Book P, pt. I, July 1611–Jan. 1617, p. 27.   [2] *Ibid.*, p. 41.
[3] *Ibid.*, p. 106.   [4] *Ibid.*, p. 145.
[5] *Ibid.*, p. 151.   [6] *Ibid.*, p. 248.

in 1607, was made a freeman of the Company in October 1616, shortly after his master's death.[1] With that entry Lockey's name disappears from the Minutes of the Goldsmiths' Company.

When "Rowland Lockey, Citizen and Gouldsmith of London" made his will on 15 February 1615/16, he resided within the parish of St. Dunstan's in the West, but according to Churchwarden Accounts for Westminster, he was in 1605/6 in residence in St. Martin-in-the-Fields, when 4s. was paid by "Rouland Lockey".

In his will[2] he made his wife Martha executrix of his testament and left everything, certain legacies excepted, to her. It emerges clearly from the will that Nicholas Lockey, who, it may be remembered, had entered Rowland's workshop as an apprentice in 1600, was his brother, a fact which had not been known hitherto.[3] This Nicholas was apparently very much younger than Rowland and it would seem that he was mainly active as a painter—he became a member of the Painter-Stainers' Company—and there is no trace, as far as I know, of his having practised the craft of the goldsmith.

The most interesting bequests of Rowland's will run as follows:

20s. is to be given to his appentice John Langton, who, as we have seen, became a freeman after Lockey's death.

Item I give vnto my Brother Nicholas Lockey all my Italian Printes and all my plasters...

Rowland apparently realised that his collection which probably contained classic patterns would prove most useful to Nicholas, his younger brother, who was also a painter.

Item I give to my Brother Nicholas Lockey the lease of the house wherein my father dwelled in Fleete lane, . .

Thus, he wanted the tradition to be carried on. The testator also bequeathed 20s. to his "loving friend John Davis . . . to make him a Ringe". He also made him one of the overseers of his will. Dr. Kurz has shown that the poet and writing-master John Davies of Hereford had written a poem in praise of Lockey and the "loving friend John Davis", mentioned in the will, can therefore be identified with this well-known author of "The Scourge of Folly", a collection of epigrams, one of which is addressed to no less important a personality than "Mr Will. Shakespeare".

[1] *Ibid.*, p. 268.
[2] P.C.C., 26 Cope. See Burl. Mag., XCIX (1957), p. 60.
[3] See Dr. Kurz *loc. cit.*, and p. 254, *ante*.

Epigram 258 may be repeated here:

To the rare Painter mine approoved friend, and good neighbor, M. Row: Locky.
>   As Nature made; so, thou dost make my Face
>   Yet, with a better, and a worser grace.
>   With better; sith thy Worke hath glory got:
>   With worse; sith thou giv'st life that moves it not.
>   Yet, when crosse-Fortune makes me move the Brow,
>   Thine, without motion, better farre doth show.
>   But by ill fortune (oft) though marr'd it bee,
>   It had good fortune to be made by Thee:
>   For, thou dost Fortunes furrowes quite out-strike,
>   And, mak'st it in all fortunes, looke alike.

A deep appreciation for the sympathetic and able portrait painter is expressed in this epigram, and one could not wish for a better contemporary testimonial to Lockey's artistic abilities. Both Francis Meres and Richard Haydocke give Lockey's name amongst the best contemporary English painters. The latter gives the Christian name as Rowland and credits him with "oil and limning in some measure". Again, Edward Norgate speaks of Rowland Lockey, the disciple of Hilliard, who practised the technique of crayon drawing.[1] There is indeed ample proof of Lockey's versatility as an artist.

More important, however, is what William Burton, the antiquary (1575–1645) says about Lockey in his notes,[2] as it leads to the actual identification of some examples of his work:

> Nicholas Hilliard . . . left . . . another expert scholler, Mr Rowland Lockey (one whom I knew very well when he dwelt in Fleet-street), who was both skilful in limning and in oil-works and perspectives; at whose house I once saw a neat piece in oil, containing in one table the picture of Sir John More, a judge of the king's bench, temp. Henry VIII, and of his wife; and of Sir Thomas More, lord chancellor, his son, and his wife; and of all the lineal heirs male descended from them; together with each man's wife, until that present year living.

This description seems to refer to the oil group portrait in the National Portrait Gallery, but also to the miniature version, formerly in the Sotheby Collection (*Pl. 227*).[3] Both the oil painting and the miniature make use of Holbein's group portrait of the family of Sir Thomas More, the original of which is lost and only the drawing in Bale has survived, but the important point for the reassessment of Lockey is his addition of likenesses of younger members of the family, giving us a good idea of his personal style. Generally speaking, the

---

[1] *Miniatura*, p. 72. See p. 220, *ante*.
[2] *Descriptions of Leicestershire* in J. Nichols, *History and Antiquities*, p. 490. Kurz, p. 15.
[3] Sotheby's, 11 Oct. 1955, Lot 67. Now in Col. of The Rev. and Mrs. J. I. Strickland.

Plate 227. Sir Thomas More and his Family, by Rowland Lockey, c. 1600

259

composition of the miniature agrees with that of the oil painting, the figures are posing alike, but there is a slight difference in the turning of the face of Anne, wife of John More, who is placed between Sir John and Sir Thomas, and is conceived in a more frontal position. One of the younger generation, John, represented between his parents, grandchildren of Sir Thomas, is bearded on the miniature, but clean-shaven on the painting. The main difference,

Plate 228. An Unknown Lady with a Dog, by Rowland Lockey (?)

however, lies in the background. The miniature gives a much clearer representation of the room, which is seen in perspective with foreshortened columns, a subdivided ceiling is visible, the figure of More's jester, Henry Patenson, is added as pushing the green curtain aside and an archway, on the right, opens on to a lovely garden view, probably identical with the garden of Sir Thomas

More's house at Chelsea. Altogether, the detailed rendering of the curtains and the surrounding, the much clearer treatment of the figures and their costumes, and the more spatial conception of the interior make the miniature superior in quality to the oil painting, and if one considers the gold lettering giving a key to the identities of the sitters, it would appear rather as the original version and not as a replica as has been suggested. Anyhow, it is a most charming work of art, of an extremely high standard, and one that shows Hilliard's influence in the minute care for clearly formulated features, and adds a certain atmosphere which may be claimed to be Lockey's own.

Plate 229.　An Unknown Man, by Rowland Lockey (?)

Plate 230.　Called Lady Hay, perhaps by Rowland Lockey

The question arises whether other miniatures which are now generally ascribed to "Hilliard's School" in various collections, might, on the strength of their similarity with the limning of *Sir Thomas More's family*, be ascribed to Rowland Lockey. Two of these works closely resemble Lockey's style, as already noted by Mr. Reynolds:[1] one is the lovely three-quarter length of *An Unknown Lady* (*Pl. 228*), standing in front of a curtain, opening into a landscape view, with a dog at her side, in the National Gallery of Victoria at Melbourne, a most charming and impressive portrait; the other is *An Unknown Man* (*Pl. 229*), wearing a bold hat and a stiffly piped ruff, at Windsor. This very well executed miniature certainly shows a particularly precise manner of modelling related to the group portrait and different from that usually seen on either Hilliard's or Oliver's works. I also think that the lovely Lady, *Called*

[1] *Conn. Guide*, p. 134, pl. 76(b). MSS. Cat. of the Royal Collection, No. 19.

Lady Hay (*Pl. 230*), from the Sotheby Collection[1] might be from Rowland Lockey's hand.

As to oils, the question of attribution is more difficult and the collection at Hardwick Hall, though well documented, presents problems which can only be

Plate 231. An Unknown Gentle-man, by John Bettes II (?), 1580, Oil on vellum

solved by further lengthy research. However, the oil portrait of Elizabeth, Countess of Shrewsbury appears to be near in style to what is known to be Lockey's miniature manner. The difficulty lies in the fact that Lockey, as in the More family portrait, copied partly or wholly from earlier pictures. An excellent example of this his method is *Margaret, Lady Beaufort*, signed at the back, at St. John's, Cambridge, which Mr. Goodison has published.[2] From all the documentary evidence and from the few examples of miniatures and oils that can be attributed to Rowland Lockey with more or less certainty, it would appear that he was a worthy disciple of his great master and an artist who enjoyed considerable esteem during his lifetime. It is to be hoped that further research will reveal more of this, at present, elusive personality.

[1] Called Hilliard's School. Lot 58.
[2] "Cambridge Portraits—I", *Connoisseur*, XXXIX, pp. 213–18, pl. 3.

JOHN BETTES II

There is still some confusion about this artist's name, John Bettes, and it has to be assumed that there were two painters of that name.[1] John Bettes I apparently died before 1576 and does not interest us in this connection. John Bettes II, however, was supposed to have been a pupil of Hilliard's and may be identified with a "picture maker" who was resident in Grub Street in 1599. Francis Meres, in 1598, gives his name as that of one of the best-known contemporary English painters and couples it with that of "Thomas Bettes". Haydock too mentions a limner of that name, but this reference is more likely to the older John Bettes. That is all the documentary evidence which is available at the present moment.

As to an attribution of work to John Bettes II, we are on even less safe ground. The letter B or the monogram I.B., appearing on a miniature and an oil portrait, have given some support to a tentative suggestion, but not one seems to fit the other. There is a well-painted oil miniature of a forceful, bearded man, wearing a black cap and a doublet of the same colour with a white close fitting ruff, at Drumlanrig Castle (*Pl. 231*), which is dated 1580 and signed with the

Plate 232. Sir Francis Walsingham, by John Bettes II (?)

Plate 233. Catherine de Balzac, Duchess of Lennox, by John Bettes (?)

monogram B. It was attributed to John Bettes. It is of good quality and clearly in the Holbein tradition. Thus, it seems to continue the style of the oil portrait of *A Man in a black cap*, in the Tate Gallery, of 1545, which is dated and inscribed at the back, definitely under the name of John Bettes, who, however, is more likely to be the older of the two artists. Three other miniatures in the collection

[1] *Burl. Mag.*, XCIII (1951), p. 45. *Tudor Artists*, pp. 153-4.

Plate 234. An Unknown Girl, by John Bettes II (?), 1587, oil on panel

of the Duke of Buccleuch were attributed to what must be John Bettes II, but as Sir Basil Long has pointed out[1] they are surely by different hands. One *Called Robert Devereux, Earl of Essex*, can be attributed to Isaac Oliver. *Sir Francis Walsingham* (*Pl. 232*), is most charming in its precise execution, and so is the still more linear treatment of *Catherine de Balzac*, Duchess of Lennox (*Pl. 233*). The most attractive attribution to John Bettes II is, however, the enchanting, truly Elizabethan portrait in large, which is signed I.B. and inscribed *Ætatis Suae 20, 1587*[2] (*Pl. 234*), where the intricate pattern of the standing wheel-shaped collar creates a splendid basis for the light-coloured enamelled face. Huge sleeves of a lovely embroidered material complete the fascinating impression. The decorative effect and the flat but brilliantly shaded handling of face and figure are akin to Hilliard's manner and could very well be based on a training with him.

ARNOLD VAN BROUNCKHURST

Until quite recently this Flemish painter, who resided in this country from *c.* 1565 onwards and is reported to have been at the Scottish Court in 1580, was only known from documentary evidence. By an amazing stroke of luck one portrait, at least, dated and signed, has now been found; it might prove the key to this painter's *œuvre*.

It may be recalled that Arnold van Brounckhurst was one of the two Flemish painters who, as partners of Hilliard, prospected for gold in Scotland in the late seventies.[3] He thus must have known Nicholas personally. He can possibly be identified as the "Arnold" who received 4*l.* 6*s.* 10*d.* for the picture of Sir Henry Sidney in 1565/6.[4] This portrait was, according to the price, presumably a miniature. Arnold was the cousin of Cornelis Devosse and in May 1573 took a letter to London which the latter had written at Liège and addressed to the Lord Mayor. On 19 September 1580 he was made principal painter to the King of Scotland to draw all his portraits, small or large. He was actually paid for a full-length of young *James VI* and for a half-length of the same minor on the Scottish throne as well as for a portrait of Buchanan. At Christmas 1573 he received the first instalment of his remuneration for a picture of *Andromeda* which he painted for the royal revels. In 1598 "Arnolde" was mentioned by Francis Meres amongst the important English contemporary painters in his

---

[1] *Miniaturists*, p. 28.

[2] R.A., *British Portraits*, 1956/7, No. 36. Repr. Auerbach, *Tudor Portraits*, pl. 8.

[3] See pp. 17–18, *ante*; *Tudor Artists*, pp. 117 and 151/2, where all the documentary material is given.

[4] *Ibid.*, p. 117.

Plate 235(a).   Oliver, 1st Baron St. John of Eletso, by Arnold van Brounckhurst, 1578, oil

266

Palladis Tamia. Whether by that time he had returned to this country, or whether he was still resident in Scotland, we do not know. So far no other documentary reference to him has been found.

Now we come to the key picture which gives us the clue to the appreciation of his work. A short time ago the bust portrait of *Oliver, 1st Baron St John of Bletso* (*Pls. 235 a and b*), was sold at Christie's under the name of "Key". On the strength

Plate 235 (b). Signature

of an unmistakably identical nineteenth-century water-colour copy by G. P. Harding in the National Portrait Gallery it could be assigned to Brounckhurst, as it is stated on the former that it was taken from "the original by AR. Brounckorst. 1578. at Melchbourn House, Beds". In January 1957, in an article in the *Burlington Magazine*, I mentioned this fortunate find[1] and regretted the picture's disappearance into the hands of its unknown private owner. However, the painting has surprisingly reappeared and it now belongs to the Hon. Hugh de B. Lawson Johnston, and it has emerged, not only cleaned but also bearing the following signature, running vertically in neat Roman letters: *AR. BRONCKORST. FECIT. 1578.* It represents a beautifully painted bust portrait of a bearded man, wearing a tall embroidered hat and a close fitting piped ruff. He turns three-quarter to the right and the lively eyes look in the opposite direction towards the onlooker. The features are brought out clearly, and the foreshortened side is softly shaded and modelled. It shows a sensitive portrait conception and a fine feeling for colour which is dominated by a silvery grey. On the whole it is decisively Flemish, though something in its composition may be inspired by Hilliard.

Two groups of portraits may be tentatively linked with Brounckhurst's *Oliver, 1st Baron St John of Bletso*, though the last word on this matter cannot yet be spoken. The first one concerns two oil portraits of *William Cecil*, Lord Burghley, at Hatfield House. One is signed with the monogram AB and dated 1573 (*Pl. 236*), the other represents the sitter at a younger age and must have been painted in the late 'sixties. With the former we are on fairly safe ground

[1] *Tudor Portraits*, p. 10.

Plate 236. William Cecil, Lord Burghley, by Arnold van Brounckhurst, 1573, oil

in view of the signature; the latter, which has recently been cleaned and exhibited,[1] resembles it in style and in addition is different in manner from Eworth, to whom it might otherwise have been attributed. Connected with this oil portrait is a miniature of the same sitter (*Pl. 237*), formerly wrongly called *Ambrose Dudley, Earl of Warwick*, at Drumlanrig Castle, which was attributed to Isaac Oliver before, but which is more probably, in Sir Basil Long's words,

Plate 237. William Cecil, Lord Burghley, by Arnold van Brounckhurst (?)

"by a foreign artist". Lord Burghley appears slightly older in the miniature compared with the oil portraits, but the combination of strong lines and a soft shading of the foreshortened side of the face make them appear related in manner. In any event the excellent miniature is neither by Hilliard nor by Oliver.

The second group of portraits that can be attributed to Brounckhurst leads us to Scotland. The style of two portraits of *James Douglas, 4th Earl of Morton*, Regent of Scotland during the minority of James VI, in the Scottish National Portrait Gallery (Nos. 839, L. 110), conforms closely to the style of Brounckhurst's signed picture. In particular, it is now possible to ascribe with confidence the impressive three-quarter-length to the Flemish painter, who resided in Scotland. The same may be said for the lovely, though slightly rubbed, portrait of *King James VI as a boy* (*Pl. 238*), in the same gallery. In this case it is not only the similarity of the style which makes the attribution likely, but in addition, there is documentary evidence existing of payments for portraits of young James VI to Brounckhurst.[2] Other portraits, such as the charming miniature representing the bust likeness of the Scottish boy king at The Hague (*Pl. 239*), can be linked with it. Quite a considerable number of portraits can thus be assigned

[1] *British Portraits*, No. 26.
[2] See p. 18, *ante*.

Plate 238.   King James VI as a boy (James I), by Arnold van Brounckhurst, oil

to an artist who was a competent portraitist in the Flemish manner and apparently had patrons amongst families connected with the English and Scottish Courts.

SEGAR

In 1598, when Francis Meres in his *Palladis Tamia* gave a list of the most eminent painters working in this country at that time—a list to which we have repeatedly referred—he mentioned "William and Francis Segar brethren".

Plate 239. King James I (James VI of Scotland) as a boy, by Arnold van Brounckhurst

In the present state of our knowledge the brothers are almost impossible to disentangle one from the other, at least in their work. William is undoubtedly the greater personality and may be the more important artist. Often the name Segar alone appears and we are left in the dark about the Christian name, so that we must try to reconstruct in the work of one of these artists an *œuvre* which might have been the product of their co-operation as a team.

The mere mention of the brothers Segar by Francis Meres would not, however, alone warrant their inclusion here in the list of Hilliard's contemporaries, followers and pupils, were it not for the fact that the portrait miniature of *Dean Colet (Pl. 240)*, decorating a statute book of St. Paul's School and preserved at Mercers' Hall, London, is documented as the work of "Segar",

271

Plate 240. Dean Colet on Statute Book of St. Paul's School, by Segar, 1585/6

who was paid for the drawing of the picture in 1585/6.[1] Further, the oil por-trait representing *Robert Devereux, 2nd Earl of Essex (Pl. 241)*, in the National Gallery of Ireland in Dublin, has recently been attributed to (Sir William?) Segar by Mr. Piper and the style of this painting as well as of some others which can be grouped round it is decisively Hilliardesque.[2] It is, therefore, possible that William, who is said to have been trained by a scrivener and patronised by Sir Thomas Heneage, came into close contact with Hilliard during the early years of his training or even later after he had finished his schooling.

William is certainly identifiable with Sir William, who became Somerset Herald in 1588/9 and Garter King of Arms in 1607: in a letter to Lord Willough-by he refers to his brother Francis.[3] Numerous documentary references to his heraldic offices exist. As early as 1603/4 he was advanced to be Garter Principal King,[4] but only in 1606/7 was he definitely appointed and had to procure a new patent.[5] There are payments to him for heraldic work in 1604, 1606/7, 1608 and 1609.[6] One more interesting reference to him occurs in the Household Accounts of Sir Thomas Egerton, Lord Keeper of the Great Seal: on 15 May 1597 we read the following entry "paid Mr Seeger alias Somersett the hearold for her Maties picture—9*l*. 10*s*."[7] Here is another proof of the identity of the painter with the herald. But here, too, as in the case of Lockey, we are not sure how far these portraits were based on studies from life and how far they were copies from other artists' designs. Besides, Sir William wrote various works on heraldry and his *Honor Military and Civil* was published in 1602. It is illustrated with engravings of full-length figures by William Rogers which may be based on Segar's drawings.[8] His own portrait was engraved by F. Delaram.

As a heraldic artist Segar had considerable abilities, as we can judge from several illuminated documents which bear his signature as Garter King of Arms and which one would therefore assume to have been composed and drawn by him. There is notably the elaborate Pedigree of the Weston family in the British Museum,[9] which has well-shaded and finely executed marble tombs and monu-ments with full-length figures. They show a great fluency of style and a clever representation of architectural views which might even suggest that he was

---

[1] *Tudor Artists*, pp. 121 and 185.
[2] Piper, *Essex, II*, p. 300, pl. 13.
[3] *Tudor Artists*, p. 122.
[4] Index 6801, January.
[5] C. 66/1692.
[6] S.P. 14/211 (5), f.89, (7), f.142. E. 403/2727, f.158.
[7] Piper, *Essex, II*, p. 300.
[8] Hind, I, pp. 277/8, pl. 150.
[9] Add. MSS. 31890.

Plate 241. Robert Devereux, 2nd Earl of Essex, by Segar, oil on panel

Plate 242.   (?) Frances Walsingham, Countess of Essex, by Segar, oil

perhaps also the artist who illustrated the *Lumley Inventory*, the drawings of which have always been greatly admired. However that may be, the portrait of *Dean Colet*, taken from the lost bust at Old St. Paul's, and seen in the terms of a miniature locket, embedded in the arabesques of the title page of a Statute Book, gives us a clear idea of his ability as a miniaturist, even though this is a posthumous likeness. The ground is blue and the face is clearly built up in a three-quarter turning to the right with eyes in the opposite direction, and it is rather more modelled than Hilliard would have made it. Especially the fore-shortened side shows shadows contrasting and clearly weighed against each other to produce a certain roundness. The delicate handling of lines in the hands and in the silhouette of the figure are related to Hilliard's method. Altogether it is a most attractive miniature.

The second work which now can be safely ascribed to one or both of the Segars is an oil portrait: *Robert Devereux, 2nd Earl of Essex*, in Dublin. This painting is labelled: *Robert Devereux, Earle of Essex 1590*. On the strength of the following entry in the Lumley Inventory of 1590: "Of the second Earle of Essex Robert Devereux Mr of the horse doone by Seigar" it has been plausibly identified as just that portrait by Mr. Piper,[1] and we therefore have now a reliable and dated oil painting by Sir William or Francis Segar. The three-quarter length, which may be a version of a full-length, was exhibited in the recent Royal Academy Exhibition of *British Portraits* and, like the miniature portrait of *Dean Colet*, is most attractive. Both have much in common, and it is interesting to see that Segar's style "in little" and in large was quite alike. A similar conception of the view of the face, a related treatment of the upper lip and mouth, the neck line, and the gestures of the hands are common features to be noted. In addition, the *Essex* portrait shows a black uniform covered by a splendid white embroidery which recalls Hilliard's minute technique, though in a definitely stiffer and more pedantic execution. In spite of the careful reproduction of the embroidered pattern it appears strangely lifeless and rather dull, when compared with the charm and sensitiveness that breathes from every single detail which is characteristic of Hilliard's rendering of material on his miniatures. There is, however, a certain tenseness in the general attitude deriving from the outstretched arms and the rather affected and pointed movement of the hands in their relationship to the straight standing figure and the head, poised in the centre.

Mr. Piper's suggestion that the so-called *Mary Queen of Scots* (*Pl. 242*) from the Ashburnham Collection, now in the Mildred Anna Williams Collection, California Palace of the Legion of Honor, San Francisco, represents *Frances Walsingham, Countess of Essex*, may well be correct.[2] He identifies it with her

[1] *Essex, I*, p. 231.   [2] *Ibid.*, p. 231 and *Essex, II*, p. 300.

Plate 243. (?) Queen Elizabeth I, by Segar (?), oil

portrait, as it appears in the Lumley Inventory: *the Countesse of Essex wife to the 2 Earle of Essex and widow to Sir Philip Sidney*. In this case no name of an artist is mentioned. The nineteenth-century inscription not only made it a portrait of Mary, Queen of Scots, but there also appears something which might be read conveniently as a monogram N H. It has, however, not much to do with Hilliard and a motif like the pose of one hand hidden behind the back, which occurs on one of his miniatures and also elsewhere on work connected with him,[1] could have easily been copied by any artist of his school and would merely be of a superficial resemblance. When Mr. Piper states that it is "very close" to Segar's *Essex*, I certainly agree, but I should like to go further than that and instead of ascribing it to "an unknown artist" and in spite of the restored condition, I think, it could really be by the same artist as the portrait of Essex, namely by Segar. In both cases there is an identical manner of expressing the attitude in which the head is carried on the neck, which, incidentally, is repeated on the miniature portrait of *Dean Colet*, the same rendering of the features with the pointed and slightly pinched expression of the upper lip, and the closely related rather dull, linear and pedantic treatment of the surface pattern of lace and other material. One needs only observe the way in which the long chain, hanging vertically down in the centre, is gliding through two fingers of the woman's left hand—it is more mechanical than studied from life—to appreciate the enormous difference from Hilliard's similar poses. The same characteristics distinguish it clearly from the *Ermine* portrait at Hatfield House which is so much closer to Hilliard in the always varied and imaginative handling of the embroidered dress, the jewellery and the veils, the charming and sensitive ermine, the smooth treatment of the hands and the delicately graded, more enamelled and soft rendering of the face which comes so unmistakably near to Hilliard's miniatures.

Another portrait, by tradition ascribed to Hilliard and likewise supposed to be the portrait of *Queen Elizabeth I* (*Pl. 243*) belongs, in my opinion, closely to the group of portraits ascribed to Segar: it is the property of Lord Verulam and hangs at Gorhambury. It is a most dignified and stately oil portrait and the attribution to Hilliard, as well as the identification with Elizabeth has been doubted. The former is easy to answer, as it definitely has no resemblance to Hilliard's miniatures. The latter is a more difficult problem. If it is Elizabeth—and there is just a possibility—it is the aged queen, painted *c.* 1595, in the realistic way which Isaac Oliver indicated in his unfinished miniature of her or William Rogers in his engravings, such as in *Rosa Electa*.[2]

[1] It appears on the unfinished miniature, pl. 99, and on the *Visit to the Blackfriars*.
[2] Repr. Hind, I, pl. 145.

Within the portrait (handwritten inscription, upper right):

Robert Dudley Erle of Leicester & Stewart of howsshold to Queene Elizabeth, for his singuler gyfts of the mynde & graces of his person was aduaunced, honored, and followed more then others. He dyed the [ ] yeare of his age. Anno 1588.

Plate 244. Robert Dudley, Earl of Leicester, by Segar (?)

Here we also find the long and prominent aquiline nose and the tight mouth with the projecting lower lip. But usually on these types of royal portraits the eyes show the heavy eyelids which are absent from the Gorhambury painting. There is, on the other hand, the Phoenix Jewel pinned to her sleeve and all the indications of royal dignity in the posture and the richly bejewelled attire, including the long strings of pearls.

The style of the portrait can be closely linked with (?) *Frances Walsingham* and with the *Earl of Essex* by Segar. Although the neckline of the dress with the lace collars is different in detail, the arrangement of the long chains and strings of pearls is very much alike. So is the way in which the string of pearls is gliding through the fingers of her left hand. The hands on the portrait at Gorhambury might be compared with those of Essex, and one will notice that the movements of the fingers are very similar and that, in particular, the hand touching the staff may be compared with that holding the fan. The modelling

Plate 245. Judith Norgate, by
Edward Norgate

of the face, however, seems to be stronger on the Gorhambury picture, though we find again the typical, rather pointed expression of the upper lip. Whatever one may think about this portrait, it has to be kept apart from Hilliard's works and cannot be linked with any of his miniatures.[1]

[1] I am not so sure about the companion picture at Gorhambury, called *The Earl of Essex* by Hilliard. Perhaps it represents a member of the Bacon family. It is not by Hilliard, but though it resembles in some ways the Boston *Essex*, ascribed to Segar by Mr. Piper, I am not sure if it belongs to the same group.

Another work, this time a miniature, often ascribed to Hilliard, has a considerable affinity with Segar's *Essex*. It is the rather large rectangular full-length *The Earl of Leicester* at Drumlanrig Castle (*Pl. 244*). Something in the modelling of the face, the attitude of the hands, the precise and clear handling of the pattern on the Earl's costume and the column, curtain and tablecloth,

Plate 246.   A Man, Member of the Harryson Family, by Edward Norgate

Plate 247.   His wife, by Edward Norgate

with its complete absence of the reflection of light, would suggest Segar rather than Hilliard. In addition, the whole colour scheme with the strong red in the curtain is more colourful and rich in contrasts than is usual in Hilliard's works. On the other hand, it is very near to the latter's compositions and it may be based on one of his patterns, especially as a portrait of that description was mentioned in Laurence Hilliard's will.[1]

To sum up, the portraits, miniatures as well as oil paintings, grouped round the name of Segar show something of Hilliard's manner, while having a typical style of their own, which is different from Hilliard's style and common to all of them.

[1] Two portraits of Leicester by Segar are mentioned in the Lumley Inventory. See pp. 227–8, *ante.*

EDWARD NORGATE

As the author of *Miniatura,* an important essay on the art of limning, we already know Edward Norgate, and when dealing with Hilliard's *Treatise* we discussed various problems connected with Norgate's written work.[1] Were it not for the fact that Hilliard's name is often mentioned by the author of *Miniatura*—thus pointing clearly to some kind of acquaintance with the master's

Plate 248. An Historical Piece of Our Saviour, by Nicholas Hilliard (?) (enlarged)

working methods—and for a lovely miniature of his wife Judith, inscribed and signed at the back by the artist and dated 1617, his name would not have to be included here. This miniature, which is in the Victoria and Albert Museum, has great charm and is of excellent quality. It shows an attractive woman with soft fair hair, a beautiful lace collar and headgear, a pale-blue dress against the usual crimson curtain, and it is generally conceived in the tradition of Hilliard's School, though in detail it appears also much influenced by Oliver, as can be seen, for instance, in the modelling of the mouth and eyes.

Edward Norgate, who was born in 1581 and was therefore approximately of the same age as Laurence Hilliard, emerges as a tangible personality, well known in Court circles and entrusted with many offices and commissions. He was

[1] See pp. 219 *et seq., ante. Tudor Artists,* pp. 135–6, 138–9, 179, pl. 49. Reynolds, *Miniatures,* p. 38.

tuner and "keeper of His Majesties Organs" and payments to him for repair of organs at Greenwich are frequently recorded from 1623 onwards. He was sent with letters to Paris, Venice, and Ireland, the first being mentioned in 1612. He was appointed Windsor Herald in 1633 and Clerk of the Signet in 1638. Already in 1613 he received payments for writing and limning of royal letters to the King of Persia and the Great Mogul. These proved so successful

Plate 249. Called Princess Mary, by an
unknown follower of Hilliard

that, on 10 March 1630, he was granted the monopoly to write, limn, and prepare letters to be sent to princes abroad. He was a man of high culture who instructed Lord Arundel's sons in the art of drawing, entertained van Dyck in his house at Blackfriars, was a close friend of Sir Balthazar Gerbier, took part in the Scottish expedition, was sent to the Low Countries in 1639 to purchase pictures for Queen Henrietta Maria's cabinet, and was generally consulted as an art connoisseur.

Apart from a duplicate of the portrait of his wife (*Pl. 245*), two miniatures representing members of the Harryson family (*Pls. 246, 247*)—identifiable by a coat of arms—and a more Baroque-looking allegorical female figure, in private hands, are attributed to Norgate by Mr. Winter.[1] They show the same precision of rendering the pattern of dress, lace and hair and give a competent and attractive likeness.

Slightly different and more Flemish in manner, in the sense of being nearer to van Dyck's style, is the admirable and beautifully executed illuminated

Plate 250.   An Unknown Lady, aged
19 in 1608, Hilliard School

Plate 251.   Catherine Carey, Countess of
Nottingham, by an unknown follower
of Hilliard

Plate 252.   Catherine Carey, Countess of
Nottingham, by an unknown follower
of Hilliard

initial letter on the grant given to William Alexander, Earl of Stirling, at Audley End,[2] which I ascribed to Norgate and which is compatible in style with his miniatures.

[1] They belong to The Hon. H. Lawson-Tancred.
[2] *Tudor Artists*, pl. 49.

Altogether, a most charming and competent miniaturist emerges, who may not have only drawn on Hilliard as the founder of a new English tradition in painting miniatures, but also on his master's knowledge of illuminating great letters on documents and manuscripts.

UNKNOWN FOLLOWERS OF HILLIARD'S STYLE

Some of the few miniatures listed below have at one time or other been attributed to Hilliard himself. They have in common a certain adherence to the English School of the end of the sixteenth and the beginning of the seventeenth century, but are in each case by a different artist.

It is almost impossible to say whether the minute *An Historical Piece of Our Saviour* (*Pl. 248*), preserved in a contemporary turned jet box, is, as tradition had it, by Nicholas himself.[1] It shows a charming arrangement of a group of tiny figures in front of a precisely characterised open fire-place, slightly reminiscent of those early Tudor hat badges which gave similar scenes in goldsmiths' work. That in itself would point to Hilliard as the author, just as a certain resemblance to his miniature portraits of Sir Christopher Hatton, but the somewhat angular treatment of the child and the gesticulating attitudes of the figures make his authorship doubtful in the absence of any other comparable work by Hilliard.

The charming portrait of the full-length figure of a child, seated in an armchair, wrongly called *Princess Mary* (1662/95), at Drumlanrig Castle (*Pl. 249*),[2] has also been ascribed to Hilliard. There is, however, in this case no doubt that this, to quote Sir Basil Long's word, "gauche" miniature is not a genuine work by our master. Though the rendering of the surroundings, the hair and the flowers decorating it are very much in the Hilliard tradition, the face is broad and flat in an exaggerated way, the hands are small and clumsy, and these features bring it close to *William Hawtrey* by an unknown artist at Chequers,[3] so close indeed, that they must be by the same hand.

There remain a few miniatures of the beginning of the seventeenth century which are slightly retouched in certain places, but which clearly show a continuation of the Hilliard school. There is first *An Unknown Lady*, aged 19 in 1608 (*Pl. 250*), at Drumlanrig Castle, which has been described by Sir Basil Long as "possibly by one of Hilliard's pupils". It shows a most attractive

---

[1] Sotheby Sale, No. 49 as Hilliard. Reynolds, *Catalogue*, 1947, No. 101, *c.* 1595. Now Coll. of Mr. and Mrs. E. H. Heckett.

[2] 10/33, Mackay ascribes it to Hilliard.

[3] Reynolds, *Conn. Guide*, pl. 76a.

and precise conception of a figure holding a dagger against a blue background inscribed with lovely Hilliardesque gold letters giving the motto: *Si Pergis Perio*. There are, further, two miniatures, both called, without any foundation, *Catherine Carey, Countess of Nottingham* (*Pl. 251*), one at Stockholm, the other at Drumlanrig Castle (*Pl. 252*). The former is ascribed to Hilliard, but is probably by a younger artist working in his tradition. Again, the latter is by an unknown artist of the seventeenth century; it shows more colour and ornamentation than is usual on Hilliard's authentic miniatures.

From all these examples, whether they were life-size works or miniatures, whether they were executed by any of the known followers and pupils of our master or by some unknown artists, there emerges the tradition of a clearly defined English school which, but for the inspiring initiative of Nicholas Hilliard, would not have come into being.

CATALOGUE

I. PRE-HILLIARD PERIOD ([1])

1. *Henry VIII* (Pl. 1), by Luke Horenbout, Fitzwilliam Museum, Cambridge. P.D. 19–1949.
Rectangular 2″ × 1¾″. Inscribed: +HR++VIII+AN[O]+XXXVI+
PROV.: Buccleuch, bought in 1949.
LIT.: Winter, *The British School of Miniature Portrait Painters*, 1948, p. 7, pl. 1a. N. Colding, *Aspects of Miniature Painting*, 1953, pl. 100. Reynolds, *Conn. Guide*, pp. 127–8, pl. 69. E. Auerbach, *Tudor Portraits*, p. 13. Hugh Paget, "Gerard and Lucas Hornebolt in England", *Burl. Mag.*, CI, pp. 396–402, pl. 44.
EXH.: B.F.C.A., 1909, case C, No. 7, pl. 33. R.A., British Portraits, 1956–7, No. 604. There are two versions of the miniature in the Royal Coll., Windsor Castle

2. *Henry VIII* (Pl. 2), by Luke Horenbout, Royal Coll., Windsor Castle. No. 1.
Circular, dia. 1¾″. Inscribed: HR VIII Ano Ætatis XXXV.
LIT.: as for pl. 1.

3. *Catherine Howard* (Pl. 3), by Hans Holbein the Younger, Royal Coll., Windsor Castle.
Circular, dia. 2¼″.
LIT.: Cust, p. 12, No. 13. Winter, *Burl. Mag.*, LXXXIII, p. 266. Parker, 53, Ganz, p. 257, No. 141.

EXH.: South Kens. Mus., 1862, No. 2405, Tudor, 1890, No. 1067. B.F.A.C., 1909, Case C, No. 4, pl. 33. R.A. 1950, No. 192. Kings and Queens, 1953, No. 79.

4. *Unknown Young Girl* (Pl. 4), by an unknown artist, Victoria and Albert Museum. P. 21–1954.
Circular, dia. 2″. Inscribed: 1549.
LIT.: Reynolds, *Conn. Guide*, p. 131.

5. *Queen Mary I* (Pl. 5), in the manner of Hans Eworth, formerly ascribed to Anthony Mor. The Duke of Buccleuch, Drumlanrig Castle.
Circular, dia. 2⅛″. Oil on copper.
PROV.: Given by Earl of Suffolk to Charles I; taken to France by Charles Lennox, 2nd Duke of Richmond; sold *c.* 1860 to Colnaghi's; bought by 5th Duke of Buccleuch.
LIT.: Vanderdoort's *Cat.* "Done by Anthony More given to the King by my Lord Suffolk".
EXH.: South Kens. Mus. 1865, No. 307. B.F.A.C., 1909, case C 8, F. R.A., British Portraits, 1956–7, No. 163.

6. *An Elizabethan Maundy* (Pl. 6), by an unknown artist of the middle of the 16th century. Coll. the Earl of Beauchamp, Madresfield Court. No. 9.
Oval, 2¾″ × 2½″.
This miniature, which looks more like an illumination which has been cut to fit a frame, was attributed to Hilliard. It is, however, close in

([1]) This part of the Cat. includes only miniatures referred to in the text.

style to the Ghent-Bruges school of manuscript painters. Cf. Auerbach, *Tudor Artists*, p. 97, pl. 28.
LIT.: Long, p. 211.
EXH.: Brussels, 1912, No. 181, p. 19, repr. Pl. I, No. 3.

7. *Young Girl* (Pl. 7), by an unknown artist of the middle of the 16th century. Royal Coll. Windsor Castle, No. 16.
Circular, dia. 2".
A most attractive miniature which has been called "Lady Jane Grey" or "Queen Elizabeth as Princess", but the sitter cannot be identified.
LIT.: Cust, No. 16. Reynolds, *Miniatures*, p. 17. *Tudor Artists*, pp. 76–7.

8. *Katherine, Countess of Hertford*, wife of Edward Seymour, *with her Son* (Pl. 8), by an unknown artist of the middle of the 16th century. The Duke of Rutland, Belvoir Castle. No. 8.
Circular, dia. 2". On card.
In the catalogue of Belvoir Castle it was ascribed to Nicholas Lockey (?) which, because of Lockey's dates, is quite impossible. The style is close to that of pl. 7, so that both are probably by the same hand.

9. *Robert Dudley, Earl of Leicester* (Pl. 9), in the manner of Nicholas Hilliard when he was young, or by an unknown artist of the mid-16th century. The Duke of Rutland, Belvoir Castle, No. 14.
Circular, dia. $1\frac{7}{8}$". *c.* 1565.
In the catalogue of Belvoir Castle it is ascribed to Nicholas Hilliard.

II. HILLIARD'S WORK
(a) Miniatures

10. *Self-Portrait* at the age of 13 (Pl. 10). The Duke of Portland, Welbeck Abbey.
Circular, dia. 1". Inscribed on band round the portrait: OPERA QUEDAM IPSIVS NICHOLAS HELIARD IN ÆTATIS SVÆ 13. Signed with monogram on the left-hand side, NH 1550.
The second 5 has been altered from 6, at a later date, and appears smudged. Dull terracotta background, yellowish doublet, mouth and hair already in Hilliard's manner. Face round.
Circular band recalls portraits on *Preux de Marignan*.
LIT.: Goulding, No. 12.
EXH.: Reynolds *Catalogue*, 1947, No. 1.

11. *Self-Portrait* at the age of 13 (Pl. 11). The Duke of Buccleuch, Drumlanrig Castle. No. VII/4.
Circular, dia. $1\frac{1}{8}$". Inscribed in gold Roman letters on band round portrait: OPERA QUÆDAM IPSIUS NICHOLAIS HELLIARD IN ÆTATIS SVÆ 13. Signed with monogram on the left-hand side: NH 1550.
The frame is Spanish 17th century and similar to that of *Henry VIII* (Pl. 1) and *Edward VI* (Buccleuch, VII, 24). Dark patches on monogram and on the second 5 which differs from the first 5. Traces of an earlier and smaller monogram under present NH. Bright red background, face not quite as round as on that of *Self-portrait* (Pl. 10), otherwise a replica. Forehead slightly repainted, blue turquoise sleeves.
PROV.: Hollingworth Magniac.
LIT.: Mackay, AA 15.
EXH.: Reynolds *Catalogue*, 1947, No. 2.

12. *Edward Seymour, Duke of Somerset* (Pl. 12). The Duke of Buccleuch, Drumlanrig Castle, VII/7.
Circular, dia. $1\frac{1}{4}$". Inscribed on round band between thin gold lines

in gold Roman letters: EDWARDE, DVKE OF SOMERSET, ANNO DOMINI. 1560 NH.

Mellow gold background, traces of some red on cheeks and mouth. Good drawing. Posthumous painting, probably from an original by Holbein. Flatness of roundel reminiscent of Jean Clouet.

LIT.: Kennedy, plate V Mackay, DRA 18.

EXH.: South Kens. Mus., 1865, No. 1602. Reynolds *Catalogue*, 1947, No. 3.

13. *Queen Elizabeth I in robes of state* (Pl. 13). The Duke of Portland, Welbeck Abbey.
Rectangular, $3\frac{1}{2}'' \times 2\frac{1}{8}''$. *c.* 1569. Painted on playing-card. (This was established by Mr. Francis Needham in 1955 after having examined the reverse.)
Probably the earliest miniature Hilliard painted of the Queen and one which still shows in its iconic conception the influence of manuscript illuminations. The execution is most refined and all the accessories including a genuine little diamond, are treated with minute care.

LIT.: Goulding, No. 10, pl. 1. Farquhar, *Nicholas Hilliard*, p. 7. O'Donoghue, p. 26, No. 1. Pope-Hennessy, *Lecture*, p. 17, pl. 7. *Tudor Artists*, pl. 35.

EXH.: Manchester 1857, b. 34. B.F.A.C., 1889. B.F.A.C., 1926, p. 56, No. 13, pl. 21. Reynolds *Catalogue*, 1947, No. 4.

14. *A Gentleman, perhaps Oliver St. John, 1st Baron St. John of Bletsho* (Pl. 16). The Duke of Portland, Welbeck Abbey.
Circular, dia. $1\frac{5}{8}''$. Inscribed: Anno Dni 1571. Ætatis Suæ 35.
The identification is based on the

likeness to a portrait at Melchbourne Park, according to Goulding. This is probably the portrait by Brounckhurst, copied by Harding, but it is of a later date. Cf. Pl. 235a.

LIT.: Goulding, No. 18.

EXH.: B.F.A.C., 1926, pl. XXI. Reynolds *Catalogue*, 1947, No. 5.

15. *An Unknown Man, aged 24 in 1572* (Pl. 17). Victoria and Albert Museum. P.1–1942.
Rectangular, $2\frac{3}{8}'' \times 1\frac{7}{8}''$. Inscribed: Ætatis Sue. XXIIII. Ano Dni. 1572. Very fine quality, light blue background. The sitter's identity is not established. The lettering is in Hilliard's hand. Gold is also used in the bow of pale green ribbon.

PROV.: From the collection of the Duke of Buccleuch. Given to the Museum by the National Art Collection Fund in 1942.

LIT.: Kennedy, pl. XXII. Mackay. B. 21. Winter, *Eliz. Miniatures*, p. 12, pl. 2b. Pope-Hennessy, *Lecture*, p. 18, pl. 8. Reynolds, *Miniatures*, p. 18.

EXH.: Reynolds *Catalogue*, 1947, No. 8.

16. *An Unknown Lady, aged 18 in 1572* (Pl. 18), companion miniature to pl. 17. The Duke of Buccleuch, Drumlanrig Castle.
Rectangular, $2\frac{1}{8}'' \times 1\frac{3}{4}''$. Inscribed: Ætatis Suæ XVIII. Ano Dni. 1572. Blue background, ruff is slightly damaged. Face partly repainted, but eyes, forehead, hair, bonnet, and elaborately painted ornaments of dress in Hilliard's manner.

LIT.: Long, *Notes*, "Very likely a Hilliard". Mackay, C. No. 9, ascribed to Oliver.

EXH.: R.A., 1879, F.3. B.F.A.C., 1909, Case C, No. 9.

17. *An Unknown Man* (Pl. 19), formerly called *Edward Courtney, Earl of*

Devon. Fitzwilliam Museum, Cambridge. Misc. 12.

Circular, dia. $1\frac{3}{4}''$. Inscribed: Año Dni. 1572. Ætatis Sue

The rest is covered by a patch of darker blue in the right hand corner of the background. A very fine miniature. The head is relatively large within the picture area. Light blue background, light grey doublet. The end of white ribbon with bow just visible. Features clearly outlined, hair and beard indicated in fine lines. Inscription in Hilliard's manner.

PROV.: From the Buccleuch Collection, 1942.

LIT.: Kennedy, pl. 3.

EXH.: Reynolds *Catalogue*, 1947, No. 7.

18. *An Unknown Lady, aged 52 in 1572* (Pl. 20). The Duke of Buccleuch, Drumlanrig Castle. VII/26.

Circular, dia. $1\frac{7}{8}''$. Inscribed: Ætatis Sue 52, curved, on the left, and Anõ Dni 1572 on the right.

Blue background, dressed in widow's weeds. Bust, face three-quarter to the left, eyes opposite. Face large in relation to surround. Black dress and bonnet relieved by white in chemise and ruff and narrow brim of bonnet. Clear, protruding features. Writing in Hilliard's hand. Gold brilliant and standing out.

LIT.: Kennedy, pl. 3. Long, *Notes*, "I do not see why this should not be a Hilliard."

19. *Queen Elizabeth I* (Pl. 21). National Portrait Gallery. No. 108.

Oval, $2'' \times 1\frac{3}{4}''$. Inscribed in curved letters on the left: Anõ Dni 1572, and on the right: Ætatis Suæ 38. Across in horizontals: E surmounted by a crown on the left, and R sur-

mounted by a crown on the right. On the back of playing card, the Queen of Hearts. A very fine and well-preserved miniature. Blue background. To the waist. Three-quarter turning to the right. Elaborately adorned black dress with white embroidered sleeves, partlet, and small frill ruff. Rich jewel hanging from pink ribbon. A white rose attached to her left shoulder. Features clearly rendered with pale blue shading. Brilliant gold lettering rounding off the composition. Very important early portrait of the Queen, clearly painted *ad vivam*.

LIT.: O'Donoghue, p. 26, No. 3. *Walpole Society* I, p. 43. Winter, *Eliz. Miniatures*, p. 11. Auerbach, *Portraits of Elizabeth I*, p. 202, pl. 35. *Tudor Artists*, p. 126, pl. 40a.

EXH.: Reynolds *Catalogue*, 1947, No. 6.

20. *Queen Elizabeth I, playing the lute* (Pl. 23). Berkeley Castle.

Oval, $2'' \times 1\frac{1}{4}''$.

This beautiful miniature confirms Hilliard's link with the illumination of manuscripts. The musical instrument and the throne are given with the same minute care as the figure of the Queen herself.

Mentioned in 1796 as at Berkeley Castle.

EXH.: South Kens. Mus., 1862, No. 2, 294 as Mary Stuart, Queen of Scots, by an unknown artist, lent by Lord Fitzhardinge. South Kens. Mus., 1865, No. 1473 under the same description.

21. *A Woman, called Isabel, Countess of Rutland née Holcroft* (Pl. 24). The Duke of Rutland, Belvoir Castle.

Circular, dia. $2''$. Inscribed: Anno

Dni 1572, curved, on the left, and Ætatis Sua 20, on the right.

The sitter was the wife of the third Earl of Rutland. Modelling of features in Hilliard's manner. Elaborate headwear and dark dress with richly embroidered chemise and wide close-fitting ruff. A miniature locket is pinned to the dress at her breast.

EXH.: Reynolds *Catalogue*, 1947, No. 9.

22. *Jane Coningsby, aged 21* (Pl. 25). Mrs. Ward-Boughton-Leigh.
Circular, dia. 1¾". Inscribed: Anno Dni 1574 on the left, and Ætatis Sua 21, on the right.
It has always been in the family.
EXH.: Reynolds *Catalogue*, 1947. No. 10.

23. *An Unknown Man, aged 45 in 1574,* (Pl. 26). The Duke of Buccleuch, Drumlanrig Castle, No. VII/13.
Circular, dia. 1¾". Inscribed on the left Ano Dni 1574; on the right Ætatis Suæ 45.
Gold letters on dark blue ground in Hilliard's writing.
Bust. Three-quarter to the left. The man wears black garment and cap. Small frilled close-fitting, wide ruff. A gold ring hangs on short gold chain. Straight nose, in typical perspective. Eyes in Hilliard's manner. Brown beard indicated in fine lines. Good quality, Holbein inspired. Between pl. 19 and pl. 27, according to the style.
LIT.: Mackay, B. No. 20. Long, *Notes*, "This may be by Nicholas Hilliard." For pose and costume he compares it with portrait by Clouet, *Gaz. des Beaux Arts*, April 1924, p. 250.

24. *An Unknown Man, aged 37 in 1574* (Pl.

27). Fitzwilliam Museum, Cambridge. PD20–1949.
Circular, dia. 1⅝". In a modern gilt locket. Inscribed in gold letters following circle: on the left, Ano Dni 1574, and on the right, Ætatis Sue 37. Pale green background. Black dress with grey pattern. Black cap and feather plume. Some gold in hatband. Black coat thrown over shoulder. Gold chain just visible. Light brown beard and moustache, darker brown curls. Face small in proportion.
PROV.: Coll. of the Duke of Buccleuch (Mackay, B.19). Bought in June 1949.
EXH.: Reynolds *Catalogue*, No. 11.
At one time thought to be Hilliard's Self-Portrait, which led to the misdating of his birth.

25. *An Unknown Woman, (?) Lady Margaret Douglas* (Pl. 28). Mauritshuis, The Hague, from Rijksmuseum, Amsterdam, No. 2875A.
Circular, dia. 1¾". Inscribed in gold letters following circle on the left, Anõ Dni 1575; on the right, Ætatis Suæ (the rest covered by blue patch) in Hilliard's writing.
Blue background. Short half-length. Small face in proportion, three-quarter to the left. Black coat over black patterned wide sleeves. Closely-fitting white ruff, white bonnet, completely covering hair with long white bands hanging down over coat. The lady is in mourning. Good modelling in Hilliard's manner. Slightly damaged round her left eye. Formerly considered to be Lady Hunsdon by Levina Teerlinc, but the style is unmistakably Hilliard's. The tentative identification of the sitter is based on entry in Vanderdoort's Cat. see p. 69 *ante*.

26. *An Unknown Woman.* Another version of Pl. 28, but much repainted, with faked writing. Fitzwilliam Museum, Cambridge. C. 80 as *Lady Hunsdon* by Hilliard. Inscribed (by later hand): Anno Dni 1576. Ætatis suæ 25.

Anne Morgan married Lord Hunsdon in 1545 and died in 1606, very aged and weak. This cannot represent her.

PROV.: From Bignor Park Coll., Hawkins Coll., 1904. Pierpont Morgan Coll., Cat. I, no. 16. Sold at Christie's, 24 June 1935. Lot 103. (Cunliffe Beq.)

27. *Called Henry Howard, Earl of Northampton, aged 39 in 1576* (Pl. 29). Formerly Viscount Morpeth, now Cleveland Mus. of Art, Greene Coll. Slightly oval, $1\frac{7}{8}'' \times 1\frac{5}{8}''$. Inscribed following the curve of the frame: Anõ Dnĩ 1576 on the left, and Ætatis Suæ 39 on the right.

Bust. Three-quarter to the left. Grey doublet with high collar and closely-fitting lace ruff. Buttons and gold chain visible. Black hat with white feathers and a little gold. Blond beard and moustache, light flesh tints. Features very well modelled in Hilliard's hand. Good quality.

PROV.: Coll. of Earl of Carlisle.

LIT.: Gower, II, attr. to Oliver.

EXH.: Leeds, Temple Newsam House, 1947. Sold at Sotheby's on 14 May 1959, Lot 114.

28. *Self-Portrait* (Pl. 30), at the age of 30. Victoria and Albert Museum. P.155–10. Salting Bequest.

Circular, dia. $1\frac{5}{8}''$. Inscribed: Anõ Dnĩ 1577. Ætatis Suæ 30. Signed with cursive monogram NH.

This miniature is one of the most important works by Hilliard. The curving gold lettering surrounds the bust and stands out on a pale blue background. It was painted whilst Hilliard was staying in France.

PROV.: In 1640 this miniature or another version is mentioned in Laurence Hilliard's will. Before 1744 the property of Jocelyn Sidney, Earl of Leicester; then Sir Robert Rich, Bart., passed to his son. In 1843 owned by the Hon. Mrs. Thomas Liddell, then Mrs. Sartoris; sold at Christie's, 27 June 1906.

LIT.: De Piles' *Art of Painting*, 1706. Walpole, *Anecdotes*, I, p. 151. Winter, *Eliz. Miniatures*, pl. IIIa. According to De Piles, it had a border with the inscription *Nicholas Hilliardus aurifaber, sculptor et celebris illuminator serenissimæ reginae Elizabethae, anno 1577, aet suae 30.*

EXH.: Reynolds *Catalogue*, 1947, No. 14.

29. *Self-Portrait* at the age of 30. Version of No. 28. Formerly Bertram Currie, sold at Christie's, 27 March 1953, Lot 24.

Circular, dia. $2\frac{3}{4}''$.

PROV.: From Penshurst, Lord de Lisle.

LIT.: Walpole, *Anecdotes*, 1826, I., p. 289. Williamson, *Portrait Miniatures*, pp. 27–8.

EXH.: South Kens. Mus., 1862, No. 2215. B.F.A.C., 1889, p. 32, Case IX, No. 10, Pl. III. B.F.A.C., 1926, pl. 20.

30. *Richard Hilliard* (1518/19–1594) (Pl. 31). Father of the artist, aged 58 in 1577. Victoria and Albert Museum, Salting Bequest. No. P.154–1910.

Circular, dia. $1\frac{5}{8}''$. Inscribed: Ætatis Suæ 58. Anno Dni 1577.

Companion picture of Self-Portrait in Victoria and Albert Museum, probably also painted in Paris. For its provenance see notes on Self-

Portrait in Victoria and Albert Museum, pl. 30. According to De Piles it had a border with the inscription *Ricardus Hilliardus quondam vicecomes civitatis et comitatus Exoniae, anno 1560, aetatis suae 58, annoque Domini 1577*.

EXH.: Reynolds *Catalogue*, 1947, No. 13.

31. *Richard Hilliard*. Copy version of No. 30. Duke of Buccleuch, No. VII/16. Pale, oval, bigger in size, $1\frac{7}{8}'' \times 1\frac{1}{2}''$. Inscribed: Ano Dni 1577, Ætatis Suæ 58.

LIT.: Mackay, D.R.A. No. 1. Long, *Notes* "Perhaps 18th century copy or earlier". A. D. Edwards, *Photographic Historical Portrait Gallery*, 1864, pl. XXVII.

EXH.: South Kens. Mus., 1862.

32. *An Unknown Man, aged 52 in 1577* (Pl. 32). Formerly in the Warneck and T. Hugh Cobb Coll. Sold at Sotheby's, 31 January 1956, No. 399. Oval, $2\frac{1}{8}'' \times 1\frac{3}{4}''$. Inscribed: Anõ Dnĩ 1577. Ætatis Suæ 52.

EXH.: Reynolds *Catalogue*, 1947, No. 12.

33. *Alice Hilliard, née Brandon, aged 22 in 1578* (Pl. 33). Portrait of artist's wife. Victoria and Albert Museum, No. P2–1942.

Circular, dia. $2\frac{3}{8}''$. Inscribed Ano Dni 1578 Æs S. 22, and signed twice, on left and on right, with monogram NH.

This lovely miniature, painted in France, has been enlarged with a border which is inscribed (Alicia. Brandon. Nicolai. Hillyardi. Qvi Propria Manu Depinxit Vxor Prima.) On the left is Hilliard's coat of arms and on the right that of Robert Brandon.

PROV.: Formerly in the Buccleuch

Coll. Bought by the National Art Collections Fund.

LIT.: Kennedy, pp. 4, 5, Pl. XII. Winter, *Eliz. Miniatures*, p. 14, pl. 3c.

EXH.: Reynolds *Catalogue*, 1947, No. 15.

34. *Mademoiselle de Sourdis*. Present owner not known. Oval, $2\frac{1}{2}'' \times 2''$. Inscribed: Ano Dni 1577.

PROV.: C. H. T. Hawkins Esq. 1904. J. Pierpont Morgan, No. 23. Sold on 24 June 1935, Lot 101, to Dr. Beets. Fred. Müller, 9–11 April 1940.

LIT.: Williamson, *Pierpont Morgan Cat.* I, No. 23.

35. *François Hercule, Duc d'Alençon* (Pl. 36). Chantilly, Musée de Condé, No. 3.

Oval, $1\frac{3}{4}'' \times 1\frac{1}{2}''$, on card.

This fine miniature is exhibited in Chantilly, as *François Duc d'Alençon* by an unknown artist. It is certainly by an English miniaturist and the attribution to Hilliard is based on stylistic reasons.

PROV.: Bought by the Duc d'Aumale in 1862 or 1865 probably in London from Colnaghi.

EXH.: South Kens. Mus., 1865, No. 386 as *François Duc d'Alençon*, afterwards Duc d'Anjou. Card. No name of an artist. It was lent by H.R.H. the Duc d'Aumale to the exhibition.

36. *François Hercule, Duc d'Alençon*, after Nicholas Hilliard (Pl. 37). Kunsthistorisches Museum, Vienna. Rectangular, $4'' \times 3''$. Oil. Inscribed on top: Dux Alenconne.

This rectangular miniature portrait of the Duc d'Alençon belonged to the Coll. of Archduke Ferdinand and was probably painted from a miniature by Hilliard, such as No. 35.

LIT.: Fr. Kenner, *Die Porträtsamm-*

lung des Erzherzogs Ferdinand von Tirol. Jahrb. der Kunsthist. Samml. des Allerh. Kaiserhauses, XIX, Vienna 1898. No. 172.

37. *Mary Queen of Scots* (Pl. 38). Mrs. Doris Herschorn.
Oval, $2'' \times 1\frac{5}{8}''$. *c*. 1578. In a mount probably from the 17th century.
This miniature gives an authentic likeness of the Queen and is supposed to be the original from which the Sheffield portrait was painted.
PROV.: Sold from the Coll. of Capt. J. H. Edwardes-Heathcote at Christie's on 13 June 1928. Formerly in the English Royal Coll., taken to France by James II in 1688. Then in the Coll. of Louis XIV until the Revolution, when brought back into England, afterwards in the Coll. of 2nd Earl Spencer; James Edwards; Rev. Thomas Butts; the Edwardes family.
LIT.: Cust, *Notes on the Authentic Portraits of Mary Queen of Scots*, 1903.
EXH.: Reynolds *Catalogue*, 1947, No. 16.

38. *Mary Queen of Scots*. Royal Coll. at Windsor Castle. No. 52.
Oval, $1\frac{3}{4}'' \times 1\frac{1}{2}''$. Another version of No. 37.
LIT.: Cust, No. 52.

39. *Mary Queen of Scots* (? by Nicholas Hilliard.) Present whereabouts not known.
PROV.: Bale Collection.
EXH.: B.F.A.C., 1889, p. 31, Case IX, No. 3, Pl. IV. Then in the possession of Mr. Jeffery Whitehead.

40. *François Hercule, Duc d'Alençon* (Pl. 41). Kunsthistorisches Museum, Vienna.
Oval, $1\frac{3}{4}'' \times 1\frac{1}{4}''$ (4.5×3.7 cms.)
This miniature by Hilliard has wrongly been assumed to represent Walter Raleigh. From the minia-

tures, grouped here together, with that decorating the Prayer Book (pl. 39) it is evident that it represents the same sitter. It belonged to the Coll. of the Archduke Ferdinand, and is mentioned as Walter Raleigh, No. 219, in the Cat. of the Museum.
LIT.: Fr. Kenner, *Die Porträtsammlung des Erzherzogs Ferdinand von Tirol. Jahrb. der Kunsthist. Samml. des Allerh. Kaiserhauses*, XIX, Vienna, No. 219.

41. *An Unknown Lady* (Pl. 45). Victoria and Albert Museum, *c*. 1580. Given by Mr. E. Peter Jones.
Oval, $1\frac{1}{2}'' \times 1\frac{1}{4}''$.
EXH.: Reynolds *Catalogue*, 1947, No. 17.

42. *An Unknown Lady, aged 21 in 1580* (Pl. 46). Coll. of Duke of Portland.
Oval, $1\frac{5}{8}'' \times 1\frac{3}{8}''$. Inscribed: Ætatis Suæ 31 or 21. Anõ Dnĩ. 1574 or 1580.
The dates of the inscription may have been altered to fit the dates of *Mary Queen of Scots* and to render her a probable sitter.
LIT.: Goulding, No. 6, pl. III.
EXH.: B.F.A.C., 1926, p. 57, No. 16. Reynolds *Catalogue*, 1947, No. 18.

43. *Sir Francis Drake, aged 42 in 1581* (Pl. 47). Kunsthistorisches Museum, Vienna. No. 216.
Oval, $2'' \times 2\frac{1}{2}''$ (5.6×4.5 cms.) Inscribed: Ætatis Suæ; 42 Anno Dni 1581.
This is certainly a very good miniature by Hilliard which was part of the portrait gallery in miniature of well-known Englishmen, commissioned by the Archduke Ferdinand of Tyrol.
LIT.: Reynolds, *Conn. Guide*, p. 133, pl. 73b. Fr. Kenner, *Die Porträtsammlung des Erzherzogs Ferdinand*

von Tirol, Jahrb. des Kunsthist. Samml. des Allerh. Kaiserhauses, XIX, Vienna 1898, pp. 95–6. Nos. 210, 217.

44. *Sir Francis Drake* (1540?–1596) (Pl. 48). Coll. of Earl of Derby, Knowsley Hall.
Circular, dia. $1\frac{1}{4}''$. Inscribed: Ætatis suæ 42, Ano dni: 1581.
Probably an authentic likeness, very delicate in colours.
LIT.: Scharf, No. 224.
EXH.: Tudor, 1890, No. 1103. B.F.A.C., 1889, p. 60, Case XX, No. 6. Reynolds *Catalogue*, 1947, No. 19.

45. *Called Sir Francis Drake* (Pl. 49). Nat. Maritime Mus., Greenwich.
Circular, dia. $1\frac{1}{8}''$, in ivory case. Inscribed on the miniature: Viue ut Viuas and on border: ÆTATIS SVÆ 42. ANO DNI 1581 in Roman letters.
This portrait shows a likeness that differs from those in the Coll. of the Earl of Derby and in Vienna.
PROV.: C. Sackville Bale, sold on 23 May 1881. The Duke of Buccleuch.
EXH.: B.F.A.C., 1889, Case II, No. 9 (Duke of Buccleuch). Reynolds *Catalogue*, 1947, No. 20.

46. *An Unknown Man*, aged 28 in 1852 (Pl. 50). Coll. Earl Beauchamp, Madresfield Court.
Oval, $2\frac{1}{4}'' \times 1\frac{3}{4}''$. Inscribed: Anõ Dnī 1582 Ætatis Suæ 28.
This miniature was formerly ascribed to Isaac Oliver, but is certainly by Hilliard.
EXH.: Reynolds *Catalogue*, 1947, No. 21.

47. *Called Sir George Carey, aged 51 in 1581* (Pl. 51). Duke of Buccleuch, Drumlanrig Castle. No. VII/6.
Inscribed: Free from all filthy fraude, and across, Anõ Dnī. 1581

Ætatis Suæ 51 (?) the last figure almost covered by the frame.
This miniature has been ascribed to Isaac Oliver but it is definitely in Hilliard's style, though the face is slightly retouched.
PROV.: The Earl of Westmorland.
LIT.: Mackay, AA No. 14. Kennedy, pl. 15.
EXH.: B.F.A.C., 1889, Case II, No. 2 as *Isaac Oliver*.

48. *Unknown Man aged 25 in 1581* (Pl. 52), probably by Nicholas Hilliard. Coll. Duke of Buccleuch, Drumlanrig Castle, No. VII/18.
Oval, $1\frac{1}{2}'' \times 1\frac{1}{4}''$. Inscribed: Anõ Dnī 1581. Ætatis Suæ 25, and across: post umbra corpus.
According to Long's *Notes* it was formerly called *Sir Philip Sidney* and attributed to Isaac Oliver. It is, however, very close to Hilliard's manner.
LIT.: Mackay, EE No. 3.

49. *An Unknown Man* (Pl. 53). Nat. Mus. Stockholm. No. Bih. 1169.
Oval, $2\frac{1}{2}'' \times 2''$. *c.* 1582.
LIT.: Karl Asplund, *Hjalmar Wicanders Miniatyrsamling*, 1929, *Cat.* No. 161, pl. 63.

50. *John Croker and his Wife* (Pl. 54). Double portrait consisting of two miniatures framed together. Victoria and Albert Museum. No. P. 139–1910, Salting Bequest.
Oval: husband, $1\frac{7}{8}'' \times 1\frac{1}{2}''$; wife, $2'' \times 1\frac{5}{8}''$. *c.* 1580/5.
John Croker was the son of Sir Gerard Croker; his marriage to Frances, 5th daughter of Sir William Kingsmill, may have been the cause for this double portrait to be painted. The frame was probably made in the 19th century.
EXH.: Reynolds *Catalogue*, 1947, No. 24.

51. *An Unknown Man* (Pl. 55a), dated 1583. Nat. Mus. Stockholm. Bih. 1312.
Oval, $1\frac{7}{8}'' \times 1\frac{1}{2}''$. Inscribed: Non poco de Chese Medissimo dona.
It is enclosed in a locket, the back of which has the enamelled representation of the Crucifixion.
LIT.: N. Colding, *Aspects of Miniature Painting*, 1953, pp. 52, 82, 84, pl. 36–37.

52. *Elizabeth I* (Pl. 57). Earl Beauchamp, Madresfield Court.
Oval, $1\frac{3}{4}'' \times 1\frac{3}{8}''$. *c.* 1584.
EXH.: Tudor, 1890, No. 1097 (3). B.F.A.C., 1926, p. 55, No. 6, pl. 23.

53. *Elizabeth I* (Pl. 58). Duke of Buccleuch, Drumlanrig Castle, No. VII/27.
Oval, $1\frac{1}{4}'' \times 1\frac{3}{8}''$. Inscribed in gold: ......Dni...... Water colour on card.
There is no doubt that this charming miniature was painted by Nicholas Hilliard *c.* 1585.
LIT.: Mackay, C. No. 10. Kennedy, pl. V. Long, *Notes*, "I am inclined to regard this as a genuine Hilliard".
EXH.: South Kens. Mus., 1862. R.A.W.E. 1879.

54. *Elizabeth I* (Pl. 59). Mauritshuis, The Hague. No. 2837.
Oval, $1\frac{3}{4}'' \times 1\frac{3}{8}''$. *c.* 1585.
PROV.: From the Rijksmuseum, Amsterdam.
This is a very nice miniature and shows Hilliard's colouring and minute detail at its best.
EXH.: The Hague, *The Age of Shakespeare*, 1958, No. 37.

55. *Queen Elizabeth I* (Pl. 60). Royal Collection, Windsor Castle.
Circular, dia. $1''$. *c.* 1590.
LIT.: Cust, No. 25.
EXH.: Reynolds *Catalogue*, 1947, No. 49.

56. *Queen Elizabeth I in minute Tudor Rose*. Royal Collection, Windsor Castle, No. 23. *c.* 1590.
Circular, dia. $\frac{3}{4}''$.
LIT.: Cust, No. 23. O'Donoghue, p. 28, No. 8.
EXH.: Reynolds *Catalogue*, 1947, No. 48.

57. *Henry, 8th Earl of Northumberland* (Pl. 62). The Duke of Rutland, Belvoir Castle, No. 10.
Oval, $2'' \times 1\frac{1}{2}''$, on card. Inscription Anõ Dni. 1585, Ætatis Suæ 54, a frame $\frac{1}{4}''$ thick bears in Roman letters the inscription: HENRICUS PERCY NORTHVUMBRIAE COMES. VERE NOBILISSIMVS ET MAGNANIMVS.
This miniature was formerly ascribed to Isaac Oliver but is certainly by Hilliard. It is an excellent specimen of his mature work.
EXH.: South Kens. Mus., 1865, No. 337 as by an unknown artist.

58. *Sir Francis Knowles* (Pl. 63). The Duke of Buccleuch, Drumlanrig Castle, No. VII/14.
Oval, $2'' \times 1\frac{3}{4}''$. Inscribed: Anõ Dni. 1585. Æs. 29. At the back is written on paper in ink: Sir/Francis Knowles/Father to Mrs. Hamond/Mother to Colonel Hamond2/Father to Mrs. Ford4/ Mother to Mr. Preston5/ Father to Mrs. Ludlow6/ Mother to Mrs. Preston7/ Mother to Master John Preston8/.
There are some yellow spots on the face. Nevertheless Hilliard's modelling can be recognised. Light eyes and a clearly drawn neck-line. A very well painted radiating lace ruff supports the fine likeness, gold colour in the doublet, neat small gold lettering on a blue ground.
LIT.: Mackay, AA 4.

EXH.: B.F.A.C., 1889, Case II, No. 6. Reynolds *Catalogue*, 1947, No. 22.

59. *An Unknown Young Man* (Pl. 64). The Earl of Radnor, Longford Castle. In contemporary turned ivory box.
Oval, $2'' \times 1\frac{3}{8}''$. *c.* 1585.
This is a very fine miniature in delicate colours with great expression, enhanced by one hand tucked into his coat; the hair is specially well drawn.
PROV.: This miniature was kept and still is with four other miniatures in a small carved and gilt cabinet. All five miniatures are enclosed in contemporary turned ivory boxes. The cabinet is said to have been given with the miniatures by Queen Elizabeth I to Lady Rich.
LIT.: Radnor, II, p. 109, No. 4.
EXH.: Reynolds *Catalogue*, 1947, No. 27.

60. *An Unknown Young Man* (Pl. 65). The Earl of Radnor.
Oval, $2'' \times 1\frac{5}{8}''$. *c.* 1585. In contemporary turned ivory box.
There is a very precise rendering of the portrait likeness and of the lace and the pattern of the doublet to be seen. An excellent quality.
PROV.: The same as No. 59 (Pl. 64).
LIT.: Radnor, II, p. 109, No. 3.
EXH.: Reynolds *Catalogue*, 1947, No. 28.

61. *An Unknown Young Man*. The Duke of Rutland, Belvoir Castle, No. 29.
Oval, $2'' \times 1\frac{5}{8}''$. *c.* 1585.
This is a replica of the miniature No. 60 (pl. 65). The colouring is different but otherwise it is the same likeness.
EXH.: South Kens. Mus., No. 335. Reynolds *Catalogue*, 1947, No. 29.

62. (?) *Anne, Lady Hunsdon*, formerly called *Queen Elizabeth* (Pl. 66). The Duke of Portland, Welbeck Abbey.
Oval, $2\frac{1}{8}'' \times 1\frac{5}{8}''$. *c.* 1585.
The letter S appears as an ornament in the lace and in the jewel in the hair. It is a very typical portrait of that period especially in the modelling of the face and the treatment of the lace collar. The identification with Anne, Lady Hunsdon, whose husband was Henry Carey, 1st Lord Hunsdon and who died in 1606/7 is based on the resemblance to a portrait of that lady at Hatfield House.
LIT.: Goulding, No. 4.
EXH.: B.F.A.C., 1889, p. 91, No. 13, Pl. III, "called Queen Elizabeth". Reynolds *Catalogue*, 1947, No. 26.

63. (?) *Anne, Lady Hunsdon* (Pl. 67). Mrs. E. H. Heckett, Valencia.
Oval, $2\frac{1}{4}'' \times 1\frac{7}{8}''$. On card. *c.* 1585.
PROV.: The Earl of Feversham.

64. *William Barbor* (died in 1586) (Pl. 180). Victoria and Albert Museum. No. 878–1894. Bequeathed by Miss Blencowe.
Oval, $1\frac{1}{2}'' \times 1\frac{1}{4}''$. In contemporary turned ivory box. *c.* 1585.
The profile is quite exceptional within Hilliard's work. William Barbor, a grocer, had Protestant sympathies and was condemned to death during the reign of Mary. He was saved by the news that Elizabeth had come to the throne. In gratitude he had the Barbor jewel (Pl. 179) made and his portrait painted, and arranged that they should remain in the family. Both descended in the family and were finally given to the Victoria and Albert Museum. The attribution to Hilliard was suggested by Mr. Reynolds in 1947.

EXH.: South Kens. Mus., 1865, No. 1319. Reynolds *Catalogue*, 1947, No. 30.

65. *Sir Walter Raleigh* (Pl. 68). Formerly Viscount Morpeth Coll., now National Portrait Gallery.

Oval, $1\frac{7}{8}'' \times 1\frac{5}{8}''$. 1588.

This is undoubtedly one of the best miniatures Hilliard painted. The way in which the radiating ruff supports the clearly built-up head is typical of his style. The sitter was formerly wrongly called Henry Howard, Earl of Northampton. C. S. Emden, *Oriel Record, 1953*, identified it as Raleigh, because of a rectangular oil-miniature in the collection of the Archduke Ferdinand in Vienna, which shows the same likeness and the name of Raleigh in an old inscription.

PROV.: Coll. of the Earl of Carlisle.

LIT.: J. D. Milner, *Burl. Mag.* 1918, Pl. 157. Reynolds, *Miniatures*, pl. 1. Piper, *The English Face*, pl. 29.

EXH.: Leeds, Temple Newsam House, 1947. Amsterdam, The Triumph of Mannerism, 1955, No. 69. R.A., British Portraits, 1956–7, No. 621. The Hague, The Age of Shakespeare, 1958, No. 87.

Sotheby's sale, 14 May 1959, Lot 116.

66. *An Unknown Lady* (Pl. 69). The Duke of Buccleuch, Drumlanrig Castle, No. IX/17.

Oval, $2\frac{5}{8}'' \times 2''$, in contemporary turned ivory case. *c.* 1585–90.

Here again the oval face is set off well against the radiating ruff. She wears a black and white dress. The ivory box has no lid. The sitter was formerly called Princess Elizabeth.

LIT.: Vanderdoort's *Cat.* Mackay, C.14. Kennedy, pl. 5. Long, *Notes*,

"This appears to me a genuine and excellent miniature by Hilliard".

EXH.: B.F.A.C., 1909, Case C, No. 14. Reynolds *Catalogue*, 1947, No. 25.

67. *A Gentleman of the Family of St. John of Bletsho* (Pl. 70). The Duke of Portland, Welbeck Abbey.

Oval, $2\frac{1}{4}'' \times 1\frac{7}{8}''$. Inscribed: Anõ Dni. 1586, Ætatis Suæ 24.

Mr. Reynolds calls this miniature "an exceptionally well-preserved, unfaded, example of Hilliard's mature style".

PROV.: Lord St. John. Bought by second Earl of Oxford in the first half of the 18th century.

LIT.: Goulding, No. 15.

EXH.: Manchester, 1857, B.22, No. 23. B.F.A.C., 1926, pl. XXI, p. 59. Reynolds *Catalogue*, 1947, No. 31.

68. *An Unknown Lady*, (Pl. 71). The Earl of Radnor, Longford Castle.

Oval, $1\frac{3}{4}'' \times 1\frac{1}{2}''$. Kept in its original turned ivory box, with lid.

Perhaps the most sophisticated expression of all the portraits Hilliard painted, a most enchanting likeness.

PROV.: Kept with four other miniatures in a carved and gilt cabinet said to have been given by Queen Elizabeth to Lady Rich. It descended to Mrs. Ann Lewis; bought by second Earl of Radnor in 1796.

LIT.: Radnor, II, 1909, No. 2. Pope-Hennessy, *Lecture*, p. 23, pl. 19.

EXH.: Reynolds *Catalogue*, 1947, No. 41. R.A., British Portraits, 1956–7, No. 625.

69. *Mary Queen of Scots* (1542–1587) (Pl. 72). The Duke of Portland, Welbeck Abbey.

Oval, $2\frac{1}{2}'' \times 2''$. Inscribed Virtutis Amore.

A deeply moving miniature because of the white and grey shades which are wrapped round the Queen.

There is a touch of red in her curls and the book she is holding, otherwise everything is pale. The features are like those on the miniature Hilliard painted in 1578 of the same sitter. The inscription can be interpreted as the anagram Marie Stouart. The date is *c.* 1587, and it may be a memorial portrait.

PROV.: Coll. of Edward Lord Harley, later second Earl of Oxford.

LIT.: R. A. Lang, *Portraits and Jewels of Mary Stuart*, 1906, p. 23. Goulding, No. 8, pl. 1. Auerbach, *Tudor Portraits*, p. 13.

EXH.: R.A. 1934, No. 921. Reynolds *Catalogue*, 1947, No. 32. R.A., British Portraits, 1956–7, No. 619.

70. *Charles Blount, Earl of Devonshire.* The Earl of Beauchamp, Madresfield Court.
Oval, $1\frac{5}{8}'' \times 1\frac{5}{16}''$. Inscribed: In Servitute Dolor In Libertata Labor. *c.* 1586.

EXH.: Tudor, 1890, frame No. 1097, No. 1. Brussels, 1912, pl. V, No. 22. B.F.A.C., 1926, No. 11, pl. 23.

71. *Charles Blount, Earl of Devonshire* (*c.* 1562–1606) (Pl. 73). Coll. Sir John Carew Pole, Bt., Antony House.
Oval, $2'' \times 1\frac{1}{2}''$. Inscribed: Amor Amoris Premium Ano Dni. 1587.
Lord Mountjoy, by which name he was very well known, was one of the Queen's favourites and very good-looking. One of the finest portraits with excellent lettering and an exquisite rendering of armour and lace collar.

PROV.: The picture has always been in the family.

EXH.: Reynolds *Catalogue*, 1947, No. 34. Manchester, 1953, No. 34. R.A., British Portraits, 1956–7, No. 622. The Hague, The Age of Shakespeare, 1958, No. 8.

72. *A Man Clasping a Hand from the Cloud*, sometimes called *Earl of Essex* (Pl. 74). Formerly Viscount Morpeth, now Coll. Lord Wharton.
Oval, $2\frac{3}{8}'' \times 2''$. Inscribed: Attici amoris ergo. Anõ Dnĩ 1588.
A very well preserved miniature and one of the best known by Hilliard. The two hands are characteristic of Hilliard's manner. The colouring, based on a light mauve in the head and an orange in the beard, is lighter than that of the replica in the Victoria and Albert Museum. The allegorical inscription is difficult to explain. The writing is of the finest quality. Transparent shades. There is a replica in the Victoria and Albert Museum.

PROV.: The Earl of Carlisle. Viscount Morpeth. Sold at Sotheby's, 14 May 1959, Lot No. 115.

LIT.: Gower, II, as *Earl of Essex* by Isaac Oliver. Winter, *Eliz. Miniatures*, p. 24, note IVb.

EXH.: Leeds, Temple Newsam House, 1947. Amsterdam, The Triumph of Mannerism, 1955, No. 68. The Hague, The Age of Shakespeare, 1958, No. 110.

73. *A Man Clasping a Hand from the Cloud*, Victoria and Albert Museum. No. P21–1942.
Oval, $2\frac{3}{8}'' \times 2''$. Inscribed: Attici amoris ergo. Anõ dnĩ. 1588.
This replica of Pl. 74 is not so well preserved and is damaged on the left cheek of the face.

PROV.: Transferred from the B.M., Sloane, No. 272.

LIT.: Winter, *Eliz. Miniatures*, p. 24, pl. IVb. Pope-Hennessy, *Lecture*, p. 23.

EXH.: Reynolds *Catalogue*, 1947, No. 35.

74. *A Lady Called the Countess of Essex* (Pl. 75). Formerly Viscount Morpeth, now Coll. Harry G. Sperling, New York.
Oval, $2\frac{3}{8}'' \times 1\frac{7}{8}''$. Card.
The delicate colours and the minute rendering of the accessories of the dress and the slim hand and characteristic light modelling of the face are typical of Hilliard. It is a miniature of the first importance. The name of the sitter cannot be ascertained beyond doubt.
PROV.: Coll. of the Earl of Carlisle. Sold at Sotheby's, 14 May 1959, Lot 113.
LIT.: Gower, II, 1882, as Companion Picture to a Man Clasping a Hand from the Cloud, called Earl of Essex, also as Oliver.
EXH.: Leeds, Temple Newsam House, 1947. Amsterdam, The Triumph of Mannerism, 1955, No. 78. R.A. British Portraits, 1956–7, 624.

75. *An Unknown Lady* (Pl. 76). Victoria and Albert Museum. No. P.8–1945. R.A. Stevenson Bequest.
Oval, $2'' \times 1\frac{3}{4}''$. *c.* 1588. The bust portrait and the radiating ruff fills the frame almost completely.
EXH.: Reynolds *Catalogue*, 1947, No. 40.

76. *An Unknown Youth* (Pl. 78). The Duke of Rutland, Belvoir Castle.
Oval, $2'' \times 1\frac{5}{8}''$. *c.* 1588.
Another version of this miniature is at Madresfield Court, but this is by Isaac Oliver after Hilliard.
EXH.: Reynolds *Catalogue*, 1947, No. 33.

77. *An Unknown Young Man* (Pl. 79). Mr. J. N. Bryson.
Oval, $2\frac{1}{8}'' \times 1\frac{3}{4}''$. *c.* 1588.
An excellent example of Hilliard's best period and one that shows his modelling very well.

EXH.: Reynolds *Catalogue*, 1947, No. 39. R.A., British Portraits, 1956–7, No. 626.

78. *An Unknown Youth* leaning against a Tree among Roses (Pl. 80). Victoria and Albert Museum. No. P163–1910. Salting Bequest.
Oval, $5\frac{3}{8}'' \times 2\frac{3}{4}''$. Inscribed: DAT POENAS LAUDATA FIDES, transl. by Winter "My praised faith procures my pain", by Reynolds, "My praised faith causes my sufferings", and by Piper "My praised loyalty brings my penalty".
It is taken from Lucan's *De Bello Civili*, viii, lines 485 *et seq.* (Loeb ed.). The miniature of this typically Elizabethan portrait has always been praised as one of the masterworks of English art. Apart from the elongated figure, the roses and leaves are beautifully captured in their natural growth.
LIT.: Winter, *Eliz. Miniatures*, p. 26, pl. 7. Pope-Hennessy, *Lecture*, p. 20, pl. 15. Piper, *Essex*, pl. 16, as portrait of Essex.
EXH.: Reynolds *Catalogue*, 1947, No. 38.

79. *An Unknown Young Man* (Pl. 81). Metropolitan Museum of Art, New York. No. 35. 89. 4.
Oval, $1\frac{5}{8}'' \times 1\frac{3}{8}''$. Inscribed: Anõ. Dni. 1588. Ætatis Suæ 22.
Mr. Winter suggested that the sitter is the same as the youth among roses, and another bust portrait in the Duke of Rutland's Collection. Mr. Piper suggests the identification with the Earl of Essex for all three miniatures (pls. 80, 81 and 82). The date inscribed on this miniature would fit that of Essex, but I am not absolutely convinced that all three represent the same identity.

PROV.: Warwick Castle, and Pierpont Morgan collection, No. 48.

LIT.: Piper, *Essex*, pp. 300–3, pl. 17. Winter, *Eliz. Miniatures*, p. 26.

EXH.: Reynolds *Catalogue*, 1947, No. 36.

80. *An Unknown Young Man*, formerly called Sir Fulke Greville, 1st Lord Brooke (Pl. 82). The Duke of Rutland, Belvoir Castle, No. 9.

Oval, $1\frac{3}{4}'' \times 1\frac{3}{8}''$. *c.* 1588.

Supposed to be the same sitter as Pls. 81 and 80. But the features do not seem to be quite the same. According to the Belvoir Castle Catalogue this miniature was ascribed to Isaac Oliver, but is certainly by Hilliard. The identification with Sir Fulke Greville may be based on the resemblance with the young man in the Metropolitan Museum which originally came from Warwick Castle.

LIT.: R. C. Strong, "Queen Elizabeth, the Earl of Essex and Nicholas Hilliard", *Burl. Mag.*, CI, p. 146, pl. 34, as (?) Robert Devereux, Second Earl of Essex.

EXH.: Reynolds *Catalogue*, 1947, No. 37.

81. *An Unknown Lady*, (Pl. 83). The Marquess of Anglesey. On loan to Nat. Mus. of Wales, Cardiff.

Oval, $2\frac{3}{4}'' \times 2\frac{1}{4}''$. Inscribed: AnõDni. 1589, Ætatis Suæ 24.

The sitter appears elongated and elegant. Beautiful lettering.

EXH.: Reynolds *Catalogue*, 1947, No. 43.

82. *An Unknown Lady* (Pl. 84). The Marchioness of Cholmondeley, *c.* 1590.

A very fine miniature with a sweet expression.

EXH.: Reynolds *Catalogue*, 1947, No. 45. Agnews, 1959.

83. *Queen Elizabeth I* (Pl. 85). Mrs. Doris Herschorn.

Oval, $1\frac{3}{4}'' \times 1\frac{1}{2}''$, in a mount probably from the 17th century. *c.* 1590.

A beautiful portrait of the Queen, showing fine shading and altogether Hilliard at his best.

PROV.: Sold from coll. Captain J. H. Edwardes-Heathcote at Christie's, 13 June 1928. Formerly in the English Royal Collection, taken to France by James II in 1688, then in Coll. Louis XIV, until Revolution, when brought back into England. Afterwards Coll. second Earl Spencer; James Edwardes; Rev. Thomas Butts; the Edwardes family.

PROV.: As stated for Mary Queen of Scots, also in possession of Mrs. Herschorn.

EXH.: Reynolds *Catalogue*, 1947, No. 47. The Hague, The Age of Shakespeare, No. 39.

84. *Queen Elizabeth I* (Pl. 86). The Earl of Radnor, Longford Castle.

Oval, $2\frac{1}{2}'' \times 2''$, in contemporary turned ivory box. *c.* 1590.

An extremely good likeness of the Queen.

PROV.: This miniature was kept and still is with four others in a small carved and gilt cabinet. The cabinet is said to have been given with the miniatures by Queen Elizabeth I to Lady Rich. The others are Nos. 59, 60, 68, 108.

LIT.: Radnor, II, p. 109, No. 1.

EXH.: Reynolds *Catalogue*, 1947, No. 42.

85. *Robert Dudley, Earl of Leicester* (1532–1588) (Pl. 87). Formerly Mr. Bertram Currie.

Rectangular, $10\frac{1}{4}'' \times 7''$. *c.* 1586.

A genuine miniature by Hilliard, though it has been attributed to

Oliver. The elongated full-length figure and the modelling of the face are typical of Hilliard's style.

PROV.: Coll. of Lord de Lisle and Dudley. Sold Currie Sale, Christie's, 27 March 1953, No. 21.

EXH.: B.F.A.C. 1926, pl. 19, as Isaac Oliver. Reynolds *Catalogue*, 1947, No. 23.

86. *Sir Robert Dudley*, called Duke of Northumberland (Pl. 88). National Museum, Stockholm. No. Bih. 1669. Rectangular, $7\frac{1}{2}'' \times 4\frac{1}{2}''$.

A very good example of Hilliard's full length miniatures.

PROV.: From Coll. of Lord de Lisle and Dudley and Currie Coll. and sale, Christie's 27 March 1953, Lot 22.

LIT.: Reynolds, *Conn. Guide*, p. 133, pl. 71.

EXH.: South Kens. Mus., 1862, No. 2210. B.F.A.C., 1926, p. 53, No. 3, as attributed to Isaac Oliver. (Lent by Lawrence Currie.)

87. *George Clifford, third Earl of Cumberland* (1558–1605) (Pl. 89). National Maritime Museum, Greenwich. Rectangular, $10\frac{1}{8}'' \times 7''$. *c.* 1590.

This is one of the most ambitious full-length portraits by Hilliard. The Earl was the Queen's champion and this miniature may, to quote Winter, "commemorate the tilting on 17 November 1590 when he was first accepted as champion". He wears the Queen's glove attached to his hat. His shield hanging from the tree is decorated with an *impresa* of the earth between sun and moon with a Spanish motto *Hasta quan*.

PROV.: Buccleuch Coll.

LIT.: Kennedy, pl. 17. Winter, *Eliz. Miniatures*, pl. 5. Pope-Hennessy, *Lecture*, pl. 31.

EXH.: Reynolds *Catalogue*, 1947, No. 54.

88. *George Clifford, third Earl of Cumberland* (1558–1605) (Pl. 90). Formerly Sotheby Coll., now Starr Coll. Oval, $2\frac{3}{4}'' \times 2\frac{1}{4}''$. Inscribed: *Fulmen aquasque fero.* (I bear lightning and water.) *c.* 1590.

There is also the emblem of a thunderbolt which together with the motto alludes to the naval achievements of the Earl. The armour is identical with that of the Greenwich School, which was formerly in the collection of Lord Hothfield in Appleby Castle and is now in the Metropolitan Museum, New York. It was exhibited in R.A. 1934, No. 1477. A drawing for this suit of armour is in the Jacob Album in the Victoria and Albert Museum. It is one of the finest and most famous miniatures Hilliard painted.

PROV.: Northwick Coll. 1859, Lot. 779. Bought by Whitehead. Bought by C. Sotheby, 1862. The Sotheby Heirlooms, Part I, Sale Sotheby's 11 Oct. 1955, Lot. No. 74, sold to Leggat, now in Nelson Gallery, Starr Foundation, Kansas City.

EXH.: South Kens. Mus. 1862, No. 2642. B.F.A.C. 1889, p. 61, No. 4, pl. IV. Tudor, 1890, No. 1112. Manchester, 1926, No. 242. R.A., 1934, No. 927. Reynolds *Catalogue*, 1947, No. 54. Remained on loan to the Victoria and Albert Museum until 1955.

89. *George Clifford, third Earl of Cumberland*, after Hilliard. Formerly Laurence Currie Coll. Rectangular, $11'' \times 7\frac{1}{4}''$. There is a motto "Hasta quanto". Replica of the rectangular miniature in Greenwich.

PROV.: Coll. of Lord de Lisle and Dudley.

EXH.: South Kens. Mus., 1862, No. 2206. B.F.A.C., 1926, P.52, No. 3. Sold at Christie's, 27 March 1953, Lot No. 20.

90. *Sir Christopher Hatton* (1540–91) (Pl. 91). Victoria and Albert Museum. No. P.138–1910. Salting Bequest.
Oval, $2\frac{1}{2}'' \times 1\frac{3}{4}''$. *c.* 1590.

A full-length portrait of one of the favourites of Elizabeth's Court, and in spite of the small size a very lively portrait. Another version is at Belvoir Castle. See No. 91.

EXH.: B.F.A.C. 1889, P.99, No. 23, pl. III, from Lumsden Propert Coll. Tudor, 1890, No. 1131. Reynolds *Catalogue*, 1947, No. 50.

91. *Sir Christopher Hatton.* The Duke of Rutland, Belvoir Castle.
Oval, $2\frac{1}{4}'' \times 1\frac{7}{8}''$. *c.* 1590. A replica of the portrait in the Victoria and Albert Museum. There are differences in colour and in the background.

The figure on the miniature at Belvoir Castle is $\frac{1}{8}''$ shorter than that in the Victoria and Albert Museum.

EXH.: Reynolds *Catalogue*, 1947, No. 51.

92. *A Lady Called Anne Clifford, Countess of Pembroke* (1590–1676) (Pl. 92). Royal Coll., Windsor Castle.
Oval, $2\frac{1}{4}'' \times 1\frac{7}{8}''$. *c.* 1590.

The identity of the sitter is impossible, because of the date, which is defined by costume and style. It is a full-length figure, and the manner in which it is represented within an interior speaks for Hilliard's authorship.

PROV.: From Lord de Roos Coll.

LIT.: Cust, No. 22.

EXH.: Reynolds *Catalogue*, 1947, No. 46.

93. *Sir Anthony Mildmay* (died 1617) (Pl. 93), Cleveland Museum of Art, Ohio.
Rectangular, $9\frac{1}{4}'' \times 6\frac{7}{8}''$. *c.* 1595.

One of Hilliard's most interesting full-length miniatures. Sir Anthony Mildmay was the son of Sir Walter, and it will be remembered that Hilliard knew him personally. This miniature was formerly attributed to Oliver, but it is a genuine miniature by Hilliard.

PROV.: Coll. of Sir Miles Stapleton, Bart.; a descendant of Sir Anthony Mildmay.

LIT.: Pope-Hennessy, *Lecture*, pp. 18–19, pl. 13.

EXH.: Reynolds *Catalogue*, 1947, No. 57.

94. *Henry Percy, Ninth Earl of Northumberland* (?) (1564–1633) (Pl. 94). Dr. M. E. Kronenberg, Rotterdam.
Rectangular, $8\frac{3}{4}'' \times 5\frac{3}{4}''$. Water colour on vellum.

The whole length figure is reclining within a formal garden. He lies horizontally right in front and the garden with its wall and trees recedes into the depth. In the background some hills, and a pale sky. The foliage is painted in different shades of green; from one branch a cross-bar is suspended from which hangs a ball on the left and a feather on the right. TANTI in Roman letters written underneath. This device may be interpreted as scales with a writing-pen balanced against the world or a cannon-ball. It can be taken as an allusion to the power of a poet. A most ambitious and attractive miniature. It is slightly retouched on the lawn, just above the figure on the right hand side.

PROV.: The Earl of Aylesford, sold

at Christie's 23 July 1937, No. 45. Dr. Beets, Amsterdam, sold 9–11 April 1940, No. 66; bought by Dr. M. E. Kronenberg as *Sir Philip Sidney* by Nicholas Hilliard.

LIT.: Vertue, V, 84, describing Coll. of Duke of Somerset, predecessor of Earl of Aylesford, "a Lord Percy, a limning lying on the ground". Pope-Hennessy, *Lecture*, pl. 32.

95. *Henry Percy, Ninth Earl of Northumberland* (?) (Pl. 95). Fitzwilliam Museum, Cambridge, No. P.E.3–1953.

Oval, $2'' \times 2\frac{3}{8}''$. On a playing card, with narrow gold rim enclosing the oval.

A most attractive miniature and one which shows clearly that the whole composition fits the oval frame in a perfect arrangement. Excellent quality.

PROV.: Coll. of Lord de Lisle and Dudley. Captain Bertram Currie, sold Christie's 27 March 1953, Lot. No. 23, partly donated by Mr. E. Evelyn Barron to Fitzwilliam Museum.

LIT.: Williamson, *Portrait Miniatures*, pl. 7. Reynolds, *Conn. Guide*, pl. 74A.

EXH.: South Kens. Mus. 1862, No. 2212, as Henry, Ninth Earl of Northumberland. B.F.A.C. 1926, II (4) pl. 20, as Sir Philip Sidney by Isaac Oliver. Treasures of Cambridge, 1959, No. 327. For a whole-length version see pl. 93, Coll. Dr. M. E. Kronenberg, Rotterdam.

96. *Called Sir Philip Sidney* (Pl. 96). Private Collection bought from Sotheby's sale, 24 June 1948, Lot 188.

Rectangular, $5\frac{3}{8}'' \times 4\frac{1}{8}''$. *c.* 1590.

97. *Sir Henry Slingsby* (died 1634) (Pl. 97). The Fitzwilliam Museum,

Cambridge. Cunliffe Bequest, 1937.

Oval, $3\frac{3}{8}'' \times 2\frac{1}{2}''$. Inscribed: 1595, Æs. . 35. And at back in a seventeenth century hand, Sr Hen Slingsby father to Sir Henry Slingsby beheaded by Oliver Cromwell. An imposing miniature on which the sitter appears in a bigger size than usual against a crimson background.

PROV.: Coll. of H. J. Pfungst, Esq.

LIT.: Cat. of the Pfungst Coll. 1914–1918. Victoria and Albert Museum. pub., No. 110, pp. 12, 13.

EXH.: Brussels, 1912, No. 185, repr. Pl. V, No. 15, B.F.A.C., 1926, p. 58, No. 21, pl. XXIV. Reynolds *Catalogue*, 1947, No. 62. Treasures of Cambridge, 1959, No. 332.

98. *Robert Devereux, second Earl of Essex* (Pl. 98). Lady Lucas, Burhunt Farm, Selborne.

Rectangular, $9\frac{7}{8}'' \times 8''$. Water colour on vellum. Inscribed on the sitter's sword belt: "DVM FORMAS . . . VM EOR . . . MV? . . . NV". *c.* 1595.

The inscription may be read as: Dum Formas Minvis, which Essex used as an *impresa* at a tournament (Camden, *Remaines Concerning Britaine*, 1614, p. 228). This confirms identification of the sitter with Essex as suggested by Mr. Piper. The style points certainly to Hilliard as the painter. Formerly called *Sir Philip Sidney*. On the back a letter by Vertue, 1750, "*Sidney* by Oliver".

PROV.: Coll. of James West Esq., Philip, Earl of Hardwick, by descent to Baroness Lucas of Wrest Park, then to her daughter, Lady Lucas.

LIT.: Vertue, V, p. 84. Add. MSS. 23091. fols. 56 and 60. See p. 126, *ante* B. Siebeck, *Das Bild Sir R. Sidneys in der Englischen Renaissance*, 1939,

p. 168. Piper, *Essex*, p. 303, pl. 18. Roy C. Strong, "Queen Elizabeth, Earl of Essex and Hilliard," *Burl. Mag.* 1959, p. 146.

EXH.: R.A., British Portraits, 1956–57, No. 545.

99. *An Unknown Lady* (Pl. 99). Dr. Louis C. G. Clarke. Lent to the Fitzwilliam Museum, Cambridge.

Rectangular, $7\frac{1}{4}'' \times 4\frac{7}{8}''$. Unfinished, *c.* 1590.

An excellent miniature which, because it is unfinished, gives us a clear idea of Hilliard's method of working. In the background a crimson curtain which in itself is already complete in its colouring and reflections of the light on the material. The full-length figure is sketched against this with a black and white effect. The likeness of the face is already clearly recognisable.

EXH.: Reynolds *Catalogue*, 1947, No. 44.

100. *An Unknown Lady* (Pl. 100). Victoria and Albert Museum. Bequeathed by Mr. E. Peter Jones.

Oval, $2\frac{3}{8}'' \times 1\frac{7}{8}''$. *c.* 1595.

All the characteristics of Hilliard's style. Note the arched forehead, the eyes and the precise treatment of the hair.

PROV.: Coll. Mrs. Wyndham Cook. Mr. E. Peter Jones.

EXH.: Reynolds *Catalogue*, 1947, No. 63.

101. *An Unknown Lady* (Pl. 101). Cleveland Museum of Art, Ohio. Edward B. Greene Bequest, 1940.

Oval, $1\frac{1}{2}'' \times 1\frac{1}{4}''$. *c.* 1590–95.

A good characterisation of the woman's likeness.

PROV.: The Earl of Moray.

EXH.: Reynolds *Catalogue*, 1947, No. 59.

102. *Mrs. Holland* (Pl. 102). Victoria and Albert Museum, No. P.134–1910. Salting Bequest.

Oval, $2\frac{3}{8}'' \times 2''$. Inscribed: Anõ Dni 1593. Ætatis Suæ 26.

A fine miniature with beautiful writing. The details of the costume are brought out with minute care.

PROV.: Mr. S. Addington in 1865, sold Christie's, 26 April 1883, as Lady Elizabeth Russell, Maid of Honour to Queen Elizabeth. Lady Russell was afterwards Mrs. Holland.

LIT.: Winter, *Eliz. Miniatures*, pl. 11a.

EXH.: South Ken. Mus., 1865, No. 309. B.F.A.C., 1889, p. 101, case XXXIV, No. 51. Lumsden Propert Coll. Reynolds *Catalogue*, 1947, No. 60.

103. *An Unknown Lady* (Pl. 103). The Metropolitan Museum of Art, New York. No. 35.89.2.

Oval, $1\frac{7}{8}'' \times 1\frac{1}{2}''$. Inscribed: 1597.

The sitter was called Catherine Charlotte de la Trémoille, Princesse de Condé, but her identity cannot be established.

PROV.: John Pierpont Morgan Coll.

LIT.: Williamson, Pierpont Morgan Cat., No. 25. Christie's, June 24, 1935, 102.

EXH.: Reynolds *Catalogue*, 1947, No. 65.

104. *Called Lady Arabella Stuart* (Pl. 104). Museum of Fine Arts, Boston.

Oval, $2'' \times 1\frac{1}{2}''$. *c.* 1590.

PROV.: Given to the Museum in 1938 as "Attributed to Hilliard".

EXH.: South Kens. Mus., 1865, No. 651.

105. *An Unknown Lady*, called Mrs. Hilliard (Pl. 105). National Museum, Stockholm. No. Bih. 932.

Oval, $2'' \times 1\frac{1}{2}''$. The identity is doubtful.

PROV.: Thorsten Laurius Coll.

LIT.: Asplund, *Wicanders Col.*, pl. 286.

106. *A Lady, called Lady Arabella Stuart* (Pl. 106). Formerly Sotheby Coll.
Oval, $2\frac{1}{8}'' \times 1\frac{3}{4}''$.
A charming miniature of a young girl.
PROV.: The Maskell Coll. Bought by Sotheby in 1868 from Whitehead.
EXH.: B.F.A.C. 1889, No. 8. Ascribed to Isaac Oliver. Reynolds *Catalogue*, 1947, No. 69. Lent by Lieut.-Col. H. G. Sotheby to the Victoria and Albert Museum from 1947–55. Sold at Sotheby's 11 October, 1955, No. 65. Bought by Thos. Agnew.

107. *Catherine Carey, Countess of Nottingham* (died 1602) (Pl. 107). The Duke of Buccleuch, Drumlanrig Castle. No. IX/41.
Oval, $2'' \times 1\frac{5}{8}''$. *c.* 1595–1600.
A delightful miniature.
LIT.: Long, *Notes*, "This is a good miniature and may be by Hilliard". Mackay, D.R.A.20.
EXH.: Reynolds *Catalogue*, 1947, No. 71.

108. *An Unknown Man* (Pl. 108). The Earl of Radnor, Longford Castle.
Oval, $2\frac{3}{8}'' \times 1\frac{7}{8}''$. *c.* 1590.
Contained in contemporary turned ivory box with lid. A crimson curtain background. Much expression in face.
PROV.: Kept with four other miniatures in a carved and gilt cabinet said to have been given by Queen Elizabeth to Lady Rich. It descended to Mrs. Lewis, bought by second Earl of Radnor in 1796. The other miniatures are Nos. 59, 60, 68 and 84.
LIT.: Radnor, II, No. 5.
EXH.: Reynolds *Catalogue*, 1947, No. 52.

109. *Leonard Darr* (Pl. 109). The Duke of Portland, Welbeck Abbey.
Oval, $2\frac{3}{4}'' \times 2\frac{1}{2}''$. Inscribed: Anõ Ætatis Leonarde Darr. 37. Anõ Dni 1591.
An interesting miniature of an excellent quality. The modelling is achieved by bright red cross lines.
PROV.: Halstead Coll.
LIT.: Vertue, II, p. 13. Goulding, No. 16, pl. 1.
EXH.: Manchester, 1857, No. B.8. B.F.A.C. 1926, pl. 21. Reynolds *Catalogue*, 1947, No. 53.

110. *An Unknown Man*, called Charles Blount, Earl of Devonshire. The Earl of Beauchamp, Madresfield Court.
Oval, $3'' \times 2\frac{1}{4}''$. Inscribed: Anõ Dni 1593 Ætatis Suæ 26.
A very fine miniature.
EXH.: Brussels, 1912, pl. III. No. 11. B.F.A.C., 1926, p. 54, No. 5.

111. *Henry Wriothesley, third Earl of Southampton* (1573–1624) (Pl. 110). Fitzwilliam Museum, Cambridge. Cunliffe Bequest, 1937.
Oval, $1\frac{5}{8}'' \times 1\frac{3}{8}''$. Inscribed: Anõ Dni. 1594. Ætatis Suæ 20.
The Earl of Southampton was a patron of Shakespeare and was known for wearing his hair so long as to fall on his shoulders. One of the best examples of this period, with a crimson curtain background. A miniature of a *Young Man* called the same sitter, was sold at Sotheby's, 14 May 1959, Lot 13. The inscription, however, is different: Ano Doni. 1594, Ætatis Suæ 32.
PROV.: Cunliffe Coll.
LIT.: Goulding, Walpole Society VIII. R. C. Strong, "Queen Elizabeth, The Earl of Essex and Nicholas Hilliard", *Burl. Mag.*, CI (1959), p. 146, pl. 36.

EXH.: Reynolds *Catalogue*, 1947, No. 61. Treasures of Cambridge, 1959, No. 334.

112. *An Unknown Gentleman*, called Sir Walter Raleigh (Pl. 111). Musée de Condé, Chantilly. No. 216.
Oval, 2½″ × 1⅞″. Inscribed: In noua fert animus. Ano Dni 1595. On playing card.
Called *Walter Raleigh* by an unknown artist. The identity of the sitter is difficult to establish, though there is a faint likeness and the inscription would fit. There is however no doubt that Nicholas Hilliard painted this miniature.
PROV.: Coll. of the Duc d'Aumale.
EXH.: South Kens. Mus., 1865, No. 388. The whereabouts of this miniature were not known since.

113. *An Unknown Young Man*, aged 22 in 1596 (Pl. 112). National Museum, Stockholm. Bih. 931.
Oval, 2″ × 1¾″. Inscribed: Anõ Dni 1596, Ætatis Suæ 22.
Though I have not seen this miniature in the original, it seems to be a genuine Hilliard.
PROV.: Bukowski's Art dealers 1919.
LIT.: Karl Asplund, *Wicanders Coll.* attr. to Hilliard. Cat. No. 287, pl. 110.

114. *George Clifford, third Earl of Cumberland* (Pl. 113). Mr. Alan Evans, No. 21a, in Alan Evans Loan to Victoria and Albert Museum.
Oval, 2″ × 1⅝″. Inscribed: Anõ . . . ætatis suæ 3- 1593 (?).
The background is very much repainted. Traces of the old inscription are visible and the date can be more or less guessed as 1593 or 94.
EXH.: Reynolds *Catalogue*, 1947, No. 56.

115. *An Unknown Man* (Pl. 114). Victoria and Albert Museum. Bequeathed by Mr. U. Copp, No. P.5-1944.

Oval, 2″ × 1⅝″. Inscribed: Anõ Dni 1597, Ætatis Suæ 22.
Much expression in this portrait. One hand visible.
EXH.: Reynolds *Catalogue*, 1947, No. 66.

116. *Sir Thomas Bodley* (1545-1613) (Pl. 115). The Bodleian Library, Oxford.
Oval, 2″ × 1⅝″. Inscribed: Anõ Dnĩ 1598, Ætatis Suæ 54. In a contemporary turned ivory box.
A very good specimen of Hilliard's calligraphy. The Bodleian was founded in 1598 by Sir Thomas Bodley and it is interesting that this was the year in which the miniature was painted.
PROV.: Bodleian Library, Oxford.
LIT.: Roy C. Strong, "Queen Elizabeth, the Earl of Essex and Nicholas Hilliard" *Burl. Mag.*, CI, 1959, pl. 35.
EXH.: Reynolds *Catalogue*, 1947, No. 67.

117. *An Unknown Young Man* (Pl. 116). The Earl of Leicester.
Circular, dia. 1¼″. Signed at back N. Hilliarde, Fecit 1599.
The signature in gold at the back is a unique feature. The calligraphy is specially fine. I tentatively suggested that this miniature may represent Laurence Hilliard as a young man, as such a picture is mentioned in the latter's will.
EXH.: Reynolds *Catalogue*, 1947, No. 70.

118. *An Unknown Gentleman* (Pl. 117) in the manner of Nicholas Hilliard. The Duke of Buccleuch, Drumlanrig Castle. No. VII/8.
Oval, 1⅞″ × 1½″. Inscribed: Ano Dni 1599. Ætatis suæ 28.
Light colouring, the face is much retouched. The lettering in Hilli-

ard's manner. There is however a certain smoothness which makes the attribution to Hilliard himself slightly doubtful.

LIT.: Mackay, D.R.B. 35.

119. *An Unknown Man against a background of Flames* (Pl. 118). Victoria and Albert Museum. No. P.5–1917. Captain H. B. Murray's Bequest. Oval, $2\frac{5}{8}'' \times 2\frac{1}{8}''$.

The burning flames in the background are taken from a well-known motif often mentioned in Renaissance literature. The playing card upon which the parchment is stuck is the ace of hearts.

PROV.: Henry J. Pfungst Coll. Described in his catalogue of 1914–15.

LIT.: Victoria and Albert Museum, *Annual Review* 1917, pp. 44–45. It was formerly ascribed to Oliver. Winter, *Eliz. Miniatures*, pl. 6b. Pope-Hennessy, *Lecture*, pl. 20. Reynolds, *Conn. Guide*, p. 133, pl. 74b.

EXH.: Reynolds *Catalogue*, 1947, No. 64. South Kens. Mus., 1865, No. 1934. The Hague, The Age of Shakespeare, 1958, No. 107, pl. 13.

120. *Edmund Spenser* (1533–99). Present whereabouts are unknown.

EXH.: South Kens. Mus., 1862, No. 2,306 (Lord Fitzhardinge). South Kens. Mus., 1865, No. 1,485, repr.

121. *George Carey*, second Lord Hunsdon, 1547–1603 (Pl. 119). Berkeley Castle.

Oval, $1\frac{7}{8}'' \times 1\frac{1}{2}''$. Inscribed: Anõ Dnĩ. 1601, Ætatis suæ 54.

The penetration of the character true to Hilliard's best style. Pale blue background.

PROV.: Apparently always in the family.

EXH.: South Kens. Mus., 1862, No. 2,292 as "Portrait of a man in

black dress" etc. by "I. Oliver"? Lent by Lord Fitzhardinge.

122. *Elizabeth Spencer, Lady Hunsdon*, 1575–1611 (Pl. 120). Berkeley Castle. Oval, $2\frac{1}{4}'' \times 2''$.

It is not quite so well preserved as that of the husband, and bigger in size. It must have been painted at approximately the same time. 18th century frame.

EXH.: South Kens. Mus., 1862, No. 2,309. She was the mother of Elizabeth, Lady Berkeley. Lent by Lord Fitzhardinge. South Kens. Mus., 1865, No. 1487.

123. *Frances Howard, Duchess of Richmond and Lennox*, 1576–1639 (Pl. 121). The Duke of Buccleuch, Drumlanrig Castle, No. IX/37. Oval, $3'' \times 2\frac{3}{8}''$. c. 1600.

Red curtained background. Pattern of flowers on dress. Excellent quality. Reflections of light in background. Likeness full of character. One hand visible.

LIT.: Mackay, D.R.A. No. 27. Kennedy, pl. 22.

EXH.: Reynolds *Catalogue*, 1947, No. 72.

124. *Frances Howard, Duchess of Richmond and Lennox* (Pl. 122). National Museum, Stockholm. No. Bih.1694. Oval, $3'' \times 2\frac{3}{8}''$. c. 1600.

Identical with the miniature of the same sitter in the Coll. of the Duke of Buccleuch, pl. 121, but slightly different in colours and she holds in her left hand a posy of white flowers.

PROV.: The Sotheby Coll. Bought by Charles Sotheby from Colnaghi in 1861, sold 11 October 1955 at Sotheby's, No. 66.

EXH.: Reynolds *Catalogue*, 1947, No. 73. On loan to Victoria and Albert from 1947–55.

125. *An Unknown Lady* (Pl. 123). The Duke of Buccleuch, Drumlanrig Castle, No. I,16.
Oval, $2\frac{1}{4}'' \times 1\frac{7}{8}''$.
This is definitely by Hilliard. A pale green thistle with a mauve flower pinned to her grey and black dress. White flowers in her hair. Excellent quality.
LIT.: Mackay, C.18. Kennedy, pl. V. Formerly called Queen Elizabeth I by Isaac Oliver. Long, *Notes*, "Doubtful whether by Oliver or Hilliard."
EXH.: South Kens. Mus., 1862, No. 2,037. B.F.A.C. 1909. Reynolds *Catalogue*, 1947, No. 68.

126. *An Unknown Lady* (Pl. 124). The Fitzwilliam Museum, Cambridge.
Oval, $2\frac{7}{8}'' \times 2\frac{1}{8}''$. *c.* 1595–1600.
Bought in May 1942 from the Buccleuch Coll.
A most attractive miniature in a grey-blue costume with a Fleur-de-Lys jewel. A red cherry brooch relieves the grey of the dress. The curls and the bonnet are characteristic of Hilliard's manner. Formerly called Anne Clifford, Countess of Dorset and Pembroke, who was however born only in 1590; this date makes the identification questionable.
PROV.: Coll. of the Duke of Buccleuch.
LIT.: Kennedy, pl. 13. Ascribed to Isaac Oliver. Winter, *Eliz. Miniatures*, pl. 10a.
EXH.: Reynolds *Catalogue*, 1947, No. 47.

127. *Queen Elizabeth I* (Pl. 125). Ham House.
Oval, $3\frac{3}{4}'' \times 2\frac{3}{4}''$ on card. *c.* 1600.
One of the most ambitious portraits of the Queen. Three-quarter length, both hands visible, pattern of sleeves, open ruff, the hair and all details beautifully executed. In the background indication of the throne
PROV.: Coll. of the Earl of Dysart. On the back is written "Queen Elizabeth, by Hilliard. Pret. 5£."
LIT.: O'Donoghue, p. 32, No. 30. Reynolds, *Conn. Guide.*, p. 132, pl. 72a.

128. *Queen Elizabeth I* (pl. 126). Fitzwilliam Museum, Cambridge, bequeathed by Leverton Harris, 1926.
Oval, $2\frac{1}{8}'' \times 1\frac{5}{8}''$. *c.* 1600.
A very colourful portrait of the Queen. Half length figure, the face relatively small, one hand with slim fingers visible, the costume beautifully rendered.
PROV.: A. Wylie, Esq.
EXH.: Reynolds *Catalogue*, 1947, No. 77. Treasures of Cambridge, 1959, No. 331.

129. *Queen Elizabeth I*, Fredericton Art Gallery, New Brunswick.
Oval, $2\frac{3}{8}'' \times 1\frac{7}{8}''$. In a gilt frame of *c.* 1700.
An extremely fine miniature.
PROV.: Acquired by James Sotheby *c.* 1720. Sold 11 October 1955, at Sotheby's, Lot 73.
LIT.: Vertue, 1741. O'Donoghue, p. 29, No. 16. *Country Life*, 28 August 1927, p. 314. Auerbach, *Portraits of Elizabeth I*, pl. 38.
EXH.: South Kens. Mus., 1862, No. 2645. B.F.A.C., 1889, p. 61, Case XXI, No. 6, pl. III. Tudor, 1890, No. 1105. Reynolds *Catalogue*, 1947, No. 75. Exh. V. & A., 1947-55.

130. *Queen Elizabeth I* (Pl. 127). The Earl of Derby, Knowsley Hall.
Oval, $2'' \times 1\frac{5}{8}''$, *c.* 1600.
Short bust. The face shows a good likeness against a crimson background.
PROV.: Family Coll.

LIT.: Scharf, No. 221.

EXH.: B.F.A.C., 1889, p. 60, Case XX, No. 3. Reynolds *Catalogue*, 1947, No. 76.

131. *Queen Elizabeth I* (Pl. 128). Victoria and Albert Museum, Jones Bequest, No. 622–1882.
Oval, $2\frac{3}{8}'' \times 2\frac{1}{2}''$.
Very colourful and a most lively portrait.
PROV.: Jones Coll.
LIT.: Cat. Jones Coll., part III, p. 18. Winter, *Eliz. Miniatures*, pl. 6a. Pope-Hennessy, *Lecture*, pl. 24a.
EXH.: Reynolds *Catalogue*, 1947, No. 78.

132. *Queen Elizabeth I* (Pl. 129). Victoria and Albert Museum, No. 4404–1857.
Oval, $2\frac{1}{2}'' \times 1\frac{7}{8}''$.
This splendid miniature is kept in its locket. The Queen's bust portrait is seen against a crimson curtain. At the back of the case there is a design of dolphins and foliage in champlevé enamel on black ground after a design by Daniel Mignot. The lid is of pierced gold.
LIT.: J. Evans, *English Jewellery*, 1921, p. 101, pl. XX. Winter, *Eliz. Miniatures*, pl. IVa.

133. *Queen Elizabeth I* at the back of a cameo. The Duke of Devonshire, Chatsworth.
Apart from this badly damaged miniature there is a second one, said to represent the Earl of Leicester. Both seem to be cut to fit the cameos.
LIT.: O'Donoghue, p. 28, No. 11.
EXH.: Reynolds *Catalogue*, 1947, No. 105.

134. *Peregrine Bertie*, 1st Baron Willoughby de Eresby (1555–1601). Victoria

and Albert Museum, No. 5–1947. R.H. Stephenson Bequest.
Oval, $1\frac{1}{4}'' \times \frac{3}{4}''$, c. 1600.

135. *King James I* (1566–1625) (Pl. 131). Royal Coll., Windsor Castle.
Oval, $1\frac{5}{8}'' \times 1\frac{3}{8}''$. c. 1605.
A short half length, turned three-quarters to the right, the king wears a black hat and a white embroidered doublet. This was a popular type.
LIT.: Cust, No. 43. Reynolds, *Walpole Society*, No. A.3.
EXH.: Reynolds *Catalogue*, 1947, No. 80. R.A., Kings and Queens, 1953, No. 114.

136. *King James I* (Pl. 132). Victoria and Albert Museum. No. P.3–1957.
Oval, $2\frac{1}{8}'' \times 1\frac{5}{8}''$. Inscribed in Roman letters round the edge of the background, IACOBVS. DEI. GRA-[C]IA MAGNAE. BRITANIAE FRAN ET. HIBE REX.
The miniature was not painted before 1604, when James I substituted the wording Brit. Rex for Ang. Sco . . . Rex on his coins. The King is shown as a good half-length with the right hand visible, white doublet and white hat, and he wears the Garter ribbon and lesser George. A good likeness of the earlier portrait type.
PROV.: Bought by the Museum from Commandant F. Besançon, Châlons, to whose family the miniature had belonged for a number of years.
LIT.: Reynolds, *Walpole Society*, No. A.1., pl. V, A.
EXH.: Reynolds *Catalogue*, 1947, No. 87.

137. *King James I* (Pl. 133). Kunsthistorisches Mus., Vienna. No. 215.
Oval, $1\frac{5}{8}'' \times 1\frac{1}{4}''$. c. 1604.
The bust portrait of the king is represented in front of a cerise cur-

tain. He wears a white doublet and a plumed hat, the lesser George is visible.

PROV.: Added to the coll. of Archduke Ferdinand in 18th century, perhaps from the Wiener Schatzkammer.

LIT.: F. Kenner, "Die Portratsämmlung des Erzherzogs Ferdinand von Tirol", *Jahrb. der Kunsthist. Samml. des Allerh. Kaiserh.*, XIX, 1898, No. 215, p. 94 Reynolds, *Walpole Society*, No. A.2.

138. *King James I.* The Duke of Buccleuch, Drumlanrig Castle, No. IX/2.
Oval, $1\frac{1}{2}'' \times 1\frac{1}{4}''$.
Crimson curtain in background. Similar to Pl. 131, but with a different hat plume.
LIT.: Mackay, D.2. Reynolds, *Walpole Society*, No. A.4.

139. *King James I* (Pl. 134). The Marchioness of Cholmondeley.
Oval, $1\frac{5}{8}'' \times 1\frac{1}{4}''$. Inscribed Anõ Dnĩ. 1608. Ætatis suæ 42.
Good lettering in gold stands on a blue ground. The king wears the Garter ribbon and part of the lesser George is visible. A good likeness. He wears the usual hat, this time with a light plume.
PROV.: Lent by Baronne G. de Rothschild to Brussels Exh. 1912, No. 840.
LIT.: Goulding, p. 35. Farquhar, *Portraiture of Stuart Monarchs*, p. 160 et seq., points to similarity with likeness on "The Peace with Spain medal", 1604—see p. 325, post and Pl. 184a. Reynolds, *Walpole Society*, No. A.3.
EXH.: Brussels, 1912, No. 840. Reynolds *Catalogue*, 1947, No. 94.

140. *Anne of Denmark* (1574–1619). (Pl. 135). Kunsthistorisches Museum, Vienna. No. 215A.

Oval, $1\frac{5}{8}'' \times 1\frac{1}{4}''$.
Companion picture to James I (Pl. 133) in Vienna. Crimson curtain background.
PROV.: Same history as for Pl. 133.
LIT.: Kenner, *loc. cit.* No. 215A. Reynolds, *Walpole Society*, No. B.3.

141. *Anne of Denmark* (Pl. 136). The Marchioness of Cholmondeley.
Oval, $1\frac{5}{8}'' \times 1\frac{1}{4}''$.
A very fine miniature and a good likeness of the Queen.
PROV.: Baronne G. de Rothschild.
LIT.: Reynolds, *Walpole Society*, No. B.4.
EXH.: Brussels, 1912, No. 94. Reynolds *Catalogue*, 1947, No. 95.

142. *Henry VII* (Pl. 137). Royal Coll., Windsor Castle, inscribed Ano Dni 1509 Ætatis Suæ 54.
Circular, dia. $1\frac{1}{4}''$. *c.* 1600–1610.
This miniature and three others representing Henry VIII, Jane Seymour, and Edward VI belonged together and were part of a jewel which was fully described by Vanderdoort in his Cat. At the top there was originally an enamelled representation of the battle of Bosworth Field, between Henry VII and Richard III. The miniature is probably based on a contemporary oil portrait. It is precise and very fine in its execution.
PROV.: Coll. of Charles I, given by Laurence Hilliard to the King.
LIT.: Vertue IV, p. 67. Cust, No. 3.
EXH.: Tudor, 1890, p. 209, No. 1065, Reynolds *Catalogue*, 1947, No. 81.

143. *Henry VIII* (Pl. 138). Royal Coll., Windsor Castle,
Circular, dia. $1\frac{1}{4}''$. Inscribed 1536 Ætatis Suæ 46. *c.* 1600–10.
This miniature was also a part of the jewel which was given to Charles I.

by Laurence Hilliard, mentioned in Vanderdoort's Cat. The likeness seems to be based on Holbein's drawing. Of an excellent quality.
PROV.: Coll. Charles I.
LIT.: Cust, No. 10. Vertue, IV. p. 67.
EXH.: Reynolds *Catalogue*, 1947, No. 82.

144. *Edward VI* (Pl. 139). Royal Coll., Windsor Castle.
Circular, dia. 1¼". Inscribed Ætatis Suæ 14. Regni 6. *c.* 1600–10.
The portrait likeness of this excellent miniature is clearly based on Guillam Scrotes' image of the King. It is like the other three miniatures of this jewel of an excellent quality.
PROV.: Coll. Charles I.
LIT.: Vertue, IV, p. 67. Cust, No. 12.
EXH.: Reynolds *Catalogue*, 1947, No. 84.

145. *Jane Seymour* (Pl. 140). Royal Coll., Windsor Castle.
Circular, dia. 1¼". Inscribed Ano Dni 1536, Ætatis Suæ 27, *c.* 1600–10.
A part of the jewel which was decorated with the battle of Bosworth Field and given to Charles I by Laurence Hilliard. (Vanderdoort's Cat.) An exquisite miniature, based on Holbein's portrait of Jane Seymour in Vienna, the original drawing of which is preserved in Windsor Castle.
PROV.: Coll. Charles I.
LIT.: Vertue, IV, p. 67. Cust, No. 5.
EXH.: Reynolds *Catalogue*, 1947, No. 83.

146. *Called Sir Walter Raleigh* (Pl. 141). Mr. A. D. R. Caröe.
Oval, 2⅛" × 1¾". *c.* 1605.
The identity of the sitter is difficult to establish. The features are well

modelled and the tall hat gives it a most imposing appearance.
EXH.: Reynolds *Catalogue*, 1947, No. 92.

147. *An Unknown Gentleman* (Pl. 142), by Nicholas Hilliard (?). The Duke of Buccleuch, No. IX/16.
Circular, dia. 1⅝". Inscribed Ano Dni 1603. Ætatis Suæ 26.
The miniature with its calligraphic writing is attractive but not definitely Hilliard's work. It might be by Laurence. The sitter has been wrongly identified as Henry Wriothesley, K.G., 3rd Earl of Southampton.
LIT.: Mackay, Frame B. No. 12. *Burl. Mag.*, VIII, p. 317. *Walpole Society*, 1919–20. Kennedy, pl. XI. Williamson, *Portrait Miniatures*, I, pl. VI.

148. *Sir Walter Raleigh* (?), by Nicholas Hilliard (?). The Duke of Buccleuch. Drumlanrig Castle, No. VII/20.
Oval, 1¾" × 1½".
The face has much faded; the dull pink of the head and the doublet bring a touch of colour into the miniature. It is in Hilliard's style, though his authorship cannot be established beyond doubt. The identity of the sitter cannot be ascertained.
LIT.: Mackay, A.A. No. 2.
EXH.: S. Kens. Mus., 1862, No. 2,795.

149. *Henry Frederick*, Prince of Wales (Pl. 143). Royal Coll., Windsor Castle.
Oval, 1⅜" × 1⅛". *c.* 1603.
The Prince is portrayed here as a boy in armour. The back of the card bears the monogram H.F.P. and the Prince of Wales feathers on a black ground.
PROV.: Believed to be part of the English Royal Coll. and to have

been taken to France by James II in 1688; from him to Louis XIV; brought back to England. Coll. of 2nd Earl of Spencer, James Edwardes, Rev. Thomas Butts, the Edwardes family, Earl of Eglinton and Winton, sold Christie's 13 July 1922 to Mr. Harry Seal. Sold Christie's 16 February 1949, bought for King George VI.

LIT.: Reynolds, *Walpole Society*. No. C.2.

EXH.: Reynolds *Catalogue*, 1947, No. 85.

150. *Charles I* as a boy (Pl. 144). Victoria and Albert Museum. No. P.10–1947.

Oval, $1\frac{3}{8}'' \times 1\frac{1}{8}''$.

The young prince wears a white doublet with silver stripes.

PROV.: Bought by Mr. Peter Jones in 1928 from Coll. of Capt. J. H. Edwardes Heathcote, 13 June, 1928 (formerly in the Royal Coll.), taken to France, brought back to England, in Edwardes family. Given by Mr. Peter Jones to the Museum in 1947.

LIT.: M. R. Toynbee, "Some early portraits of Charles I", *Burl. Mag.*, XCI, pp. 4–9, dates the miniature *c.* 1608–9. Reynolds, *Walpole Society*, No. D.1.

EXH.: Reynolds *Catalogue*, 1947, No. 86.

151. *Charles Howard*, Baron Howard of Effingham (Pl. 145). Nat. Maritime Mus. Greenwich.

Oval, $2'' \times 1\frac{5}{8}''$. Inscribed Ano Dni. 1605.

The portrait of a knight wearing the Garter, therefore identified as Baron Howard of Effingham who lived from 1536–1624. A fine picture of Hilliard's late phase.

PROV.: Coll. of the Duke of Buccleuch, Mackay, AA5. Wrongly

called *Henry Carey, 1st Baron Hunsdon* (d. 1596).

LIT.: Winter, p. 27, pl. Xb.

EXH.: South Kens. Mus., 1862, No. 1939. South Kens. Mus., 1865, No. 1646. B.F.A.C., 1889, Case II, No. 1 as Henry Carey, Lord Hunsdon. Reynolds *Catalogue*, 1947, No. 91.

152. *An Unknown Lady* (Pl. 146). The Marquess of Salisbury, Hatfield House. Oval, $1\frac{3}{4}'' \times 1\frac{1}{2}''$. Inscribed S qui bien aim(e) tard oublie S. 1605.

An exquisite miniature with beautiful colouring and well composed within the oval frame.

EXH.: Reynolds *Catalogue*, 1947, No. 90.

153. *Lady Elizabeth Stanley* (1586–1632/3). (Pl. 147). Viscount Bearsted.

Oval, $2\frac{1}{2}'' \times 2''$. Inscribed: facies mutabilis/sed amor stabilis/semel missa/semp fixa, and at back Demitte michi deus/parce Deus; *c.* 1605–10.

In the clouds in the background a pierced-through heart. One of the most beautiful miniatures of this late period, typically mannerist in conception.

PROV.: Coll. of Horace Walpole, given by him to Sir H. W. Huntingdon.

LIT.: G. C. Williamson, *Apollo*, 1926, July, pl. 32. Pope-Hennessy, *Lecture*, p. 24, pl. 25a. Reynolds, *Miniatures*, pl. III, No. 9.

EXH.: Reynolds *Catalogue*, 1947, No. 96. Manchester, 1953, No. 6. R.A., British Portraits, 1956–7, No. 634. Amsterdam, The Triumph of Mannerism, 1955, No. 70.

154. *Called Lady Arabella Stuart* (Pl. 148), Victoria and Albert Museum, P.15–1941. Given by Mrs. S. S. Joseph. Oval, $1\frac{1}{4}'' \times 1''$.

In spite of the small size it is pre-

cisely drawn and full of expression.
EXH.: Reynolds *Catalogue*, 1947, No. 93.

155. *An Unknown Lady* (Pl. 149). The Earl of Derby, Knowsley Hall.
Oval, $1\frac{7}{8}'' \times 1\frac{1}{2}''$. *c.* 1605–10.
A beautiful portrait with loose hair and a deep expression.
PROV.: Coll. of Horace Walpole.
LIT.: G. Scharf, No. 219, as *Elizabeth of Bohemia* by I. Oliver. By comparison of this likeness with authentic portraits of the Queen of Bohemia, her identification here cannot be maintained.
EXH.: Reynolds *Catalogue*, 1947, No. 97. R.A. British Portraits, 1956–7, No. 633.

156. *Mrs. Mole* (Pl. 150). Miss M. R. Bulkeley.
Oval, $2'' \times 1\frac{5}{8}''$.
She was Elizabeth, wife of Mr. John Mole and her miniature was found in Mr. Mole's possession when he was imprisoned. It was returned to his family by an English gentleman who visited him in Rome.
PROV.: Lord Clinton, 1905, the Hon. Mrs Fane, 1950.
LIT.: Pope-Hennessy *Lecture*, p. 24. pl. 23. Piper, *The English Face*, pl. 27.
EXH.: Reynolds *Catalogue*, 1947, No. 97b. R.A. British Portraits, 1956–57, No. 628.

157. *Mr. John Mole* (Pl. 151). Miss M. R. Bulkeley.
Oval, $1\frac{7}{8}'' \times 1\frac{1}{2}''$. *c.* 1605.
Slightly stiff in conception but probably quite a good likeness. Mr. John Mole of Molton, Co. York, travelled with the grandson of Thomas, Earl of Exeter, but as a Protestant he objected to crossing the Alps. When they arrived at Rome, he was imprisoned for 30 years and died there *c.* 1640 (P.R.O., S.P.23/101).

PROV.: Lord Clinton 1905, the Hon. Mrs. Fane 1950.
EXH.: Reynolds *Catalogue*, 1947, No. 97a. R.A., British Portraits, 1956–7, No. 627.

158. *Henry Frederick, Prince of Wales* (Pl. 152). Royal Coll., Windsor Castle.
Oval, $2\frac{3}{8}'' \times 2''$. Inscribed in gold on the curtain Ano Dni. 1607. Ætatis Suæ 14.
An exquisite miniature of Hilliard's late phase, and a most attractive and rare likeness. Half-length with one hand akimbo. The armour is given in transparent shades and most accomplished in Hilliard's style. A helmet with white plumes on the left against a dark background. A red curtain on the right.
PROV.: Coll. Charles I, Vanderdoort's Cat. No. 20 as "done by the old Hilliard".
LIT.: Cust, No. 53. Reynolds, *Walpole Society*, 1958, C.I., pl. VI, E.

159. *An Unknown Young Man* (Pl. 153). Royal Coll., Windsor Castle.
Oval, $1\frac{3}{4}'' \times 1\frac{3}{8}''$.
An excellent example of Hilliard's late style. Clearly-drawn features are shown in this bust portrait against a red curtain background. Undoubtedly a genuine Hilliard as emerges from the modelling of the forehead and the hair.
LIT.: Ascribed to Hilliard by Reynolds in typewritten catalogue in the library of Windsor Castle.

160. *James I* by Nicholas Hilliard. Mr. and Mrs. Eric H. Heckett, Valencia, Pennsylvania.
Oval, $1\frac{3}{4}'' \times 1\frac{1}{2}''$, inscribed Ano Dni. 1609, Regni 43.
The earliest of the second type.
PROV.: Coll. Lord de Lisle and Dudley. Mr. Lawrence Currie, sold Christie's 1953, No. 26.

LIT.: Williamson, Portrait Miniatures I, p. 33, repr. Pl. VII. No. 4 as Oliver. Reynolds, *Walpole Society*, A.6. Goulding, p. 35. "Four Centuries of Portrait Miniatures from the Heckett Collection", Pittsburgh, 1954, No. 28, pl. III.

EXH.: B.F.A.C., 1926, p. 52, pl. 20.

161. *King James I*, Mr. George Howard. Oval, $1\frac{7}{8}'' \times 1\frac{1}{2}''$. Inscribed on background Ano Dni 1610. Ætatis Suæ 45.

PROV.: Coll. of the Earl of Carlisle.

LIT.: Gower, II, Pl. 6, by I. Oliver. Goulding, p. 35. Reynolds, *Walpole Society*, A.7.

162. *King James I* (Pl. 154). Royal Coll., Windsor Castle.

Oval, $1\frac{7}{8}'' \times 1\frac{1}{2}''$. c. 1610.

Short half length, the King's doublet is lavender blue, and he wears the lesser George suspended from the Garter ribbon. Red curtain background. Mr. Reynolds identified this miniature as No. 44 of Vanderdoort's Cat., described as follows: "Done by old Hilliard, bought by the King ... Another of King James's of famous memory, a picture without a hat, in a bone lace falling band in a lavender cloth suit."

PROV.: Coll. Charles I.

LIT.: Cust, No. 48, as by Oliver. Reynolds, *Walpole Society*, No.A.8., pl. V, c.

EXH.: R.A., Kings and Queens, 1953, No. 115.

163. *King James I* (Pl. 155), formerly Mr. Harry Seal.

Oval, $2\frac{1}{8}'' \times 1\frac{5}{8}''$. In contemporary locket. c. 1610.

Half-length; the King is wearing a black doublet, and the lesser George is suspended from the Garter ribbon. Curtained background. One hand visible.

PROV.: Earl of Eglinton and Winton. Sold Christie's, 13 July 1922, Lot 78; bought by Mr. Seal. Sold Christie's, 16 February 1949, Lot No. 106; bought by H. E. Backer.

LIT.: Reynolds, *Walpole Society*, No. A.9.

EXH.: Reynolds *Catalogue*, 1947, No. 98.

164. *King James I* (Pl. 156). Scottish National Portrait Gallery. No. L. 153. Oval, $2'' \times 1\frac{5}{8}''$. Inscribed IACOBVS. D:G... MAG.BRIT. FR.ET. HIB.REX.

The king wears a white doublet and is seen in good half length. One hand is visible, blue background. A most impressive portrait.

PROV.: W. G. Buchanan, Esq., bought in Stirling in 1935.

LIT.: Reynolds, *Walpole Society*, No. A.10.

165. *King Charles I as a young man* (Pl. 157 and Pl. 160). Victoria and Albert Museum. No. P.150–1910. Salting Bequest.

Oval, $2'' \times 1\frac{5}{8}''$.

As King Charles I did not receive the Garter until May 1611, which he is here represented as wearing, this miniature must have been painted shortly after 1611.

He wears a white doublet and a tall hat seen against a red curtained background. This miniature is one of six included in a 17th-century frame. The latter resembles a black ebony frame in the Buccleuch Coll. which is supposed to have been in the Royal Coll. at the beginning of the 17th century.

PROV.: Salting Bequest.

LIT.: Hand-list of miniatures of the Victoria and Albert Museum, 1930,

as Oliver. Toynbee, *ibid.*, p. 9.
Reynolds, *Walpole Society*, No. D.2,
pl. VI, C.

EXH.: Reynolds *Catalogue*, 1947, No.
89.

166. *Charles I as Prince of Wales* (Pl. 158).
The Duke of Rutland, Belvoir
Castle. Vellum,
Oval, $3\frac{1}{4}" \times 2\frac{3}{4}"$. Inscribed round
the rim; ILLVSTRISSIMVS ET
SERENISSIMVS. CAROLVS
WALLIAS PRINCEPS MAGNAE
BRITANIAE MAXIMA SPES
ANNO ÆTATIS SVA 14.

A most ostentatious and attractive
miniature with an elaborate background; on the right, above the
Prince of Wales feathers a cloud
with rays of light emerging from it,
on the left an iris against a distant
landscape and the sky. The Prince
is of a good half-length, his left arm
akimbo, wearing the Garter ribbon
and lesser George, and a huge cart-
wheel ruff; the face is well modelled
in Hilliard's manner.

LIT.: Toynbee, *ibid.*, p. 9. Reynolds,
Walpole Society, No. D.3.

167. *Called Henry Carey, 2nd Earl of Monmouth* (Pl. 159). The Duke of
Portland, Welbeck Abbey.
Oval, $2\frac{1}{2}" \times 2"$. Inscribed Encores
vn* Luit pour moy (still one star
shines for me) round the rim, on
separate mount, inscribed quadragessimo ano dni 1616 vera effigies
Ætatis Suæ 20.

An excellent miniature painted
three years before Hilliard's death.
The black and white costume has
led to the suggestion that the sitter
has been represented in mourning:
Williamson, *Miniatures*, pl. X, 2.
Perhaps it is therefore identifiable
with the miniature of one "Mr.
Hearne" which Laurence Hilliard

left in his will to his daughter.
The identification with Henry
Carey is doubtful.

LIT.: Goulding, No. 14, pl. III.

EXH.: Reynolds *Catalogue*, 1947, No.
100.

168. *Frederick, Elector Palatine and later
King of Bohemia* (Pl. 160e). Victoria
and Albert Museum. No. P.151–
1910. Salting Bequest.
Oval, $2\frac{1}{4}" \times 1\frac{7}{8}"$.

A short half-length wearing an embroidered doublet, a standing lace
collar and the Garter ribbon with
the lesser George against a blue
background. A most spontaneous
and excellent likeness, probably
taken *ad vivam*. It is one of the six
miniatures, representing members of
the family of James I mounted together in a 17th-century frame. There
are repetitions of this miniature in
Windsor Castle, Cust, No. 64, as by
Isaac Oliver, and one in the Buccleuch Coll., ascribed to Peter Oliver.

LIT.: Hand-list of miniatures, Victoria and Albert Museum, 1930, as
a copy after Isaac Oliver. Reynolds.
Walpole Society, No. F.1.

169. *Elizabeth, Queen of Bohemia* (Pl. 161),
Victoria and Albert Museum. No.
P.4–1937.
Oval, $2\frac{1}{8}" \times 1\frac{3}{4}"$.

The graceful figure of the young
girl in a white embroidered dress
and standing collar is seen against a
red background curtain. Typical of
Hilliard's manner. Formerly called
a *Lady of the Family of King James I.*
The identification of the sitter as
Elizabeth of Bohemia, suggested by
Mr. Reynolds, can be accepted.

PROV.: Bought from Commandant
F. Besançon, Châlons, to whose
family the miniature had belonged
for a number of years.

LIT.: Reynolds, *Walpole Society*, No. E.1, pl. VI, D.

EXH.: Reynolds *Catalogue*, 1947, No. 88.

170. *Called James I* (Pl. 162). Barber Institute of Fine Arts.
Oval, 2″ × 1⅝″. In frame of *c.* 1700, engraved at back with a monogram J. S. James Sotheby.
A very good work of Hilliard's late manner. The identity as James I is unlikely. A very strong portrait.
PROV.: Bought by James Sotheby as "of Old Hilliard ye picture of K. James I. £2–10s." Bought at Sotheby's sale 11 October 1955, Lot No. 71, by Professor Bodkin for Barber Institute of Fine Arts, Birmingham.
LIT.: Vertue, V, p. 10, 1741.
EXH.: South Kens. Mus., 1862, No. 2646. B.F.A.C., 1889 p. 31, Case IX. R.A., 17th Century Art, 1938, No. 759, Pl. III. Reynolds *Catalogue*, 1947, No. 99, on loan at Victoria and Albert Museum, 1947-55.

171. *King James I* (Pl. 160a.), Victoria and Albert Museum, Salting Bequest, No. P.147–1910.
Oval, 2⅛″ × 1¾″.
The King wears white doublet, pleated lace ruff and Garter ribbon with lesser George half cut off; background: on the left cerise curtain, on the right an iris against the sky. The face itself is well modelled, as always on this type. The miniature is mounted with five others depicting members of the family of James I in one frame of *c.* 1630–40. See the miniature in The Hague (Pl. 163).
LIT.: Reynolds, *Walpole Society*, No. A.13, Pl. V, D.

172. *Queen Anne of Denmark* (Pl. 160b). Victoria and Albert Museum, Salting Bequest, No. P.148–1910.

Oval, 2″ × 1⅝″.
Bust portrait seen against a red background. Mounted with five others in 17th-century frame as companion picture of James I.
LIT.: Reynolds, *Walpole Society*, No. B.2, pl. VI, B.

173. *King James I* (Pl. 163), Mauritshuis, The Hague.
Heart-shaped, 2″ × 1¾″.
As characteristic of this type the head is relatively big in size as compared with the surroundings. An excellent miniature, seen against a red curtained background. In a three-quarter turning to the right.
PROV.: From the Rijksmuseum. Amsterdam, No. 2861, as I. Oliver, in Cat. of 1927.
LIT.: Reynolds, *Walpole Society*, No. A.14.
EXH.: Brussels, 1912, pl. VI as Oliver. The Hague, The Age of Shakespeare, 1958, No. 68.

174. *King James I* (Pl. 164). Royal Coll., Windsor Castle.
Oval, 1¾″ × 1½″.
The king looks older and is without a hat; this is the 3rd portrait type, according to Reynolds, that Hilliard created of James I. Short bust, white doublet, and pleated lace ruff. The lesser George half cut off by the frame of the miniature, red curtained background. On the back of the playing card on which the miniature is laid there is the date 1614 painted in gold paint, probably in Hilliard's own hand.
LIT.: Cust, No. 57 (as by Oliver). Reynolds, *Walpole Society*, No. A.12.

175. *James I* Royal Coll., Windsor Castle, No. 50.
Oval, 1¾″ × 1⅞″. This is a miniature of an extremely small size.

LIT.: Cust, No. 50, as by I. Oliver. Reynolds, *Walpole Society*, No. A.15.

176. *Anne of Denmark.* Formerly Lady Northcote.
Oval, $2\frac{1}{4}'' \times 1\frac{7}{8}''$, probably by an assistant. 19 July, 1934, Sotheby's, Lot 99.
LIT.: Reynolds, *Walpole Society*, No. B.5.

177. *King James I.* Formerly Lady Northcote.
PROV.: The Propert Coll. Sotheby's, 29 July, 1934, Lot 100. Sale of Lady Northcote.
LIT.: Reynolds, *Walpole Society*, No. A.16.

178. *Anne of Denmark*, style of Nicholas Hilliard. Royal Coll., Windsor Castle, No. 45.
Oval, $1\frac{5}{8}'' \times 1\frac{3}{8}''$. Round the rim in italic letters inscribed: *Gaudea falsa iuvant. dum carcam veris.*
Quite a nice miniature but not of the very best quality.
LIT.: Cust, No. 45. Reynolds, *Walpole Society*, No. B.6.

179. *James I* (Pl. 165). Painted on vellum within the Lyte Jewel. British Museum. Bequeathed by Baron Ferdinand Rothschild, the Waddesdon Bequest, 1902.
Oval, $1\frac{3}{4}'' \times 1\frac{3}{8}''$.
Short bust, gold doublet, the Garter ribbon, standing lace collar, dark cerise curtain. The type of the king's portrait is nearest to the heart-shaped likeness in the Hague. This close affinity makes Hilliard's authorship probable. The miniature is embedded in a most elaborate jewel.
PROV.: Hamilton Palace Sale, Lot No. 1615.
LIT.: Cat. of the Works of Art, The Waddesdon Bequest, 1902, No. 167. Sir H. Maxwell Lyte, *Proceedings*

of the Somerset Archaeol. Soc., 1892, II, 60. G. Evans, *Engl. Jewellery*, 108, XX, 6.
EXH.: South Kens. Mus., 1862. No. 2, 383, James I by N. Hilliard, lent by the Duke of Hamilton and Brandon. "This exquisite miniature is set in a jewelled and enamelled case and bears the royal cypher."

180. *Anne of Denmark, wife of James I* (Pl. 166). The Fitzwilliam Museum, Cambridge.
Oval, $2\frac{1}{4}'' \times 1\frac{3}{4}''$.
Half-length figure. Her right hand is laid across her décolleté dress, she has a standing collar and a richly arranged hair dressing, a blue curtained background. The most elaborate of Hilliard's portraits of the Queen. It is kept in its original jewelled case of *c.* 1610.
PROV.: Formerly Coll. of Earl of Eglinton and Winton. Sold Christie's 13 July, 1922, Lot 77, lent anon. to B.F.A.C., 1926, case II, No. 14, as probably by Isaac Oliver, bequeathed by L. D. Cunliffe, 1937, to the Fitzwilliam Museum.
LIT.: Reynolds, *Walpole Society*, 1958, B.1, pl. VI, A.
EXH.: Treasures of Cambridge, No. 333.

b. *Oil paintings connected in style with Hilliard's miniatures.*

181. *Queen Elizabeth in robes of state* (Pl. 15) in the manner of Nicholas Hilliard. The Earl of Warwick, Warwick Castle. Oil on panel, $48'' \times 39''$.
Frontal figure of the Queen in majesty. Dark blue background with white horizontals and verticals. Golden coat. Pale face with light blue modelling. Red in necklaces, orb and sceptre. Close connection

with miniature at Welbeck Abbey, from which probably derived.

PROV.: Probably from Coll. of Sir Fulke Greville.

LIT.: O'Donoghue, p. 2, No. 4. Pope-Hennessy, *Lecture*, p. 17.

EXH.: National Portrait Exhibition, 1866, No. 257. Tudor, 1890, No. 354.

182. *Queen Elizabeth I* (Pl. 22), in the manner of Nicholas Hilliard. Pelican portrait. Walker Art Gallery, Liverpool. Oil on panel. $30\frac{1}{4}'' \times 23\frac{1}{2}''$. Shortly after 1572.

To the waist, turning to the right, eyes opposite. Figure frontal. The left hand holding glove, below big pelican jewel suspended from chains of pearls. The right hand hidden behind large fan. Richly embroidered dress, closely fitting ruff, elaborate head-wear and many jewels.

Warm colours, a scarlet rose, pink in the fan. A crowned Tudor rose and a crowned fleur-de-lys in the background on either side of the face. Conception and treatment of features (see typical line of forehead) very close to Hilliard's style.

PROV.: Coll. Mr. E. Peter Jones, from Charlton Park (1930), thought to be given by the Queen to a Howard ancestor.

LIT.: C. R. Beard, *Conn.*, XCII, 1933, p. 263. E. Alfred Jones, *Conn.* CXII, July 1943, p. 2. Auerbach, *Portraits of Elizabeth I*, p. 202, pl. 32.

EXH.: Reynolds *Catalogue*, 1947, No. 108. Walker Art Gallery, Liverpool, 1953. Kings and Queens of England, No. 13.

183. *Queen Elizabeth I* (Pl. 43), in the manner of Nicholas Hilliard. Cambridge University, panel, $24'' \times 19\frac{1}{4}''$ 1575-80. Given to the University by

Sir Vincent Skinner, Treasury Official, 1588-9.

This portrait, painted in delicate grey colours, shows close affinity with Hilliard's miniatures of 1572-75. It belongs to a group of oil portraits that have Hilliard's influence as a feature in common.

LIT.: O'Donoghue, p. 4, No. 10 as by Gheeraerdts. F. M. Kelly, "Queen Elizabeth and her Dresses", *Conn.*, Vol. CXIII, 1944, pp. 71-9. Auerbach, *Portraits of Elizabeth I*, p. 205, pl. 33 J. W. Goodison, *Cat. of Cambridge Portraits*, I., 1955, No. 12, pl. 3.

EXH.: Nat. Portraits, 1866, No. 363, C.A.S., 1884, No. 73. Tudor, 1890, No. 460. Reynolds *Catalogue*, 1947, No. 109. Treasures of Cambridge, 1959, No. 24.

184. *Queen Elizabeth I* (Pl. 44) by Nicholas Hilliard(?). Lord Rothschild, Cambridge, panel $32\frac{1}{2}'' \times 24''$. *c.* 1580.

This oil portrait has much in its style extremely close to Hilliard's manner in miniatures. It is strong in colours and gives a clear conception of the likeness.

PROV.: The Earl of Westmorland.

LIT.: O'Donoghue, p. 6. Auerbach, *Portraits of Elizabeth I*, p. 205. pl. 34.

EXH.: Reynolds *Catalogue*, 1947, No. 108a.

185. *Elizabeth I* (Pl. 61) by Nicholas Hilliard(?), the "Ermine" portrait. The Marquess of Salisbury. Oil on panel, $37\frac{1}{2}'' \times 34''$, dated 1585 on the sword.

In style and treatment this oil portrait comes so close to Hilliard's manner that it can be attributed to him with some confidence. Traditionally it is ascribed to him.

PROV.: An inventory of Hatfield

House of 1611 mentions two pictures of the Queen in the Marble Hall. This painting appears to have always been in the collection of the Marquess of Salisbury from the beginning of the 17th century.

LIT.: O'Donoghue, p. 9, No. 25. F. M. Kelly, "Queen Elizabeth and her Dresses", *Conn.*, Vol. CXIII, 44. Auerbach, *Portraits of Elizabeth I*, p. 202, pl. 40 and *Tudor Artists*, p. 132.

EXH.: Tudor, 1890, No. 1410 A. Reynolds *Catalogue*, 1947, No. 110.

186. *Queen Elizabeth I* (Pl. 77). The "Armada" Portrait in the manner of Nicholas Hilliard. The Duke of Bedford, Woburn Abbey. Panel, $62\frac{1}{2}'' \times 41\frac{1}{2}''$, c. 1588.

This oil portrait commemorates the defeat of the Spanish Armada; it shows the Queen life-size to the knees. The colouring of the huge sleeves and all the details of the elaborately ornamented dress are near to Hilliard's style. The mask used for the face which is shaded in transparent colours is based on Hilliard's pattern. In the background on the left-hand side appears the English Fleet in calm waters and on the right-hand side the Spanish Armada overthrown by a furious sea.

LIT.: O'Donoghue, p. 8, No. 23, ascribed the painting to M. Gheeraerts. Cust, "Marcus Gheeraerts" *Walpole Society III* (1914), pl. IVa. Auerbach, *Portraits of Elizabeth I*, p. 205, pl. 39.

EXH.: R.A., Woburn Abbey, 1950. Liverpool, Walker Art Gallery. Kings and Queens of England, 1953. The Hague, The Age of Shakespeare, No. 35.

187. *Queen Elizabeth I* (Pl. 130), detail of the visit of Queen Elizabeth to

Blackfriars 1600, after Nicholas Hilliard. The painting itself attributed to Marcus Gheeraerts II. Coll. Mr. Simon Wingfield Digby, canvas $52'' \times 75''$.

The portrait of the Queen is in its light colouring completely different from the rest of the painting; it is probably based on a pattern by Hilliard and may even have been painted by him.

LIT.: Walpole Soc. III, 1914, pp. 22–3 and 1921 pp. 1–20, pl. 44. Auerbach, *Portraits of Elizabeth I*, p. 205, pl. 44.

EXH.: Tudor, 1890, No. 368. R.A., Kings and Queens, 1953, No. 100.

(c) Drawings

188. *An Elizabethan Lady* (pl. 176). Victoria and Albert Museum. P. 9 — 1943, given by the Nat. Art Coll. Fund. Pen and ink drawing over pencil. The signature in lower right hand corner is rendered invisible by a tear and collector's mark. Rectangular, $5\frac{3}{8}'' \times 4\frac{1}{2}''$.

An especially fine drawing.

PROV.: Francis Wellesley, A.G.B. Russel.

LIT.: *Conn.*, 1924, pp. 137–8, Vasari Soc. II, No. 30., pp. XI, 11. John Woodward, *Tudor and Stuart Drawings*, 1949, No. 6.

EXH.: B.F.A.C., 1926, pl. 19, Reynolds *Catalogue*, 1947, No. 106.

189. *Queen Elizabeth I* (pl. 177), drawing, design for the obverse of (?) Third Great Seal of the Queen. British Museum. No. 1912–7–17–1. Circ. dia. 5'', inscribed Elisabet D.G. ANGLIE FRA. ET. HIBERNIE REGINA, pen and ink and wash over pencil.

It is possible that the pattern originally designed for Elizabeth's Third Great Seal was transformed into the drawing for the Great Seal of Ireland by adding in pencil the faint Irish emblems, the harp, and the three crowns. Otherwise, it is near in style to the Second Great Seal and shows unmistakably Hilliard's refined drawing.

PROV.: From the P. Gellatly Coll.

LIT.: C. Dodgson, *Burl. Mag.*, V (1904), pl. II. Farquhar, *Nicholas Hilliard*, pp. 342, 346, 347, pl. XXVI. C. Dodgson, *Vasari Soc.*, Series I. part 3. Sir Hilary Jenkinson, *Archaeologia* LXXXV, pp. 316–23. Blakiston, *Nicholas Hilliard and Queen Elizabeth's 3rd Great Seal*, p. 107. Brinsley Ford, *Apollo*, May 1947. J. Woodward, *Tudor and Stuart Drawings*, 1949, No. 5.

EXH.: Reynolds *Catalogue*, 1947, No. 107.

190. *A Queen with a little boy* (Pl. 185), perhaps by Nicholas Hilliard. The monogram N.H. in left hand corner, wash and ink over pencil. B.M. Print Room.

Rectangular, $4\frac{7}{8}'' \times 3\frac{1}{2}''$.

The Queen has been identified with Mary Stuart or with Elizabeth of Bohemia. It is the drawing for an engraving and near in style to Hilliard's drawing for the (?) Third Great Seal.

LIT.: B. M. Print Room, No. T15–18.

(d) *Engravings*

191. *Titelborder*, wood engraving, with initials N.H., and the date 1574. Twisted columns and a lamb with legs bound within circular frame embedded in the design.

LIT.: McKerrow and Ferguson: "Title-page Borders," etc. *Bibliographical Society*, XXI, 1932, pl. 148. Auerbach, *More Light on Nicholas Hilliard*, p. 167.

192. *Louis de Gonzague, The Duke of Nevers* (Pl. 34), wood engraving. On the title page of the *Fondation du duc de Nivernois, 1578*. Paris, Bibliothèque Nationale, Département des Imprimés, Velins, No. 999, LK² 71. Oval, $1\frac{1}{8}'' \times 1''$.

LIT.: Henri Bouchot, "La préparation de la publication d'un livre illustré au XVIe siècle," *Bibliothèque de l'école des Chartes*, vol. LIII, Paris 1892, p. 612 *et seq.*
L. Dimier, *Histoire de la Peinture de Portrait en France au XVIe. siècle*, (1924–6), I, p. 125.
L. Dimier, *French Painting in the 16th century* (1904), p. 254.
Williamson, *Pierpont Morgan Cat.*, I. p. 24.
J. Adhémar, *Inventaire des Fonds Français Graveurs du 16me siècle* (1939), p. 403.
E. P. Goldschmidt, "Nicholas Hilliard as Wood Engraver". *The Times Literary Supplement* (Aug. 9, 1947), p. 403.
Auerbach, *More Light on Nicholas Hilliard*, pp. 166–7, pls. 27 and 28.
N. Blakiston, "Nicholas Hilliard in France", *Gazette des Beaux Arts*, June 1958, pp. 298–300.

193. *Henriette de Cleves, Duchess of Nevers,* (Pl. 35), wood engraving. On the title page of the *Fondation du duc de Nivernois, 1578*. Département des Imprimés, Velins, No. 999, LK² 71. Oval, $1\frac{1}{8}'' \times 1''$.

LIT.: The same as mentioned in the entry for the Duke of Nevers, No. 190.

194. *Queen Elizabeth I*, after Nicholas Hilliard (?) (Pl. 42). Frontispiece, Saxton Atlas, 1st state, B.M. Print room. Wood engraving.

The Royal image is related to the portrait of the Queen, enthroned, as it appears on Charter headings, and particularly on Hilliard's Second Great Seal.

LIT.: O'Donoghue, p. 43, No. 35. A. M. Hind, *Engraving in England in 16th and 17th Centuries*, I, p. 73 as by Remigius Hogenberg. Sir Sidney Colvin (*Early Engraving and Engravers in England*) 1905, Frontispiece, p. 29, is in favour of Augustine Ryther. E. Auerbach, Review of Hind's book, *Burl. Mag.*, 1952, p. 330. *Portraits of Elizabeth I*, p. 202, pl. 36.

195. *Queen Elizabeth I* (Pl. 186) engraved by Francis Delaram after Nicholas Hilliard. Print Room, Brit. Mus.

Rectangular, $7\frac{1}{2}'' \times 5\frac{1}{4}''$. A posthumous portrait, engraved between 1617 and 1619. In lower right corner is Hilliard's signature and copyright; NIC: HILLIARD DELIN: ET EXCUD: CUM PRIVILEGIO MAIEST: Inscribed in the Clouds PER TAL VARIAR SON QUI above stars which encircle her crown. The Queen is holding an ostrich feather fan in her right hand, her left hand touches a jewel at her breast; she is surrounded by clouds. In 1617, Hilliard was granted Royal Patent, for twelve years to issue portraits of James I and his family. See p. 40 *ante*.

LIT.: Auerbach, *Portraits of Elizabeth I*, pl. 37, p. 205n. Hind, *Engraving in England*, II, pp. 219–20, pl. 124.

(e) Illuminations

196. *Queen Elizabeth I* (Pl. 14), on indenture of 30 August 1559, in the manner of Nicholas Hilliard, P.R.O., E.36/277.

LIT.: Tudor Artists, p. 120, pl. 35c.

197. *François Hercule, Duc d'Alençon* (Pl. 39). In front of a lilliputian Prayer Book. Fac. 218. in B.M.

Oval, within a Wreath, $2'' \times 1\frac{1}{2}''$, standing on a page which was originally a gold ground, powdered with Fleurs de Lys. The whereabouts of the original are unknown. The Prayer Book contained manuscript prayers written by Elizabeth I in different languages. At the end of the book appears the miniature of the Queen.

PROV.: James II, Duke of Berwick, James West, Duchess of Portland for 21 gns. According to Mr. W. S. Lewis it was not bought by Horace Walpole, as often assumed, from Portland Sale, 24 May 1786, Lot 2950. See note in Walpole's Cat., now at Farmington. Bought for Queen Charlotte, left to the Dowager Duchess of Leeds, passed to Mr. Jeffrey Whitehead in 1884. It did not appear in the sale of his Coll. at Christie's 5 August, 1915.

LIT.: Universal Mag. 79, 1786. O'Donoghue, pp. 31–2. Williamson, *Portrait Miniatures*, p. 16. Williamson, *The Miniature Collector*, 1921, pl. V. F. Chamberlain, *Private Character of Queen Elizabeth*, 1921, states that the original is now lost, repr. from facs. on p. 94, No. 6.

EXH.: B.F.A.C., 1889, p. 136, on centre table. Fine Art Society, 1902.

198. *Queen Elizabeth I* (Pl. 40) on Prayer Book, on the last page of facsimile 218 in B.M.

Oval, within a Wreath, $2'' \times 1\frac{1}{2}''$. The portrait of the queen is of the type that follows her portrait on the Saxton Atlas of 1579 and precedes the type on the Ermine portrait of 1585, it can therefore be dated between 1581–83.

For provenance and other details see entry for Pl. 39 and No. 197.

199. *Queen Elizabeth I.* (Pl. 56) by Nicholas Hilliard (?). Emmanuel College, Cambridge.

The Queen's image appears within the great letter E starting the top border of the Foundation Charter for Emmanuel College, Cambridge, in 1584. Sir Walter Mildmay, who was Chancellor at that period, had founded Emmanuel College, and this was the Foundation Charter which he may have commissioned from Hilliard.

LIT.: Sir John Neale, *Elizabeth I and her Parliaments, 1559–81*, vol. I, 1953, repr. as frontispiece.

(f) Goldsmiths' work

200. *Tudor Hat badge, Samaritan at the Well* (Pl. 167), by an unknown English goldsmith, British Museum, Dept. of British Antiquities.
Circular, dia. 2″.
Inscribed on the well in roman letters: OF. A. TREWTHE. THOW. ART. THE. TREW. MESSIAS. gold enamelled work. *c.* 1535.
LIT.: G. H. Tait, "Tudor Jewellery", (in prep.).

201. *Joseph in the Well* (Pls. 168a and b) a pendant, by an unknown English goldsmith of *c.* 1542. British Museum, Dept. Brit. Antiquities.
Oval, $1\frac{3}{8}″ \times 1\frac{5}{8}″$. Round the well, in the centre, figures are crowded, abrupt movements. The framework is composed of grotesques and cartouches. The back shows a translucent enamel design. Work in gold and enamel.
LIT.: Tait, *ibid.*, see No. 200.

202. *Communion Cup* by Richard Hilliard (Pl. 169), *c.* 1570, St. Sidwell's, Exeter.

203. *Font-shaped Standing Dish* (Pl. 170) by Richard Hilliard, Private Coll., 1560–65.
LIT.: N. M. Penzer, "Tudor Font-shaped Cups—III", *Apollo*, 1958, pp. 82–86. repr. Figs. II and III.
EXH.: Exeter, 1957, No. 43.

204. *Seal-topped Spoon* (Pl. 171) by Richard Hilliard, Exeter Museum.
EXH.: Exeter, 1957, No. 66.

205. *Edmund Withipoll* (Pl. 172), 1562, medallion by Stephen Van Harwick, British Museum.
Circular, dia. $1\frac{3}{4}″$.
LIT.: *Med. Ill. Eliz.*, No. 34.

206. *Maria Dimock* (Pl. 173) by Stephen Van Harwick, 1562. Brit. Museum.
Circular, dia. $1\frac{1}{2}″$.
LIT.: *Med. Ill. Eliz.*, No. 36.

207. *The Phoenix Jewel* (Pl. 174a and b). Gold ornament. Queen Elizabeth I, framed by a wreath of Tudor Roses in gold and enamel. Brit. Mus., bequeathed by Sir Hans Sloane in 1753, the reverse shows the Phoenix amid flames, surmounted by the crowned Royal cypher.
Circular, dia. 2″. *c.* 1574.
This is very close to the style of Hilliard's miniatures and possibly by him. Related to it is the Phoenix Badge, *Med. Ill. Eliz.*, No. 70.
LIT.: Farquhar, *Phoenix Badge*, p. 278, and "Portraiture of our Tudor Monarchs on their Coins and Medals". *Brit. Numismatic Journal and Proceedings of the Brit. Numismatic Soc.* 1907, 1st series, IV, 1908 pp. 79ff. Joan Evans, *English Jewellery*, pp. 91–3.

208. *The Second Great Seal of Queen Elizabeth I* (Pl. 175a and b), designed and engraved by Nicholas Hilliard, in conjunction with Charles Anthony.
Circular, dia. $4\frac{3}{4}″$. P.R.O.
On the obverse the queen is

enthroned, she fills the height of the frame completely and holds the orb and the sceptre; she wears the crown, and two hands appear from clouds drawing the royal coat apart. On either side there is a coat of arms. The reverse shows the heavy figure of the queen on horseback. As to the documentary evidence for the designing and engraving of the Seal by Nicholas Hilliard, see text p. 20 *ante*.

LIT.: Blakiston, *Nicholas Hilliard and Queen Elizabeth's Third Great Seal*, pp. 101–7.

209. *The Drake Pendant* (Pls. 178a and b), gold and enamelled. A cameo in the centre; rubies, diamonds and pearls decorate the Renaissance setting; behind the cameo the lid opens and there is a miniature of Queen Elizabeth by Nicholas Hilliard, inscribed with gold letters, 1575, but according to the costume it must have been painted later. Lt.-Col. Sir George Meyrick. The miniature is oval, $1\frac{7}{8}'' \times 1\frac{1}{2}''$.

The cameo shows a classical head in white behind the head of a negro, a cluster of pearls with one big pearl is suspended from it.

PROV.: Queen Elizabeth gave this pendant to Sir Francis Drake in 1579, and on his portrait of 1591, in the Nat. Marit. Mus., Greenwich, he is wearing it.

LIT.: Clifford Smith, *Jewellery*, *1908*, pl. 34. Joan Evans, *English Jewellery*, *History of Jewellery*, pl. A.5. p. 130.

EXH.: Reynolds *Catalogue*, No. 102.

210. *The Barbor Jewel* (Pl. 179), perhaps by Nicholas Hilliard. Victoria and Albert Museum, bequeathed by Miss Blencowe.

Oval, $1\frac{3}{8}'' \times 1''$. It is said to have been made in commemoration of Barbor's deliverance from the flames

with the accession of Elizabeth I. Her portrait appears in shape of a small cameo in the centre of an enamelled setting with square cut stones; a bunch of grapes is suspended from the Renaissance setting.

LIT.: Joan Evans, *English Jewellery*, 1921, pp. 4, 97, pl. XIX, 4.

EXH.: South Kens. Mus., 1865, No. 1319, the Rev. E. E. Blencowe.

211. *Armada Jewel* (Pls. 181a, b, c). The Queen's Badge, enamelled gold, set in pendant, with diamonds and rubies. The legend reads in roman letters ELIZABETH. DE. G. ANG. FRA. ET. HIB. REGINA.

Oval, $2\frac{3}{4}'' \times 2''$. The front of the lid inscribed SAEVAS TRANQVILLA. PER. UNDAS. (calm through the savage waves), and the inside HEI. MIHI QUOD TANTO VIRTUTIS PERFUSE DECORE NON HABET ETERNOS IN VIOLATA DIES. (alas that virtue endued with so much beauty should not uninjured enjoy perpetual life). At the back is a lid which opens to show a much restored miniature portrait of the Queen.

PROV.: On the defeat of the Spanish Armada, Queen Elizabeth gave this jewel to Sir Thomas Heneage who was a great favourite of hers. Sold by his descendants anonymously at Christie's in 1902. Bought by J. Pierpont Morgan, given by Lord Wakefield through the Nat. Art. Coll. Fund. to the Victoria and Albert Museum in 1935. No. M. 81–1935.

LIT.: Williamson, *Pierpont Morgan Cat.*, Farquhar, *Nicholas Hilliard*, pl. XXIII, 1. Clifford Smith, *Jewellery*, pl. 34. Joan Evans, *English Jewellery*, p. 91, pl. A, 5.

EXH.: Reynolds *Catalogue*, 1947, No. 103.

212. *Armada Badge* or *Dangers Averted Badge* (Pl. 182a and b). Brit. Mus. Oval, 2″ × 1¾″. Gold.

The portrait of the queen filling the oval rim completely, shows the likeness which Hilliard had created in his Second Great Seal. The lettering round the rim is DITIOR. IN. TOTO. NON ALTER. CIRCV-LVS. ORBE. (No richer crown in the world than this.) On reverse, a bay tree grows on an Island surrounded by the waves of the sea. The island is inscribed NON IPSA PERICVLA. TANGUNT (not even dangers affect it).

LIT.: *Med. Ill. Eliz.*, No. 129.

213. *Dangers Averted Medal* (pl. 183), celebrating the defeat of the Spanish Armada of 1588. Fitzwilliam Museum, Cambridge. Given by A. W. Young, 1936.

Oval, 2¼″ × 2″. Inscribed in Roman letters round the rim. DITIOR. IN. TOTO. NON. ALTER. CIRCV-LVS ORBE (No richer crown in the world than this). On reverse, NON IPSA . PERICVLA . TAN-GVNT. (not even dangers affect it). Gold cast and chased, perhaps a naval award.

The portrait likeness is very well executed in the round and true to Hilliard's style.

PROV.: from the Charles Butler Coll., one of three known specimens.

LIT.: *Med. Ill. Eliz.*, No. 130. *Brit. Numismatic Journal*, 2nd series vol. III, 1917, vol. XIII, p. 169. Farquhar, *Nicholas Hilliard*, p. 338.

EXH.: Reynolds *Catalogue*, 1947, No. 104. Treasures of Cambridge 1959, No. 371.

214. *James I, Peace with Spain Medal* (Pl. 184a and b), probably by Nicholas Hilliard, 1604, in gold. Brit. Mus.

Circular, dia. 1¾″. The obverse shows the likeness of the king, as it was created by Hilliard in type I. James I wears a hat, the legend reads JACOBVS . D.G. . ANG . SCO' . FR.' ET . HIB' . REX. The reverse shows two classical figures, Peace and Religion, standing opposite each other. The legend reads HINC. PAX. COPIA. CLARAQ. RELIGIO. and it is dated A'1604.

LIT.: *Med. Ill*, pl. XLV, Nos. 14 and 15. John Pinkerton. *The Medallic History of England to the Revolution*, 1790, ascribes it to Hilliard. Farquhar, *Portraiture of Stuart Monarchs*, pp. 159ff; *Nicholas Hilliard*, XIII, 3. Reynolds, *Walpole Society*, pp. 18-19.

SOME LOST WORKS

Entries from Vanderdoort's Cat.: p. 45. No. 41.

215. Done by old Hilliard, which the King had of my Lord of Arundel.

Item Another of the aforesaid Queen Elizabeth's picture, being side-faced in the clouds, with one hand, and a little landskip by it, with some golden letters in the clouds, being under a crystal, in a black round turned jet-box, the light coming neither from the right nor the left side, being done without any shadows, in an open garden light. 1¼″ × 1½″.

p. 53. No. 72.

216. Done by old Hilliard, which he had of Sir James Palmer.

Item. The Spanish fleet or Armada in limning of 1588, in a black frame with a cover, without a glass, done upon the right light. 6″ × 1f. 1½″.

The painting of the Spanish Armada in the Apothecaries'

Hall, London, is different in style from Hilliard's work.

References from documents:

217. New Year's gift roll for 1584 (Egerton Ms. 3052), published by Roy C. Strong, "Queen Elizabeth, The Earl of Essex and Nicholas Hilliard", *Burl. Mag.*, CI (1959), p. 145.

By Nicholas Hillyarde a faire Table being pyctores conteyninge the history of the fyve wise virgins and the fyve foolysshe virgins.

218. Lumley Inventory 1590, *Walpole Society*, VI (1918), p. 27.

A table on the conyng perspective of death and a woman, doone by Hilliarde.

Some likely miniatures, known only from engravings:

219. Francis Bacon, inscribed: *1578, Si tabula daretur digne, animum, mallem.* Ætatis Suæ 18, engraved by W. H. Worthington "from a miniature by Hilliard".

LIT.: Noel Blakiston, "Nicholas Hilliard as a Traveller", *Burl. Mag.*, XCI (1949), p. 169. See p. 74, *ante*.

220. John Donne, engraved by William Marshall, inscribed ANNO DNI 1591. ÆTATIS SVÆ 18 can be based on a miniature by Hilliard. See p. 45, *ante*. Strong, *ibid.*, pl. 38.

SELECTED WORKS BY HILLIARD'S CONTEMPORIES, FOLLOWERS AND PUPILS[1]

221. *An Unknown Man* (Pl. 187), by Laurence Hilliard. Fitzwilliam Museum, Cambridge, bequeathed by L. B. Cunliffe, 1937.
Oval, $2\frac{1}{4}'' \times 1\frac{5}{8}''$. Signed with monogram L.H. Inscribed: Ano Dni 1640 Ætatis Suæ. . . .
A very fine miniature of a man, with a lively expression, standing against a crimson background.

LIT.: Reynolds, *Miniatures*, p. 36, pl. VI, No. 15.

EXH.: *Treasures of Cambridge*, 1959, No. 339.

222. *A Lady wearing a wide-brimmed Hat* (Pl. 188) by Laurence Hilliard. Victoria and Albert Museum. P. 23–1945.
Oval, $2\frac{1}{4}'' \times 1\frac{1}{4}''$. Signed with monogram in Roman letters H.L., transferred from British Museum.
A lively miniature of a woman whose expressive face is overshadowed by a wide hat. She wears a huge wheel ruff, and is seen against a golden background. The composition fits well into the oval frame.

LIT.: Winter, *Eliz. Miniatures*, pl. XVI A.

223. *A Lady* (Pl. 189) *wearing a velvet cap*, by Laurence Hilliard. Victoria and Albert Museum, No. P. 10–1946.
Oval, $3'' \times 2\frac{3}{8}''$. Inscribed on top *Constant in the midst of inconstancey*, within clouds, signed with monogram L.H.
A most ambitious miniature which clearly shows Laurence Hilliard's decorative qualities. It is interesting that the sky is the background.

224. *Unknown Man* (Pl. 190), by Laurence Hilliard. Formerly Sotheby Coll.
Oval, $1\frac{7}{8}'' \times 1\frac{1}{2}''$. Inscribed Ano Dni. 1622, Ætatis Suæ 26.
The bust portrait of a man in a green doublet with a falling ruff, and reddish brown hair, standing in front of a red curtained background.

PROV.: Bought by James Sotheby (1655–1720) and recorded in a list of *c*. 1720 as "a man's head and part of ye body clothed in green spotted,

---

[1] As far as they are reproduced.

1622, ætatis 26, set in a gold frame". The original frame has been preserved, sold in the Sotheby Sale, 11 October 1955, Lot No. 56.

225. *An Unknown Man* within a richly enamelled gold contemporary locket, (Pls. 191a and b), by Laurence Hilliard. Nat. Mus. Stockholm, No. Bih. 930.
Oval, $1\frac{1}{2}'' \times 1\frac{1}{4}''$. Signed L. H. (Monogram). Inscribed: Ano Dni 1644. Ætatis Suæ. The portrait resembles in style that which was formerly in the Sotheby Collection. If the locket is really Laurence Hilliard's work, it would testify to his ability as a goldsmith.
PROV.: From the Wicander Coll.
LIT.: Asplund, *Wicanders Miniatyr-samling*, II, pp. 64-5, No. 166, pl. 68.

226. *An Unknown Man* (Pl. 192), by Laurence Hilliard. The Earl of Beauchamp, Madresfield Court.
Oval, $2'' \times 1\frac{1}{2}''$. Inscribed: Ano Dni 1636 Ætatis Suæ 37 and signed with monogram L.H.
A strikingly broad treatment gives a pleasant impression.

227. *An Unknown Man* (Pl. 193), by Laurence Hilliard. The Earl of Beauchamp, Madresfield Court.
Oval, $1\frac{1}{2}'' \times 1\frac{1}{4}''$. Inscribed: Ano Dni 1638 ætatis suæ 31, signed with monogram L.H. in the left hand corner.
It shows Hilliard's training and gives a lively likeness.

228. *An Unknown Man* (Pl. 194), perhaps by Laurence Hilliard. Duke of Buccleuch, No. IX/10.
Oval, $2'' \times 1\frac{5}{8}''$. Inscribed: Ano Dni 1620. En. vo. Fi. con. ma. sub. Ætatis Suæ 30.
Definitely Hilliard's manner, but probably not by himself. The broad treatment of the face would agree with that used by Laurence.
LIT.: Mackay, B. No. 2.

229. *An Unknown Gentleman*, perhaps by Laurence Hilliard. The Duke of Buccleuch, Drumlanrig Castle, No. IX/3. Formerly called Robert Earl of Essex.
Oval, $1\frac{3}{4}'' \times 1\frac{1}{4}''$. Inscribed: Ano Dni 1611 Ætatis Suæ 33. Three-quarter length.
The young man appears in a yellow silk doublet and red trousers. He wears a pink écharpe and a falling lace collar, one hand visible. The writing in gold letters resembles Nicholas' manner and stands on a blue ground.
LIT.: Mackay, E.E.6. Long, *Notes*, "perhaps by Laurence Hilliard".

230. *Unknown Girl* (Pl. 195), by Isaac Oliver. The Duke of Buccleuch, Drumlanrig Castle.
Oval, $2\frac{1}{4}'' \times 1\frac{5}{8}''$. Inscribed Ano Dni 1587 Ætatis Suæ 20, signed with monogram in gold on blue ground IO. In contemporary black carved frame.
A charming miniature, never mentioned in literature before, three-quarter length, both hands visible, the girl wears a tall hat. Flemish manner. The earliest known signed and dated miniature by Oliver.

231. *Unknown Youth* (Pl. 196), ascribed to Isaac Oliver. The Earl of Beauchamp, Madresfield Court.
Oval, $1\frac{3}{4}'' \times 1\frac{5}{8}''$, c. 1588. Probably copied from Hilliard's *Unknown Youth* in the Duke of Rutland's collection. In spite of the affinity with Hilliard's style it already shows Oliver's modelling.
EXH.: Reynolds *Catalogue*, 1947, No. 123.

232. *Unknown Man* (Pl. 197), by Isaac Oliver. The Queen of the Netherlands.
Oval, $2\frac{1}{8}'' \times 1\frac{5}{8}''$. Inscribed: Ano Dni 1588 Ætatis Suæ 59, and signed with monogram.
Typical of Oliver's early style.
LIT.: Frits Lugt, *Le Portrait-Miniature* . . . . 1917, p. 4.

233. *An Unknown Man* (Pl. 198), formerly supposed Self-Portrait, by Isaac Oliver. The Queen of the Netherlands.
Oval, $2\frac{1}{8}'' \times 1\frac{5}{8}''$.
A very powerful miniature.
LIT.: Williamson, *Portrait Miniatures*, I, pl. XIII. F. Lugt, *Le Portrait-Miniature*, 1917, pl. 5.
EXH.: Brussels, 1912, No. 997. Paris 1938, *La peinture anglaise XVIIIe et XIXe siècles*, No. 309. Reynolds *Catalogue*, 1947, No. 134, Amsterdam, *The Triumph of Mannerism*, 1955, No. 84.

234. *An Unknown Man* (Pl. 199), by Isaac Oliver. Victoria and Albert Museum. No. P.37–1941.
Oval, $2\frac{1}{8}'' \times 1\frac{3}{4}''$. Inscribed: Ano Dni 1590 Ætatis Suæ 27. Given by Mrs. S. S. Joseph.
Plenty of shade and light, the lettering in Hilliard's style.
LIT.: Winter, *Eliz. Miniatures*, pl. IX A.
EXH.: Reynolds *Catalogue*, 1947, No. 131.

235. *Unknown Girl*, aged 4, (Pl. 200), by Isaac Oliver. Victoria and Albert Museum. No. P.145–1910, Salting Bequest.
Oval, $2\frac{1}{8}'' \times 1\frac{5}{8}''$. Inscribed: Ano Dni 1590 Ætatis Suæ 4.
Enclosed in one half of a turned ivory box; the other half contains the miniature of a girl of 5. Three-quarter length figure, both hands

visible, she is holding an apple in her right hand.
LIT.: Winter, *Eliz. Miniatures*, pl. IX C, who ascribed them both to Isaac Oliver, whereas they were formerly attributed to Levina Teerlinc. *Tudor Artists*, p. 130.
EXH.: B.F.A.C., 1889, Case B, No. 5, pl. 32, as "Levina Teerlinck," lent by Mr. George Salting. Reynolds *Catalogue*, 1947, No. 141.

236. *Isaac Oliver* (Pl. 201), Self-Portrait. Black chalk drawing. Fitzwilliam Museum, Cambridge. No. P.W.27–1948.
This gives Oliver's authentic likeness.

237. *An Unknown Young Man* (Pl. 202), formerly called *Sir Philip Sidney*, Royal Coll., Windsor Castle.
Rectangular, $4\frac{5}{8}'' \times 3\frac{1}{4}''$, *c*.1590. Signed with IO. monogram.
PROV.: Coll. Dr. Mead.
LIT.: Cust, No. 24. Winter, *Eliz. Miniatures*, pl. 8.
EXH.: Reynolds *Catalogue*, 1947, No. 124.

238. *Unknown Lady* (Pl. 203), by Isaac Oliver. Fitzwilliam Museum, Cambridge.
Oval, $2\frac{1}{4}'' \times 1\frac{3}{4}''$.
The lady wears a tall hat, and is much related to the miniature of *An Unknown Lady* at Windsor Castle, exh. in 1947, under No. 133.

239. *Called Mrs. Holland* (Pl. 204), by Isaac Oliver, formerly Sotheby Coll.
Oval, $2'' \times 1\frac{5}{8}''$. Signed with monogram IO in gold.
A very charming portrait.
PROV.: Bought by Charles Sotheby in 1861 from Whitehead. Sold in Sotheby Sale, 11 Oct. 1955, Lot No. 69.

240. *Unknown Woman* (Pl. 205), by Isaac Oliver. The Queen of the Netherlands.
Oval, $2'' \times 1\frac{5}{8}''$, *c.* 1585-95.
Full of character, and very realistic.
LIT.: Lugt, *loc. cit.*, pl. 6.
EXH.: Reynolds *Catalogue*, 1947, No. 122.

241. *Called George Clifford, 3rd Earl of Cumberland* (Pl. 206), by Isaac Oliver. National Mus. Stockholm, No. 974.
Oval, $2\frac{1}{8}'' \times 1\frac{3}{4}''$. Signed with monogram IO. *c.* 1595.
A very good likeness. He is wearing a tall hat.
PROV.: From the Wicander Coll.
LIT.: Karl Asplund, Cat. II, No. 162, pl. 64.
EXH.: Reynolds *Catalogue*, 1947, No. 138.

242. *An Unknown Man* (Pl. 207), by Isaac Oliver, in ivory turned box. Fitzwilliam Museum, Cambridge.
Oval, $2'' \times 1\frac{5}{8}''$. *c.* 1595.

243. *Robert Devereux, 2nd Earl of Essex,* (Pl. 208), by Isaac Oliver. Royal Coll., Windsor Castle.
Oval, $2'' \times 1\frac{5}{8}''$.
This is an authentic likeness of the Earl of the period when he was wearing a beard. He is wearing the ribbon of the Garter.
LIT.: Cust, No. 27. Winter, *Eliz. Miniatures*, pl. XII B.
EXH.: Reynolds *Catalogue*, 1947, No. 151.

244. *Sir Arundell Talbot* (Pl. 209), by Isaac Oliver. Victoria and Albert Museum. No. P.4–1917. Bought from funds of H. B. Murray's Bequest.
Oval, $2\frac{3}{4}'' \times 2\frac{1}{8}''$. Inscribed at the back by the artist: adi. 13. Magio. 1596. In Venetia. Fecit m. Isacq oliuiero Francese IO. ṽ. 14. da L 8.

LIT.: Winter, *Eliz. Miniatures*, pl. XI B.
EXH.: Reynolds *Catalogue*, 1947, No. 149.

245. *Catherine Knevet* (Pl. 210), *Countess of Suffolk*, (1566–1633), by Isaac Oliver. The Duke of Buccleuch, Drumlanrig Castle, No. 1/19.
Oval, $2'' \times 1\frac{5}{8}''$. Inscribed: Infelix spectator. *c.* 1600.
The traces of a gilt signature appear under high magnification near the right edge of the background. Formerly ascribed to Hilliard, but certainly by Oliver.
LIT.: Mackay, B, 4.
EXH.: Reynolds *Catalogue*, 1947, No. 156.

246. *Called Elizabeth Bruges* (Pl. 211), *Lady Kennedy*, (1575–1617), by Isaac Oliver. The Duke of Portland, Welbeck Abbey.
Oval, $2\frac{1}{8}'' \times 1\frac{5}{8}''$. *c.* 1600. Signed with monogram IO.
LIT.: Goulding, No. 30.
EXH.: Reynolds *Catalogue*, 1947, No. 157.

247. *Elizabeth I*, (Pl. 212), unfinished, by Isaac Oliver. Victoria and Albert Museum. No. P.8–1940.
Oval, $2\frac{3}{8}'' \times 2\frac{1}{8}''$. *c.* 1600.
Bought from funds of the R. H. Stevenson Bequest.
A most realistic portrait of the Queen.
PROV.: Solly Coll. and perhaps from the Coll. of Dr. R. Mead.
LIT.: Winter, *Eliz. Miniatures*, pl. 12a.
EXH.: Reynolds *Catalogue*, 1947, No. 163.

248. *Robert Devereux, 2nd Earl of Essex* (Pl. 213), by Isaac Oliver. Mauritshuis, The Hague. From the Rijksmuseum, Amsterdam, No. 2859.
Oval, $2'' \times 1\frac{1}{2}''$. *c.* 1595–1600.

EXH.: Reynolds *Catalogue*, 1947, No. 168.

249. *An Unknown Man*, perhaps the 9th Earl of Northumberland, (Pl. 214), by Isaac Oliver. Fitzwilliam Museum, Cambridge, from funds of Cunliffe Bequest.
Oval, 2″ × 1⅝″. Signed with monogram IO.
This miniature may represent the same sitter, but with a beard, that Hilliard portrayed in his reclining poet in the Coll. of Dr. Kronenberg in Rotterdam.
EXH.: Reynolds *Catalogue*, 1947, No. 167.

250. *Called a Member of the Fanshawe Family of Ware Park* (Pl. 215), by Isaac Oliver. Mr. Brinsley Ford.
Oval, 2¼″ × 1¾″. Inscribed: Anõ Dnĩ 1608. Æta. 43.
PROV.: Colls. of Earl of Gainsborough and J. Pierpont Morgan, No. 58.
LIT.: Reynolds *Miniatures*, p. 26, pl. IV, 13.
EXH.: Reynolds *Catalogue*, 1947, No. 166.

251. *Lucy Harington, Countess of Bedford*, (Pl. 216), by Isaac Oliver. Fitzwilliam Museum, Cambridge, bought in May 1942.
Circular, dia. 5″. Signed with monogram IO. *c.* 1605.
The drawing, pen and ink, which is also in Fitzwilliam Museum, Cambridge, and was supposed to be the study for this miniature, is now considered to be copied from it by a Flemish artist.
PROV.: from Coll. of The Duke of Buccleuch.
LIT.: Kennedy, Pl. I. Reynolds, *Miniatures*, p. 29.
EXH.: Reynolds *Catalogue*, 1947, No. 165.

252. *Henry Frederick, Prince of Wales* (Pl. 218), by Isaac Oliver. Royal Coll., Windsor Castle, No. 56.
Oval, 4″ × 3¼″. Signed with monogram IO.
A very fine miniature.
LIT.: Cust, No. 56.

253. *Anne of Denmark, wife of James I* (Pl. 217), by Isaac Oliver. Royal Coll., Windsor Castle.
Oval, 2″ × 1⅝″. Inscribed: Seruo per regnare and signed with monogram IO. *c.* 1610.
PROV.: Coll. of Dr. R. Mead.
LIT.: Cust, No. 42.
EXH.: Reynolds *Catalogue*, 1947, No. 178. R.A. Kings and Queens, 1953, No. 130.

254. *Elizabeth of Bohemia*, daughter of James I, (Pl. 219), by Isaac Oliver. Royal Coll., Windsor Castle, No. 28.
Oval, 2″ × 1⅝″. Signed with monogram IO.
A very charming portrait.
PROV.: Coll. of Charles I, Vanderdoort's Cat., described on p. 49.
LIT.: Cust, No. 28. Reynolds *Walpole Society*, p. 25, where he stresses the authenticity of the portrait.
EXH.: Reynolds *Catalogue*, 1947, No. 158.

255. *Anne of Denmark* (Pl. 220), by Isaac Oliver. National Portrait Gallery.
Oval, 2⅛″ × 1¾″. Signed with monogram IO. *c.* 1610.
PROV.: Bought by James Sotheby on 2 Feb. 1691 from Mr. Barry Walton, sold Sotheby on 11 Oct. 1955, Lot 72.
LIT.: Vertue, V, p. 10. Long, p. 319.
EXH.: South Kens. Mus., 1862, No. 2647. R.A. 1938, 17th Century Art, No. 2647. Reynolds *Catalogue*, 1947, No. 183.

256. *An Unknown Man* (Pl. 221), by Isaac Oliver. Fitzwilliam Museum, Cambridge. Cunliffe Bequest, 1937.
Oval, $1\frac{7}{8}'' \times 1\frac{1}{2}''$. c. 1610.
EXH.: Treasures of Cambridge, 1959, No. 338.

257. *Dr. Donne* (Pl. 222), by Isaac Oliver. Royal Coll., Windsor Castle.
Oval, $1\frac{3}{4}'' \times 1\frac{3}{8}''$. Inscribed 1616 and signed with monogram IO.
A beautiful portrait.
LIT.: Cust, No. 21.
EXH.: Reynolds *Catalogue*, 1947, No. 194.

258. *Richard Sackville, 3rd Earl of Dorset,* in turned box. (Pl. 223). Fitzwilliam Museum, Cambridge, Cunliffe Bequest.
Oval, $1\frac{5}{8}'' \times 1\frac{3}{8}''$.
EXH.: Reynolds *Catalogue*, 1947, No. 196. Treasures of Cambridge, No. 337.

259. *Edward Herbert, 1st Baron Herbert of Cherbury* (1583–1648), (Pl. 224), by Isaac Oliver. Earl of Powis.
Rectangular, $9'' \times 7\frac{1}{8}''$. Inscribed: Magica. Sympathia.
LIT.: Pope-Hennessy, *Lecture*, p. 28, pl. XXX. Reynolds, *Miniatures*, p. 28.
EXH.: South Kens. Mus., 1862, No. 2775. Reynolds *Catalogue*, 1947, No. 197. R.A., British Portraits, 1956–7, No. 600. The Hague, The Age of Shakespeare, 1958, No. 60.

260. *Sheet of Sketches* (Pl. 225), by Isaac Oliver, drawing, wash and ink. Fitzwilliam Museum, Cambridge. No. P.D. i, 1956.
Signed in corner: *Is: Olliuieri.*

261. *Prodigal Son* (Pl. 226), by Isaac Oliver. The Duke of Portland, Welbeck Abbey.
Oval, $2\frac{7}{8}'' \times 2\frac{1}{8}''$. Signed with monogram IO.

PROV.: Coll. Charles I, Vanderdoort's Cat., p. 52.
LIT.: Goulding, No. 34.
EXH.: Reynolds *Catalogue*, 1947, No. 191.

262. *Sir Thomas More* and his family (Pl. 227), by Rowland Lockey. The Rev. and Mrs. J. E. Strickland, Jersey.
Rectangular, $9\frac{1}{2}'' \times 11\frac{1}{2}''$. c. 1600.
Members of the family who were at that time alive, are added to the family group which is based on a composition by Holbein of which only a sketch in Basle has survived.
PROV.: Bought by James Sotheby, 15 May 1705, from "Lady Gerrard" . . . . for the picture of Sir Thomas More's family in Water-colours.
LIT.: Vertue, V, p. 10, ascribed it to Holbein, Walpole, *Anecdotes* to Peter Oliver. Related oil painting in Nat. Portrait Gallery.
Burton, *Antiquities of Leicester*, mentions an oil painting of that type as by Lockey.
O. Kurz, "Rowland Lockey" *The Burl. Mag.*, XCIX (1957), p. 15.
EXH.: South Kens. Mus., 1862, No. 2650. B.F.A.C. 1889, p. 123, case IX, No. 1, as by P. Oliver. Tudor, 1890, No. 1087. Sold at Sotheby's Sale, 11 Oct. 1955, to the Rev. and Mrs. Strickland.

263. *An Unknown Lady with a dog* (Pl. 228), by Rowland Lockey (?). National Gallery of Victoria, Melbourne, Felton Bequest.
Circular, dia. $4\frac{1}{2}''$.
PROV.: From J. Pierpont Morgan Coll. as Isaac Oliver.
LIT.: Reynolds, *Conn. Guide*, p. 134, pl. 76, No. B.

264. *An Unknown Man* (Pl. 229), by Rowland Lockey (?), Royal Coll., Windsor Castle.

Oval, $2'' \times 1\frac{5}{8}''$.

A very fine distinctive miniature, formerly called School of Nicholas Hilliard. Mr. Reynolds suggested in typed list (?) R. Lockey. The attribution to Rowland Lockey on reasons of style seems to be plausible.

265. *Called Lady Hay* (Pl. 230), perhaps by Rowland Lockey. Formerly Sotheby Coll.
Oval, $2\frac{1}{8}'' \times 1\frac{5}{8}''$.
Sold at Sotheby's Sale 11 Oct. 1955, Lot 58, as School of Hilliard.

266. *An Unknown Gentleman* (Pl. 231), miniature in oil, ascribed to John Bettes II. The Duke of Buccleuch, Drumlanrig Castle, No. IX/34. Inscribed 1580, signature B.
LIT.: Mackay, Frame G. Kennedy, Pl. IX, No. 10. Williamson, pl. IV, No. 2.

267. *Sir Francis Walsingham* (Pl. 232), attributed to John Bettes II. The Duke of Buccleuch, Drumlanrig Castle, No. VII/3.
Oval, $8\frac{3}{4}'' \times 1\frac{1}{2}''$.
LIT.: Mackay, AA, No. 6. Kennedy, pl. VIII.
EXH.: B.F.A.C., 1889, Case II, No. 3 as Hilliard.

268. *Catherine de Balzac, Duchess of Lennox* (Pl. 233), ascribed to John Bettes II. The Duke of Buccleuch, Drumlanrig Castle, No. IX/40.
Oval, $2'' \times 1\frac{3}{4}''$.
LIT.: Mackay, B 35, Kennedy, Pl. VIII.

269. *An Unknown Girl* (Pl. 234), by (?) John Bettes II. St. Olave's Grammar School. Signed: I.B.
Rectangular, $27'' \times 30''$. Oil on panel. Inscribed Ætatis Suæ 20, 1587.
PROV.: Given to St. Olave's Grammar School in 1866 by Jeremiah A. Pilcher; it was overpainted to make a portrait of Queen Elizabeth and only after recent cleaning did the inscription come to light.
LIT.: Auerbach *Tudor Portraits*, pl. 8.
EXH.: R.A., British Portraits, 1956–7, No. 36.

270. *Oliver, 1st Baron St. John of Bletsho* (Pl. 235a and b), by Arnold van Brounckhurst. Signed and dated: A. Bronckorst Fecit 1578. The Hon. Hugh de B. Lawson Johnston.
Rectangular, $18\frac{1}{2}'' \times 15''$. Oil.
PROV.: Christie's, 27 May 1955, Lot 19 as *Key*.

271. *William Cecil, Lord Burghley* (Pl. 236), by Arnold van Brounckhurst. The Marquess of Salisbury, Hatfield House. Signed: 15 AB 73. Oil.
PROV.: Owned by the family of the Marquess of Salisbury.
LIT.: Old Cat., No. 34.

272. *William Cecil, Lord Burghley*, formerly wrongly called *Ambrose Dudley, Earl of Warwick* (Pl. 237), by Arnold van Brounckhurst(?). The Duke of Buccleuch, Drumlanrig Castle. No. VII. Oval, $1\frac{3}{4}'' \times 1\frac{1}{4}''$.
LIT.: Mackay, Frame B, 37. Isaac, Oliver. Long, *Notes*: "this is a very choice miniature, but I doubt if it is by Isaac Oliver. Perhaps it is by a foreign artist". Auerbach, *Tudor Portraits*, p. 10.

273. *King James I as a boy* (Pl. 238), by Arnold van Brounckhurst. Scottish National Portrait Gallery, Edinburgh. No. 992.
Rectangular, $17'' \times 11''$.
PROV.: Royal Coll., Langton Sale, 1925.

274. *King James I as a boy* (Pl. 239), by Arnold van Brounckhurst. Mauritshuis, The Hague, No. 2772.
PROV.: Rijksmuseum Amsterdam, No. 2772, as Edward VI by an unknown artist.

275. *Dean Colet* (Pl. 240), illum. by Segar

on Statute Book of St. Paul's School 1585/6. The Mercers' Company.

LIT.: *Tudor Artists*, pp. 121–2; F. Grossmann, "Holbein, Torrigiano and Some Portraits of Dean Colet", *Journal of the Warburg and Courtauld Institutes*, XIII (1950), pl. 54(a), pp. 211ff. Piper, *Essex*, p. 300, pl. 12.

276. *Robert Devereux, 2nd Earl of Essex* (Pl. 241), by Segar. National Gallery of Ireland, Dublin.
Rectangular, $44\frac{1}{2}'' \times 34\frac{1}{2}''$. Oil on panel. Inscribed on a cartouche: *Robert Devereux Earle of Essex* 1590. The portrait is very much in the style of Hilliard. The cartouche is identical with a label which, according to Mr. Piper, was used by Lord Lumley on many of his pictures *c.* 1600. Essex does not yet wear his beard.
PROV.: Probably Coll. of Lord Lumley. According to 1590 Inventory "doone by Seigar". Lumley Castle, Sale, 1785 and 1807, Lot No. 58. Earl of Stafford Sale, Christie's 30 May 1885, Lot No. 380. Bought by the Gallery in 1886.
LIT.: Cust, *Walpole Soc.*, VI. Piper, *Essex*, pp. 231, 300, 303, pl. 13.
EXH.: R.A., British Portraits, 1956–7, No. 47.

277. (?) *Frances Walsingham, Countess of Essex* (Pl. 242), by Segar, formerly Ashburnham Coll. Now Mildred Anna Williams Collection, California Palace of the Legion of Honor, San Francisco. Oil on panel.
Rectangular, $33\frac{1}{2}'' \times 29\frac{1}{2}''$. On the label: Maria Regina Scotiae. This is a false inscription of the 19th century. Mr. Piper suggests the identity with the Countess of Essex.
PROV.: probably Coll. of Lord Lumley. Sale from Lumley Castle, 1807,

Lot 27. Mentioned in Ashburnham Coll. in the 19th century. Sold Ashburnham Sale, Sotheby's, 15 July 1953, Lot 142 as "Mary Queen of Scots" by Hilliard.
LIT.: Piper, *Essex*, pp. 231, 300, and pl. 15.

278. (?) *Queen Elizabeth I* (pl. 243), by (?) Segar. The Earl of Verulam, Gorhambury. Oil on panel.
Rectangular, $46'' \times 33''$.
PROV.: always in the family, supposed to have been given by Queen Elizabeth to the Bacon family. Traditionally considered to be *Elizabeth* by Hilliard.
LIT.: O'Donoghue, p. 16, No. 49.

279. *Robert Dudley, Earl of Leicester* (Pl. 244), by (?) Segar. The Duke of Buccleuch, Drumlanrig Castle, No. XX/9. Rectangular, $9'' \times 6\frac{1}{4}''$.
The prototype of this miniature was perhaps by Hilliard as a portrait of that description was mentioned in Laurence's will. The style is close to Segar's miniatures and oils.
PROV.: Coll. 5th Duke of Buccleuch, from Colnaghi (1848) as "by Hildyard".
LIT.: Kennedy, as Leicester by Hilliard. Mackay, Frame A, No. 12 as Hilliard. Williamson, *Portrait Miniatures*, I, IX, 2. Piper, *Essex*, p. 300, n. 8.
EXH.: The Hague, The Age of Shakespeare, 1958, No. 29, pl. 8.

280. *Judith Norgate* (Pl. 245) by Edward Norgate. The Hon. H. Lawson-Tancred.
Oval, $2\frac{1}{8}'' \times 1\frac{3}{4}''$.
The miniature was identified by Mr. Winter from another version in the Victoria and Albert Museum. No. P.71–1935. See Winter, *Eliz. Miniatures*, pl. XVIb.

281. *A Man*, a member of the Harryson

family (Pl. 246) by Edward Norgate. The Hon. H. Lawson-Tancred.

Oval, $2\frac{1}{4}'' \times 1\frac{3}{4}''$

282. *His Wife*, (Pl. 247), by Edward Norgate. The Hon. H. Lawson-Tancred.

Oval, $2\frac{1}{4}'' \times 1\frac{3}{4}''$

These miniatures were identified as works by Norgate by Mr. Carl Winter. The miniature of Judith Norgate is in the same Private Collection as well as two further miniatures: one, representing an allegorical female figure in a Baroque style, the other illustrating a Coat of Arms which is identifiable as that of the Harryson family.

283. *An Historical Piece of Our Saviour* (Pl. 248), by Nicholas Hilliard (?), coll. Mrs. E. H. Heckett, Valencia. Circular, dia. $\frac{3}{4}''$. In a contemporary turned jet box.

Traditionally ascribed to Hilliard, but his authorship cannot be established beyond any doubt.

PROV.: Acquired by James Sotheby, 1655–1720 as "An Historical Piece of our Saviour with several Figures in a Jet Box 15 (shillings)".

EXH.: Reynolds *Catalogue*, 1947, No. 101. Sale at Sotheby's, 11 October 1955. Lot 49 as Hilliard.

284. *Called Princess Mary* (Pl. 249), by an unknown follower of Hilliard. The Duke of Buccleuch, Drumlanrig Castle. No. X/33.

Oval, $2\frac{7}{8}'' \times 2''$. Top rounded. Dated 1607 on the back of the chair.

The identity of the sitter is not established. Princess Mary lived much later, namely, from 1662–1695. The style is near to that of *William Hawtrey* at Chequers, ascribed by Reynolds, *Conn. Guide*, p. 134, pl. 76a to an unknown artist.

Both miniatures appear to be by the same hand.

LIT.: Mackay, A. No. 27, ascribes it to Hilliard. Long, *Notes*: "A 16th century miniature, but very gauche."

285. *An Unknown Lady*, aged 19 in 1608, (Pl. 250). Hilliard School. The Duke of Buccleuch. Drumlanrig Castle. No. x/6. Oval, $1\frac{5}{8}'' \times 1\frac{1}{4}''$. Inscribed *Si pergis pereo* in gold italics on blue ground. Ano 1608. Ætatis 19 in usual writing. Light blue background and pale flesh tints. The lady holds in one hand a grey dagger and has been assumed to represent Lucrecia. The face has been slightly retouched.

LIT.: Mackay, Frame A, No. 16. Long, *Notes;* "Possibly by one of Hilliard's pupils".

286. *Catherine Carey, Countess of Nottingham*, (Pl. 251), by an unknown follower of Hilliard. National Museum, Stockholm. No. Bih. 1582.

PROV.: Coll. Harry Seal, Christie's February 1949, 105 as Anne of Denmark by Hilliard.

LIT.: C. Nordenfalk, "Miniatyrsamlingen", *National musei Årsbok* (1949–50), pp. 74–5, pl. 20 as Elizabeth (?) Carey, Countess of Nottingham, by Hilliard.

287. *Catherine Carey, Countess of Nottingham* (Pl. 252), by an unknown follower of Hilliard. The Duke of Buccleuch, Drumlanrig Castle, No. IX/12.

Oval, $2\frac{1}{4}'' \times 1\frac{7}{8}''$. On label in pencil: I. Oliver.

A most attractive miniature in light, dusty pink colours. Near in style to Hilliard, but probably by a younger artist.

LIT.: Mackay, B.24.

Catalogue

ADDENDA

288. *An Unknown Man* by Nicholas Hilliard. Mr. and Mrs. E. H. Heckett, Valencia.
Circular, dia. $1\frac{1}{2}''$. Inscribed Anõ Dnĩ, 1572. Ætatis sue 33.
PROV.: H. E. Backer.
LIT.: *Four Centuries of Portrait Miniatures* from the Heckett Coll., Cat. No. 26.

289. *An Unknown Lady* by Nicholas Hilliard. Mr. and Mrs. E. H. Heckett.
Circular, dia. $1\frac{7}{16}''$. Inscribed Año dnñ 1576 Ætatis sue 31.
PROV.: S. J. Phillips, London.
LIT.: *Four Centuries of Portrait Miniatures* from the Heckett Coll., Cat. No. 27, pl. II.

290. *Unknown Lady* by Nicholas Hilliard. Cleveland Mus. of Art, Greene Coll. *c.* 1590.
Oval, $2\frac{1}{2}'' \times 1\frac{1}{2}''$.
PROV.: K. Ticher, Dublin.
LIT.: Cat. Greene Coll., No. 14, pl. II.

291. *Unknown Man* by Nicholas Hilliard. Cleveland Mus. of Art, Greene Coll.
Oval, $1\frac{3}{8}'' \times 1\frac{1}{8}''$.
LIT.: Cat. Greene Coll., No. 16, Frontispiece.

292. *An Unknown Young Man* attributed to Nicholas Hilliard. Mrs. E. Cartwright, Aynhoe Park, Banbury.

293. *Called Robert Cecil*, 1st Earl of Salisbury, by Nicholas Hilliard. The Duke of Northumberland, Alnwick Castle, No. 33.
Oval, $1\frac{3}{4}'' \times 1\frac{1}{2}''$.
Inscribed Ætatis Suae 39 A° 1594. The date does not agree with the age of the 1st Earl of Salisbury.

294. *Called Queen Elizabeth I*, by Nicholas Hilliard. The Duke of Northumberland, Alnwick Castle, No. 34.
Oval, $2\frac{3}{4}'' \times 2''$.
The sitter is not Queen Elizabeth.

295. *Queen Elizabeth I*, by Nicholas Hilliard. The Duke of Northumberland, Alnwick Castle, No. 35.
Oval, $1\frac{1}{4}'' \times 1''$, in locket.
Cerise curtain background.

296. *Elizabethan Jewel*, gold enamelled with rubies and emeralds, perhaps by Nicholas Hilliard.
Coll. Lord Wharton.
The goldsmith's work is near in style to the *Armada Jewel*. This is a cameo attached to one side, and a locket to the other. The latter opens to show two miniatures by Nicholas Hilliard. On the left: *An Unknown Gentleman* (oval, $1'' \times \frac{3}{4}''$); on the right: *Queen Elizabeth I* (oval $\frac{9}{10}'' \times \frac{3}{4}''$).
The miniature of the man may represent the portrait of Robert Devereux, 2nd Earl of Essex.

335

BIBLIOGRAPHY

1. ASPLUND, KARL, *Hjalmar Wicanders Miniatyrsamling* (1920, 26), 2 Vols.

2. AUERBACH, ERNA, "Holbein's Followers in England," *Burl. Mag.*, XCIII (1951), pp. 44–51.

3. — — "An English Indenture", *Burl. Mag.*, XCIII (1951), pp. 319–23.

4. — — "Early English Engravings," *Burl. Mag.*, XCIV (1952), pp. 326–30.

5. — — "English Engravings in the Reign of James I", *Burl. Mag.*, XCIX (1957), pp. 97–8.

6. —"More Light on Nicholas Hilliard", *Burl. Mag.*, XCI (1949). pp. 166–8.

7. —"Notes on Flemish Miniaturists in England", *Burl. Mag.*, XCVI (1954), pp. 51–3.

8. — — "Portraits of Elizabeth I", *Burl. Mag.*, XCV (1953), pp. 197–205.

9. — — *Tudor Artists*, A Study of Painters in the Royal Service and of Portraiture on Illuminated Documents from the Accession of Henry VIII to the death of Elizabeth I, London, 1954.

10. — — "Some Tudor Portraits at the Royal Academy", *Burl. Mag.*, XCIX (1957), pp. 9–13.

11. BLAKISTON, NOEL, "Nicholas Hilliard and Queen Elizabeth's Third Great Seal", *Burl. Mag.* XC (1948), pp. 101–7.

12. — — "Nicholas Hilliard as a Traveller", *Burl. Mag.*, XCI (1949), p. 169.

13. "Nicholas Hilliard at Court", *Burl. Mag.*, XCVI (1954), pp. 17–18.

14. — — "Nicholas Hilliard in France", *Gazette des Beaux Arts*, 1958, pp. 298–300.

15. — — "Nicholas Hilliard: Some Unpublished Documents", *Burl. Mag.*, LXXXIX (1947), pp. 187–9.

16. BOON, K. G., "De Passe's prent van Koningin Elisabeth I". *Bulletin van Het Rijksmuseum*, 1958, No. 1.

17. BOUCHOT, HENRI, "La Préparation et la Publication d'un livre illustré au XVIe siècle" *Bibliothèque de l'École des Chartes*, LIII, 1892, pp. 612 *et seq.*

18. COLDING, TORBEN HOLCK, *Aspects of Miniature Painting* (1953).

19. CUST, SIR LIONEL, *Windsor Castle, Portrait Miniatures*, privately printed, London, 1910.

20. DIMIER, LOUIS, *French Painting in the XVIth Century*, London, 1904.

21. — — *Histoire de la Peinture de Portrait en France au XVIe siècle* (1924–6), 3 Vols, Paris.

22. DONALD, M. B., *Elizabethan Copper*, 1955.

23. EVANS, JOAN, *English Jewellery*, London, 1921.

24. — — *A History of Jewellery, 1100–1870*, London, 1953.

25. FARQUHAR, HELEN, "Nicholas Hilliard: Embosser of Medals of Gold", *Numismatic Chronicle*, 4th Series, VIII, No. 32 (1908).

26. — — "John Rutlinger and the Phoenix Badge of Queen Elizabeth", *Numismatic Chronicle*, 5th Series, iii (1923), pp. 270–93.

27. — — "Portraiture of our Stuart Monarchs on their Coins and Medals" (1909), pp. 159 *et seq.*

28. GOLDSCHMIDT, E. P. "Nicholas Hilliard as Wood Engraver", *The Times Literary Supplement*, 9 August, 1947, p. 403.

29. GOODISON, J. W., *Catalogue of Cambridge Portraits*, I, 1955.

30. GOULDING, R. W., "The Welbeck Abbey Miniatures", *Walpole Society*, IV (1914–15).

31. GOWER, LORD RONALD, *The Great Historic Galleries of England*, Vol. II, 1882.

32. HAYDOCKE, RICHARD, *Tracte containing the Artes of curious Paintinge, Caruinge, Buildinge*, Oxford, 1598. (Transl. of part of Giovanni Lomazzo, *Trattato dell'arte della pitura*, Milan, 1584.)

33. HIND, ARTHUR M., *Engraving in the Sixteenth and Seventeenth Centuries*, I, *The Tudor Period*, 1952, and II, *The Reign of James I*, 1955.

34. HOSKINS, W. G., *Devon*, London, 1954.

35. JONES, ALFRED E., "Some Notes on Nicholas Hilliard, Miniaturist and Goldsmith", *Conn.*, XCII, pp. 3–6.

36. KENNEDY, H. A., "Early English Portrait Miniatures in the Collection of the Duke of Buccleuch", *The Studio*, 1917.

37. KURZ, OTTO, "Rowland Locky", *Burl. Mag.*, XCIX (1957), pp. 13–16.

38. LONG, BASIL S., *British Miniaturists 1520–1860*, London, 1929.

39. MACKAY, ANDREW, *The Collection of Miniatures in Montagu House*, 1896.

40. MCKERROW, R. B. AND FERGUSON, F. S., *Tile-page borders used in England and Scotland*, 1485–1640, Bibliographical Society, ill. Monograph, XXI (1932).

41. *Medallic Illustrations of the History of Great Britain and Ireland to the Death of George II*, compiled by E. Hawkins and edited by A. W. Franks and H. A. Grüber. Text, British Museum, London, 1885. 19 Portfolios, Brit. Museum, 1904–11.

42. MERES, FRANCIS, *Palladis Tamia*, Wit's Treasury, being the second part of Wit's Commonwealth, London, 1598.

43. NEALE, SIR JOHNE, *Queen Elizabeth*, 1st edition, London, 1934. Latest ed. 1960.

44. NORGATE, EDWARD, *Miniatura or the Art of Limning*, edited by Martin Hardie, Oxford, 1919.

45. O'DONOGHUE, F. N., *A Descriptive and Classified Catalogue of Portraits of Queen Elizabeth*, London, 1894.

46. OMAN, C.C., *Church Plate*, London, 1957.

47. PENZER, N. M. "Tudor Font-shaped Cups" III, *Apollo* 1958, pp. 82–6.

48. PIPER, DAVID, *The English Face*, London, 1957.

49. — — "The 1590 Lumley Inventory: Hilliard, Segar and the Earl of Essex", I and II, *Burl. Mag.*, XCIX (1957), pp. 224–31 and 299–303.

50. POPE-HENNESSY, JOHN, *A Lecture on Nicholas Hilliard*, London, 1949.

51. — — "Nicholas Hilliard and Mannerist Art Theory", *The Journal of the Warburg and Courtauld Institutes*, VI (1943), pp. 89–100.

52. — — Review, *Burl. Mag.*, LXXXV (1943), pp. 259–260.

53. Radnor, The Earl of, Catalogue of the pictures in the Collection of the Earl of Radnor, 1909.

54. ROWSE, A. L., *Tudor Cornwall*, London, 1941.

55. —— *The West in English History*, London, 1949.

56. REYNOLDS, GRAHAM, *Nicholas Hilliard and Isaac Oliver*, an Exhibition, Victoria and Albert Museum, Handbook, London, 1947.

57. —— "Portrait Miniatures", *The Connoisseur Period Guides*, The Tudor Period 1500–1603, pp. 127–35.

58. —— *English Portrait Miniatures*, London, 1952.

59. —— "Portraits by Nicholas Hilliard and his Assistants of King James I and his Family", *Walpole Society*, (1952–4), XXXIV, 1959, pp. 14–26.

60. SCHARF, GEORGE, *A Descriptive and Historical Catalogue of the Collection of Pictures at Knowsley Hall*, London, 1875.

61. STRONG, ROY C., "Queen Elizabeth, Earl of Essex and Hilliard", *Burl. Mag.*, CI (1959), pp. 145–8.

62. The Devon and Cornwall Record Society, II, 1919.

63. TOYNBEE, M. R., "Some early portraits of Charles I", *Burl. Mag.*, XCI (1949), pp. 4-9.

64. Transactions of the Devonshire Association, Vol. 44. (1912).

65. *Treatise* by Hilliard, Nicholas, "A Treatise concerning the Arte of Limning", with Introduction and Notes by Philip Norman, *Walpole Society* I (1911–12), pp. 1–54.

66. VANDERDOORT, ABRAHAM, *A Catalogue and Description of King Charles the First's Capital Collection of Pictures and Limnings*, etc., printed for W. Bathoe, London, 1757.

67. VERTUE, GEORGE, "Note Books", *Walpole Society*, 6 volumes (1930–55).

68. WATERHOUSE, ELLIS K., *Painting in Britain, 1530–1790*, London, 1953.

69. WILLIAMSON, GEORGE C., *La Miniature Anglaise*, 1913, Catalogue de l'Exposition de la Miniature à Bruxelles en 1912.

70. —— *The History of Portrait Miniatures*, London, 1904.

71. —— Catalogue of the Collection of Miniatures, the Property of John Pierpont Morgan, I, London, 1906.

72. WINTER, CARL, *The British School of Miniature Portrait Painters*, Annual Lecture on Aspects of Art, British Academy, 1948.

73. —— *Elizabethan Miniatures*, London, first published 1943, latest edition 1956.

74. —— "Hilliard and Elizabethan Miniatures," *Burl. Mag.*, LXXXIX (1947), pp. 175–83.

75. PAGET, HUGH, "Gerard and Lucas Hornebolt in England", *Burl. Mag.*, CI (1959), pp. 396–402 (publ. after the present book went to press).

INDEX

Titles of portraits are indicated as such; titles of other pictures and of books are printed in italics.

Names of museums and of private owners are printed in small capitals.

The numbers in italics refer to the plates; the numbers in bold type to entries in the Catalogue of this book.

Index

St. Edmund on the Bridge, 2; St. George, 4, 5, 16; St. Pancras, 4, 27; ST. SIDWELL, 2, 173

Fabius Quintus Pictor, 202
Fanshawe family of Ware Park, miniature of member, 246, *215*, **250**
Feckemann, Abell, goldsmith, 26-7, 170, 193
Ferdinand, Archduke, Coll. of, 79, 85
Fialletti, Odoardo, 221, 223
FITZWILLIAM MUSEUM, *see* CAMBRIDGE
Flemish, apprentice, 2; artists in England, 50, 53-4, 63, 223, 234, 251, 265, 269; influence, 62, 235-6, 241-2; pattern book, 242; style, 50, 236, 244, 267, 271
Flore, Maître de, 155
FORD, BRINSLEY, 246, 330
Font-shaped standing dish, 2-3, 173, *170*, **203**
Fortescue, Sir John, 29-30
France, 10-17, 61, 70, 73-9, 80, 86, 170, 232
Franke, William, goldsmith, 10, 13
Frederick, Elector Palatine, later King of Bohemia, miniature of, 162, *160e*, **168**
FREDERICTON ART GALLERY, NEW BRUNSWICK, 309
Freeman, William, 21
Fynch, Mrs., picture of, 171

Garter King of Arms, 273
Gaultier, Jacques, 14
—, Léonard, 14
Georges, Master, 15
Gerbier, Balthazar, 283
Gerhard, of Bruges, 223n.
Gheeraerts, Marcus, the elder, 47, 110
—, the younger, 110, 146, 222-3, 235, 251, *130*, **187**
GHENT, MUSÉE DES BEAUX-ARTS, 50
Goldsmiths' Company, London, Minutes, 2-13, 18, 22-3, 25-6, 28-30, 33-5, 38, 40, 169, 171-2, 224-5,

233, 254, 256-7; Bequest to, 25, 228; Rent Book, 30, 225
—, work, 169-197, 285
Goldwell, Henry, goldsmith, 172
Goltzius, Hendrick, 204, 214
GORHAMBURY, *see* VERULAM, EARL OF
Gower, George, 20, 41, 110
GREENWICH, NATIONAL MARITIME MUSEUM, 86, 112, 152, 283, 295, 302, 313
Greville, Sir Fulke, miniature of (formerly called), 100, 106, *82*, **80**
Grigg, Thomas, 223
Guildhall, Banquet at, 256
Gylberd, Edward, goldsmith, 8
Gysard, Susan, 40

HAGUE, THE, MAURITSHUIS, 92, 164, 246, 269, 291, 296, 317, 328-9, 332
HAM HOUSE, 146, 309
Harding, G. P., water colour by, 267
Hardwick, Bess of, Countess of Shrewsbury, 24, 44, 254-6, 262
HARDWICK HALL, 256, 262
Harington, Sir John, 44, 198, 212
—, Lucy, Countess of Bedford, *see* Bedford
Harrington, Lord, Account Book, 234
Harrison, Thomas, 32
—, at Fleetlane, 234
Harryson, family, miniatures of, 283, *246*, **281**, *247*, **282**
Harwick, Steven van, goldsmith, 178-9, *172*, **205**, 173, **206**
HATFIELD HOUSE, *see* SALISBURY, MARQUESS OF
Hatton, Sir Christopher, 33, 43, 198, 210-11, 222; miniatures of, 115-16, 285, *91*, **90**, **91**
Hawtrey, William, miniature of, 285
Hay, Lady, miniature of, 265, *230*, **265**
Haydocke, Richard, 18, 41, 46, 198, 204-5, 212, 214-15, 219, 221, 223, 258, 263
Hearne, Mr., miniature of, 227-8, 316
HECKETT, MR. AND MRS. E. H., 94, 157, 285, 297, 314, 334-5

343